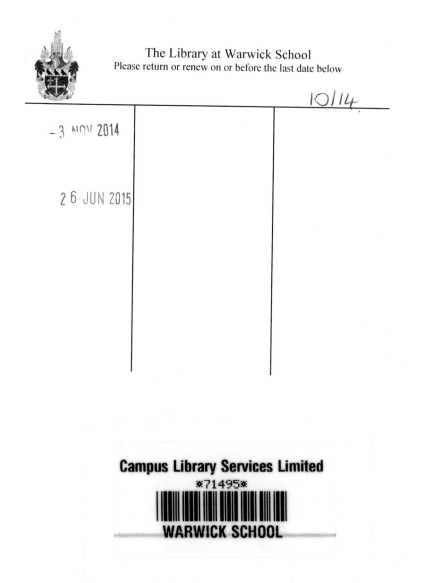

The Library at Warwick School
Please return or renew on or before the last date below

10/14

Rough Justice

Rough Justice

The International Criminal Court in a World of Power Politics

DAVID BOSCO

OXFORD
UNIVERSITY PRESS

OXFORD
UNIVERSITY PRESS

Oxford University Press is a department of the University of Oxford.
It furthers the University's objective of excellence in research, scholarship,
and education by publishing worldwide.

Oxford   New York
Auckland   Cape Town   Dar es Salaam   Hong Kong   Karachi
Kuala Lumpur   Madrid   Melbourne   Mexico City   Nairobi
New Delhi   Shanghai   Taipei   Toronto

With offices in
Argentina   Austria   Brazil   Chile   Czech Republic   France   Greece
Guatemala   Hungary   Italy   Japan   Poland   Portugal   Singapore
South Korea   Switzerland   Thailand   Turkey   Ukraine   Vietnam

Oxford is a registered trademark of Oxford University Press
in the UK and certain other countries.

Published in the United States of America by
Oxford University Press
198 Madison Avenue, New York, NY 10016

Catalogue record is available from the Library of Congress.

ISBN 978–0–19–984413–5

1 3 5 7 9 8 6 4 2
Printed in the United States of America
on acid-free paper

For Shana

Contents

Acknowledgments

AMERICAN UNIVERSITY'S SCHOOL of International Service has been my very happy home throughout the research and writing of this book. The university generously provided resources for research and travel, and SIS's former and current deans, Louis Goodman and James Goldgeier, supported me at every stage.

I benefited from the generosity and insight of numerous current and former officials at the International Criminal Court, only some of whom I can acknowledge publicly. Luis Moreno-Ocampo was remarkably generous with his time and responded courteously to my frequent pestering. Judge Hans-Peter Kaul, David Koller, Paul Seils, Darryl Robinson, Alex Whiting, and Béatrice le Frapper du Hellen provided valuable insight into the court's inner workings. On the US government side, John Bellinger and Harold Koh provided important insights. Stefan Barriga was a frequent source of expertise and advice and commented incisively on an early draft.

Special thanks go to former ICC president Philippe Kirsch, who not only endured hours of interviewing but provided shelter and food. In The Hague, Susanne Malmstrom generously offered a place to stay, and Steve Kostas served as an early sounding board for ideas.

I had the good fortune of having Jacinth Planer as my research assistant for most of this project. Even as she completed a demanding Master's degree, Jacinth was an indefatigable researcher and an indispensable source of advice, insight, and constructive criticism. Laura Bosco pitched in expertly in the final stages of the project. Thanks also go to Michael Brune, Wanlin Ren, and Natalia Suvorova.

I owe a special thanks to the participants in a day-long session on the book manuscript hosted by the School of International Service and supported by James Goldgeier. Michael Barnett, Tamar Gutner, David Kaye, Shannon Powers, Chris Rudolph, Sharon Weiner, and Erik Voeten took time out of their busy schedules to participate. I am grateful to Mana Zarinejad and the team at the International Affairs Research Institute for expertly planning the event.

Another wonderful group of colleagues and friends read and provided insightful comments on all or parts of the manuscript, including Boaz Atzili, Stefan Barriga, Jeff Colgan, Conor Dugan, Mark Kersten, Sikina Jinnah, Victor Peskin, Michael Schroeder, Jordan Tama, and Christian Wenaweser. I am especially grateful to Jack Goldsmith for his encouragement and insights as the manuscript neared completion.

I greatly enjoyed working again with the skilled and professional team at Oxford University Press, including David McBride and Alexandra Dauler.

My wife, Shana Wallace, commented expertly on multiple versions of the book and, as always, sustained me through the highs and lows of research and writing. Our two children, James (4 years) and Lael (11 months), scribbled and chewed on several draft chapters with impunity.

D.B.

Rough Justice

Introduction

IN MAY 2011, an Argentine lawyer stood at a podium in a quiet Dutch suburb and accused Libya's dictator of committing serious crimes. Luis Moreno-Ocampo, the chief prosecutor of the International Criminal Court (ICC), described how Muammar Gaddafi had ordered his forces to assault unarmed protesters and wage a brutal military campaign against regime opponents. "The evidence shows that Muammar Gaddafi, personally, ordered attacks on unarmed Libyan civilians," the prosecutor charged.[1] Just a few months after violence began in Libya, and as fighting raged between government forces and rebels, the machinery of international justice was turning. And it was targeting not low-level perpetrators, but individuals at the very top of the Libyan regime.

It was the kind of moment that advocates of international justice had long sought. Instead of being deemed a regrettable but inevitable feature of conflict, abuses by Gaddafi's forces were being treated as crimes. The story of the International Criminal Court is in many ways the story of this simple aspiration: that those guilty of serious crimes, even those individuals who command armies or occupy high office, should be held accountable. The letter and spirit of the court's governing statute reject the idea that power or political influence should influence the course of justice.

But the new court operates in a turbulent world where power matters. Even as the prosecutor leveled legal charges at Gaddafi, NATO warplanes had the dictator's armed forces in their sights. With Britain, France, and the United States in the lead, the Western alliance was in the midst of a complex military and political operation. That intervention had its own political logic and imperatives that did not necessarily correspond to the demands of international justice. In the abstract, the powerful states leading the intervention had all endorsed international justice. In practice, as the prosecutor discovered, there were distinct limits to their support.

This book examines how the world's most serious attempt at achieving international justice meshes with the realities of power politics. It focuses in particular on the relationship between the ICC and states with global interests and influence. In many contexts, these states will have reason to support the court's work. But because of its formal independence, the ICC is also a potential challenge to their prerogatives and interests. In certain circumstances, the court claims the right to investigate their activities and those of close allies. It can judge whether their domestic justice systems have adequately investigated possible crimes. Ultimately, it could indict their top political and military leaders. Recognizing the institution's risks, several powerful states at first resisted the court. The United States even launched a worldwide diplomatic campaign to limit its reach. That tension has abated in the decade since the court opened its doors. It has rapidly become part of the international architecture and has grown from a hollow shell to a bustling institution with an annual budget of more than $100 million. The United States has turned from the court's principal adversary to an ally. Other skeptical powers have grudgingly acknowledged that the court has an important role to play.

This book tells the story of how powerful states and a potentially revolutionary court learned to get along. It argues that both key states and the court have given ground to avoid a direct clash between power and international justice.

Independence and Dependence

The International Criminal Court represents a remarkable transfer of authority from sovereign states to an international institution. The investigation and prosecution of individuals, particularly senior military, political, and security officials, is a sensitive function even for countries with strong and stable domestic institutions. In the context of internal or external conflict, that sensitivity increases markedly. Yet more than a hundred states have given an international body the ultimate say over whether these individuals should be prosecuted. "The development of the ICC represents a stunning change of course," conclude scholars Beth Simmons and Alison Danner. "Not only does the ICC promise more stringent enforcement of international crimes, it also takes away from sovereign states the discretion to decide when to initiate prosecutions—a right they have heretofore jealously guarded."[2]

For decades, the radical nature of that idea confined discussion of an international criminal court to a handful of devoted lawyers and activists. Those advocating a court were inspired, in particular, by the Nuremberg trials after the Second World War.[3] If international justice should apply to senior German officials, they insisted, why not perpetrators of similar crimes around the world? In the wake of Nuremberg, states signed a treaty outlawing genocide, and international lawyers set to work drafting a charter for a permanent court that might prosecute future perpetrators. But by the early 1950s, the Nuremberg moment had passed and the momentum dissipated. National sovereignty reasserted itself, and the Cold War precluded the construction of such an ambitious new international structure. For decades, the project lay dormant.

The idea's rapid reemergence after the Cold War's end reflected new political flexibility and a renewed determination to address conflict and bloodshed with the tools of international law. In the early 1990s, the UN Security Council created special tribunals to prosecute atrocities committed in the former Yugoslavia and Rwanda. Their launch set in motion a broad diplomatic and activist campaign for a permanent court. In 1998, a mere five years after those tribunals began operating, more than one hundred states signed the Rome Statute of an International Criminal Court.

Many advocates saw the court as more than just a mechanism for punishing excesses during conflict; it was designed to help prevent conflict and replace the rule of force with the rule of law. William Pace, the leader of an influential coalition of nongovernmental organizations, declared: "[T]he ICC will deter; the ICC will prevent.... The ICC will save millions of humans from suffering unspeakably horrible and inhumane death in the coming decades."[4] Then UN Secretary-General Kofi Annan echoed the theme. "The establishment of the Court is a gift of hope to future generations, and a giant step forward in the march towards universal human rights and the rule of law."[5]

That march toward the rule of law was conceived of as a march away from something else: politics and expediency. During the negotiations that produced the court's founding document, diplomats and advocates repeatedly insisted that the new court must be independent, impartial, and fundamentally apolitical. "The Court should be a strictly independent and impartial judicial organ of the international community, independent of any political influence, and its judgments should be given exclusively on the basis of law," said a Japanese delegate.[6] The court "must not become a tool for the political convenience of states," insisted an African negotiator.[7] Another diplomat asked the conference to "overcome selfish national interests" and create an "effective, permanent court, independent of any political structures."[8]

Many of these diplomats were drawing on a strain of thought that has been described by the scholar Judith Shklar as "legalism." As described by Shklar, "[p]olitics is regarded not only as something apart from law, but as inferior to law," for "[l]aw aims at justice, while politics looks only to expediency. The former is neutral and objective, the latter the uncontrolled child of competing interests and ideologies."[9] That legalist sensibility suffused the

debate about the new court, but it long predated the ICC. The desire to channel messy and sometimes violent international relations into a system of binding law extends back centuries and has spawned other institutions, including
the UN's International Court of Justice (ICJ), a collection of regional courts,
and, even more recently, a dispute settlement mechanism at the World Trade
Organization (WTO).

On paper at least, the International Criminal Court is a striking advance
for the legalist worldview against the traditional concept of sovereignty.
Indeed, the court was created in the face of significant opposition from several powerful states. Some of these states questioned the value of international
judicial intervention, while others argued for greater political control of the
judicial process. Their efforts mostly failed. The ICC is designed to be largely
free from political control. The court's prosecutor and its judges are asked to
work on the basis of the court's governing statute, a set of carefully defined
crimes, and the court's rules of evidence and procedure. Their work does not
require formal political input or the approval of states. By design, states have
few levers to influence the prosecutor or judges.

Yet the Rome Statute also made clear that the court would be entirely
dependent on state resources to succeed. Negotiators gave the court no
enforcement tools of its own. Investigations on national soil require official
permission and access. To apprehend suspects, the court leans on state police
and military forces. Financially, the court relies on annual dues from members. As the court's prosecutor said shortly after taking office, "the ICC is
independent and interdependent at the same time."[10] In this sense at least, the
ICC is very much like other international organizations. States in the past
century have consented to create dozens of these institutions, but they rarely
endow them with permanent resources or enforcement power. They are quite
intentionally left dependent on state resources.[11]

If the court needs the support of states in general, those major powers that
enjoy global reach and influence are particularly important. These states have
the economic, diplomatic, intelligence, and military resources needed to help
turn the court's writ into reality either directly or via pressure on those whose
cooperation is essential in particular cases.[12]

The End of Great-Power Privilege?

As a result of design choices, the International Criminal Court was born with
a weak connection to major powers whose support it needs. Those major
powers who are court members—the United Kingdom, France, Germany,

Japan, and Brazil—are accorded no special powers or privileged place in the institution. In large part because of this lack of deference and protection, other major powers have chosen not to join the court at all. Those states outside the court include the world's uncontested superpower, the United States, and its most rapidly growing power, China. Nuclear-armed giants Russia and India have not joined the court. (Regional powers including Turkey, Egypt, Israel, Saudi Arabia, Pakistan, and Indonesia have also kept their distance.) Together, nonmembers account for two-thirds of the world's population and almost three-quarters of its armed forces (see figures I.1-I.3).

This dynamic is in tension with traditional accounts of how international organizations are shaped. Scholars have generally assumed that international organizations are, at their core, the product of major-power interests. As Kenneth Abbott and Duncan Snidal have written, "powerful states structure [international] organizations to further their own interests but must do so in a way that induces weaker states to participate."[13] In making concessions to less powerful states, however, major powers generally award themselves enough formal influence to safeguard their interests.

When the principal allied nations drafted the United Nations Charter in the wake of the Second World War, they secured the right to veto decisions in the UN's powerful Security Council. At the World Bank and the International Monetary Fund, major powers have their status recognized

Global Participation in ICC

▨ ICC Members (121)   ▨ Nonmembers (72)

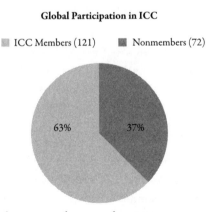

FIGURE I.1 ICC member states and nonmember states

Source: The list of 193 UN member states is available at http://www.un.org/en/members/. The list of 122 ICC states parties is listed at http://www.icc-cpi.int/en_menus/asp/states%20parties/Pages/the%20states%20parties%20to%20the%20rome%20statute.aspx. Please note that the Cook Islands is not included in this dataset. The Cook Islands became a party to the ICC on July 18, 2008, but is not a United Nations member state.

World Population

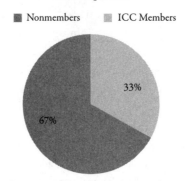

FIGURE I.2 Percentage of world population in ICC member states

Source: Population data for this analysis drawn from World Bank World Development Indicators for 2012, last updated July 2, 2013. Total population was 7,023,106,813. The populations of ICC member states and of semi-autonomous territories to which Britain, the Netherlands, and Denmark have extended Rome Statute ratification totaled 2,330,948,656. Combined population of nonmember states was 4,692,158,157. Between December 31, 2011, and June 1, 2013, Guatemala and Côte d'Ivoire joined the ICC, and the populations of these two states are included in the "ICC Members" category. ICC membership data is drawn from the list of ICC states parties, last updated March 15, 2013, by the ICC Assembly of States Parties, at http://www.icc-cpi.int/ en_menus/asp/states%20parties/Pages/states%20parties%20_%20chronological%20list.aspx. Membership information is cross-checked and adjusted to include semi-autonomous regions using the United Nations Treaty Series Online Collection at http://treaties.un.org/pages/ ShowMTDSGDetails.aspx?src=UNTSONLINE&tabid=1&mtdsg_no=XVIII-10&chapter=1 8&lang=en#Participants. The interactive World Bank World Development Indicators database is available at http://databank.worldbank.org/data/home.aspx.

through large voting shares that give them effective control of institutional decision-making. Other major organizations, including the World Trade Organization and NATO, operate on a consensus basis, meaning that no major decisions can be taken without state acquiescence.

Courts are a distinct kind of international organization, and independence (or at least the appearance of independence) from state influence is much more central to their identity.[14] But the ICC is unique even in this smaller universe. Its ability to investigate and issue arrest warrants for even senior government officials is unprecedented. At the same time, states have fewer means to control its activities than in other international courts. The ICJ, for example, can only hear cases against states when they have in some form consented to have them heard.[15] ICJ processes are also state-driven, and court officials cannot initiate cases. By custom, moreover, the permanent Security Council members always hold one judgeship each on that court.[16]

Global Armed Forces

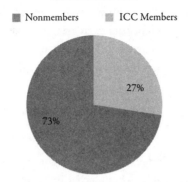

FIGURE I.3 Percentage of global armed forces in ICC member states

Source: Data for total armed forces personnel drawn from the World Bank World Development Indicators for 2011 (more recent data was not available at the time this book went to press). Available data for armed forces personnel in all countries and territories surveyed by the World Bank totaled 27,713,079. Armed forces in ICC member states totaled 7,600,975. Armed forces in nonmember states totaled 20,112,104.

The WTO's adjudication process is also state-driven, and there is no WTO official capable of initiating investigations without state action. The WTO's processes incorporate required "waiting periods" during which diplomatic processes may work. Its system of remedies also effectively privileges powerful states.[17] The UN's Law of the Sea Tribunal is highly constrained in its ability to hear cases. In all these institutions, major states have mechanisms to exert their influence or, at the very least, protect their vital interests.

In key respects, the International Criminal Court rejects this model. Its uniqueness derives in large part from the negotiating process that produced it. The Rome conference marked an important departure from the traditional process of building international institutions. A group of smaller and mid-size states—the "like-minded group"—was the dominant presence in the lead-up to the conference. Before and during the conference, civil society groups both helped shape and amplify the message of these smaller states. By contrast, no group of major powers emerged as an effective or coherent negotiating bloc.

In this context, attempts to include in the evolving document privileges for powerful states met strong resistance. This occurred most notably on the question of what role the UN Security Council—a body dominated by its powerful five permanent members—should play. During the negotiations, state after state inveighed against according the Council members special power, and the final statute gave the body only a limited role. The like-minded group and civil-society activists also fiercely defended the ability of the court's prosecutor to launch investigations without a request from states. The court's supporters saw judicial independence as critical to keeping power politics at bay, and scholars have concurred. "The more independent a court is, the less likely its decisions cater to the wishes of powerful states," Erik Voeten has noted.[18]

For those major states that choose to join the ICC, formal influence in the body is limited. The court's judges and prosecutor are elected by a majority vote, on a one-state, one-vote process numerically dominated by small and mid-size states. No two judges may be from the same state, so major powers can only have one national on a bench that includes eighteen judges. Because judges and the prosecutor cannot be reappointed, states cannot implicitly threaten them with a withdrawal of support. The only way in which the status of major powers is recognized is through higher budget assessments, but the budget is also approved by a simple majority vote. Once elected, and assuming the court has jurisdiction, the prosecutor and the judges have almost complete discretion as to which situations to investigate and which individuals to prosecute. Even when the UN Security Council refers a situation to the court, the prosecutor and judges may choose not to investigate or bring any charges.

Those major powers that have chosen not to join the court lack even the limited formal influence member states enjoy, while still facing the possibility—reduced but still real—that the court could investigate and prosecute their citizens and even their leaders. Nonmembers cannot nominate or vote upon candidates for court prosecutor and judgeships. They have no direct influence over its budget process. More than any other major international organization, the ICC keeps its distance from state power.

Approach of the Book

This book constructs an analytical account of the ICC's first decade that seeks to illuminate the relations between the court and major states. Its theoretical ambition is modest. It does not seek to test a general theory but instead deploys existing theory to help understand and analyze the court's first decade. Its approach is narrative and historical.[19] A chronological approach here has several advantages over a thematic or case-study based treatment. While the court's major investigations (in places including Sudan, the Democratic Republic of Congo, and Kenya) would appear to be natural case studies, they do not capture effectively the trajectory of the institution or its relations with major states, which weave between cases and often involve matters not encompassed by any of the court's investigations. A chronological approach also allows for the work of the ICC to be placed in the context of other developments in international and transnational justice. The ICC is a unique institution, but it is also part of a broader international justice project that has influenced both states and the young court.

The book draws on official government documents, court documents and filings, diplomatic histories and memoirs, and the extensive scholarly and specialist literature on the court, including many reports issued by nongovernmental organizations. At the core of the book, however, are dozens of interviews with court officials, major-power diplomats, and international organization officials. These interviews were essential to shed light on the often opaque processes by which state and court officials interact. I conducted these interviews on a semi-structured basis; most interviews included set questions on the relationship between the court and major powers, but they also featured queries based on the particular experiences and role of the interview subject. Most of these interviews were conducted on a background basis to allow diplomats and court officials to speak candidly about ongoing investigations and sensitive diplomatic matters.[20]

Throughout the book, I place particular emphasis on the relationship between the court and the United States. There are several reasons for this focus. US opposition to the court has been the most pronounced and articulated, and its early effort to limit the court's reach was the most developed. The US stance toward the court has also changed considerably in the past decade and describing that transformation requires sustained attention. The United States also stands alone in terms of its global interests and capabilities. Whether its military and intelligence resources and its diplomatic weight are deployed to assist the court is a critical factor in the institution's trajectory.

Chapter 1 provides a conceptual framework for analyzing the relationship between the court and major powers, outlining several possible major-power and court behavior patterns. Chapters 2 through 6 present and analyze the historical record. Chapter 2 centers on the roots of the ICC and the diplomatic process that created the court. Chapter 3 begins by briefly explaining the Rome Statute's key provisions. While this book is not a study of the court's jurisprudence, certain legal concepts and distinctions must be addressed in order to understand the contours of the court's work. After doing so, this chapter then documents the period between the signing of the Rome Statute and the court's opening, with a particular focus on US policy and the often acrimonious interactions between the European Union and the United

States over the court. Chapters 4 through 6 move through the court's first decade in operation, focusing on key decision points and critical interactions between the court and major states. The conclusion systematically assesses the evidence presented and considers the implications in both theoretical and policy terms.

I

A Conceptual Framework

THIS CHAPTER ESTABLISHES a framework for analyzing the International Criminal Court's relationship with the world's most powerful states. I have argued that the court's structure and rules create a significant distance from these states, and that this distance is both an important departure in design from other major international organizations and a daunting practical challenge for the ICC. Drawing on existing theory, this chapter outlines and discusses several ways in which powerful states and the court might behave toward each other. (Tables 1.1 and 1.2 summarize these behaviors.) The chapter then expands on the book's central argument: that major powers and the court have engaged in an interactive process of mutual accommodation.

State Behavior

Important strands of international relations and legal scholarship suggest that major powers are unlikely to empower or materially support a court over which they do not exercise significant control. Realists view international organizations largely as extensions of existing power realities. To the extent these organizations can be relevant, it is by drawing on and reflecting the influence of powerful states.[1] Legal scholars working in this tradition have argued that international courts not controlled by powerful states will usually be ineffective.[2] Several scholars have argued, in particular, that the International Court of Justice lost major-power support when, through its judicial decision-making, it moved beyond their control.[3] While generally more sanguine about the impact of international organizations and courts, leading neoliberal scholars have concurred that major powers will demand influence in exchange for membership and that institutions will be constrained by that influence.[4] This understanding yields two likely patterns of major-power behavior toward the court: marginalization and control.

Table 1.1 Potential Major-Power Behavior Patterns

Strategy	Expected Major-Power Behavior
Active Marginalization	• Attack the perceived defects of the institution and its personnel in an effort to delegitimize the organization • Deploy political and other resources to undermine the support the court receives from the rest of the international community • Use power to assert the primacy of political processes over judicial ones led by the ICC. Use Rome Statute's Article 16 provision liberally to assert the Security Council's institutional dominance
Passive Marginalization	• Avoid steps that would confer legitimacy or additional authority on the court, including Security Council referrals • When international judicial action is deemed useful, seek to circumvent the court by working through other, more readily controlled institutions such as ad hoc tribunals[a] • Avoid deploying political, economic, and diplomatic resources to help enforce court decisions and rulings
Control	• Use Security Council referrals and deferrals regularly to guide the court toward certain investigations and away from others • Lend resources and support to the court on the basis of whether state supports the court activity in question • Communicate to court officials concerns about certain activities and even suggest that there are "red lines," which if crossed would trigger marginalization behavior • Major-power court members could use their influence in annual budget negotiations to direct the court toward certain activities and away from others
Acceptance	• For nonmembers, move toward membership • Offer resources and support for the court's investigations even when those investigations do not serve other political or diplomatic interests • Refer situations to the court through the Security Council • Avoid deferring court investigations through the Council • Consistently deploy diplomatic and other resources to help enforce court judgments

[a] Koremenos, Lipson, and Snidal contend that major powers used this approach when they shifted intellectual property issues from the World Intellectual Property Organization to the World Trade Organization. See Barbara Koremenos, Charles Lipson, and Duncan Snidal, "The Rational Design of International Institutions," *International Organization* 55, no. 4 (2001): 767.

Active or Passive Marginalization

The most obvious possibility is that powerful states will ensure that the court remains weak and ultimately fades into irrelevance. Their motive for doing so is straightforward: an institution that they cannot control might prove inconvenient—even dangerous. As Jacob Katz Cogan has argued, the phenomenon of mostly unchecked judicial bodies "means that States are more likely to avoid courts, abandon them, or disregard their decisions, potentially condemning them to irrelevance."[5] For powerful states, marginalizing international courts minimizes the risks associated with their independence.

Marginalization behavior could come in several forms. The major powers who feel most threatened by the court might actively work against the institution, seeking to limit its reach and delegitimize it through formal and informal means. "The more unhappy powerful states are about [international court] independence and influence," Karen Alter has predicted, "the more we will hear about the illegitimacy of international legal bodies."[6] Major powers could also discourage states from joining and seek to circumvent the court through more readily controlled bodies. Powerful states could also opt for a less aggressive approach that can be termed passive marginalization. They might not attack the court or actively seek to undermine its support, but they could consciously avoid deploying their resources to support the institution, even when some of their interests might suggest doing so.

It is intuitive that powerful states that have not joined the court might choose to pursue its marginalization, but what about those major powers that *have* become court members? One logical possibility is that these states will seek to support the institution they have embraced and in which they have invested. If this is correct, there would be two competing major-power strategies: one group of powerful states would seek to marginalize the institution while another seeks to empower it.

However, it is possible that even major powers that have joined might have an incentive to marginalize the institution. The diplomatic and financial investment these states have made in the court is relatively small. The court's success and influence will not often accrue to their direct benefit. As Christopher Rudolph has argued, the court's expected advantages—providing accountability, stability, and deterrence in conflict zones—may be too diffuse to compete with the sovereignty and other costs it exacts.[7] In specific situations, moreover, major-power members may find that the court's work complicates their diplomatic, political, and military strategies and relationships.

Control

There is a second likely pattern of major-power behavior toward the court: efforts to control it and shape its activities. As Randall Stone has argued in the context of international financial organizations, "powerful states will always find a way to control outcomes of interest to them, if they are not explicitly prevented."[8] Control of international judicial institutions has been defined as a process by which states "ensure that the organization acts within its assigned mandate."[9] The term is used here in a more expansive sense. It encompasses not only efforts to keep the court within its mandate but also to ensure that the court does not interfere with important state political or diplomatic interests.

Powerful states pursuing a control strategy could seek to guide the court toward activities that serve their interests and away from those they deem unhelpful. Control behavior would likely reflect a major-power belief that the ICC can be a useful instrument in certain cases but not in all. It would look different from the marginalization behavior outlined above. Major powers seeking control have no incentive to systematically deprive the institution of resources or undermine its legitimacy, as doing so would diminish the court's utility in those situations where they desire its involvement. Instead, major powers should be selective in their support and should seek to guide the court toward favored activities.

What are the most likely control mechanisms? The implicit threat that states might exit or abandon an international court like the ICC is a potentially powerful tool. States displeased by the activities of an international court to which they belong may simply withdraw their consent to jurisdiction and their membership. For international courts in need of cases and clients, this can be a serious threat, and there is recent precedent.[10] In the 1970s and 1980s, respectively, France and the United States withdrew the broad jurisdiction they had granted the ICJ after that court considered sensitive cases. Yet exit is an exceptionally blunt tool that can likely only be employed once. Moreover, several major powers are not ICC members and so cannot wield exit as a threat. Nor does exit offer the protection it does with other international courts; in some situations, the Rome Statute allows for the possibility of jurisdiction over nonmember states.

For these reasons, major powers may reach for other levers, including deploying their political, diplomatic, and economic influence to direct the court. The most direct formal mechanism for control is the UN Security Council. The Council cannot compel the prosecutor to launch an investigation or force the court's judges to issue arrest warrants, but through its referral power it can communicate its desires and accord the court additional jurisdictional reach. The Council may also defer investigations for up to a year, allowing its members to take a particular situation out of the hands of the court (at least temporarily).

The Security Council has distinct limits as a control mechanism however. It can only use its referral and deferral powers when its permanent members are in agreement. Major powers without Council seats, moreover, may not be able to use the institution to control the court at all. Given these limits, states might also use other, less obvious, mechanisms to direct the court. Scholars of international courts have identified an array of possible tools including limiting court discretion by providing precise rules, restricting funding, setting up alternative adjudication mechanisms, informal signaling, and failing to comply with court judgments.[11]

Acceptance

In essence, the marginalization and control behaviors outlined above seek to restore the traditional relationship between powerful states and international institutions. The former does so by rendering the anomalous institution impotent, the latter by submitting it to major-power influence. However, there is a third possible behavior pattern: acceptance.

Major powers might embrace a court they cannot control for several reasons. They might calculate that the benefits of supporting the institution outweigh the costs and decide that they cannot reap those benefits without offering support. They might determine that these institutions make their commitments more credible and thereby help them resolve important coordination problems with other states. As Lawrence Helfer has argued, "[b]y increasing the probability of both material sanctions and reputational harm, international tribunals raise the cost of violations, thereby increasing compliance and enhancing the value of the agreement for all parties."[12]

There is an alternative mechanism that might lead even skeptical major powers to accept the court: the governments of these states—and the publics to which they respond—might be influenced by the norms that the ICC embodies. Kathryn Sikkink has argued that a "norm cascade" is already well underway as regards accountability for international crimes. She identifies a "dramatic new trend in world politics toward holding individual state officials, including heads of state, criminally accountable for human rights violations."[13] The ICC represents the idea of individual accountability for serious crimes. Because no other institution can claim to advance this principle at a global level, the ICC occupies unique and potentially powerful moral ground.

There are several ways that normative power could be brought to bear in major-power capitals. Influential civil society organizations may pressure governments to support the institution. Through bilateral and multilateral diplomacy, states that back the court may be able to convince less supportive states to alter their stance. Support for, or at least acquiescence to the court, might become a condition for intrastate cooperation on a host of other issues. Officials from other international organizations may be able to exert pressure on states to accept and respect the court. The aggregated weight of international support for the court's work could gradually push the major powers who are not members to accept the value of an independent court. As the court's activities develop and as its reputation grows, powerful states that imagined they could marginalize or control the court might instead find themselves adjusting to its activities. The ICC's first prosecutor predicted just such a dynamic. Shortly after assuming his post, he expressed confidence that the court would gradually win over the skeptics. "We have to show how seriously we are working, and slowly people who today are reluctant will start to trust us."[14]

These alternative behaviors—marginalization, control, and acceptance— each assume a different dynamic between the court and states. The marginalization route assumes that major-power skepticism, indifference, or outright hostility will lead them consciously or unconsciously to weaken the institution. Control behavior assumes that the major powers will use their influence to direct and manage the court. Acceptance assumes that the interests of states are at least somewhat variable and subject to reinterpretation, and that the existing fault lines on the value of the court may shift.

By analyzing the diplomatic record of the past decade, this book attempts to understand which, if any, of these behaviors are evident in the policies of major states toward the court. There are potentially important theoretical and policy implications to the findings. From a theoretical perspective, evidence of marginalization and control behavior would tend to vindicate those skeptical that powerful states will support independent international judicial institutions. Evidence of acceptance—particularly by nonmember major powers—may suggest that other dynamics are at work.

In policy terms, evidence of sustained marginalization would cast doubt on the viability of constructing institutions without granting major powers greater control. Acceptance, by contrast, would indicate that the ICC model may be effective, and that it is possible to construct institutions around power—and then leverage the normative power of those institutions to induce major-power support. Particularly if it is effective, control behavior by major powers may be most complex from a policy perspective. Major-power control of a judicial institution, even if incomplete, raises important questions about how to balance legitimacy and effectiveness.

Court Behavior

To this point, the focus has been on how major powers will react to an unprecedented and anomalously designed institution. That singular focus on state behavior is in fact characteristic of much scholarship on international institutions. "[I]nternational relations scholars have not given systematic consideration to how IOs actually behave," Michael Barnett and Martha Finnemore have noted. "IOs have no agency and cannot act in any meaningful way under most theoretical constructs in the field."[15] Barnett and Finnemore insist that, in fact, international organization officials can employ different kinds of authority to alter the trajectory of the institution they represent, perhaps even in the face of contrary state preferences.

At least in formal terms, the ICC should have a robust ability to set its own course. The Rome Statute created a prosecutor who has "broad discretionary power"—much broader than other international and some domestic prosecutors—to choose situations to investigate and individuals to indict.[16] The court could accentuate and defend that already considerable formal autonomy through its moral authority. The Rome Statute's preamble describes the court as a response to "unimaginable atrocities that deeply shock the conscience of humanity."[17] ICC officials can plausibly insist to states and the public that they are apolitical and advancing the principles of the Rome Statute rather than narrow national interests. Led by lawyers and judges rather than diplomats, the ICC has a particularly strong claim to be considered apolitical, or at least capable of more disinterested judgment. As Karen Alter has argued, "even if judges are political actors, not truly neutral or even unbiased, they can still be seen as better decision-makers than politicians."[18]

Court officials may be able to deploy the urgency of their mission and their reputation as disinterested officials both to win support from skeptical states and to shield themselves from political pressure. Senior court officials could educate national policymakers about the court's work, build political support for the institution in civil society, and encourage states that have not joined the court to do so. They could also challenge those states that fail to support the court. In short, court officials could pursue their mandate apolitically while using their authority to build the institution's credibility, expand its freedom of action, and generate support from states.

Yet there is no reason that court officials must employ their discretion, formal autonomy, and moral authority in this way. They might instead tailor their rhetoric and activities to cultivate relations with key states. The possibility that ICC officials would allow political and strategic considerations to influence their work is anathema from a legalist conception. But international judicial officials operate in a complex environment, and it is important to take seriously the possibility that they are influenced by non-legal considerations. In the context of other courts, scholars have found evidence that international judges can be influenced by political and strategic considerations.[19]

There has been much less work on how these considerations may impact international prosecutors, and that question is vital for the ICC. The most important discretionary authority—whether to open investigations and seek arrest warrants—centers on the prosecutor rather than judges. While the judges do review prosecutorial behavior in several respects, the prosecutor alone takes the critical decision to trigger a full investigation and request arrest warrants. No other actor can compel the prosecutor to do so. Yet research on how international prosecutors use their discretion is scant. A few international law scholars have addressed the issue, but international relations scholars have not.[20] In part, this gap is due to the relatively recent arrival of prosecutors as actors on the international stage. There are also significant challenges to research in this area; prosecutors rarely document their decision-making process on discretionary questions. Yet the breadth of the ICC prosecutor's discretion makes an enquiry into how it has been used essential. Below, I elaborate several different ways in which the ICC prosecutor might use discretionary authority to manage relations with major powers.

The legalist expectation forms an important baseline possibility: that the ICC prosecutor will be essentially apolitical. On this view, the court should examine information about potential crimes with little reference to the political realities surrounding them and to the preferences of major powers. The prosecutor's only job is to determine whether crimes of sufficient gravity have been committed, whether the court has jurisdiction, and whether relevant domestic judicial institutions are handling the matter adequately. The political dynamic in the country, the region, or globally is only relevant to the extent it sheds light directly on these issues. Understanding the political context, for example, could help the ICC to determine whether key actors had genocidal intent or to understand how chains of command operated. But politics should not be relevant in any broader sense.

An alternative, more pragmatic view is that the prosecutor has no choice but to consider diplomatic realities in selecting situations, if only to ensure that an investigation will be feasible. In most cases, some level of support from the state where the alleged crimes had occurred, or at least from neighboring states, would be necessary to conduct complex investigative work. Court personnel typically need visas, permits, and sometimes security. In cases where crimes have occurred across borders, the prosecutor's office might require cooperation from multiple states. In the event the court issues arrest warrants, states would have to provide the resources to enforce them. Without this official support, an investigation could be a futile gesture. On this view, the prosecutor should include an assessment of likely state support before launching an investigation. He or she might choose not to open an investigation if the prospects for that support appeared weak. Pursuing an ideal apolitical form of justice by ignoring the need for state support would only sap the institution's credibility.

An even more permissive view of the role of politics and diplomacy in the court's investigative strategy is possible. Given the ICC's fragility and dependence on state support, its officials might decide that they have no choice but to actively build support among states with global power and reach. Doing so might mean taking seriously their preferences about where ICC investigations were advisable and where they might complicate diplomatic efforts or impinge on strategic interests. In this more strategic mode, the court might, within reason, take into account the political interests of key states in order to help build relationships. The ultimate goal of doing so, however, would be to build up the court and allow it to eventually pursue its mandate independently.

By focusing on those areas of the world where major powers support the court's involvement—or at least do not oppose it—the prosecutor may be able to convince even skeptical countries that the court poses little danger to their interests and that it can be a useful instrument for conflict resolution. It should be clear that there are significant dangers to this approach however. Most fundamentally, it incorporates political considerations into decisions that are supposed to be made on the basis of law. In appearing to tread carefully with the major powers, the court may anger other states. To the extent it becomes apparent that the court is according major states special consideration, the court's authority would likely weaken.

There is an even more extreme possibility: that the prosecutor will effectively take direction from major states. This could happen either directly or indirectly. The prosecutor might decide that he or she cannot oppose the clearly expressed wishes of major powers on issues ranging from which investigations to open to the timing of individual prosecutions. As this book

Table 1.2 Potential Prosecutor Behavior Patterns

Prosecutor Behavior	Relevance of Political and Diplomatic Considerations	Likely Outcomes
Apolitical	None, other than as needed to assess criminal intent or nature of complex crime	Investigations and prosecutions based entirely on jurisdiction and relative gravity of situations and crimes
Pragmatic	Assessed to determine whether full-scale investigation can be effective and likelihood arrest warrants will be implemented	No prosecutions where state support is too weak for investigation and/or enforcement
Strategic	Taken into account to help strengthen the court by building key diplomatic relations	Case-by-case analysis of situations in light of geopolitical realities. Goal is to maximize court autonomy but without provoking damaging clash with powerful states
Captured	Prosecutor will take direction from leading states in system	Investigations and prosecutions will respond to political interests of leading states

makes clear, the prosecutor and his staff engage in a regular dialogue with key member and nonmember states, and there are ample opportunities for state officials to communicate state preferences. A more subtle process, through which the prosecutor internalizes the preferences of key states, is also possible.

Mutual Accommodation

This book argues that the interaction of major-power and prosecutorial behavior has resulted in mutual accommodation. The result has been an exceptionally cautious court that even skeptical major powers can tolerate and, to a degree, support. This accommodation is incomplete, fragile, and reversible, but it is also creating precedents and expectations likely to influence the court's future trajectory.

The historical evidence suggests that the process of mutual accommodation has been dynamic and interactive. The ICC prosecutor has operated strategically, sending conciliatory signals and orienting early court investigations so as to avoid tension with major powers. During the court's first several years, that strategy had an impact. It helped undercut the marginalization strategy that several major powers—led by the United States—were attempting. In the face of innocuous court activity, US officials skeptical of the institution had difficulty elevating their concerns above competing policy priorities.

As important, national diplomats and activists supportive of the court— sometimes working from within skeptical states—were able to use the principles the court represents to further undermine these marginalization efforts. In several cases, major powers who had joined the court either directly or indirectly sought to counter the US-led campaign against the court. The success of these efforts highlighted the deep reluctance of states to publicly oppose the court's work. Even non-democratic states such as China have hesitated to do so.

If the court's own caution and the institution's normative power curtailed marginalization efforts, they did not produce broad major-power acceptance of the institution. While there is some important evidence of acceptance, I argue that control behavior has been more prevalent. In their attempts to manage the court, major powers have employed several different mechanisms. The UN Security Council—a locus of great-power privilege— has been a key tool in this effort. Because three of the permanent Council members are not court members, and because the United States adamantly opposed the court's creation, few observers expected the Council to refer situations to the court. Remarkably, the Council did so in March 2005, less than three years after the court opened its doors. The Council did so again, this time unanimously, in early 2011. To a limited extent, these referrals legitimized the court and invested key major powers in the work of the court. But they have also allowed the major powers to exercise considerable control over the court's docket.

The ICC has limited funds and personnel for investigations, and the referrals produced resource-intensive investigations that consumed years of court activity. The referrals have therefore allowed the Council members to indirectly guide the court away from investigations that its members would consider more hostile to their interests. Moreover, in referring situations, the Security Council's members have not limited their own freedom of action. These referrals did not oblige them to take any specific actions in support of the court's work, to expose their own nationals to broader jurisdiction, or even to cover the court's costs for the requested investigation. In a broad sense, the referrals have allowed powerful states an element of control without extracting from them deep or lasting support for the institution.

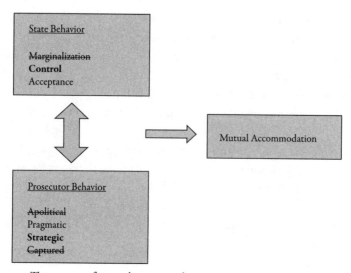

State Behavior

~~Marginalization~~
Control
Acceptance

Mutual Accommodation

Prosecutor Behavior

~~Apolitical~~
Pragmatic
Strategic
~~Captured~~

FIGURE 1.1 The process of mutual accommodation

Certain major powers—although certainly not all—have also employed other mechanisms of control. They have on several occasions sent signals to the court officials about whether to open new inquiries and how to conduct ongoing investigations. Even more subtly, they have used the power of information they possess to guide the court away from investigations they would find inconvenient. They have offered diplomatic and other resources to the court in certain situations but have withheld them when court activity clashed with other priorities. Through an amendment process to the Rome Statute, they have sought to limit the court's ability to prosecute the crime to which their senior officials would be most exposed.

For the most part, the prosecution officials have not resisted these efforts at major-power control. They have not challenged the Security Council's restrictions on the court's freedom of action or campaigned for expanded jurisdiction. Meanwhile, the court's cautious and even deferential behavior in selecting situations to investigate has continued. The historical record does not suggest that leading states have "captured" the prosecutor or other court officials. Indeed, there are notable examples of the prosecutor rejecting major-power pressure and advice. But these assertions of independence have occurred within a broadly conciliatory framework (see figure 1.1).

The chapters that follow describe and place in context that process.

2

Origins

THE STORY OF modern international criminal justice begins with the Nuremberg trials in the wake of the Second World War and then, after an almost fifty-year pause, continues with the tribunals created in the early 1990s to address crimes in the former Yugoslavia and Rwanda. The International Criminal Court, the long-awaited permanent home for international justice, appears as the logical and almost natural next step. There are several important twists in this overarching narrative however. For the purposes of this book, the most critical of these is how, with the advent of the ICC, some of the world's most powerful states lost ownership of international justice.

"Trial of the Century"

On April 20, 1945, Adolf Hitler and his inner circle quietly celebrated what would be the Führer's last birthday. The German leader accepted a glass of champagne before retiring early. A couple hundred miles from that Berlin bunker, the American 7th Army was sweeping into Nuremberg, the city where Hitler many times had rallied the Nazi faithful. The American forces entered a city that had already been devastated from the air. By some estimates, more than 90 percent of the city's buildings were destroyed or damaged in the fierce campaign that American and British bombers had been waging for months. The city's population had been reduced from 450,000 to 160,000, and 30,000 people may have been entombed under the rubble. Many of Nuremberg's remaining citizens were scavenging to survive.[1]

Less than a month later, American general Lucius Clay flew into the city with US Supreme Court justice Robert Jackson. At the highest levels, the victorious Allies had determined that Germany's senior wartime leaders would face a court of law, and President Truman had designated Jackson as the lead

American prosecutor. In the course of the visit, Clay convinced Jackson that Nuremberg was the right spot for the trials. Critically, it was in the American occupation zone, which would give the United States significant control over the proceedings. Despite the enormous destruction, Nuremberg's imposing Palace of Justice had been left mostly intact and a nearby prison facility was standing as well.[2]

In the midst of the city's deprivation, the occupying powers began their experiment in international law. Throughout the summer, the Allies hurriedly readied the Palace for what the press was already describing as the "trial of the century." German prisoners of war cleaned up the rubble around the courthouse. Allied officials located intact structures able to house the court's officials and the press covering the trials. The Allies remodeled the main courtroom and imported the latest simultaneous interpretation technology. On November 21, 1945, the Nuremberg trials began.

It was not inevitable that the leaders of the Nazi regime would face judicial proceedings. At many moments in the war's final months, a firing squad appeared just as likely. Soviet leader Josef Stalin advocated summary executions of thousands of German political and military leaders. British Prime Minister Winston Churchill vigorously opposed the Soviet plan and even stormed out of a meeting with Stalin over the issue. But Churchill's objection appeared to be about the scale of the proposed executions rather than the principle. As Gary Jonathan Bass has documented, British leaders agreed that a judicial process was inappropriate. The fate of German leaders, Churchill wrote, "is a political and not a judicial one." Foreign minister Antony Eden was convinced that "the guilt of such individuals is so black that they fall outside and go beyond the scope of any judicial process." The prime minister advocated executions of senior leaders within six hours of their being detained and positively identified.[3]

Many Americans felt the same way. Polls indicated that an overwhelming percentage of Americans favored summary executions or the immediate imprisonment (without trial) of top Nazi leaders. In some polls, as many Americans favored torturing Axis leaders as putting them on trial (2 percent for each option).[4] That view was well represented in cabinet meetings. Treasury Secretary Henry Morgenthau advocated a harsh postwar policy that included summary executions of German leaders and a thorough deindustrialization of the country. In Morgenthau's view, the erstwhile aggressor needed to be ground down much more comprehensively than after the First World War to prevent its reemergence as a threat. At various points, General Dwight Eisenhower and President Roosevelt himself were inclined toward this view.

Roosevelt appeared particularly unsympathetic to an approach that diminished the collective guilt of the German people:

> Too many people here and in England hold to the view that the German people as a whole are not responsible for what has taken place—that only a few Nazi leaders are responsible. That unfortunately is not based on fact. The German people as a whole must have it driven home to them that the whole nation has been engaged in a lawless conspiracy against the decencies of modern civilization.[5]

Morgenthau was opposed most actively by Secretary of War Henry Stimson, who championed the idea of trials for German leaders.[6] Several concerns appeared to animate Stimson. He worried that large-scale executions would taint the war effort—"mar the page of our history," as he put it in one memorandum. He was also convinced that a policy of large-scale imprisonment or execution without due process would embitter the German people against the Allies. Public trials, by contrast, would educate Germans about the crimes of the Nazi regime. "[T]he very punishment of these men in a dignified manner consistent with the advance of civilization," he wrote in late 1944, "will have all the greater effect upon posterity. Furthermore, it will afford the most effective way of making a record of the Nazi system of terrorism and of the effort of the Allies to terminate the system and prevent its recurrence."[7]

At least outwardly, the debate in Washington was not about legalism. Stimson did not insist on the inherent superiority of a legal approach over a political one. He did not contend that the would-be defendants somehow had a right to a trial. Instead, he argued that a legal approach would yield long-term political benefits. Those arguments proved potent. Although Roosevelt initially supported Morgenthau's proposal, Stimson ultimately prevailed. With Washington's weight behind the trials, Moscow and London reluctantly acquiesced to the creation of what was called the International Military Tribunal (IMT). Meeting in London, the Allies approved the charter for the tribunal in August 1945.[8]

American, French, British, and Soviet judges presided over the trials of twenty-one senior Nazi officials and military leaders (three more individuals were tried *in absentia*). The defendants sat on raised benches, ringed by military police and facing the Allied judges. Robert Jackson opened his case with a plea that the defendants receive a fair hearing and characterized the trials as "the most eloquent compliment that power has ever paid to justice." Even more grandly, Jackson insisted that the law being applied at Nuremberg must ultimately apply to all, including those doing the judging. "[L]et me make clear that while the law is first applied against German aggressors, the law includes, and if it is to serve a useful purpose, it must condemn, aggression by any other nation, including those which sit here now in judgment."[9] Seven months later, the sentences were handed down. Ten of the twenty-one defendants present were condemned to death by hanging; most others received long prison sentences. Several were acquitted.

In Japan, with less public attention, a similar project played out. The Tokyo trials, which included judges from eleven different countries that had fought against the Japanese, ultimately convicted twenty-five Japanese political and military leaders, including several former prime ministers and foreign ministers. Six of those convicted were sentenced to death, and the rest to lengthy prison terms. Only the Emperor was placed beyond the reach of the trial. During the negotiations preceding the Japanese surrender, the Americans agreed to preserve the Emperor's position. They exempted him from prosecution and worked to avoid implicating him personally during the trials.[10]

As these several dozen German and Japanese defendants met their fates, the Allies faced the question of whether to continue the justice initiative. They knew that the initial trials had only scratched the surface; investigators were uncovering caches of documents that meticulously documented Axis crimes and implicated thousands of officers and officials. But the international trials had been slow and costly, and Allied patience for the enterprise was wearing thin in both Germany and Japan. Robert Jackson urged President Truman to oppose more international trials and instead permit each occupying power to pursue cases independently. British diplomats privately encouraged the Americans to not pursue additional trials in Japan. "Experience has shown that the present type of international tribunal with eleven different countries represented on the tribunal and on the prosecution is slow and inefficient."[11]

As Kevin Jon Heller has documented, there was also a political dimension to the American and British reluctance to continue the enterprise. Key American officials, including Jackson, had qualms about jointly prosecuting more cases with the Soviets. That concern was particularly acute because a new round of international trials in Germany would likely target German industrialists, notably the Krupp and Farben enterprises. British and American officials did not relish the prospect of Soviet judges prosecuting corporate leaders and worried that the trials might become a "wrangle between the capitalist and communist ideologies."[12]

By early 1947, the experiment in international justice was over. The Allies continued prosecuting individuals within their respective occupation zones in Germany. The Soviets conducted thousands of summary trials, most of which led to quick executions. British and French military tribunals prosecuted several thousand Germans and sentenced several hundred to death. The Americans proved particularly zealous about documenting the scale of Nazi crimes and the culpability of an array of professions. US prosecutors brought a series of complicated cases against a total of 185 Nazi doctors, lawyers, concentration camp guards, and industrialists.[13]

Precedents and Politics

The Nuremberg and Tokyo trials represented a revolutionary development in international law on several fronts. Most remarkably, German and Japanese political and military leaders were charged with the crime of waging aggressive war. While the horrors of the Holocaust played a part at Nuremberg, the sin of launching an unprovoked and expansionary war had pride of place in the indictments. "For those who conceived of the trial," David Luban has written, "its great accomplishment was to be the criminalization of aggressive war, inaugurating an age of world order."[14]

That accomplishment occurred by fiat. For centuries the right of states to wage war for essentially any reason they saw fit had been a feature of international life. The experience of the First World War had only partially eroded that concept. The Treaty of Versailles included a provision "publicly arraign[ing]" the German Kaiser for "a supreme offence against international morality and the sanctity of treaties."[15] But no tribunal ever convened, and the Kaiser eventually died in exile. In 1928, a dozen countries, including the United States, France, Germany, and Great Britain, foreswore war as an instrument of national policy. The so-called Kellogg-Briand pact excited imaginations, but it included no enforcement provisions and not even a hint that waging aggressive war would lead to individual criminal liability. After the 1934 assassination of Yugoslavia's King Alexander, the French government advocated international trials for terrorists.[16] Delegates meeting in Geneva drafted a convention to do so, but only a few states signed and it never came into force.

Nuremberg's leap to criminalizing aggressive war was breathtaking, and the charge that the Allies had created *ex post facto* a new principle of international law is difficult to deny. Whatever the legal propriety of charging Germany's leaders with aggression, the Nuremberg and Tokyo trials made that crime part of the international landscape. The trials also advanced other important legal doctrines, including the largely inchoate concept of "crimes against humanity," which were defined to include peacetime abuses against civilian populations. The IMT's charter defined these crimes as "murder, extermination, enslavement, deportation, and other inhumane acts committed against any civilian population, before or during the war."[17] The Nuremberg and Tokyo trials also added important detail to the established body of war crimes law formed by the Hague Conventions and other instruments.

Taken together, the strands of Nuremberg law seemed to represent a dramatic triumph for law over force. If Robert Jackson's words were to be believed, even powerful national leaders who unleashed illegal wars would in the future be met with not only the force of arms but also the force of law. Governments that massacred their citizens—even in peacetime—could be called to account for crimes against humanity. Military commanders who targeted civilians or grossly violated the rules of war would have to answer for their crimes. The work of the tribunal, one Nuremberg participant wrote decades later, "laid the basis for a law-ordered world society by the declaration of principles of law applicable to future aggressors."[18]

However powerful that precedent, these trials occurred in a specific historical context: they were conducted by victorious states against the leaders of countries they had vanquished and occupied. The judicial process was under the firm control of the occupying powers. Crucially, it was clear that the variant of international justice employed in Germany and Japan would not threaten the power or reputation of the occupiers; the trials were explicitly limited to the crimes committed by the Axis powers. The indictments did not reference the Nazi-Soviet pact of 1939 that divided Poland between the two powers. They ignored the British and American carpet-bombing of German and Japanese cities, including Nuremberg itself. The indictments did refer to the 1941 massacre (by the Soviets) of thousands of Polish officers in the Katyn Forest, but the Soviets insisted on including this crime in the indictment against the Germans (despite American and British objections).[19]

Clear-eyed Allied officials knew that certain of their own wartime and postwar tactics were morally and legally dubious. In 1945, a British Foreign Office official wrote that Royal Air Force commander Arthur Harris "must have got more victims on his conscience than any individual German General or Air Marshal."[20] Moreover, certain Allied violations continued even as the trials began. Robert Jackson expressed concerns about the double standard in a letter to President Truman:

[The Allies] have done or are doing some of the very things we are prosecuting Germans for. The French are so violating the Geneva

Convention in the treatment of prisoners of war that our command is taking back prisoners sent to them. We are prosecuting plunder and our Allies are practicing it. We say aggressive war is a crime and one of our allies asserts sovereignty over the Baltic States based on no title except conquest.[21]

The question of Allied conduct arose only briefly. One of those charged during the initial round of Nuremberg trials was Karl Doenitz, the commander of Germany's submarine fleet during much of the war. In addition to a broad array of other crimes, Doenitz was accused of waging unrestricted submarine warfare by targeting unarmed ships. The German admiral and his lawyer demonstrated to the judges that the Allied powers had also targeted unarmed merchant ships and often left survivors of sunken ships to their fate. Doenitz's lawyers even solicited statements from senior Allied naval commanders attesting to the similarity in tactics. He was not found guilty on that charge.[22] But the admiral's case was an exception; the Nuremberg and Tokyo trials otherwise remained firmly fixed on the massive sins of the German and Japanese leadership.

The high degree of Allied control—and the certainty that their interests and image would not be threatened—allowed the vast resources of these powerful states to serve the tribunal. The thousands of Allied troops on German and Japanese territory helped secure access to witnesses, archives, and documents. Occupation forces stood ready to arrest those individuals the prosecution sought to put on trial. For a brief moment, and in a very limited context, the world's most powerful states had pursued international legal accountability. As those trials ended, the critical question was whether that precedent would be incorporated into the network of international institutions being constructed in the wake of the war.

Accountability in the Architecture?

The Nuremberg and Tokyo trials were a small part of a much broader, Western-led effort to construct institutional bulwarks against renewed conflict and instability. The United Nations began meeting in early 1946 with a mandate to maintain international peace and security, through the application of collective force if necessary. In The Hague the next year, a new International Court of Justice (ICJ)—designed to resolve disputes between states, rather than to prosecute individuals—heard its first case, brought by the United Kingdom against Albania.[23] In the financial realm, the

International Monetary Fund and the International Bank for Reconstruction and Development (soon to become known as the World Bank) sought to rebuild war-torn societies and prevent another spiraling financial crisis like the one that had laid the foundations of political extremism and war.

Many observers saw the creation of a permanent instrument to punish aggression and atrocities as a natural extension of this institution-building exercise. As he left the post of president of the Nuremberg tribunal in November 1946, the American lawyer Nicholas Biddle urged President Truman to support the rapid codification of the Nuremberg precedents and the development of an international criminal code. The president responded positively, but cautiously. "The setting up of such a code as that which you recommend is indeed an enormous undertaking, but it deserves to be studied and weighed by the best legal minds the world over."[24] A month later, the UN General Assembly instructed a committee to formulate an International Criminal Code to codify the Nuremberg principles.[25]

Support for establishing a system of international criminal justice expressed itself in other ways. In December 1948, again under the auspices of the United Nations, countries negotiated and signed a convention on the prevention and punishment of genocide, a crime that the Holocaust had defined. The document evinced some optimism about the prospects for an international court. Article 6 instructed signatories to prosecute individual perpetrators before national courts or "such international penal tribunal as may have jurisdiction."[26] In the drafting of the convention, that reference to a possible future court had almost been stripped out by the Soviet Union, which voiced objections based on national sovereignty. The United States and several European allies managed to reinsert it.[27]

During the next several years, multiple UN-appointed committees developed draft statutes for a permanent international tribunal to punish war crimes and crimes against humanity. The UN's top legal official hopefully touted the Nuremberg principles and described the "crumbling of the old doctrine that international law is a system which concerns states alone." Citing the work of the high-level commission, he predicted "we are about to witness a conscious and well-prepared effort at large scale progressive development and codification."[28]

The momentum dissipated, however, for a variety of reasons. Public attention, briefly captured by senior Nazis and Japanese officials in the dock, faded as the trials proceeded slowly and with little drama. (By the end of the initial proceedings, only a few journalists were regularly attending court sessions.[29]) The determination of the Allies to seek punishment for key perpetrators also diminished considerably as the trials progressed. The emerging Cold War made turning western Germany and Japan into reliable allies a strategic imperative. With US acquiescence, some of those convicted and imprisoned in Germany and Japan were quietly released before their sentences expired.[30]

More important, the states that had created the Nuremberg precedent showed little enthusiasm for a court that might be able to scrutinize their own behavior. The universality that Robert Jackson had ringingly promised soon seemed hopelessly impractical to the Allies. In August 1951, speaking to the UN's legal committee, Britain's attorney general inveighed against the idea of a permanent international criminal court in terms that made clear how narrowly circumscribed the Nuremberg legacy might be: "Who is going to bring such men before an international court? If they were brought to court how could judicial proceedings take place in an atmosphere of political tension that would be bound to prevail? Would not this court bid fair to become the focus of international discord?"[31]

Discussion of a permanent court continued fitfully in New York through 1952. The British, in particular, insisted upon the impracticality of the venture. The potential court faced a "simple dilemma," a British official said in November 1952. "If the [proposed] statute imposes obligations, governments will not sign it, and if it does not the court will not work."[32] A permanent court was not necessary to try individuals for ordinary war crimes, which were best handled by national courts or by ad hoc mechanisms established after a conflict. The real gap was a mechanism to prosecute aggressive war and crimes against humanity. But in these areas, London argued, an international court was not feasible. These crimes were almost always committed by senior state officials under the color of state authority, and states would simply not surrender their senior leaders for trial. Only in rare circumstances—such as a country's utter defeat or an internal revolution—might an international court be able to get hold of a suspect. British officials concluded that the push for a court was the result not of practical analysis but of emotion.

> [B]elief in the project of an international criminal court…is largely the result of the deep impression created on the public mind by the successful and striking action of the Nürnberg and Tokyo tribunals. This feeling has not, however, always been accompanied by a corresponding recognition of the peculiar circumstances under which those tribunals functioned, and which alone made their successful operation possible.[33]

While no other country mounted as robust an assault, the British skepticism was widespread, particularly among larger powers. Brazil's delegate doubted that the idea was practical. India's ambassador agreed. "Only the establishment of world government could secure and guarantee the jurisdiction of the court," he said.[34] The Soviet Union and its allies objected to the notion as a threat to national sovereignty. With the project obviously stillborn, the United States took a somewhat detached view, insisting that debate was healthy, but strongly suggesting that the issue should remain in the realm of discussion. Of the traditional major powers, only France was broadly supportive.[35]

The UN's International Law Commission finally produced a draft statute for an international criminal court in late 1953. It called for a mostly toothless court that could only take cases when all states involved had acquiesced.[36] In the political climate of the early Cold War, even this unthreatening draft had little chance of success. In the West, the belief in the prospects of international institutions that had been so strong immediately after the war had been shaken by the UN's early paralysis, and particularly by the Soviet Union's frequent use of the veto power in the Security Council. For their part, the Soviets had no interest in a body designed to punish national leaders for using force.

The blueprints for a permanent war crimes court were shelved, and the idea of a permanent court attracted attention only sporadically during the 1960s and 1970s. Antiwar activists floated the idea as a means of prosecuting those they deemed responsible for the Vietnam War.[37] Associations of lawyers and judges, supported in some cases by smaller countries, occasionally tried to revive interest in the project. In 1977, delegates from twenty-seven countries convened in Barbados to draft a statute for a court that could try international terrorists. In 1979, the UN General Assembly asked a group of experts to draft a plan for implementing international instruments like the apartheid convention.[38] These efforts culminated in a plan for an international criminal court and a series of mostly unread reports.

Around that time, a diminutive but intense New York lawyer named Benjamin Ferencz devoted himself to reviving the idea of a permanent court. As a young man, Ferencz had served in General George Patton's army and walked through liberated German concentration camps. As the war ended, the Harvard Law School graduate served on Robert Jackson's staff in Nuremberg. In the spring of 1946, an investigator alerted him to newly discovered and quite meticulous records that had been kept by German *Einsatzgruppen* units operating in Eastern Europe and the Soviet Union. Ferencz convinced Jackson that the revelations warranted a separate trial, and the 29-year-old lawyer himself became lead prosecutor in that case, brought by the United States alone after the main Nuremberg trial ended.

Several decades later, Ferencz was frustrated that the project of international justice to which he had devoted years of work had such dim prospects. Even as US-Soviet tension escalated, and as the prospects for meaningful international cooperation appeared to be at a low ebb, he began a lonely campaign. In 1980, he published a two-volume monograph documenting the historical roots of an international criminal court.[39] In 1985, he wrote a *Common Sense Guide to World Peace*, which included calls for a permanent court. As a living link to Nuremberg, Ferencz had embarked on a path that would make him the unofficial patron saint of the international justice movement.

In his writings, Ferencz insisted that an international criminal court was an essential step toward lasting world peace. Even in a dark international landscape, he detected signs that "humankind is experiencing an erratic and turbulent evolutionary movement toward a more rational order."[40] His conception of the project encompassed two purposes: (1) to regulate the conduct of hostilities and (2) to judge national decisions to use force in the first place. For Ferencz, the enemy was not just atrocities or abuses committed during war, but war itself.

Given his involvement at Nuremberg, it was not unnatural that Ferencz would see these two imperatives as part of one coherent project. Conceptually, however, they were distinct. Theologians, philosophers, and lawyers who had grappled with the justice and legality of war had usually distinguished two concepts. The *jus ad bellum* set certain conditions for when it was moral to use force, including having a just cause, a reasonable chance of success, and proper authority. The *jus in bello* provided related but distinct principles for how force could be used morally. Combatants had to distinguish between combatants and noncombatants, for example, and obey rules of proportionality.[41]

The latter branch had developed considerably and been codified in a variety of ways by the time of the Nuremberg trials. Even powerful states found it in their interest to create basic rules of warfare, not least to ensure that their forces would be treated decently if captured. In part because of the Nuremberg and Tokyo jurisprudence, the rules for conduct in warfare advanced even further shortly after the Second World War. In 1949, dozens of states signed the Fourth Geneva Convention, which provided new detail on the obligations of combatant states to protect civilians during conflict.[42]

By contrast, the law on the right to use force remained murky. The Allies prosecuted German and Japanese leaders for waging aggressive war, but no clear definition of aggression emerged from the tribunal's work. The UN's early attempts to define aggression also foundered, and the United States, in particular, grew suspicious of the effort. Powerful Western states worried that the concept might be turned against the United States and its allies. One US official described the push for a definition as "absolute nonsense." Britain's UN ambassador labeled the effort "undesirable, unacceptable, and unnecessary."[43]

It was not until 1974 that the UN General Assembly managed to approve even a non-binding definition.[44] That text won only lukewarm support from several major powers. The British insisted that the definition merely upheld provisions of the UN Charter. Soviet diplomats expressed skepticism about the new definition, and the Chinese delegate said it would not alter his country's position on the issue.[45] Moreover, the actual practice of states showed widely diverging views on when force was permissible. While states could agree on basic principles of conduct during conflict, consensus on when it was lawful to use force was much more elusive, particularly for major powers with a taste for intervention.[46] With the broad project of international justice essentially frozen, however, that fissure between the different elements of the Nuremberg legacy was mostly obscured.

The Legacy Revived

It took the new flexibility of post-Cold War diplomacy and the atrocities that accompanied the disintegration of Yugoslavia in the early 1990s to bring the idea of a permanent court back to life. The violent break-up of that country became bloodiest in the ethnically jumbled province of Bosnia and Herzegovina. In April 1992, Serb forces in the country began to carve out an ethnically pure area of the country. Thousands of Bosnian Muslims were expelled from their homes, and some were herded into makeshift camps. As footage leaked out of eastern Bosnia showing emaciated prisoners behind barbed wire, the parallels to Holocaust images were haunting. Journalists, activists, and citizens' groups in the West pressured reluctant Western governments to respond, insisting that the nature of the post-Cold War order was at stake.[47]

The demands for an institutional response fell mainly on the doorstep of the United Nations and its Security Council. In the early 1990s, the fifteen-member body, which the UN Charter gives responsibility for "maintaining international peace and security," was enjoying a remarkable renaissance. The Council had often been peripheral during the Cold War. Serial vetoes by the superpowers transformed the body into little more than a debating society. By 1990, that often reflexive obstructionism had ended. A united

Security Council even authorized the use of military force against Iraq after its August 1990 invasion of Kuwait. In the wake of the successful Gulf War, the Council dispatched tens of thousands of peacekeepers around the globe and began experimenting with other tools for maintaining order.[48]

The frenetic activism did not imply the end of discord on the Council. Its members split, in particular, over how to respond to the violence in the Balkans. The Council had sent a large peacekeeping force to Croatia and Bosnia, but it was lightly armed and incapable of stopping the conflict or preventing atrocities. As news of fresh horrors streamed out of Bosnia, the United States agitated for a more robust response against the Bosnian Serbs but balked at committing its own forces. The British and French, who had contributed thousands of peacekeepers, opposed more aggressive steps, concerned that their forces would become combatants. Russia, meanwhile, began to chafe at the opprobrium heaped on the Serbs, their co-religionists and historical allies.[49]

Even as it hesitated on more dramatic steps, the Council in October 1992 managed to authorize an investigation of atrocities in the former Yugoslavia.[50] Soon after, the United States advocated that the Council create a tribunal to prosecute those responsible for abuses. The US initiative met with a mixed response. British diplomats initially saw little utility in a judicial instrument that might complicate political negotiations. Other countries disliked the idea that the Security Council could, with a stroke of its collective pen, create an international court, something that normally would be accomplished by drafting a treaty. In the end, these objections yielded to the strong American preference for trials and the perceived necessity of an international response to the violence. The lead American negotiator, State Department official David Scheffer, concluded "[t]he 'soft' option of an international criminal tribunal represented a form of action much less costly...than the 'hard' option of military intervention."[51]

In February 1993, the Security Council voted to create a special tribunal to investigate and prosecute atrocities committed during the conflict. With a seat in The Hague, the International Criminal Tribunal for the Former Yugoslavia (ICTY) had the mandate to investigate and prosecute those individuals responsible for crimes committed on the territory of that fragmenting country. The Security Council gave the court primary responsibility for these prosecutions; it would have priority over any national courts in the region.[52]

The atrocities in the Balkans were soon dwarfed by those in Rwanda. In April 1994, a massive killing campaign began in that country. An extremist ruling faction unleashed a well-planned campaign of violence that ultimately took the lives of more than 800,000 people. In late 1994, after the genocidal regime had been deposed and most killing had ended, the Security Council authorized another tribunal to investigate the massacres. The court would sit in Arusha, Tanzania, and would share a prosecutor, although not judges, with the Yugoslav tribunal.[53]

Supporters saw a variety of potential benefits to these courts. It was argued that prosecuting those responsible for atrocities would help individualize guilt and thereby mitigate or even prevent new cycles of ethnic violence.[54] Tribunals could help deter new atrocities by making clear to potential perpetrators that there would be no impunity. At a broader level, Western politicians argued that they were rekindling the powerful Nuremberg legacy and inserting the demands of justice into the cynical realm of world politics. "There is an echo in this chamber," US ambassador Madeleine Albright intoned after the Council voted to create the Yugoslavia tribunal, "the Nuremberg principles have been reaffirmed."[55]

The tribunals for Rwanda and the former Yugoslavia echoed Nuremberg in another way: these were instruments fashioned by certain of the most powerful states—through the mechanism of the UN Security Council, rather than by the international community as a whole. And like the Nuremberg court, they were narrowly focused on crimes committed by others. The tribunals' reach was territorially and temporally limited to the particular episodes of violence that the Council wanted to address. Neither court was expressly proscribed from investigating and indicting individuals of any particular nationality. In theory, an American or Russian who signed up with one of the factions in Bosnia and committed crimes might come under the jurisdiction of the court. But that possibility appeared so remote that it was not even considered by the Council during negotiations on the resolution.[56]

Even with the endorsement of the Security Council, and strong support from the United States in particular, both tribunals stumbled. The Yugoslav tribunal had no prosecutor for eighteen months as Security Council members politicked fruitlessly over an appropriate individual to lead investigations. A leading candidate, the Egyptian-born academic Cherif Bassiouni, fell afoul of Russia, which did not want a Muslim prosecutor. The United States proposed the Argentine lawyer Luis Moreno-Ocampo, who had become prominent by helping to prosecute his country's *junta* leaders, but his own government declined to back him. The Council eventually settled on the Venezuelan Ramon Escovar Salom. He reported to The Hague in early 1994—only to immediately resign his position and accept a ministerial post at home. Finally, in July 1994, a consensus candidate emerged who was willing to serve. With strong prodding from the tribunal's chief judge, South Africa's Richard Goldstone accepted the post.[57]

Goldstone encountered a grim reality in The Hague. The tribunal was operating on a shoestring budget and struggling to attract qualified applicants. The willingness of powerful states to create the court, he quickly discovered, did not imply commitment to its success. On budgetary and logistical matters, the court faced obstructionism from the United Nations bureaucracy, of which the court was nominally a part. Frustrated by red tape, the prosecutor at least once relied on the support of a private foundation to secure equipment that his field investigators required.[58] Few member states—even the Security Council members who had created the tribunal—seemed enthusiastic about its work. The tribunal only got hold of its first suspect—a low-ranking Bosnian Serb named Duško Tadić—in 1995. Goldstone knew that pursuing that case was almost perverse given Tadić's minor role, but the prosecutor was desperate to show that the tribunal was in motion. "We had an empty prison. There was a great deal of frustration. The judges were frustrated. We were all frustrated."[59]

Even as the Tadić trial proceeded, the combination of NATO airstrikes and a Croatian military offensive finally brought an end to the Bosnian war. The Dayton peace accords cleared the way for a large and well-armed NATO stabilization force, which arrived in December 1995. For the tribunal, the presence of such a muscular force in Bosnia should have been a boon. To that point, apprehending senior indictees had been almost impossible; now thousands of Western soldiers with the authority and wherewithal to arrest these individuals were pouring into Bosnia. But NATO proved reluctant to arrest indicted war criminals, even those its forces encountered during routine operations. For its part, neighboring Serbia showed no interest in supporting the work of the tribunal that was focusing heavily on Serb crimes, and Serbian politicians regularly railed against its work.[60]

Meanwhile, the Rwandan tribunal was beset with political and managerial problems. The post-genocide Rwandan government fully supported prosecuting the perpetrators of the mass killings, but its vision of a tribunal was quite different from that of the Council. The Rwandan government wanted a court that would be located in Rwanda, could impose the death penalty, and would allow government participation. Unable to secure these objectives, Rwanda had ultimately voted against the resolution creating the court.[61] As the tribunal became operational, its relationship with the Rwandan authorities soon descended into "rancor and bitterness."[62] Goldstone—at that time, the Rwandan and Yugoslav tribunals shared a prosecutor—clashed with

Rwandan officials over who should get custody of key suspects. Leading human rights figures were also dissatisfied with the court, charging that its work was characterized by "bumbling and delays."[63]

By the mid-1990s, the ad hoc tribunals were works in progress. Blessed by the Security Council, major-power support for the institutions was nonetheless episodic. Nor was there clear evidence that the tribunals had contributed to stability in the region or to reconciliation between the warring parties. In the Balkans, and particularly in Bosnia, ethnic tension and recriminations continued to dominate national politics. Explicit warnings about future prosecutions did not prevent low-level violence in the disputed province of Kosovo. Near Rwanda, fresh atrocities occurred as Rwandan government forces hunted down extremists and as militia groups battled for control in eastern Congo. Human rights groups charged the new Rwandan government with a range of abuses, including massacres of political opponents.[64]

Despite their shaky beginnings, the special tribunals galvanized a broader movement for international justice. Mechanisms created by certain major powers acting through the Security Council had helped to generate a broad movement that was beyond the direct control of those states. Key human rights organizations, including Human Rights Watch and Amnesty International, made international justice one of their priorities. Major foundations and private donors poured funds into advocacy efforts aimed at governments and the general public.[65]

The Road to Rome

For this gathering group of advocates, the Yugoslav and Rwandan tribunals raised a simple question. If the United Nations was willing to create special courts to address specific conflicts, why not create a permanent version that could stand ready to investigate future crimes? Not only would a permanent court be more efficient than separate tribunals, it was argued, but it would be a more effective deterrent against future atrocities. Potential perpetrators would know in advance that an international court stood ready to address crimes they might commit.[66] The ad hoc tribunals, argued Amnesty International, "are not a substitute for a permanent international court able to try people accused of gross violations of humanitarian and human rights law wherever the crimes are committed."[67]

In late 1994, as interest in international justice grew, the UN's International Law Commission produced a new draft statute for a permanent criminal court.[68] Soon thereafter, an ad hoc group of states emerged to work on the draft and advance the idea of a permanent court. They dubbed themselves the "like-minded group" and began meeting in early 1995. Initially, the group was heavily European, but it enjoyed the support of several Latin American states. Australia, New Zealand, and Canada were also enthusiastic. Two Canadian diplomats described the like-minded as dominated by "middle powers that were not directly involved in any conflicts, and had relatively little historical baggage to compromise the credibility of their search for humanitarian solutions."[69]

This quality of the like-minded was not incidental to their goal. The key members of the group conceived of themselves as depoliticized in an important sense: they lacked strong political interests and strategic entanglements in many parts of the world. Because they were not global powers, they thought of themselves as more able to construct international architecture that would be perceived as fair and legitimate by the rest of the world. The usually unstated corollary of this thesis was clear: powerful states with complex interests had limited ability to advance impartial international justice.

As diplomatic support for the court firmed up, the energy of influential human rights organizations and justice advocates took a more concentrated form. In early 1995, a group of nongovernmental organizations met in New York to coordinate advocacy efforts. The resulting Coalition for an International Criminal Court (CICC) developed a public relations strategy and began reaching out to supportive governments. Funding arrived from the well-heeled MacArthur and Ford Foundations as well as from sympathetic governments. The European Commission and Canada provided support that allowed the coalition to hold conferences and coordinate the work of its several dozen members.[70]

In the UN committee where negotiations were proceeding, the ongoing atrocities in the Balkans and in central Africa created a sense of urgency. John Washburn, a former US diplomat and UN official who watched the negotiations closely identified a "psycho-emotional" need to respond:

> There was a very strong feeling worldwide, including in the United States, that we can't have Rwanda and Bosnia again. We screwed it up, we had these unspeakable situations, we now have to recognize that there are leaders out there who will try to do these things again. We have to have some way of dealing with this.[71]

That sense of urgency collided, however, with the interests of some of the most powerful states. The permanent members of the UN Security Council

(P5)—the United States, the United Kingdom, France, Russia, and China—
were all wary of the project, although to different degrees. Their apprehen-
sions had spoken and unspoken elements. Outwardly, the P5 expressed
concern that an independent and permanent court might complicate ongoing
Security Council attempts to manage conflict. The concern was plausible: by
the mid-1990s, the Council had authorized large peacekeeping missions and
regularly passed resolutions and issued statements regarding more than a
dozen situations around the world. These efforts at global stabilization often
involved facilitating negotiations between and among disaffected political
leaders, dictators, and militia commanders. A fully autonomous international
tribunal might derail, or at least complicate, these initiatives. Not often articulated in public was the more parochial worry that a court not controlled
by the Council might target the P5 or their allies. The veto power effectively
immunized the permanent members and their close allies from criticism by
the only international authority with binding power. A criminal court independent of the Council and its veto power would threaten that privilege.

Because an ICC seemed to be a natural extension of the ad hoc tribunals,
however, skeptical major powers were reluctant to openly oppose the initiative. Instead, they expressed concern at the quick pace of negotiations. In
October 1995, the Chinese negotiator insisted that "[i]t would be premature
to set a date for a diplomatic conference or to begin preparing for that conference."[72] The United Kingdom emphasized the amount of work that remained
before a convention could be drafted.[73] As they sought to manage the process,
some P5 officials insisted that the proposed court not infringe on Security
Council territory. Russian officials warned that an ICC "should not, in any
way, limit the powers of the Security Council."[74]

For their part, US officials often voiced concerns about the political fea-
sibility of the project. A US official warned in 1995 "if we approach the court
from an academically pure perspective, without regard for political realities
and what States are willing to participate in and fund, we will have wasted our
time. The United States has consistently cautioned against unrealistic propo-
sitions that would create a court that would be ineffective."[75] For the United
States, "political realities" meant that the Council had to have the decisive
say over the court's activities. Without that element of control, US officials
implied, the court would lack the support and resources it would need to
function.

The French shared the general P5 desire to preserve their privileges and
suggested that the Council "screen all state complaints to see if they involve
a situation of threat to or breach of international peace and security."[76] The

French military had an even more specific concern, arising out of the recent Balkans conflict. For several critical years, the commander of UN forces in Bosnia had been a French general. When the Srebrenica massacre occurred as NATO planes flew lazy circles over Bosnia, outraged observers asked whether senior UN and NATO officials could be charged with complicity. While the notion was a stretch legally, it created sharp sensitivity and led French officers to briefly limit their cooperation with the Yugoslav tribunal.[77] As the ICC negotiations advanced, French military officials insisted that these concerns be addressed.

The P5 suggestion that any new court be effectively controlled by the Security Council met stiff resistance from civil society activists, the like-minded group of states, and other states wary of the Council's powers. William Pace, the leader of the Coalition for an International Criminal Court, warned in 1996 that "some countries...want the court to be controlled by the Security Council, reducing an ICC to a sham status of a 'permanent' *ad hoc* tribunal; one which would dispense international criminal justice only to small and weak countries, never to violators in powerful nations."[78] One small-country diplomat saw in the entire ICC negotiation process a reflection of the 1945 debates that had produced a Security Council dominated by powerful states:

> [A]lthough nobody ever articulated it was that there was a bit of a re-run of the 1945 negotiations in San Francisco about the veto, and the feeling was that the large guys weren't going to get away with it this time. The smaller people had a better bargaining position at this stage and the numbers were much bigger and there were people with more clout.[79]

One powerful state disrupted this pattern. Germany emerged as a stout defender of the court's independence from the Council. As Ronen Steinke has documented, the German position on the idea of a court shifted decisively in the mid-1990s. "Germany began to voice concerns that a 'UN Court'...would perpetuate unjustified privileges for the five veto-wielding members of the UN Security Council." For German policymakers, Steinke has argued, "the risk of an ICC prosecutor running wild was ultimately seen as a lesser evil than a court which would be seen from the beginning as distributing unequal justice."[80]

The insistence that international justice must reach the powerful as well as the weak echoed Justice Jackson's opening statement at Nuremberg. The experience of that tribunal was frequently cited in the negotiations surrounding the court, and Benjamin Ferencz's energetic presence provided a constant reminder of its legacy. But in at least one respect the focus of the project had changed considerably. Nuremberg had as its centerpiece the prosecution of aggressive war. By the time the ICC negotiations began in the mid-1990s, there was no longer consensus that prosecuting aggression was a feasible or profitable endeavor. Most major powers (with the notable exception of Germany) opposed giving an international court the means to prosecute aggression.

Surprisingly, several prominent human rights advocates shared that skepticism. Human Rights Watch worried that "[t]he very process of the court's determining when aggression is not self-defense would have the potential of undermining the court's appearance of impartiality."[81] The first several years of the post-Cold War era had brought about an important change in how the human rights movement, in particular, viewed the use of force. During the Cold War, the use of force by major powers threatened global conflagration. After the Cold War, those fears receded. In Somalia and Bosnia, international forces had intervened forcefully to address humanitarian crises. In those cases, the intervening forces had permission from the Security Council. But it was becoming apparent that there might also be cases in which humanitarian intervention would occur without UN approval (as it did during the Kosovo conflict in 1999). In such a situation, a mission to end atrocities and defend human rights might also qualify as an act of aggression. For the human rights community, events were prying apart two important legacies of Nuremberg.

In spite of the P5 admonitions, the drive for a permanent court continued to clear procedural hurdles. In December 1995, the UN General Assembly established a preparatory committee to prepare for a formal diplomatic conference.[82] It met six times between 1995 and the spring of 1998. The momentum of the project surprised some observers. "Countries that hoped to bog down the drive toward an international criminal court with more studies…found instead that this momentum had extraordinary power. The court's supporters were deterred neither by the difficulty of drafting a long and complicated statute nor by conventional concerns about sovereignty and the unknown."[83]

In the summer of 1997, diplomats from Singapore offered an important compromise on the relationship between the court and the Security Council. They suggested that the Council should have certain limited powers over the court's work. If the Council agreed that a particular inquiry would be counterproductive, for example, it could instruct the court to halt the investigation for a set period of time. Singapore also suggested that the Council have the power to refer situations to the court. It was a deft proposal: the Council acting as a whole would retain certain privileges, but individual P5 members would be unable to block court action on their own.

The Singapore compromise fell on increasingly fertile political ground in several key states. In November 1996, Americans had reelected Bill Clinton. Madeleine Albright, who had championed the Yugoslav and Rwandan tribunals as UN ambassador, became secretary of state and appointed David Scheffer as the first-ever US ambassador-at-large for war crimes issues.[84] In May 1997, Britain's Labor Party, out of office for almost two decades, swept back into power and Tony Blair became prime minister. In France, a snap National Assembly election a few weeks later produced a socialist majority and compelled President Jacques Chirac to "cohabitate" with a socialist prime minister, Lionel Jospin.

These political shifts had important effects on the ICC negotiations. In late 1997, the United Kingdom broke ranks with the other permanent members of the Security Council by joining the like-minded group and supporting the compromise suggested by Singapore.[85] The more or less united front of the P5 had splintered, and the British decision reverberated through the UN conference rooms where diplomats were laboring over a draft text. At the same time, the French government became serious about winning over the court skeptics (mostly military) within its ranks. "There was a decision to join, to be in favor—and then there was a political agreement between Jospin and Chirac to join but protect the military, to give something to the military," recalled Gilbert Bitti, who served on the French negotiating team.[86] A French official named Beatrice le Frapper du Hellen—later to become a key figure at the ICC—was told that France had to end up on the "right" side of the negotiations, but that the concerns of the military had to be addressed.[87]

The Clinton administration's position on the court was more ambivalent. President Clinton had called for "nations around the world who value freedom and tolerance [to] establish a permanent international court to prosecute, with the support of the United Nations Security Council, serious violations of international law."[88] The statement evidenced a clear desire to be associated with the project, but Clinton's reference to the Security Council was a critical caveat. Unlike the British and the French, the Americans showed few signs of weakening on their insistence that the Council remain in control of international judicial interventions. The Pentagon was paying close attention to the negotiations, and key Defense officials warned that they would oppose any court that could have jurisdiction over Americans. The Clinton administration was therefore divided on the issue: it could not abide a court that might scrutinize US behavior but supported the advance of international justice. In three of the P5 states then, the political stars had aligned to produce governments receptive to multilateral initiatives like the court, or at least not openly opposed to such projects. Gilbert Bitti contends that absent those shifts, the project would likely have stalled: "If we didn't have that very specific combination of socialists in United Kingdom and France plus Democrats in the United States, the ICC was doomed. It's a very bizarre combination. It's a little bit of luck. [Absent that] you would have had all the P5 skeptical and that would have been the end of the story."[89]

Standing in the way of the process carried diplomatic and reputational costs that several of these governments were reluctant to incur, not least because the project might founder quietly in UN conference rooms.[90] Treaty-making at the global level had long been the work of national diplomats negotiating with little public attention. Consensus was normally the rule, and drafts only became actual treaties once agreement had been reached, particularly with the most powerful states. The possibility still existed that the ICC project might expire without any major capital being the obvious cause of death.

A separate multilateral effort underway at the time—negotiations to limit the use of land mines—should have given major-power diplomats pause about the likelihood that negotiations would fail. An important change was occurring in the way that international treaties were constructed. Both the relative obscurity of multilateral negotiations and the consensus tradition came under strain in the heady days after the Cold War. In the case of land mines, a remarkable public campaign, later awarded the Nobel Peace Prize, helped propel international negotiations at unprecedented speed. When the United States and several other major powers objected to the emerging draft, dozens of states voted in December 1997 to approve the treaty without them. The outcome of the land mines negotiation was a "complete shock to the system," according to a lead US negotiator. "Professional negotiators who'd been negotiating law of war treaties for the last 50 years weren't used to seeing the superpower not be part of something. Russia, China, United States were not part of the convention, but [other states] went ahead and signed it anyway."[91]

A few months after the land mine treaty was signed, the UN committee working on the ICC transmitted its own, more developed draft statute to the conference delegates. The draft had changed considerably from the version that the International Law Commission prepared, moving primarily toward more independence from the control of states. The new draft strengthened the powers of the court's prosecutor in particular, granting that official the authority to initiate prosecutions without any state action (the so-called *proprio motu* power). As diplomats prepared to negotiate the final text in Rome, a court that could hold even powerful leaders to account was tantalizingly close.

Endgame

Delegates traveling to the Rome Conference in June 1998 had received a consolidated draft that included more than 1,700 bracketed items, each marking some point of difference between states. The differences ranged from core issues of jurisdiction and crimes to more detailed issues of procedure, evidence, and the court's proposed budget procedures. The speed with which the ICC project had moved was unusual, and many government officials "had little time to study the text, brief their superiors, and obtain appropriate instructions on the political and complex legal issues."[92] Even as the Yugoslav and Rwandan tribunals struggled to establish themselves, a major diplomatic conference convened to construct a permanent court.

The significant work that remained on the draft did not dampen expectations. A huge billboard at the conference center read simply, "We Expect Results." The conference generated excitement among activists, international lawyers, and many world leaders. Kofi Annan, then the UN Secretary-General, cast the delegates' efforts in epochal terms. "Until now, when powerful men committed crimes against humanity, they knew that as long as they remained powerful no earthly court could judge them."[93]

As the conference began, the British decision to join the like-minded group gave the court's advocates hope that major-power opposition might dissolve. The NGO coalition lauded what it described as a process of "steering Britain away from the other four permanent members of the Security Council to accept a more limited Council role over the Court's work."[94] But the British shift had not triggered any broader movement by major powers. The United States, France, China, and Russia remained skeptical, as did Japan and India. Of the major powers, only Germany and Brazil appeared fully committed to the like-minded group's vision of a court.

A key feature of the conference diplomacy was the inability of these powerful states to construct a united front. Even the P5, with their shared interest in preserving the Security Council's prerogatives, failed to form an effective negotiating position. The like-minded group, by contrast, had produced a detailed guide for its members to help guide them through the maze of bracketed text. In the weeks before the conference, leading like-minded states circulated a text indicating the group's preferences on most disputed points.

Germany, together with a number of other delegates, went through the entire draft and we bolded all articles which were good and positive and we did not bold all provisions and proposals which were not

good in our view. I sent this version of the draft statute to the German
UN mission in New York. We duplicated it and bound it and gave it
to all like-minded delegations. We told them, you just have to look at
the bolded text, which in our view is the best option for the provision
in question.[95]

During the Rome negotiations, the large NGO coalition kept careful watch
on the assembled diplomats, often advising them on what language to support. The activists combined private counsel with public pressure. At one
point during the conference 300 protesters laid down on a street in front
of the Coliseum to symbolize the victims of crimes against humanity. Their
determined advocacy and expertise allowed them to influence matters that
had once been the exclusive province of diplomats.[96] Over the course of the
conference, the NGO coalition proved particularly effective in defending the
prosecutor's *proprio motu* powers.

The Rome Conference followed the pattern of most major UN treaty
negotiations in that it gave no privileged place to major powers and
attempted to respect the formal equality of participants. A so-called Bureau
of the Committee of the Whole (known simply as the Bureau) organized the
negotiations, established internal deadlines, and managed the evolving draft.
Its composition reflected the influence of states other than major powers.
Canadian diplomat Philippe Kirsch, who had stepped in at the last minute
to replace an ailing Dutch diplomat, chaired the body. Vice-chairs came from
Argentina, Romania, and Lesotho.[97]

The large American delegation that arrived in Rome still lacked a clear
bottom-line position, but it knew that key constituencies in Washington
were alarmed at the direction of negotiations. In March, the Pentagon had
called together military attachés from around the world to discuss the dangers an international court might pose.[98] Senator Jesse Helms, chair of the
Senate Foreign Relations Committee, informed Secretary of State Madeleine
Albright that he was "unalterably opposed to the creation of a permanent
U.N. criminal court" and warned that any treaty without a US veto over its
operations would be "dead on arrival" in the Senate.[99] Several staffers from
Helms's office accompanied the American delegation to Rome.

During the conference, the US delegation continued to insist on a close
link between the Security Council and the proposed court. As it had been
doing for months, the United States framed this position as an exercise in
realism. Delegates "must distinguish carefully between the ideal of an international criminal court and the reality of the world today. Negotiating the

Court's establishment should not ignore existing institutions that can support the Court's goals or vexing problems that could cause its politicization."[100] That line became even more insistent as the negotiations progressed. Scheffer warned, "[i]f there are people walking around in a dreamy sort of way about the utility of an International Criminal Court without the US and several permanent members of the Security Council and several other populous democracies…I simply beg to differ."[101]

Statements like these produced a dynamic of ongoing suspicion between the like-minded group and the NGO coalition, on the one hand, and the United States, on the other. One member of the US negotiating team recalled the tension: "You'd walk into a big meeting room and you'd see a whole bunch of people and they'd see you coming and they'd disperse or they'd whisper to each other. So you knew other things were going on that you weren't party to and that they didn't want you to know about and they were plotting against you."[102] That tension extended to interactions between US negotiators and the NGO coalition. Scheffer upbraided NGO leaders during one meeting for claiming to speak for the "international community."[103] The United States was the most vocal skeptic of the like-minded position at Rome, but not the only one. The Chinese government expressed consistent discomfort with the proposed court's power to investigate internal conflicts and insisted that the Security Council must have a key role in authorizing investigations. "[T]he Court should not become a tool of political struggles or a means of interfering in other countries' internal affairs. Meanwhile, the ICC should not compromise the principal role of the UN, its Security Council in particular, in safeguarding world peace and security." France echoed that concern. "Let's recall that the statute needs to be applied in practice.…Without the Security Council, there would simply be the law of the jungle," a French delegate said.[104]

India was a diplomatic outlier at the conference. It had not joined the like-minded group, and it rejected the notion of a court that might be able to exercise jurisdiction over non-parties. But it did not share the specific concerns of the P5. In fact, one of its principal objections was that even the limited role the draft statute gave to the Security Council was excessive. India's lead negotiator insisted that a formal role for the Council would place its members "above the law and thus possess de jure impunity from prosecution, while individuals in all other States are presumed to be prone to committing such international crimes." Indian diplomats appeared concerned that the court would become a tool of Western states, opening the door to "European neo-colonialism."[105]

Even as the largest questions of the court's reach remained unanswered, the gathered negotiators made progress on many other issues. Common law and civil law lawyers forged a hybrid system for investigations and trials in which the court's judges would supervise and approve the work of the court's prosecutor. Negotiators agreed that crimes committed entirely within a state's borders could be covered. A group of largely Catholic states pushed to include forced abortion as a crime. Arab states insisted on including language on the resettlement of occupied territories and argued in favor of including the death penalty. Issue by issue, delegates brokered compromises and crafted language.[106]

They did so in negotiating sessions that often extended late into the night. The pace and complexity of the negotiations strained the normal reporting channels between delegations and their respective capitals. Delegates often had to make compromises without explicit instructions.

> We had so many working groups, working sometimes in parallel and sometimes not. We often would find ourselves working until 11:00 at night, going back to our hotel rooms, and all of us would be too tired to write up a report to send back to capitals and then receive instructions. What tended to happen was that by the time you got to the second or third day, you were already well beyond your initial starting position. It was left up to the individuals who were in Rome to negotiate on behalf of states, which was very good.[107]

In important respects, the negotiators at Rome had formed their own community, with weak links to national capitals. The small victories achieved by this increasingly cohesive band of diplomats heartened conference organizers, but the persistent divide on when and where the court would have jurisdiction placed them in a bind. Normal procedure at UN negotiating conferences insisted that consensus should be achieved if at all possible, and voting was frowned upon. As conference president Philippe Kirsch wrote later:

> [T]he best Court in the world on paper would be stillborn if it was unable to receive the political support and resources it needed to be viable. The Bureau was therefore determined to avoid any voting as long as possible. Voting might well produce majorities around certain principles that were widely supported, but it could also permanently alienate States and groups of States whose support was essential for the effectiveness of the court.[108]

That understanding had its limits. The Bureau regularly assessed the positions of states at the conference and found broad and consistent support for an independent court with expansive jurisdictional reach. There was not majority support for the most sweeping version—universal jurisdiction, which would mean that the court could prosecute relevant crimes committed anywhere in the world. However, most states appeared willing to accept multiple bases for jurisdiction, including for crimes committed within a member state, by a member-state citizen, against a member-state citizen, and when a member state hosted a wanted individual.[109]

After two weeks of negotiations, Kirsch was convinced that consensus was no longer possible. As the conference deadline approached, Kirsch and the other organizers made a critical choice. They opted not to suspend the conference, as the United States was urging. Canadian foreign minister Lloyd Axworthy flew to Rome to help make the case for forging ahead.[110] Instead of declaring deadlock, the conference organizers assembled a text that they believed could attract the votes of an overwhelming majority of states. In so doing, they realized that it might not meet the concerns of the United States or other skeptical powers. Richard Dicker of Human Rights Watch recalled that most court supporters had no illusions that the United States or several other major powers would sign. Instead, the court's advocates hoped to set in motion a longer process:

> There was at least an implicit recognition that a number of heavyweights were going to remain outside the court and that the imperative was to push the negotiation across the finish line . . . and even with the disadvantage of several heavyweights on the outside, rely on the momentum that the like-minded group would provide, rely on that quantitative mass and that sense of momentum, to pull along those heavyweights who were not so favorably disposed.[111]

As the denouement approached, several states attempted to broker a compromise that would clear the way for the powerful dissenters to join. Japan's ambassador convened a meeting with most major powers and attempted to broker a deal involving an opt-out provision allowing states to join the court without immediately giving it jurisdiction. A few days later, drawing in part on Japan's proposal, the P5 delegates met on their own to see whether they could salvage a common approach. In the residence of the Russian ambassador, the heads of the P5 delegations dined together and discussed possible strategies. At one point, the ambassadors broke out a laptop computer and began drafting language that would prevent the court from exercising jurisdiction over the "official actions" of nonmember states and would include a broad opt-out provision. Late that night, and several long-distance phone calls later, they emerged from the Russian residence with language all governments had approved.[112]

The P5 compromise did not last long. The next day, the British and French tested the language with other European states and encountered fierce resistance. "This is a catastrophe," German delegate Hans Peter Kaul recalled telling his British counterpart that morning. The attempts by Japan's Hisashi Owada to win support for the compromise yielded nothing. By the end of the day, the P5 compromise was dead:

> The like-minded had an almost violent reaction to the P-5 proposal and challenged Owada's credibility as an honest broker. Germany, as leader of the like-minded, led the verbal assault on Owada and the proposal. Time was running out. Once Owada reported the rejection, France and Britain split off, and the Wednesday night P-5 coalition collapsed.[113]

On the evening of July 16, the Bureau worked through the night to finish a draft statute. Urged on by his colleagues, Kirsch engineered a last minute change on jurisdiction that he hoped might make the court more attractive to reluctant states and included an optional seven-year opt-out on war crimes that the French had sought. But the draft would keep open the possibility—however remote—that soldiers and leaders of states that did not join the court could still face prosecution.[114]

The final maneuvering at Rome the next day reflected the broader unwillingness to yield to major-power concerns. "This is the court we and others warned of: strong on paper and weak in reality," Scheffer told the assembled delegates. Two of the world's behemoths, the United States and India, proposed last-minute amendments. A collection of small states, including Norway, Malawi, and Chile, blocked them. The defeat of the US and Indian amendments opened the way for a direct vote on the draft statute. One hundred and twenty states voted in favor, while only seven opposed the statute (the United States, China, Israel, Syria, Iraq, Cuba, and Yemen). Another twenty-one states abstained, including India.

"Those of us who were in Rome on Friday evening July 17, 1998 will, I believe, never experience another moment like that in our lives," one participant remembered. "I have never seen such an outbreak of emotion and celebration in any intergovernmental conference."[115] Another observer recalled that "diplomats abandoned themselves to cheers and chants, tears and embraces, and rhythmic stomping and applause."[116] Kirsch himself was almost overcome. The delegates had created an "instrument that they hoped would mark the beginning of a new era in which humanitarian values and the protection of victims might finally become centre stage, and not the usual side show to the protection of sovereignty or even the exercise of raw power."[117] Five decades after Nuremberg, the most powerful states were losing their grip on the mechanisms of international justice.

3

The Phantom Court (1998–2002)

THE ROME STATUTE won broad support but left many key powers unconvinced—and the United States alarmed. In the wake of the conference, the superpower cast about for a strategy toward the embryonic institution. Several US officials struggled to somehow align the superpower with the ICC project it had spurned. With a change in administration, however, that effort yielded to a campaign to oppose the court and limit its reach. As Washington pursued that policy, based in large part on the perceived dangers of global prosecutors, other experiments in international justice demonstrated the ability of powerful states to subtly manage the work of international courts.

The Court on Paper

The final days of the Rome Conference were hectic, and negotiators cobbled together the last elements of the statute so quickly that the resulting document had several typos, inconsistencies, and other drafting errors that had to be corrected. But from the messy diplomatic process emerged a document that provided for a court with wide reach and a remarkable degree of formal autonomy from even powerful states. The negotiations had whittled down considerably the like-minded group's vision of an entirely independent court that could prosecute atrocities wherever they occurred, but what remained still constituted a significant diminution of traditional national sovereignty.

The ICC was always conceived of as a court that would handle only the most serious international crimes, and the Rome Statute reflected that judgment. For the most part, conference organizers and delegates insisted that they were not defining new international crimes, but instead fashioning a permanent mechanism to punish what international law already made criminal. Efforts by some states to include crimes that had not been clearly defined internationally, including terrorism and drug trafficking, failed.[1]

The statute gave the court jurisdiction over four broad categories of crimes: genocide, crimes against humanity, war crimes, and aggression. Of these, genocide was the least controversial. The 1948 Genocide Convention had already defined the crime and committed states, however vaguely, to its prevention and prosecution. The Rome Statute adopted word for word the Genocide Convention's definition of the crime as violence committed "with intent to destroy, in whole or in part, a national, ethnical, racial or religious group."[2]

The negotiators at Rome also included the category of crimes against humanity with little debate. The term had existed since the mid-nineteenth century but took shape most clearly at Nuremberg. As they adjudicated a grim litany of massacres, torture, and rape, the ad hoc tribunals for the former Yugoslavia and Rwanda added detail to the concept. The Rome Statute defines crimes against humanity to encompass more than a dozen acts, such as murder, deportation, rape, and torture, when committed "as part of a widespread or systematic attack directed against any civilian population."[3] Delegates negotiated at length about several points, including whether a crime against humanity could occur during peacetime (they ultimately decided that it could). South Africa and a number of other African delegations pushed successfully to include apartheid in the category.[4]

The largest and most detailed category of crimes in the Rome Statute is war crimes. Existing international law—including the several Geneva Conventions—already defined prohibited activity in detail. The Rome Statute drew on those instruments (including provisions on targeting civilians, mistreating prisoners of war, and employing prohibited weapons) as well as from the jurisprudence of the ad hoc tribunals. Notwithstanding the pre-existing body of law, there were hard-fought battles about specific war crimes. Arab states squared off with Israel (generally backed by the United States) over whether resettling populations in occupied territories should be a war crime.[5] States negotiated until nearly the last minute over whether the use of certain weapons—such as biological and chemical weapons, landmines, blinding lasers, and nuclear weapons—should in itself be criminal.[6] An influential group of women's rights organizations pushed for more explicit recognition of rape and sexual abuse as war crimes, and the Rome Statute broke new ground by explicitly criminalizing forced pregnancy.[7]

Finally, the Statute provided for possible jurisdiction over aggression. Although it was central in the Nuremberg and Tokyo proceedings, aggression barely survived in the Rome Statute. It was included only on the condition that states agree at some later date on a binding definition. Until that agreement, the court would not be able to investigate or prosecute the crime. The special sensitivity reflected the fact that aggression is the most "political" of the crimes elaborated. It addresses why a conflict was waged rather than how it was conducted. It implicates state policy in a way that other crimes need not. The United States and several other delegations wanted to strip aggression from the text entirely. As a group, the permanent Security Council members had a particular concern; their shared view was that the UN Charter gave the Council unique authority to determine when aggression had occurred, and they believed any ICC investigation of the crime would require prior action by the Council.

In addition to elaborating categories of crimes, the Rome Statute provided the blueprints for the court as a working institution. All countries that sign and ratify the Statute secure seats and a vote in the Assembly of States Parties (ASP). There, the member states provide broad oversight and approve the court's budget. In a sense, the ASP can be considered the conduit through which the political power and authority of states is funneled to the court.

However, the statute made clear that the Assembly would not be in the business of selecting investigations or directing the court's prosecutor and judges. Nor were major powers accorded any special rights in the body; the assembly exercises its functions on a one-state, one-vote basis. Negotiators chose not to include any mechanism like the Security Council veto power or the larger voting shares accorded to major powers in the IMF and World Bank. Assembly votes require either a majority or two-thirds vote (although the Statute does encourage consensus decisions).

At the heart of the court is an independent prosecutor responsible for reviewing complaints and information about possible crimes, conducting investigations, requesting arrest warrants, and prosecuting those on trial. The prosecutor is elected by a majority of the member states but, once elected, he moves largely beyond the control of the states. The statute insists that the prosecutor "shall act independently as a separate organ of the Court."[8] Because the prosecutor serves a nine-year, nonrenewable term, he or she need not worry about securing support for reelection (although a majority of member states can remove the prosecutor before the end of his term for "serious misconduct").[9]

The statute calls for eighteen judges to supervise the prosecutor's investigations, issue arrest warrants, oversee trials, and rule on appeals. Judges are to serve either on pre-trial, trial, or appeals chambers, so that individual judges do not review their own decisions. As with the prosecutor, judges are elected by a majority vote in the ASP. The Rome Statute elaborates certain basic experience that judges should have and stresses the need for "the representation of the principal legal systems of the world, equitable geographical representation and a fair representation of female and male judges."[10] But the statute does not give major powers any special right to judgeships, nor did the delegates at Rome broker any informal agreement giving major powers special privileges.

The Rome Statute outlines three mechanisms for triggering the court's involvement in a situation. A member state may refer a situation to the prosecutor, the UN Security Council may do so, or the prosecutor, on his or her own initiative, may initiate an investigation.[11] That last mechanism—the prosecutor's so-called *proprio motu* power—was the most contentious at Rome. The United States, China, and several other states argued that it would afford the prosecutor too much discretion and insisted that if neither a state party nor the Security Council referred a situation, it likely was not of international concern. A large majority of states present at Rome backed the *proprio motu* power, and they prevailed. As a form of compromise, however, the final statute required that a panel of judges review the prosecutor's decision to open an investigation without the involvement of states.[12]

The *battle royale* at Rome was over the court's jurisdiction, and the last-minute changes left two principal avenues. The Statute allows the ICC to prosecute crimes committed *on the territory* of a court member or *by a national* of a court member.[13] While this compromise left many of the court's strongest backers disappointed, it was a step too far for the United States and China, among others, which objected to the fact that their citizens could still be exposed to prosecution. US diplomats argued that the jurisdictional provisions departed dangerously from the principle that a state cannot be bound by a treaty it did not sign. For most other states, the structure was uncontroversial. States already had the right to prosecute anyone on their territory who had committed serious crimes there. Why could they not choose to delegate that right to the ICC?[14]

There was one additional route to jurisdiction: action by the UN Security Council. If the Security Council refers a situation to the court, the court acquires jurisdiction even if neither the territorial nor the nationality conditions are met. Since the UN Charter gives the Council the power to take any steps it deems necessary to maintain peace and security—and since the Council created ad hoc tribunals in the early 1990s—delegates ultimately agreed to grant the body power to expand ICC jurisdiction. Through Security Council action, therefore, a leader whose country has not signed onto the Rome Statute, and who is committing crimes entirely within his borders, could still find himself in the court's crosshairs.

Well before the Rome Conference, negotiators had settled on another key concept that would impact the court's reach: the doctrine of complementarity. In short, it made clear that the court should only investigate crimes when relevant national courts were not able to do so. If competent national authorities were investigating crimes, the statute made clear, the ICC should give way. But there was a critical caveat to that principle. If a state and the court disagreed about whether national proceedings were sufficient or genuine, a panel of ICC judges would decide the matter.[15]

The Rome Statute was much more specific on crimes and court mechanics than on the critical question of how states should support the court politically and diplomatically. The statute obligates member states to pay assessed dues, to hand over indicted individuals on their territory, and to respond to requests for information and other assistance. It is silent, however, on the broader question of how states should provide political backing to the court. Should members diplomatically and economically isolate states that do not cooperate with the court? Should they provide military and intelligence assistance to states attempting to capture indicted persons? Moreover, the statute provides several escape clauses for states facing a formal request from the court, including when cooperation would endanger classified material or cause the state to be in conflict with other legal obligations. The consequences of noncompliance for a state shirking its obligations were left vague. In a case of noncompliance, the court may refer the matter to all court members (and to the Security Council, if the Council had referred the matter initially).[16] But the statute outlined no penalties or punishments for states disregarding their obligations. Unsurprisingly, states were not enthusiastic about putting in place automatic sanctions for noncompliance.

The Rome Statute would enter into force after sixty signatories had ratified it. As the conference closed, that threshold appeared distant. The statute was an enormously complex document that required states to change their national legal systems and enact procedures for handing over individuals to the international court. William Pace, leader of the NGO coalition supporting the court, said many believed it would take "decades" for sixty countries to ratify.[17] Philippe Kirsch recalled, "When we finished the conference in Rome, the pessimists were saying 20 years and the optimists were saying ten years."[18]

The Superpower Reacts

US opposition to the court was the dominant storyline from the Rome Conference, and its stance mystified many observers. How had the United

States—which had played so central a role in Nuremberg and the tribunals for the Balkans and Rwanda—found itself opposing a permanent court that most of the world backed? The *Washington Post* labeled the conference a "diplomatic trainwreck."[19] The legal scholar Ruth Wedgewood lambasted the Clinton administration for its confused negotiating stance:

> [Only] four weeks into the five-week U.N. final conference in Rome, were cabinet debates resolved and instructions issued to the American negotiating team. But by then it was too late for American diplomats to convince frustrated friends and allies to accommodate new U.S. demands—a case study in how not to conduct multilateral diplomacy.[20]

Reaction from the rest of the world was harsh as well. A Japanese newspaper called the US performance "a stain on that country's image."[21] An Australian paper derided the American "global tantrum."[22] The *Toronto Star* editorialized that the United States had behaved "with the petulance of a failed bully."[23] British outlets bemoaned the "naked, cynical self-interest" on display in Rome and noted that the court would come into being "minus the United States, China and a handful of virtual pariah states."[24]

Inside the US government, senior officials distanced themselves from the diplomatic embarrassment. David Scheffer returned from weeks of intense negotiations in Rome and encountered a chilly silence from the secretary of state, the national security advisor, and most other senior officials. He received a much warmer welcome on Capitol Hill, where conservative senators lauded him for having stood up in defense of American sovereignty.[25]

In the months that followed the Rome Conference, the administration hunted for a strategy. At certain moments, the United States appeared to be contemplating a diplomatic offensive against the nascent court, and perhaps even a campaign to prevent it from coming into being. Scheffer insisted, in public remarks, that the provisions granting the court jurisdiction over nationals of nonmember states were "unheard of in treaty law." He promised that the United States would "actively oppose" ratification of the statute, and he warned that if the court came into existence it would have "real consequences for Congressional attitudes" toward American participation in military missions abroad.[26]

Scheffer also asked states to reopen some of the basic jurisdictional questions settled at Rome. At a UN meeting in October 1998, he warned fellow diplomats that absent significant revisions, the United States would not be able to offer the kind of logistical, intelligence, and even military support to the court that it had to other international tribunals:

> [W]e had hoped in Rome for a consensus that would allow the United States to begin planning the kind of support that the permanent court will need if it is also to be effective—to sustain a costly investigative capability, to build its infrastructure in The Hague, to achieve custody of indictees, and to work with the UN Security Council for enforcement initiatives. So long as the United States is unable to join the treaty, it would be unrealistic to expect the United States to give the court that level of support. We fear that, without the United States, the effectiveness of the permanent international criminal court will fall far short of its potential.[27]

In effect, US officials were warning other states that a court that could not accommodate American concerns would become marginal.[28] While there were occasional hints at a strategy of actively marginalizing the court—by, for example, campaigning against ratification—the Clinton administration more often suggested that marginalization would be the inevitable consequence of its disaffection. At least in public, administration officials did not acknowledge the possibility that the United States might, over time, be drawn toward a closer relationship with the court.

These predictions of the court's likely marginalization, and Scheffer's suggestion that states reconsider key jurisdictional questions, alarmed civil society groups and worried even close allies. Any change that would put the United States or other major powers beyond the court's reach, they warned, would undermine the Rome Conference's key achievement:

> This proposal is aimed at obtaining a 100-percent ironclad guarantee that no American official accused of genocide, crimes against humanity or war crimes could be ever brought before the court. Such an exemption for citizens of one nation or set of nations would destroy the universality necessary for the court to gain broad acceptance and deliver impartial justice... [Americans] are the world's only superpower and they think that gives them special privileges.[29]

US warnings of marginalization mingled with a more conciliatory approach. Most importantly, the administration chose to remain involved in the detailed negotiations that followed the Rome Conference. The final resolution of the

Rome Conference provided for the formation of a Preparatory Commission ("PrepCom") charged with arranging the court's operational details. The PrepCom would also develop guidelines on court procedure and evidence and provide additional detail on the crimes the court could prosecute. Because the Rome Statute was still open for signature, all states could participate in the PrepCom, and the United States availed itself of the option.

As the United States searched for a consistent post-Rome strategy, key ICC backers worked to prevent the discord with the superpower from becoming a permanent divide. They realized that the American bitterness had to be diluted and often tried to convince US officials that active engagement was the best antidote to the institution's perceived defects. Kofi Annan sounded this note a few months after the Rome Conference. "If any States are worried that the judges or prosecutors of this Court may be inclined to malice, or frivolity, or bias," he argued, "by far their best remedy is to sign and ratify the Statute, and to ensure that as many like-minded States as possible do the same."[30]

Court backers, like Philippe Kirsch, also tried to adjust the atmospherics of the post-Rome Conference meetings to reintegrate the United States and other states that had been most disaffected. The Canadian diplomat, who had chaired the Rome Conference and been a key figure in the US diplomatic defeat, had initially demurred when invited to chair PrepCom. He worried that his continued involvement might perpetuate animosity with the Americans. He accepted the leadership position only after receiving assurances that the United States would be comfortable with his role.[31] In February 1999, a large American delegation attended the first of what would be many sessions.

As PrepCom meetings progressed, US negotiators played a leading role in specifying what behavior constituted crimes under the Rome Statute. Kirsch praised the US delegation for its constructive contributions and consciously worked during the meetings to draw in other actors as well, including Arab states.[32] Several skeptical major powers joined as well, with Russian, Chinese, and, to a lesser extent, Indian diplomats regularly attending meetings to keep an eye on developments.

ICC supporters were pleased that the skeptical major powers were still engaged. But that relief mixed with suspicion that these countries were participating primarily to minimize the chances the court could ever touch them. Key NGOs worried that the United States, China, and certain other states would undermine the new institution by inserting restrictive language into the more detailed documents that negotiators were drafting. For example,

Russia submitted an amendment on the definition of war crimes and aggression that would have restricted both categories significantly (the provision ultimately failed).[33] The participation of the United States, Russia, China, India, and Japan in the PrepCom meetings was at least as much about limiting the court's reach as it was keeping open the possibility of cooperation.

Pinochet as Harbinger?

As the diplomatic dust from the Rome Conference was settling, the broader project of international justice took several other dramatic turns. These events both affected the political environment in which the ICC was emerging and also foreshadowed key political challenges that the institution would face once it became operational.

Three months after the Rome Conference ended, on October 16, 1998, former Chilean president Augusto Pinochet was resting in a London hospital room. He had traveled to London a few weeks earlier for back surgery, along the way paying a courtesy call on former British prime minister Margaret Thatcher. Unbeknownst to Pinochet, a Spanish judge named Baltasar Garzón had a few weeks earlier transmitted a request for the former dictator's arrest. The judge accused Pinochet of having ordered the murder and torture of several Spanish nationals and others during the 1970s. British officials determined that they were obliged to act on the arrest warrant.[34]

The Pinochet arrest threw sudden light on the role of universal jurisdiction in international politics.[35] The doctrine—that all states may prosecute individuals who have committed certain serious crimes anywhere in the world—had established roots in international law, but states had employed it infrequently. Before the end of the Cold War, national governments had invoked the principle mainly to pursue individuals, such as pirates or hijackers, who operated in the spaces between national jurisdictions.[36] The Pinochet prosecution was a much more dramatic gambit, and it set off a diplomatic firestorm. As Chileans demonstrated for and against Pinochet on the streets of Santiago, the country's politicians, even on the political Left, worried that Spain's move threatened the delicate compromise Chilean society had struck regarding past crimes. "We are returning to situations of the past, as a result of wounds in our society that have not healed," said a prominent socialist politician.[37]

Coming just months after the conclusion of the Rome Conference, Judge Garzón's move seemed to represent a new judicial challenge to the prerogatives and political choices of even powerful states. Several leading American foreign policy conservatives viewed the Pinochet arrest as further evidence that the international justice project was spinning out of the control of states. Law professor Jeremy Rabkin insisted that the Pinochet case could upend traditional diplomacy. "This [precedent] is available to be used against the United States or Israel.... If Algeria manages to get hold of Henry Kissinger or [U.S. General Norman] Schwarzkopf or Ariel Sharon, what is to stop Algeria from going forward to the prosecution?"[38]

The willingness of Judge Garzón to wreak diplomatic havoc suggested to many ICC skeptics that their concerns about a roving international prosecutor were well founded. Garzón's targeting of a former right-wing leader, who had been supported by the United States, seemed to bolster the concern that an ICC prosecutor would actively seek out cases hostile to the superpower. John Bolton, a prominent conservative lawyer, saw in the case a foreshadowing of ICC behavior. "Chileans made their choice and have lived with it. But for a self-selected Spanish official, it was not good enough," Bolton said. "However this particular affair ends, it demonstrates the moral and political arrogance that will likely permeate the ICC, contributing materially to its potential for damage."[39] If a Spanish judge operating on his own could do this, Bolton and others worried, what might an international prosecutor with a global mandate and a multi-million dollar budget accomplish? From this perspective, the Pinochet case made aggressive marginalization of the ICC an even more urgent priority for the United States.

There were several assumptions embedded in Bolton's prediction that the ICC would act with similar assertiveness. He and other critics took for granted that the new international institution would be animated by an anti-US ideology and predisposed to challenge the world's leading power. He assumed that an international prosecutor and judges would have similar incentives to those of a national judge like Garzón, who operated within an established state institution. Bolton failed to consider the possibility that the ICC prosecutor might prefer not to seek confrontations with the United States or that the United States might still find ways to manage, direct, or constrain the court.[40]

Managing Justice in the Balkans

Developments surrounding the international tribunals created for Yugoslavia and Rwanda suggested that the dynamic between international prosecutors and key states was in fact quite complex. Events in 1998 and 1999, in particular, demonstrated that powerful states could hitch international justice to a political strategy, effectively constraining the activities of international prosecutors. Yet the same events suggested that prosecutors had a limited but real ability to influence major-power calculations.

As the Pinochet case wound its way through the British legal system, the lawyers, investigators, and judges at the international tribunal for the former Yugoslavia (ICTY) were increasingly optimistic about the prospects of their own efforts at international justice. That optimism came after several dark years. As of mid-1997, fewer than ten of more than seventy individuals indicted were in custody, and those trials underway were of low-level suspects.[41] With so many suspects at large, the tribunal's prosecutor, Richard Goldstone, spent far more time badgering states for resources and support than prosecuting cases.

The powerful NATO states whose troops patrolled postwar Bosnia showed little interest in arresting prominent indictees, notably Bosnian Serb leaders Radovan Karadžić and Ratko Mladić. Fearful of instability, NATO officials reportedly quashed a proposal to set up joint arrest squads. "If politicians ask us to take action against war criminals, they should realize the operative risks may last a long time," a senior alliance official said. "We do not know what the aftermath would be because many people regard these criminals as heroes worth defending."[42] An atmosphere of gloom settled over the international justice project. Theodor Meron, a leading authority on international criminal law, argued in early 1997 that "the [Yugoslav] tribunal may soon approach the end of its working life. It should not be continued only to serve as a fig leaf for the impotence of the international community to enforce international law."[43]

Then, quite quickly, key NATO states charted a new course. In July 1997, British Special Air Service commandos captured two Bosnian Serbs indicted by the tribunal and killed another in the Bosnian town of Prijedor, where some of the war's most brutal atrocities had been committed.[44] Those captured were swiftly sent to the tribunal. A few months later, Dutch troops seized and dispatched to The Hague two more suspects. Several developments had prompted NATO's newly aggressive posture on war crimes suspects. The military situation in Bosnia had stabilized, the forces of the formerly warring parties were under strict NATO supervision, and Western leaders worried much less about an insurgency. The arrests of ICTY indictees brought political benefits. Many indictees were local power brokers and remained hostile toward the Dayton peace process. Relocating those who most threatened Bosnia's fragile stability and reintegration process to The Hague helped states enforce the peace agreement.

There was another element in NATO's shift toward enforcement: an increasingly public campaign by the tribunal prosecutor. In late 1996, the Canadian jurist Louise Arbour had succeeded Richard Goldstone as ICTY prosecutor. By late 1997, Arbour had become convinced that working exclusively behind-the-scenes with key Western governments was no longer effective. A clash between the tribunal and French defense officials in late 1997 precipitated a new and aggressive strategy from the prosecutor. In December, French defense minister Alain Richard derided the ICTY as a "show trial" and suggested that French officials might not be given leave to testify at its trials.[45] Arbour responded fiercely, pointing out to the media that the French had made no arrests of war criminals and that indictees felt "absolutely secure" in areas of Bosnia patrolled by French troops. "The French failing is pretty remarkable," she said.[46]

The scholar John Hagan has argued that during this period Arbour effectively set in motion an "esteem competition" between the various states responsible for peacekeeping in Bosnia. By publicly lauding those states carrying out arrests and criticizing those failing to do so, Arbour helped to convert the principles the tribunal represented into meaningful political pressure.[47] Combined with intense private pressure, the prosecutor's public statements appeared to produce results. In late 1998, the US military began making arrests. In December, US commandos seized Radoslav Krstić, a senior Bosnian Serb general, as he traveled between two Bosnian cities.[48] Then, about a year after Arbour crossed swords with Alain Richard, French troops carried out their first arrest of an ICTY indictee.[49] The old pattern of NATO acquiescing to the presence of indicted war criminals was crumbling fast, and new defendants were streaming into The Hague.

While there is some evidence that the ICTY prosecutor was able to influence the decision-making of certain states, events in 1999 also highlighted the larger reality that international justice in the Balkans was still tethered to the political and military strategy of the powerful Western states. By early 1999, the Western powers were moving toward open confrontation with the Serbian government, led by Slobodan Milošević. The Serbian president had been a key player during the Bosnian peace negotiations, during which Western diplomats had relied on his influence over Bosnian Serbs. As the region's attention turned to the disputed Serbian province of Kosovo, however, Milošević became a direct obstacle to Western policy.

Attacks by a shadowy resistance group on Serbian authorities in Kosovo had begun in 1996, and Serb forces responded brutally. The West, fearful of another bloodletting, pressured Serbia to loosen its grip on the province, but open conflict between Kosovo rebels and Serb security forces escalated in 1998. In September, NATO insisted that Serbia cease its crackdown and threatened military action if it did not. As Western diplomats pressured Belgrade, the ICTY prosecutor provoked a faceoff with Serb authorities. In January 1999, she appeared at the border to Kosovo and demanded access to investigate recent atrocities. Serb authorities denied her permission, and a public standoff ensued.[50] Arbour's bid to enter Kosovo apparently had been coordinated with key NATO states. According to former US official David Scheffer, the prosecutor "had been coaxed there by NATO governments and NGOs."[51] While Arbour stewed near the border, she received frequent calls from US and other NATO diplomats, who were eager to use the episode to intensify pressure on Belgrade.[52]

The prosecutor was eventually turned away, but NATO continued to play a key role in negotiations about possible ICTY access to Kosovo. In late January, NATO's top general, Wesley Clark, negotiated directly with Milošević about how Arbour could investigate. He called the prosecutor repeatedly during the session to check on whether Serbian concessions would suffice (they did not).[53] By March the negotiations between NATO and Milošević had broken down entirely. Western warplanes struck Serbian targets for the first time on March 24, 1999. Even as NATO bombs fell, Arbour and her staff raced to gather evidence for an indictment of Milošević.[54] To this point, the Serbian leader had never been accused directly of orchestrating crimes. As the crisis in Kosovo developed, that changed. During this period, the prosecutor and her top staff traveled regularly to key NATO states to collect evidence from national intelligence services and keep officials informed about the case against the Serbian leader.[55]

Arbour attributes the quick pursuit of Milošević not to the political environment but to a broader change in investigative strategy at the tribunal. Even before the Kosovo violence erupted, she said, the tribunal had shifted its focus toward senior political leaders. The fact that Serbian government forces were directly involved in Kosovo also made pursuing Milošević much easier. For the first time, there was a direct connection—through the Yugoslav military chain of command—between Milošević and crimes being committed on the ground. She rejected the notion that the tribunal was working at the behest of Western governments: "There was nobody giving marching orders to anybody."[56]

Western governments certainly smoothed the way for the tribunal's pursuit of the Serbian leader. As the Kosovo crisis developed, information from Western intelligence services poured into the tribunal. In April 1999, the United Kingdom announced "the biggest handover of British intelligence to an outside agency in history."[57] US officials worked to match their allies in helpfulness to the tribunal. When Arbour visited Washington that month, Secretary of State Madeleine Albright promised to help remove bureaucratic obstacles slowing the flow of US intelligence to the tribunal. Albright encouraged Arbour to "work at your own pace, do what you have to do, recognizing that what you do is not being done in a vacuum. It is great you are willing to consult with us."[58] Ostensibly an independent and apolitical prosecutor, Arbour was enmeshed in NATO's political and military strategy as she finished the Milošević indictment:

> Arbour was at this point deeply engaged in a dialectical process of give and take involving the final authority to make the indictment decision. The decision might ultimately be hers, but the secretary-general of the UN, Kofi Annan, also had major input, along with the leaders of the NATO nations who were now committed to the bombing campaign. Her agency derived from their authorization, even though the indictment decision was formally hers as chief prosecutor.[59]

The tribunal's hand-in-glove work with NATO raised a delicate question: whether and how prosecutors should scrutinize the alliance's own behavior. NATO forces were now combatants in an armed conflict on the territory of the former Yugoslavia, and they thus fell within the tribunal's jurisdiction. Almost unwittingly, the major powers had created an international judicial institution that could scrutinize their own behavior. Soon enough ICTY was forced to do just that. As the air campaign dragged on, and as NATO planes struck more and more aggressively, reports emerged that bombs had hit civilian targets. On the night of May 7, a bomb partially destroyed the Chinese embassy in Belgrade, killing three and injuring at least twenty.[60] In a post-conflict assessment, Human Rights Watch estimated that, in all, more than 500 civilians were killed during the air campaign.[61]

With complaints against NATO streaming into her office, Arbour established a working group to analyze information regarding the alliance's conduct. When the prosecutor broached the subject with Madeleine Albright, the secretary of state bristled. "I won't get into an argument of moral equivalence," she told the prosecutor.[62] When Carla del Ponte, a Swiss prosecutor who had tangled with the mafia, took over from Arbour that fall, she continued the inquiry into NATO's air strikes. She sent NATO a list of detailed questions regarding targeting policy. She received back a short letter with none of the specific information she had requested.

Del Ponte wrote later that she received no direct pressure from NATO members to curtail her investigation. But no direct pressure was necessary; NATO's members controlled the information vital to her investigation. The classified material that flowed into the prosecutor's office when it was preparing its Milošević indictment dried up when it came to investigating the air campaign:

> I quickly concluded that it was impossible to investigate NATO, because NATO and its member states would not cooperate with us. They would not provide us access to the files and documents. Over and above this, however, *I understood that I had collided with the edge of the political universe in which the tribunal was allowed to function.* If I went forward with an investigation of NATO, I would not only fail in this investigative effort, I would render my office incapable of continuing to investigate and prosecute the crimes committed by the local forces during the wars of the 1990s.[63]

Del Ponte was encountering a familiar dynamic; powerful states might be willing to deploy international justice in particular situations, but they would resist seeing it applied to them. Faced with NATO's unwillingness to share information, the prosecutor in June 2000 signaled the end of her inquiry into allegations of NATO's wrongdoing. "Although some mistakes were made by NATO," the tribunal announced, "the Prosecutor is satisfied that there was no deliberate targeting of civilians or unlawful military targets by NATO during the campaign."[64] A few years before the ICC opened its doors, the ICTY prosecutor's abortive Kosovo inquiry had revealed the ability of powerful states to circumscribe the work of tribunals by withholding key information. More broadly, the dynamic suggested that major powers still saw international justice as a process directed at others. Speaking about the ICC after the Kosovo war, British foreign minister Robin Cook was blunt. "If I may say so, this is not a court set up to bring to book Prime Ministers of the United Kingdom or Presidents of the United States."[65]

The question of NATO's targeting policy and precision during the air campaign was only one uncomfortable issue for the tribunal's Western backers. Even more fundamental was the legality of the resort to force. Russian opposition had prevented Security Council approval for intervention, and the Western powers ultimately chose to intervene nonetheless. NATO's action might have qualified as aggression: the alliance was, after all, using force without UN approval and not in direct self-defense. The ICTY had a straightforward answer to whether it should investigate the alliance for aggression. The tribunal's charter—drafted by the Security Council—limited it to war crimes, crimes against humanity, and genocide. In this sense, Kosovo aggravated the divide apparent at the Rome Conference between those determined to focus on conduct during conflict and those who wanted to control the resort to force itself. What kind of international justice, some observers asked, was blind to NATO's possibly illegal use of force?[66]

The NATO intervention bolstered the notion, at least in the West, that military intervention—even without UN approval—could be an appropriate and even necessary response to atrocities. Far from condemning the intervention, the UN Secretary General appeared to endorse the principle it established. Speaking to the UN General Assembly a few months after NATO's military campaign ended, Annan insisted that state sovereignty was conditional. "If states bent on criminal behavior know that frontiers are not an absolute defense...then they will not embark on such a course of action in expectations of sovereign impunity." Several human rights groups also offered their support for the intervention.[67]

The precedent of a humanitarian intervention without UN approval had potentially important implications for the ICC, and particularly regarding the crime of aggression. At the Rome Conference, most major powers—and all the P5 states—had expressed grave doubts about allowing the court to prosecute aggression. For the Western powers, the Kosovo experience accentuated sensitivity about the crime. At the International Court of Justice, Serbia accused all the NATO countries of aggression.[68] Senior Russian and Chinese officials also routinely characterized the NATO operation as illegal. Russia's foreign minister suggested that NATO leaders themselves should be held criminally responsible.[69] In major Western capitals, the Kosovo experience made granting the ICC authority to prosecute the illegal use of force even less appealing.

These complications aside, the Milošević indictment marked an important moment for the international justice movement. For the first time, an international court had indicted a sitting head of state for crimes his forces had committed. Milošević's fate after the indictment also provided an important illustration of how major-power pressure could make the court's writ run. Milošević yielded power in October 2000 after a disputed election spawned large protests in Belgrade and other cities. The new Serbian government then succumbed to heavy pressure from the United States and European Union, both of which insisted the new regime cooperate with the tribunal and hand over the ousted leader. Washington and Brussels made clear that they would withhold economic aid and other benefits until Belgrade cooperated. A resigned Milošević finally appeared before the tribunal in June 2001.[70]

The Ratification Race

The continuing momentum of the international justice project was reflected in the speed with which states ratified the Rome Statute. Few observers expected this process to move as quickly as it did. Ratification usually required domestic legislation, and sometimes constitutional changes. Without sustained high-level attention, the process could easily languish. Key international figures helped galvanize the process. "The best chance humankind has ever had to end the 'culture of impunity' is within our grasp," said Kofi Annan in 1999. "We must not let it fail."[71] ICTY prosecutor Louise Arbour, whose public profile had increased dramatically as a result of the Milošević indictment, added her voice to the chorus advocating quick ratifications. Spanish judge Baltasar Garzón, protagonist of the Pinochet prosecution, also urged ratification, insisting that "the principle of universal justice must be applied."[72] Pope John Paul II endorsed the ICC as "an important first step" in the establishment of human rights.[73]

Several European Union states and Canada advocated ratification routinely in bilateral exchanges with other states.[74] Those governments also continued to support the activist network that had played such an important role before and during the Rome Conference. The Coalition for an International Criminal Court (CICC) developed strategies for encouraging ratification by key target countries and enlisted the support of local civil society activists.[75] In 1999 and 2000, the coalition scheduled seminars in Mexico, Chile, Colombia, Costa Rica, and Brazil to build momentum for ratification among lawmakers and nongovernmental groups. In April 2000, a conference in Dhaka, Bangladesh, promoted ICC ratification in Asia. The CICC also attended an Economic Community of West African States (ECOWAS) conference on children affected by war to press participants to ratify. A June 2001 conference in Buenos Aires drew dozens of actors together to discuss implementation of the statute. The CICC also promoted subregional conferences that year in Namibia, Hong Kong, Thailand, Ghana, and Peru.[76]

The United States and other states skeptical of the court did not actively oppose these activities or try to counter them. US officials did not pressure states to delay ratification or suggest that joining the court would damage bilateral relations. Nor is there evidence that Russia, China, India, or Japan actively opposed ratification by other states. The skeptical major powers had, thus far, opted to wait and watch, apparently content to pursue a policy of passive marginalization.

Smaller states moved fastest to become ICC members. Senegal ratified in February 1999, followed that year by Trinidad & Tobago and San Marino. Fiji, a major contributor to UN peacekeeping, and Kofi Annan's native Ghana ratified next. In 2000, the pace of ratifications accelerated, and a number of major powers joined. In June 2000, France, which had negotiated carefully at Rome to ensure that its military was satisfied, became the first permanent member of the Security Council to ratify. Canada, Spain, Germany, the United Kingdom, and South Africa joined by the end of the year. South Africa not only ratified but also actively encouraged ratification throughout southern Africa.

A distinct regional pattern in ratifications appeared. Asia and the Middle East were difficult terrain for ICC supporters. By January 2001, not a single Asian or Arab state had ratified the Rome Statute.[77] But in much of the world, the idea of the ICC had significant appeal. Democratic states in Latin America and Europe provided particularly fertile ground for the court. Southern and central African states also proved quite supportive. Government statements that accompanied ratifications framed their decision as the vindication of the idea of accountability, justice, and human rights. Brazil, for example, stated that the choice to ratify reaffirmed its "commitment to the establishment of a permanent tribunal to promote the rule of law and ensure the gravest international crimes do not go unpunished."[78] South Africa's UN representative said, "As victims of the crime of apartheid, we experienced the pain and despair suffered by victims of crimes against humanity when they are without a forum from which to seek justice. It is for that reason that we have resolved not to be party to the delay in establishing the court any longer and invite other states to make the same decision and act upon it by ratifying the International Criminal Court Statute."[79]

Continued US objections notwithstanding, the desire to be formally associated with the project even reached into the upper ranks of the State Department. In the closing days of the Clinton administration, war crimes ambassador David Scheffer and several other officials worked overtime to induce President Clinton to sign the Rome Statute. A US signature would not imply membership; Scheffer knew that there was no prospect that the Senate would ratify the treaty. But signing would associate the United States with the ICC project and impose on the United States a legal obligation not to undermine the goal and purpose of the Rome Statute.[80]

With mixed success, Scheffer reached out to figures he perceived to have moral authority, including Holocaust survivor Elie Weisel, South African

leader Nelson Mandela, and former president Jimmy Carter. Other prominent ICC supporters worked through the media. In a *New York Times* op-ed,
the indefatigable Benjamin Ferencz and former US Defense Secretary Robert
McNamara beseeched Clinton to sign. The president "has a last chance to
safeguard humankind from genocide, crimes against humanity and the rav-
ages of war itself." Clinton's decision, they insisted, would decisively affect
the US image in the world: "If President Clinton fails to sign the treaty, he
will weaken our credibility and moral standing in the world. We will look like
a bully who wants to be above the law. If he signs, however, he will reaffirm
America's inspiring role as leader of the free world in its search for peace and
justice."[81] The pressure appeared to have an effect. In November, Clinton read
an article noting that the Rome Statute would soon close for signature. "I
suppose there's nothing we can do about this?" he scribbled in the margins.
The president's marginalia found its way to Eric Schwartz, a National Security
Council staffer who had previously worked for a human rights organization.
Schwartz knew that many government officials, particularly in the Pentagon,
considered the issue closed: US officials had said repeatedly that they could
not accept the Rome Statute as drafted. Schwartz nonetheless worked to
make clear to the president that signing was still possible. "I was animated
by a deep and abiding commitment to the promotion of human rights and
the principle of international accountability," he recalled. "I was driven by my
conviction that this was critically important and the president should have
the chance to review the issue."[82]

At almost the last possible moment, while hunkered down at Camp
David, Clinton decided to sign. Alerted by Schwartz to that possibility,
David Scheffer had already departed for New York. As soon as he received
word of the president's decision, he walked through the snow-covered city to
UN headquarters and signed the treaty. "I felt airborne," he wrote later.[83] The
White House released a statement outlining continuing American objections
to the statute but also emphasizing that US influence could be exercised most
effectively as a signatory. Clinton described the US signature as evidence of
America's "tradition of moral leadership." Scheffer believed that the decision
reflected the president's natural foreign policy instincts: "I think it was part of
his general nature to want to be part of something rather than not part of it.
Clinton was a participatory president not an isolationist one. So it's consistent
with his character that he would want to be part of the enterprise."[84] Clinton's
decision clearly had a tactical rationale as well. As a signatory (although still
not a member), the United States would have greater access to certain meetings and deliberations regarding the court and could attempt to influence

its development. But, as Scheffer recognized in his effort to tap figures with moral authority, Clinton's decision also reflected the way that court support-ers inside and outside government could deploy the power of the ideas that the ICC represented to align the superpower with the new institution.

The US Campaign against the Court

The court in waiting and its backers were about to face a much more sus-tained attempt at marginalization. Beginning in 2001, the new administra-tion of George W. Bush and the US Congress set in motion a multifaceted effort to limit the reach of the ICC. As the Bush administration settled into office in January 2001, it faced the unsettling reality that a court that it ada-mantly opposed was on the verge of becoming a reality and that the United States was now a signatory. John Bolton, in line for a senior administration post, warned in a *Washington Post* article that "there is every reason to believe that the ICC will shortly join the International Court of Justice as an object of international ridicule and politicized futility."[85] He and others joining the administration had plans to ensure just such a fate.

Bush administration officials briefly considered launching a diplomatic effort to prevent the sixtieth ratification that would bring the court into exis-tence. They determined that the strategy would be diplomatically costly and unlikely to succeed. On Capitol Hill, meanwhile, a different approach was taking shape. Lawmakers were drafting a bill to ensure that Americans could never be brought before the court. Titled the American Servicemembers' Protection Act (and referred to as ASPA), the legislation forbade most US support for the court and required the US government to cut military and economic aid to states not willing to pledge that they would not turn Americans over to the court. The bill's most controversial provision autho-rized the president to use "all necessary means" to free Americans held by the court.[86]

Although the new Senate bill was designed to protect Americans from a court the Bush administration opposed, the legislation itself raised concerns about the domestic balance of political power. State Department and White House lawyers worried, in particular, that the draft legislation encroached on the executive branch's control of foreign policy. For several weeks, the admin-istration negotiated changes with congressional experts. By late May, the dif-ferences had been settled and the White House expressed its support for the new legislation.[87] A key drafter, Stephen Rademaker, recalled that the law was designed to send a message to countries supportive of the court: "It *was* an objectionable bill; it was the Hague Invasion Act. It was designed to be objectionable because we found the International Criminal Court objectionable and so we tried to deal with it in a way that others found objectionable. It's not surprising the diplomats at the State Department didn't like it."[88] These US measures were in large part a function of traditional American sovereignty concerns and skepticism of international institutions that was particularly strong in conservative circles.[89] The attacks of September 11, 2001, only accentuated that distrust. As the United States hastily developed a more aggressive counterterrorism strategy, it employed a range of aggressive military, intelligence, and interrogation tactics. A year after the attacks, the CIA's lead counterterrorism official told Congress "there was a 'before 9/11' and there was an 'after 9/11'. After 9/11, the gloves came off."[90] As this effort intensified, US intelligence officials worried about the domestic legal exposure they might face. They had no desire for international scrutiny as well.

The desire to shield national officials from international scrutiny extended even to major powers supportive of the court. As it negotiated status-of-forces agreements in Afghanistan, for example, the United Kingdom insisted on language stipulating that NATO forces "may not be surrendered to, or otherwise transferred to the custody of, an international tribunal or any other entity or State without the express consent of the contributing nation."[91] To US officials, that provision was evidence that, when pressed by events, even states supportive of the ICC wanted immunity for their forces.[92]

The new dynamics of the post-9/11 period underscored that the period between the end of the Cold War and the 9/11 attacks had likely been a unique and limited window to launch the ICC. For that brief period, the security and sovereignty concerns of certain major powers were reduced enough for several of them to acquiesce to the court. According to David Tolbert, a former ICTY official, the ICC arose "in the political space between 1991 and 2001, between the fall of the Soviet Union and 9/11. Post 9/11 all of this would have been impossible and pre-1991 it would have been impossible."[93] The ICC was negotiated in a very different climate from the one in which it would operate.

By September 2001, however, the ratification process was well underway. Many states had set in motion the domestic processes needed to formally join the court. As the ratifications piled up, a competition emerged as to which states would push the Rome Statute over the sixty-ratification threshold that would bring it into force. At a ceremony in April 2002, ten countries deposited their ratifications simultaneously. With that gesture, the Rome Statute was on the cusp of becoming a functioning institution. "A page in the history of mankind is turning," exulted one senior UN official.[94]

A few weeks later, the US undersecretary of state, Marc Grossman, gave the most comprehensive account yet of the Bush administration's position on the ICC. The speech included a litany of concerns about the court, including that that it undermined the UN Security Council's authority and that it created an unchecked and unanswerable prosecutor. Grossman also insisted that the court's potential jurisdiction over nonmember states was unprecedented. "While sovereign nations have the authority to try non-citizens who have committed crimes against their citizens or on their territory, the United States has never recognized the right of an international organization to do so absent consent or a UN Security Council mandate," Grossman said.[95]

Much of the criticism of the court amounted to little more than an assertion of America's unique constitutional traditions and role in the world. But in a rudimentary form, the administration also made arguments that might have appealed to a range of states. In opposing the Clinton administration's decision to sign the Rome Statute, John Bolton had argued that the court's supporters "desire to assert the primacy of international institutions over nation-states."[96] In his speech Grossman expanded on that theme, insisting that in many contexts states must decide for themselves whether to prosecute those who have committed atrocities: "When a society makes the transition from oppression to democracy, their new government must face their collective past. The state should be allowed to choose the method. The government should decide whether to prosecute or seek national reconciliation. This decision should not be made by the ICC." As later events would demonstrate, this privileging of domestic choice had potentially strong resonance beyond the United States. Grossman was offering an alternative approach on justice that might have competed with the ideal of universal accountability backed by ICC supporters. But Grossman's argument was underdeveloped and overwhelmed by the array of objections that had limited appeal beyond the United States. It was also in tension with recent US policy. In the face of objections from the national governments, the United States had insisted on international justice for the perpetrators of the Rwandan genocide and the violence in Kosovo. What of the right of those societies to face their collective past in their own way? The US attempt to compete directly with the ICC's normative appeal was hobbled from the start.

On the day Grossman spoke, John Bolton submitted a letter to the UN Secretary General indicating that the United States had no intention of ratifying the Rome Statute; in essence, the letter "unsigned" the statute. Sending that letter, Bolton later said, was "my happiest moment at [the] State [Department]."[97] Under Bolton's direction, the United States set out

to negotiate a series of bilateral treaties—so-called "Article 98 agreements"—
that would make it difficult for the court to get hold of Americans. In dozens
of countries, US diplomats asked governments to sign agreements committing to not turn over American citizens to the court.

Many countries quickly agreed, not willing to offend the superpower over
hypothetical scenarios that seemed far-fetched. Other countries took con-
vincing. Jordan worried that Israeli settlers might commit crimes and then
pull out an American passport, ensuring that they could never be sent to The
Hague. Special language was inserted into that agreement to cover that even-
tuality.[98] Other states objected to signing an agreement that they interpreted
as an attack on the court. As the negotiations proceeded, Bolton and his colleagues invoked provisions from the Senate ASPA legislation and reminded
interlocutors that future American economic and military aid were at stake.
Although the Bush administration had originally balked at the bill's federal
balance of power questions, the law had ultimately provided valuable leverage
to secure these bilateral immunity agreements.

Bolton's campaign soon collided with other diplomatic priorities. Even as
the United States was pressuring close allies to sign the ICC immunity agreements, it was asking them for other favors related to the war on terror, including the use of military bases and airspace. The push for immunity agreements
particularly angered European officials, who strongly supported the ICC and
resented American attempts to undermine it. Their concerns were shared by
some American diplomats. One of Bolton's State Department colleagues,
assistant secretary of state for European affairs Beth Jones, was so incensed
by Bolton's crusade that she demanded a meeting with top State Department
officials. For almost an hour, undersecretary of state Marc Grossman medi-
ated a dispute between the two senior diplomats. Finally, he sided with
Bolton. The Article 98 campaign would continue.[99]

The United States pursued other avenues to extend immunity from
ICC prosecutions. At the United Nations, US diplomats threatened to end
American participation in UN peacekeeping operations unless the Security
Council agreed to immunity for countries that had not signed the ICC's
statute. "If there is not adequate protection for U.S. peacekeepers," a US
diplomat said, "there will be no U.S. peacekeepers."[100] That position led to
clashes between American diplomats and some of their closest allies, including Britain and Canada, whose diplomats charged that the United States was
engaged in an "abuse of power."[101]

While the administration had success negotiating the immunity agreements, there was little evidence that the United States was prevailing in the

broader battle of ideas that it was waging over the ICC. In the months after the Bush administration's policy was announced, US allies including Brazil, Australia, Uganda, and Colombia all joined the court. Even a few states highly dependent on the United States, including the new Afghan government led by Hamid Karzai, chose to ratify the Rome Statute.[102]

Victor's Justice in Rwanda

The increasingly contentious American battle against the ICC mostly obscured another collision between political realities and international justice. Since its creation, the international tribunal for Rwanda (ICTR) had faced a difficult dilemma: how aggressively to investigate the crimes of the serving Rwandan government. As members of the Rwanda Patriotic Front (RPF), many key Rwandan leaders had unseated the regime that had committed mass killings in 1994. That genocide was the tribunal's primary focus, but the court had jurisdiction over all crimes committed in Rwanda, including those by RPF forces and the new government. Influential human rights groups noted that RPF forces may have killed as many as 60,000 Hutu civilians during and after its struggle to overthrow the genocidal government.[103]

Relations between the tribunal and the Rwandan government were frosty from the outset, and the tribunal's prosecutors chose to pursue only cases related to the genocide itself for its first several years. Even with this strategy in place, relations between the court and the Rwandan government broke down at several points. Louise Arbour encountered a public protest when she visited the country in May 1997, and Rwandan officials at several points ceased cooperation with tribunal officials.[104] In this environment, the prosecutors had little incentive to pursue cases against government forces. Not only were RPF crimes of a different magnitude from those committed during the genocide, but tribunal officials worried that investigators might face violence or intimidation if they pursued government officials.[105]

Yet the idea that the court must not be an instrument to prosecute one side of the conflict ran deep. As Victor Peskin has argued, "The idea of prosecuting atrocities committed by all sides of an armed conflict is a foundational principle of the contemporary ad hoc tribunals as well as the International Criminal Court."[106] During her tenure as joint prosecutor, Arbour opened a discreet inquiry into RPF crimes. Her successor, Carla del Ponte, became more aggressive. In 2000, the Swiss lawyer publicly announced plans to investigate an alleged RPF massacre of Hutu civilians in 1994.[107] By early 2002, she was moving toward indicting several senior RPF officers. These steps provoked outrage and open defiance in Kigali. In April, Del Ponte condemned the Rwandan government for its failure to cooperate with the investigation, and in July the tribunal lodged a formal complaint against Rwanda with the UN Security Council.[108]

In June 2002, Del Ponte had a contentious meeting with the Rwandan president Paul Kagame. According to the prosecutor, Kagame accused her of "destroying Rwanda" and warned that the investigation "will disrupt the reconstruction of the nation."[109] The evidence suggests that powerful Western states agreed. Del Ponte received little support in her quest for RPF accountability from Washington or London, in particular. As key allies of the Rwandan government and permanent Security Council members, their stance was critical. Both governments chose not to actively pressure Rwanda into compliance with the tribunal. Instead, they supported a plan to strip Del Ponte of her responsibility for the Rwanda investigations, confining her to the Yugoslav tribunal and creating a new prosecutor exclusively for Rwanda.

The ICTY had failed in its earlier bid to investigate NATO, and Del Ponte's fruitless efforts to prosecute RPF crimes now offered further evidence of major powers' ability to circumscribe the work of international judicial bodies. This dynamic was particularly striking given the political context in which the ad hoc tribunals had been created. Both the Rwandan and Yugoslav tribunals were creations of the Security Council, and they were financially supported by the major powers. The United States was the top funder of the ICTY and ICTR and had spent hundreds of millions of dollars on the projects.[110]

That broad political and financial support did not translate, however, into the kind of concrete political support the tribunal's prosecutor needed in this instance. Faced with a choice between the demands of impartial justice and their political and regional interests, key powers chose the latter. The quiet standoff over Rwanda occurred just as the ICC was set to open its doors.

The Court Opens

The Rome Statute provided that the ICC would formally come into existence on the first day of the month, sixty days after the sixtieth ratification was received.[111] That date fell on July 1, 2002. In early 2002, the realization that the ratification process was moving much faster than anticipated had provoked alarm among diplomats and governments most closely associated with the project. "The ICC in fact faced the exact opposite of the problem usually encountered by newly born organizations: ratifications were too fast, not too slow."[112] The sixtieth ratification might give the court formal life, but there was no staff, building, or budget in place to make it real.

As that date approached, the national diplomats working on the project wanted to mark the occasion and provide evidence to the world that the court was operational. The solution was to create a small advance team comprised of administrators with experience in other international tribunals. But until the court's members formally met, the ICC had no budget to pay even this skeletal staff. The European Union and the private MacArthur Foundation stepped into the vacuum, offering funds to cover the costs of the advance team. Meanwhile, the Dutch government helped the team negotiate contracts for services and identified a headquarters building that the new court could use.[113]

The court's steering committee was struggling to pull together a staff of lawyers and investigators from around the world. Judges and a prosecutor still needed to be appointed. In all this, the office politics of the new international bureaucracy made every move complex. Most of the ICC's funding came from European nations, but the court answered to all countries that had ratified the Rome Statute, and most of these states had candidates they wanted considered for judgeships and staff positions. For the ICC's leadership, even hiring decisions involved political balancing. For almost a decade, diplomats and activists had negotiated and argued, sometimes bitterly, over the idea of the court. Now, utterly dependent on state support, the court was becoming a fragile reality.

On July 1, 2002, the ICC officially opened its doors. Two members of the advance team, a Dutch lawyer named Sam Muller, and an official from Lesotho, Phakiso Mochochoko, formally opened the court's offices in a quiet suburb of The Hague. Standing in front of the modern concrete and steel building that would house the court, they gave a short press conference. The new court appeared much more impressive than it was. Still lacking a budget, Muller had bought the court's first cell phones on his personal credit card. After the press conference, Muller and Mochochoko entered the headquarters building as camera crews filmed the moment. The two men immediately walked out a back entrance; there were no offices ready and nothing for them to do inside.[114]

4

Caution and Consensus
(July 2002–March 2005)

AS THE ICC began operating, it faced the challenge of institution-building in the face of intense and multifaceted opposition from the United States and less overt skepticism from several other leading powers. The court's early work, however, undercut major-power fears of what the institution might do in practice. Even before formally taking office, the prosecutor sought to reassure the United States. Once installed, he selected uncontroversial early investigations and proceeded carefully in conducting them. The prosecutor's office steered well clear of conflicts that directly engaged major-power interests.

An "Unaccountable" Court

The international environment in which the ICC opened its doors was very different from the one that prevailed shortly after the Rome Conference. The most obvious change was the US shift toward full opposition. The Bush administration had abandoned the post-Rome Conference ambiguity of the Clinton administration and was actively opposing the court. Shortly after the court's July 2002 opening, President Bush called the ICC "very troubling" and insisted that the United States would not join. Speaking to soldiers from the US Army's 10th Mountain Division, the president declared that "every person who serves under the American flag will answer to his or her own superiors and to military law, not to the rulings of an unaccountable international criminal court."[1]

Armed with the US Congress's new threat of aid restrictions, US diplomats pursued immunity agreements across the globe.[2] At the United Nations, US diplomats extracted from the Security Council a year-long exemption from ICC investigations for nonmember state personnel participating in UN operations. That resolution expressed the Council's intent to renew the exemption "as long as may be necessary."[3] The American strategy in part flowed from ideological currents regarding national sovereignty represented in the Bush administration, but it also recognized that international legal scrutiny of American policy was a growing possibility.

After the 9/11 attacks, the landscape of global violence had changed, and the potential "supply" of cases to the new court had changed with it. By July 2002, forces from the United States, the United Kingdom, France, Canada, and Australia were engaged in active combat in eastern and southern Afghanistan.[4] Elsewhere, US special operations forces and intelligence agents adopted newly aggressive tactics. In Yemen, Pakistan, and several other countries, US officials considered direct action against Islamic extremists. The increased use of American military force was not limited to the campaign against Islamic extremists. In March 2002, the Bush administration sought authority from Congress to expand military support to Colombia's government, which was engaged in a long-running struggle with leftist rebels. Meanwhile, pressure in Washington was growing for a more aggressive policy toward Saddam Hussein's Iraq. In a major August 2002 speech, Vice President Dick Cheney suggested that no new UN action was needed for military action there.[5]

In the months before and after the court opened, other significant military powers also flexed their muscle. In April, Israel responded to a terror attack by mounting an offensive in the West Bank and holding Palestinian leader Yasser Arafat under house arrest for several weeks. The Israeli offensive included a controversial attack on the city of Jenin. Russia's long-running battle with militants in Chechnya expanded as Vladimir Putin increasingly linked the Chechen rebels to international Islamic extremists. Russia responded to the seizure of hostages in Moscow with expanded military action and officials pledged to "wipe out the commanders of the movement."[6] In South Asia, nuclear-armed India and Pakistan clashed over extremist violence in the Kashmir region. Rhetoric between the two powers escalated dramatically before international pressure helped defuse the crisis.[7]

In this environment, international judicial scrutiny of the major powers was a significantly less abstract consideration than it had been at the time of the Rome Conference. American officials voiced their concern most openly. A Bush administration official acknowledged that the administration worried less that individual soldiers would be prosecuted and more that the court might pursue senior policymakers. "The soldiers are like the capillaries; the top public officials—President Bush, Secretary Rumsfeld, Secretary Powell—they are at the heart of our concern."[8] The anxiety was not irrational;

the legality of post-9/11 military operations, in particular, was attracting scrutiny. Shortly after the ICC opened its doors, the *New York Times* published detailed accounts of US airstrikes in Afghanistan, noting that hundreds of civilians had likely been killed.[9] In London, British government lawyers debated whether an attack on Iraq without UN approval could expose British leaders and forces to prosecution. Absent a proper legal basis for the war, one British Foreign Office legal advisor worried in an August 2002 memorandum, "individual members of the Armed Forces and civilian officials (at all levels) would also be potentially liable to charges of murder."[10]

During the years when the Rome Statute was negotiated, and indeed for most of the 1990s, Western military forces had been deployed primarily in limited missions designed, at least ostensibly, to advance humanitarian goals. The United States and several NATO allies had intervened in Somalia to staunch famine, in Bosnia to force an end to a brutal ethnic conflict, and in Kosovo to avert a fresh wave of ethnic cleansing. It was possible to imagine during this period that the world's advanced militaries were essentially vehicles for the broader global mission of restraining and civilizing conflict. After 9/11, that view was harder to maintain. The new court faced a world in which powerful countries, and the United States above all, were using force to confront what they perceived as immediate threats to their security. Moreover, the context in which they were using force—against nonstate actors—strained the established international law framework. The laws of war were originally designed to govern the activities of national armed forces in open conflicts. The military campaign against Al Qaeda was, in many respects, a war in the legal shadows.

Even as the United States and its allies expanded their military engagement and used force in unconventional ways, there was evidence that the rise in internal violence associated with the end of the Cold War had crested. Overall deaths as a result of violent conflict had declined substantially in the four years since the Rome Conference concluded.[11] The wars in the Balkans were over. While still deadly, the sprawling conflict in the Democratic Republic of Congo had eased substantially.[12] A fragile political process was ending the bloody civil conflict in Côte d'Ivoire. Several internal conflicts continued, and there were ominous signs that new ones might be beginning. By the spring of 2003, for example, a rebel group in the disaffected Darfur region of Sudan had mounted several attacks on Sudanese police and military, prompting a violent response.[13] Central Africa continued to be conflict prone. But the overall trend was toward less frequent and less intense internal violence.

Taken together, the increase in military activity by some of the world's leading powers and the decline in violence in several of the world's weakest states raised key questions about the new court. Was it designed to help eradicate conflict generally or only to curb its worst abuses? Was this an institution capable of influencing the most powerful state actors, or would its influence be limited to smaller and weaker states? Perhaps the most important question was how major powers using force in newly assertive ways would react to an institution created in a very different historical context.

Selecting Judges and the Prosecutor

In the court's early months, these questions were often subsumed by the much simpler one of how far the United States would go in opposing the institution. The new American legislation authorizing the use of "all necessary means" to free any US citizens in the court's custody heightened the sense that the court was under assault by the world's most powerful state. On the eve of the court's inauguration, several activists, including Benjamin Ferencz, manned symbolic sand bunkers on a beach near The Hague, dramatizing their willingness to defend the court from American threats.[14] Dutch politicians puckishly suggested clearing sunbathers from the shoreline to make a path for the invading American troops.[15]

Those working inside the new institution felt its fragility acutely. "We were a handful of people thrown into a suburb of The Hague and asked to play world court," one early staff member said.[16] One of the first judges elected recalled that he and his colleagues "were not at all sure about whether this new baby would be able to survive all the hostility shown by the big powers."[17] Diplomats from states that strongly supported the court worried that incautious statements by new court officials might provoke an even more severe confrontation with the United States. But the American pressure may have had a galvanizing effect as well. Some court officials recall that instead of inducing paralysis, Washington's hostility generated pressure to make the court operational as quickly as possible:

> The American pressure also played a really important role. There was the sense that this baby was about to be born but Mr. Bolton and his friends are on the warpath to kill it. So if somebody rang the [court's] doorbell and nobody was there, that would be really bad....At one point, somebody told me that the budget line that Mr. Bolton had on the State Department budget to destroy the ICC was ten times higher than the budget we had to set it up.[18]

If the hostility of nonmembers like the United States was a constant concern, the court and its members also had to consider how to recognize the status of the powerful states that had joined the institution. The United Kingdom, Germany, and France were members, and together they would pay more than 40 percent of the court's costs. Would these and other major countries receive certain privileges in exchange for their membership and support? The ICC's member states met formally for the first time in September 2002. With relatively little debate, the assembled delegates adopted the Rules of Procedure and Evidence and the Elements of the Crimes that had been negotiated at the Preparatory Commission meetings. The delegates then turned to the task of selecting the court's eighteen judges. As they did so, they faced the question of major-power privilege directly.

The Rome Statute provided detailed instructions for how judges should be selected. Successful candidates would have to secure the support of two-thirds of court members, who would cast ballots on a one-state, one-vote basis. All member states could nominate judges, and no one country could have more than one national on the bench. The statute provided that judges should be selected from two different lists: one for those with experience in criminal law and another for those experienced in international law. The statute urged states to pay due regard to gender and geographical representation.[19] At the first meeting of the Assembly of States Parties (ASP), delegates adopted a system designed to encourage the representation of different regions on the ICC bench.[20] But neither the Rome Statute nor the subsequently adopted procedures formally privileged the largest or most powerful states in any way.

Still, there was an expectation that major states should win judgeships. The venerable International Court of Justice, the UN's principal legal body, had developed a "P5 convention" that informally assured all five permanent Security Council members a judgeship.[21] Many delegates to the ASP expected that some similar form of major-power privilege would prevail at the ICC. Major powers with large military, development, and aid budgets have significant leverage, and there is evidence that they used it during the first round of ICC elections. "Votes can be traded against promises of development assistance," one delegate reported to researchers. While the Jordanian diplomat chairing the Assembly asked states to refrain from the bargaining and horse-trading that had become typical in elections for other international judgeships, it appears the practice endured.[22]

The high voting threshold to elect judges, and the novelty of the institution's processes, made the elections messy however. There was consternation when several major-power candidates did not secure the necessary votes in the early rounds. The British nominee got through on the ninth round, but the French candidate, Claude Jorda, was only elected on the thirty-third and final round.[23] One fellow candidate recalled that Jorda found the process "humiliating" and blamed the French government for not campaigning aggressively enough on his behalf.[24] Sam Muller, a member of the court's advance team, followed the voting anxiously. "There was an unspoken idea that, for example, the P5 members insofar as they were part of the court would have judgeships. The Germans paid twenty percent of the budget, so there's no way that we cannot have a German judge."[25] In the end, major powers did well. The five largest funders saw their national candidates prevail (see table 4.1).

As the elections for judgeships played out, the more immediately important process of selecting the court's first prosecutor accelerated. In contrast to the election of judges, it was a quiet, informal affair. One participant recalled "lots of behind-the-scenes talks."[26] Instead of soliciting multiple nominations at the ASP, a small group of diplomats most involved in the court's creation identified a candidate that could be selected by consensus. Some of the most obvious names were barely considered. Despite expressing interest in the position, Carla Del Ponte never gained traction as a candidate. The Yugoslav tribunal prosecutor had clashed repeatedly with key states during her tenure, and many diplomats saw her as too abrasive. There was brief consideration

Table 4.1 Leading ICC Budget Contributors and Judgeships

Country	2003 Assessed Dues (% of total)	Judgeship
Germany	19.4	Yes
France	12.8	Yes
United Kingdom	11	Yes
Italy	10	Yes
Canada	5	Yes
Spain	5	*No*
Brazil	4.7	Yes
Netherlands	3.5	*No*
South Korea	3.4	Yes

Source: Assembly of States Parties to the Rome Statute of the International Criminal Court, Third session, The Hague, September 6–10, 2004 Official Records, ICC-ASP/3/25. Part II, Programme budget for 2005 and related documents; B, Related documents, pp. 262–265, http://www.icc-cpi.int/NR/rdonlyres/EEF8F8E2-6AF9-47F7-859E-1C1AE1359ED3/140538/ICCASP325IIB_English.pdf.

of a candidate put forward by Australia, but the French were wary; French officials believed that the Yugoslav and Rwandan tribunals had been dominated by Anglo-American officials and were determined to avoid a repetition of that dynamic.[27]

Instead, the individual that quickly became the focus of the search was Luis Moreno-Ocampo. Little known outside his native Argentina, he had investigated and prosecuted abuses by the Argentine military government during the 1980s. Along the way, he developed a reputation in the country as a determined investigator not afraid to challenge the powerful. After serving as a public prosecutor, he entered private legal practice and joined efforts to battle corruption. In 1995, *Newsweek* cited his anticorruption work and predicted that he was "about to become [a] media star."[28] In Argentina at least he did just that, defending several high-profile clients, including soccer star Diego Maradona. He starred as a television judge in an Argentine version of *The People's Court*, mediating disputes over divorce, unpaid rent, and stolen property.[29] On the international stage, however, the Argentine was a newcomer. He had never prosecuted a case in an international court or managed a multinational office.

When his name emerged, Moreno-Ocampo was living in Cambridge, Massachusetts, where he had been appointed a visiting professor at Harvard Law School. With the assistance of Samantha Power, a fellow Harvard professor and an expert on genocide, he sketched out his vision for the position in a letter to Jordan's Prince Zeid, who was coordinating the search. On his own initiative—and on the very eve of the Iraq War—Moreno-Ocampo then flew to Europe to unofficially interview with key ICC member states. In Berlin, Paris, Madrid, The Hague, Oslo, and London, he answered questions about his vision for the court and his past experience. The Argentine's itinerary reflected an understanding that while more than seventy states had joined the court, the European powers were the principal movers behind the new institution. The questions varied. German officials grilled him about certain cases he had taken on as a private lawyer; French officials focused on whether he understood the civil law elements of the court's hybrid system. Reviews were mixed, and German officials were particularly doubtful that Moreno-Ocampo was right for the job.[30]

As nonmembers, the United States, Russia, China, and Japan had no formal input into the selection of the court's first prosecutor. There is no evidence that any of them sought to influence the process informally. US passivity is particularly noteworthy. Senior American diplomats and lawmakers had warned repeatedly about the dangers an unchecked and politicized prosecutor might pose to American interests. Yet Bush administration officials recalled no meetings, briefings, or serious attention to potential candidates, their backgrounds, or their political profiles. A handful of US diplomats in The Hague embassy followed the negotiations, but they sensed little interest in Washington. Consumed with other matters, the United States left the selection of the court's first prosecutor entirely to the court's members.

If US concern about the ICC was genuine, why didn't American officials work informally to ensure that the first prosecutor would be someone whose judgment the United States could trust? The answer appears to be twofold: first, American officials did not want to legitimize the institution by expressing views on its staffing. Even informally communicating views would signal to other states that the United States was reconciled to the ICC's existence. Certain American officials also realized that the choice of an incompetent or incautious prosecutor might actually help the American cause by demonstrating to the world the ICC's defects.[31] As important was a simple bureaucratic reality: dozens of issues competed for the attention of senior policymakers, and the selection of the prosecutor for a court the United States had spurned did not rank high.

US silence did not mean that the superpower's presence was not felt as a group of key ICC states considered candidates. Several of those involved in the process recalled that Moreno-Ocampo had previously received US backing. In 1993, the State Department had endorsed him for prosecutor of the Yugoslav tribunal (the Argentine government failed to back his candidacy and Richard Goldstone was ultimately selected).[32] "Even if [the Americans] were not consulted in formal terms, that fact played very much in his favor," recalled one participant in the selection process.[33] If some US officials quietly hoped for a disastrous first prosecutor, several diplomats from more supportive states were pleased that someone the United States had already decided was credible was the leading candidate.

As the court's leading members debated who should be the first prosecutor, the court's first judges took up their posts in a formal ceremony. Bruno Cathala, a French official selected as the court's lead administrator, choreographed the ceremony to achieve maximum effect. In The Hague's medieval Knights' Hall, the eighteen incoming judges would take their oath and then process to a designated area, set off from the assembled diplomats and guests. Cathala emphasized that symbolic separation to signify that the judges were "protected from influence, particularly political influence."[34]

The first act of the judiciary in every society has always been to set aside an area, to delineate a physical form in which to dispense justice. The judicial area is sacred and by its very existence defines the lay area. It is commonly symbolically protected by the presence of a "bar" or barrier in the courtroom, which ensures that the law cannot be attacked.[35]

Cathala could not shelter the judges from lofty expectations. William Pace, head of the Coalition for an International Criminal Court, declared "this is one of the greatest days for international law in all history." The European Union's representative, Chris Patten, called the ICC the "most significant development in international law since the creation of the United Nations."[36] Jordan's Prince Zeid predicted that the court would serve as "the inseparable and necessary companion to a more peaceful world, and our permanent conscience."[37]

"Iraq Is Not My Case"

On the night of March 19, 2003, American warships launched a salvo of cruise missiles at a site near Baghdad. The CIA had information suggesting that Saddam Hussein might be staying in the complex's basement, and President Bush approved the "decapitation" strike after a hastily-called meeting in the Oval Office. Shortly after the missiles struck, American bombers entered Iraqi airspace to drop bunker-busting bombs. After the blast, the Al Jazeera network aired footage of dead and wounded being pulled from the site and alleged that the attack had killed civilians.[38]

Five days later, while back home in Argentina, Moreno-Ocampo received word that he would indeed become the court's first prosecutor (he would not be formally appointed until late April). He immediately faced the question of whether he would investigate what much of the world viewed as an illegal war. As the Iraq war unfolded, complaints flooded into the court from academics, nongovernmental organizations, and lawyers' associations.[39] A prominent human rights lawyer insisted that US leaders could be prosecuted for aiding and abetting war crimes.[40] Human rights groups warned that coalition forces were using types of weapons—notably cluster munitions—that could easily violate the laws of war. In light of later investigations, some of the complaints were ironic; in April, Sudanese lawmakers called for the prosecution of George Bush and Tony Blair.[41]

The jurisdictional provisions of the Rome Statute made any investigation of the Iraq conflict unlikely. Iraq was not a court member and so the court lacked territorial jurisdiction over crimes committed within its borders. There is evidence that Saddam Hussein's government may have considered granting the new court jurisdiction in the run-up to the war. In early 2003, Iraqi diplomats contacted a prominent British expert on international law for advice on the implications of joining the court. The lawyer eventually responded with a memorandum outlining Iraq's options and suggesting that Iraq consider granting the court jurisdiction. By the time that memo reached Iraq, however, Saddam Hussein's regime had been deposed.[42]

Without territorial jurisdiction, the court's reach was limited. The principal foreign combatant, the United States, had not joined the court, and the activities of its forces could not provide jurisdiction based on nationality. The United States—and likely others—would have blocked any attempt in the Security Council to refer the situation and give the court broader jurisdiction. The only plausible route to ICC jurisdiction therefore was through the activities of coalition members who *had* joined the court, most prominently the United Kingdom and Australia. If their nationals committed crimes that the ICC believed national authorities were not pursuing adequately, the court could have an opening to investigate.

To the frustration of many activists who opposed the war, however, mere British and Australian involvement in the conflict was not grounds for ICC scrutiny. The fact that the crime of aggression remained undefined meant that invading Iraq under questionable legal authority could not be prosecuted. Some of the more legally astute observers crafted their complaints to the ICC accordingly. The Athens Bar Association attempted to make the case that British forces had indeed committed war crimes and crimes against humanity.[43] But many complaints simply ignored the limitations on the court's reach.[44]

As Moreno-Ocampo prepared to take office, his every utterance regarding Iraq was scrutinized. Both in public and in private, Moreno-Ocampo signaled that he had little interest in the case. Quietly, the incoming prosecutor reached out to Americans he knew in an attempt to allay suspicion and repair the rift. One interlocutor assured the prosecutor that he had good contacts within the Bush administration and could help smooth relations. A few weeks later, he called back, chastened. "Luis, where are you working? This place [the ICC] is radioactive!" Undeterred, Moreno-Ocampo tried repeatedly to arrange a meeting with US officials. He was rebuffed; no administration officials would meet with him, even informally.[45]

An intermediary finally put Moreno-Ocampo in contact with General John Altenburg, who had recently retired as the Army's deputy Judge Advocate General. As a top Army legal official, Altenburg was acutely aware of, and to some extent shared, the military's concerns regarding the ICC.

But he saw no reason not to talk with the incoming prosecutor. The men met at the Army-Navy Club in Washington, and Moreno-Ocampo made clear that he considered American fears about the court exaggerated. He said that with robust US domestic procedures, he could not imagine launching a case against a US citizen. While Moreno-Ocampo did not explicitly ask Altenburg to serve as an intermediary, the general had the distinct impression that the prosecutor was conveying a message. Altenburg communicated the substance of the conversation to certain government officials and lawyers he knew, but it is not clear how widely the exchange was disseminated within official circles.[46]

In April, Moreno-Ocampo was formally elected and he delivered a careful statement noting that the ICC would be respectful of sovereignty, cautious, and would operate strictly within the bounds of the Rome Statute. He signaled that the court might be most effective in prodding national court systems to take action and, to the chagrin of other court officials, he suggested that an inactive court might still be a success:

> The efficiency of the International Criminal Court should not be measured by the number of cases that reach the court or by the content of its decisions. Quite on the contrary, because of the exceptional character of this institution, the absence of trials led by this court as a consequence of the regular functioning of national institutions would be its major success.[47]

The prosecutor had huddled earlier with Prince Zeid to discuss what he should say about Iraq in his first press appearance as prosecutor. Moreno-Ocampo suggested that he might address the court's jurisdictional limitations to demonstrate the obstacles to an investigation. Zeid was alarmed; the suggestion that it was only jurisdictional limitations holding back the prosecutor from an Iraq investigation would have irritated the Americans and the British, he warned. Zeid's sensitivity was well founded. In early 2003, the Bush administration's strategy of marginalizing the court was in full stride. The US decision to ignore the process of selecting the prosecutor did not imply diminished concern about the court. The campaign for immunity agreements continued and American diplomats at the UN were planning to renew the broad immunity resolution it had achieved in 2002. In pursuing these tactics, the United States was willing to rattle diplomatic china. When European officials objected to the American immunity agreements, US officials sent stern warnings. A US demarche reportedly warned Europe that its position "will undercut all our efforts to repair and rebuild the transatlantic relationship just as we are taking a turn for the better after a number of difficult months....We are dismayed that the European Union would actively seek to undermine U.S. efforts."[48]

In other contexts as well, the United States was laboring to restrain foreign judicial scrutiny of its military activities. In Belgium, several court cases accused the United States of abuses in Iraq.[49] Those complaints—one launched by a left-leaning candidate for parliament—sparked a furious American reaction. Senior American officials saw the Belgian cases as part of a much broader phenomenon that encompassed the ICC: the use of foreign and international legal instruments to threaten US sovereignty. In early 2003, defense secretary Donald Rumsfeld sent a blistering memorandum to other senior administration officials describing "several disturbing trends in international law, including the ICC, universal jurisdiction prosecutions, and the broader judicialization of international politics and warfare." The Belgium case, he suggested, was just the tip of the iceberg, and the Iraq conflict heightened the need to respond systematically to this challenge. "It is only a matter of time before there is an attempted prosecution of a U.S. official."[50]

The Belgian piece of what Rumsfeld saw as a global trend was addressed speedily. On a visit to Brussels in June 2003, Rumsfeld inveighed against its universal jurisdiction law. Belgium, he said, "has turned its legal system into a platform for divisive politicised lawsuits against her NATO allies." He warned that the alliance might not keep its headquarters in the country unless the provision was changed. "Belgium needs to recognize that there are consequences for its actions. It's perfectly possible to meet elsewhere."[51] The pressure had the desired effect. Belgium's government swiftly modified the law.[52]

Meanwhile, US diplomats kept a watchful eye on the ICC. On July 15, the US embassy in The Hague cabled Washington with a detailed report on the new court that highlighted the extreme sensitivity on Iraq. While noting a tendency for the prosecutor to speak somewhat casually, the cable picked up on the message of caution that the Moreno-Ocampo had emphasized in his public and private statements:

> In semi-private forums and in private conversations reported to Embassy legal officers, Ocampo has indicated consistently that his initial investigative interests will focus not on Iraq but on the situation in the Congo....In public, however, Ocampo has been less restrained. At a recent presentation before a group of ICTY staff and students participating in a Humanity in Action summer course, Ocampo said that

he was looking at the actions of British forces in Iraq—which, according to one Embassy source, led a British ICTY prosecutor nearly to fall off his chair. It was, another participant said, "a complete shocker" and came without any qualifications. Such statements may contain less than meets the eye. Privately, Ocampo has said that he wishes to dispose of Iraq issues (i.e., not investigate them).

The cable also reported that another senior court official, Bruno Cathala, communicated to embassy officials his desire that the court remain narrowly focused on the most serious crimes and avoid "silly things like Iraq." These comments, embassy officials concluded, "seem designed to put the [US government] at ease and assure us that the court will proceed carefully and not launch controversial investigations."[53]

If it was clear that Iraq would not be the prosecutor's first investigation, where would he begin? The court's newly elected judges were restlessly awaiting work, and the advocacy community that had played a critical role in creating the court was eager to see it take action. The prosecutor's suggestion that the court could succeed even without launching investigations provoked a strong reaction. NGO leader William Pace bristled at the suggestion of an inactive court.[54] Several judges also objected to the vision of a court exerting influence by its mere presence rather than its caseload. From inside and outside The Hague, there was intense pressure on the new institution to become operational.[55]

Moreno-Ocampo recalled that he and several other prosecution officials proceeded methodically—almost mechanically—to rank the gravest situations over which the court had jurisdiction. They developed a chart that included major conflict zones, drawing on information from the United Nations and leading human rights groups. The key metric was violent deaths in the last several years, and the Democratic Republic of Congo was at the top of the list. Violence in Colombia was at almost the same level. Uganda, the prosecutor remembered, ranked third.[56]

In July, at his first press conference in The Hague, Moreno-Ocampo announced that he would examine closely the situation in eastern Congo. That region had been in a nearly constant state of violence and instability since 1994, when genocide in neighboring Rwanda produced a massive influx of refugees. Among the thousands that poured into the country were members of the extremist Rwandan movement responsible for the genocide. These groups established militias and assumed control of many of the region's sprawling refugee camps. Soon, Rwandan forces and allied militias began a campaign against them. With support from Rwanda and Uganda, some of these rebel forces in eastern Congo ultimately crossed the vast country and unseated the decades-old regime of Mobutu Sese Seko, who many believed had supported the genocidaires.[57]

However dramatic, regime change in Kinshasa offered little respite for Congo's eastern provinces, where violence continued. In June 2003, an independent monitoring organization described the region as a "theatre of spiraling violence bordering on genocide that urgently needs to be stopped."[58] A UN peacekeeping force deployed a few months earlier had not been able to restrain the recurrent violence. After a visit to the region in June 2003, a senior UN official explicitly raised the possibility of international prosecutions as a mechanism for managing the lawlessness:

> Whoever thinks that he can assassinate, that he can drug young children and use them for armed combat, whoever thinks they can get away with this will find himself before a tribunal one day.... There is the possibility for judgment some day, and I believe this day will come.[59]

The prosecutor's announcement made that abstract possibility much more likely. But his decision to focus on a situation so quickly surprised some in his office. He was operating with a minimal staff and faced myriad logistical challenges. In many respects, the prosecutor's office was not yet equipped to operate, let alone mount a complex investigation. Identifying one situation did have certain advantages. It could focus the work of an office that, with its global reach, faced the danger of spreading its meager resources too thinly.

Publicly announcing a focus also sent a signal—intended or not—about the kind of case the court would likely select. Faced with several conflicts in which major powers or their allies were directly involved, the prosecutor chose instead to focus on internal violence in a part of the world where these powers had few direct interests and where the United Nations was already heavily engaged. Given the limits on his jurisdiction and the nature of the crimes involved, that decision was reasonable. But the prosecutor's choice—and, as important, the reassuring signals that it sent to major powers—created an important precedent.

The Court's Foreign Policy

Even as Moreno-Ocampo selected an initial target, the work of building the ICC continued hurriedly. The various offices within the court had to recruit staff, establish procedures, develop a more detailed budget, and begin investigations. They did all this under the watchful gaze of states. In the court's hectic first months, national delegations regularly visited the modern headquarters building in a quiet suburb of The Hague. Often, diplomats were just curious to see the nascent institution. Sometimes, they gently pressured court officials to consider their nationals for key posts.[60]

To better monitor the ICC's work, several key embassies expanded their professional staffs in The Hague. Both the British and French appointed legal advisers to focus on the ICC. They and other member-state diplomats met regularly with new court officials, who were eager to establish relationships with states.[61] Silvia Fernandez, a veteran Argentine diplomat who had played a key role at the Rome Conference, became a principal point of contact. Moreno-Ocampo selected her as his *chef de cabinet* and leaned heavily on her for diplomatic advice. The court soon established the practice of offering a regular briefing on its activities to Hague-based diplomats.[62]

The frequent interactions between diplomats and court officials struck a few observers as odd. One Hague-based diplomat who had significant experience with domestic criminal courts remembered: "It was a bit strange if you consider that the ICC is a legal institution. You can ask why states intervene so much in the life of the court."[63] Other diplomats in The Hague recalled being careful not to give the impression that they were seeking to influence the court. "We didn't want them to think we're intruding on their independence," a European diplomat said. "There was great caution about that. On the other hand, for this bird to fly it needed some support and that's the reality of it."[64]

American officials in The Hague were not among those getting to know the new players at the court, at least not directly. They understood that Washington did not want them to have any official contact with ICC officials or visit the court's premises. Instead, US diplomats in The Hague stayed informed secondhand, through contacts with other national diplomats who were court members. In the institution's early days, a senior ICC official recalled meeting a US diplomat by chance at a diplomatic reception. They had an amicable conversation, but the American declined to provide his business card. "I had no proof that we met," the court official said.[65] At times, a former US diplomat recalls, the effort to remain informed about the court "had the quality of an intelligence operation."[66]

It soon became apparent to those watching that the court's architecture created potential both for internal friction and for confusion as the institution managed its relations with states. The ICC had three main power centers, each of which needed to interact regularly with states. The prosecutor was the most obvious; he had full control over the court's investigations and interacted with states as he examined allegations and developed a prosecution strategy. The Rome Statute declared that his office was independent from the rest of the court. The second power center was the court's registry, or administrative arm, led by the veteran French judicial administrator, Bruno Cathala. The registry interacted with states on budget matters and technical cooperation issues such as witness protection agreements. Finally, there was the court's president, a judge elected by all other judges. Philippe Kirsch, the chairman of the Rome Conference, was elected ICC president as soon as the judges took office.[67]

All three officials—the registrar, the president, and the prosecutor—could claim to be the face of the court. Although there is evidence that the registrar attempted to communicate a conciliatory message to the United States, he was confined to mostly technical issues and had little input into investigative strategy. The court's president and the prosecutor would have the most significant diplomatic roles. As the key player at the Rome Conference and a senior Canadian diplomat, Kirsch was a well-known figure with good diplomatic connections. His participation in conferences and media appearances could help generate awareness and understanding of the court, particularly in nonmember states. But Kirsch discovered quickly that his duties as manager of the judiciary kept him mostly tethered to The Hague and limited his ability to serve as the court's *de facto* foreign minister. He decided not to attend most of the events to which he was invited—with one notable exception:

> If I spent too much time doing academic exercises and conferences, I would never be at the court. The court was difficult enough to manage being there and I really didn't think I could be away too often. When invited to the United States, however, I tried to make myself available as much as possible. I would go to radio stations, to academia, to think tanks, whatever was necessary. There was a great deal of inaccurate information going on, we were not getting anywhere with the authorities, so we needed some kind of education going through other channels.[68]

Just as the prosecutor had attempted to repair the rift with the superpower, so too did Kirsch. As a sitting judge, however, Kirsch was constrained in even this narrow ambassadorial function. He could say little about matters on which he might have to rule. Nor was he well positioned to respond to or convey to the prosecutor concerns that diplomats might have about the court's investigative strategy or activities.

As the official who would decide where to investigate and whom to pros-ecute, the prosecutor was therefore the court's central figure in establish-ing relationships with key states. Within the quickly growing Office of the Prosecutor (OTP), there was debate about how to manage these relation-ships and, in particular, how much diplomatic activity the prosecutor should engage in as he conducted his work. The Rome Conference had featured repeated admonitions from states that the ICC should be independent and free of political influence. What that meant in practice, however, was some-thing the prosecutor and his staff had to grapple with directly.

The prosecutor's offices of the international tribunals for the former Yugoslavia and Rwanda had featured two principal elements: an investigation division and a prosecution division.[69] The former was responsible for devel-oping physical and documentary evidence and identifying and interviewing witnesses. The prosecution division then used this material to fashion indict-ments and prosecute cases. Moreno-Ocampo and his closest advisers decided quickly that the ICC prosecutor's office required a third element. Unlike the Yugoslav and Rwanda tribunals, which had prescribed areas of operation, the ICC would have to choose where to focus its investigative resources. Also unlike the ad hoc tribunals, the ICC was required to defer to national courts when they were conducting credible investigations.

These differences made the ICC prosecutor's job vastly more complex than those of his colleagues at other tribunals. He and his team would have to weigh the severity of multiple situations around the world, assess the efforts of national governments to address ongoing crimes, and ensure that the ICC had the necessary jurisdiction. They would do all this in a political environ-ment that might be far less supportive than those in which the ad hoc tribu-nals operated. As creations of the Security Council, those tribunals enjoyed the formal—if not always actual—support of powerful states. In many cases, the ICC might not.

This environment, Moreno-Ocampo realized, required sustained and often delicate interactions with a broad range of national governments. In effect, prosecution officials would have to negotiate with diplomats and, to a degree at least, speak their language. "You really cannot have the cops who are the investigators dealing with diplomats," a former prosecution official noted.[70] "[Diplomats] don't like to be dealt with by people who don't under-stand diplomacy and international relations."[71]

The institutional answer to this need was what eventually became known as the Jurisdiction, Complementarity, and Cooperation Division (JCCD).[72] Moreno-Ocampo designated Silvia Fernandez as the first director of the new unit. By the end of 2003, Fernandez had added several other officials, includ-ing former foreign ministry officials from Canada and the United Kingdom, a political scientist, and a former NGO official with experience in interna-tional justice. The prosecutor decided that JCCD would have responsibility for reviewing potential investigations, and that an official from the division would be part of all active investigations.[73]

In reviewing situations, the new division assessed not only the internal political dynamics producing violence but also the broader regional and inter-national political context.[74] Within the prosecutor's office, certain lawyers and investigators viewed JCCD with suspicion. Why was this extra layer of review necessary? Couldn't the office's investigators and prosecutors them-selves determine which situations merited the court's attention? And why was the division headed by a former foreign ministry official? For some expe-rienced national prosecutors, JCCD sometimes appeared to be a political organ at the very center of the prosecutor's office. A former JCCD official acknowledged that the office saw establishing effective relations with govern-ments as a fundamental task:

> We were sensitive to states...we wanted to show states that we were respectful, organized and that we understood the dynamics. We would try to work in a way that was as far as we possibly could be like normal diplomatic relations. In a sense, the cooperation aspect was run a little bit more like a diplomatic relations office than a prosecutor's office. It was a perfectly understandable beginning. We wanted to achieve a basic element of statecraft.[75]

Skeptics inside the office worried that in speaking the language of diplomats, senior prosecution officials might start thinking like them. Sensitivity to the political and strategic context in which the court operated might subtly influ-ence what should be purely legal and factual decisions about what investiga-tions to pursue. The court's legitimacy rested on its apolitical nature, these officials believed; hints that the office was operating politically would be corrosive.

Investigations and Openings

Even as the prosecutor designed his office, he and his closest advisors con-sidered a much more concrete question of how politics and diplomacy inter-sected with justice. The issue was how to convert the prosecutor's preliminary examination of violence in eastern Congo into a full investigation. The Rome Statute granted the prosecutor the power to initiate the investigation himself (although he would need the approval of a panel of judges). But this *proprio motu* power had been highly controversial at the Rome Conference. The United States, China, and Russia, among other states, had opposed giving the prosecutor the freedom to initiate investigations.

Given this reality, Moreno-Ocampo and Silvia Fernandez worried that using the prosecutor's *proprio motu* powers so quickly might unsettle key states. They wanted the court's first investigation to enjoy broad support, and they wanted a state, or multiple states, to initiate the process. At one point, the prosecutor considered seeking a referral of Congo from all member states, although the idea was dropped as impractical. The strategy the prosecutor settled on was to make clear his desire for a referral by Congo's own government. Not only would such a "self-referral" avoid the *proprio motu* problem, it would make the court's first investigation more an affirmation of national sovereignty rather than a challenge to it.

As Moreno-Ocampo sought Congo's support for an investigation, another conflict in the region evolved in a way that implicated the court. One of Congo's eastern neighbors, Uganda, was engaged in a long-running fight against an often brutal rebel group, the Lord's Resistance Army (LRA). Led by the cult figure Joseph Kony, the LRA drew on disaffection with the Ugandan government in the country's north but also periodically terrorized the people it claimed to defend. During the 1990s, the LRA had developed a close relationship with the Sudanese authorities, who used Kony's troops to help battle separatist rebels in southern Sudan. The LRA had become a regional fighting force adept at melting across borders. It specialized in abducting children to replenish its ranks.[76]

In 2002, the Ugandan authorities struck a deal with the Sudanese government to cooperate against the LRA. The result was a major new offensive—code-named Iron Fist—to finally root out Kony's fighters. Ugandan president Yoweri Museveni, a former guerilla commander himself, moved briefly to northern Uganda to supervise what he hoped would be a decisive campaign against the rebels. With Sudanese acquiescence, Ugandan troops pushed into areas of southern Sudan and clashed periodically with LRA units. But the offensive failed to defeat the LRA and instead generated new rounds of violence in Sudan and Uganda itself.[77]

By 2003, Museveni was casting about for other options. Often touted as one of Africa's new generation of political talent, Uganda's president already enjoyed considerable international support.[78] As president, Bill Clinton had visited Uganda and hailed its economic growth and stability, and Museveni's government was a leading recipient of US aid.[79] In 2003 the British, German, Japanese, and American governments together provided about $1.3 billion to Uganda's coffers. In all, foreign assistance accounted for almost one-quarter of Uganda's annual budget that year.[80] After the 2000 US election, Museveni worked hard to forge good relations with the Bush administration. His government supported the invasion of Iraq and quickly signed one of the bilateral immunity agreements that Washington was seeking.[81]

Yet Museveni's international backing had not translated into the kind of military cooperation and intelligence support needed to defeat the LRA. It was in this context that the notion of an ICC role arose. Payam Akhavan, a private lawyer representing Uganda, met with the prosecutor in late 2003 to discuss the court's likely Congo investigation and to ensure that Uganda, which still had forces operating in parts of that country, was not a target of the investigation. In the course of that conversation, the prosecutor suggested that Uganda consider referring the situation of the Lord's Resistance Army to the court.[82]

Akhavan passed on the idea to senior Ugandan officials. "It took some days of discussion," he recalled, "but the Ugandan government understood well that it was in the interest of the people of Uganda to internationalize the LRA case through an ICC referral."[83] Ugandan ambassador Mirjam Blaak, a confidant of president Museveni, recalled that leveraging an ICC role into concrete support made the proposal appealing. "We thought that if we could get warrants of arrest out that through collaboration with other states parties or even non-states parties, we could achieve something."[84] In late 2003, Ugandan officials quietly initiated a dialogue with the prosecutor's office about a referral.

The prosecutor's office still included only a handful of lawyers and investigators, and they had been focused on Congo, but a Uganda investigation appeared even more promising in some respects. Kony's unquestioned brutality made the case an attractive one. There was little doubt that the violence there crossed the court's gravity threshold. No powerful governments supported the LRA; Kony was as close as an individual could be to an international outcast. The case had other advantages. Given American fears of a too-powerful prosecutor, it was helpful that the Ugandan government appeared eager to initiate the case. For prosecution officials, Uganda's self-referral appeared to be an ideal way for the court to begin:

> When the referral came we thought this was a great thing because at that time and in that climate the fear, especially from a U.S. point

of view, was the frivolous, politically motivated prosecutor who was lurching out into the world to collect cases in any way and therefore trampling all over legitimate state concerns. So we saw a state referring itself as a dramatic sign that the ICC can actually be something constructive and work in partnership with states, of course the partnership can't be too close but a constructive relationship is conceivable.[85]

By early 2004, the conversation between the prosecutor and Ugandan officials had advanced considerably. In late January, Moreno-Ocampo and Museveni met at a London hotel to finalize the arrangement. Even at this late stage in the negotiations, the prosecutor worried that something might still go wrong. Perhaps another government would counsel the Ugandans against the referral. Perhaps Museveni's own generals and intelligence officials would become nervous. Eager to seal the deal, the prosecutor and the president announced the referral at a joint press conference.[86]

The sight of the ICC prosecutor all but linking arms with a national leader stirred controversy inside and outside the court. Several advocacy groups warned that the joint announcement suggested that the court would be working closely with the Ugandan government rather than impartially investigating abuses. For the population in northern Uganda, much of which was hostile to Museveni, the court appeared to be working on the president's behalf. The Ugandan government described the referral as covering "the situation of the Lord's Resistance Army" only, and the prosecutor had to later make clear that government abuses could be investigated as well.[87]

The perception that the court was working closely with a sovereign government unnerved justice and human rights advocates, but it may have helped reassure officials in the Democratic Republic of Congo. In March 2004, after several months of periodic consultations with the prosecutor's office, Congo's government finally announced that it was referring the internal violence to the court. Less than a year after the prosecutor took office, the ICC was beginning two major investigations referred by the relevant governments themselves.

It appears that the major powers played only a limited role in the referrals. Indeed, Uganda's move caught the diplomatic community in Kampala by surprise. The US ambassador to Uganda, Jimmy Kolker, recalls being "quite shocked" by the sudden announcement.[88] Other key governments also appear to have been caught off guard. The Congo referral, which the prosecutor had explicitly sought, was much less surprising. In that case, the court apparently benefited from quiet interventions by European officials, who pressed

Congo's government to accept an ICC role. The EU's status as the lead donor to Congo's fragile government ensured that its views were influential.[89]

The relatively placid major-power reaction to the court's first two investigations did not reflect unanimity in major capitals that an ICC role would be helpful. In fact, there was a diversity of views between and within governments about the wisdom of the move. But neither investigation raised red flags at the highest levels. In the foreign diplomatic community in Uganda, an ironic pattern emerged: US officials tended to be more supportive of seeking Kony's capture and prosecution than those of states that had actively supported and joined the ICC:

> Ironically, it was the European diplomats, the countries that had favored and had subscribed to the court, who were most reluctant, saying this will discourage defectors from telling where Kony is because they could be caught in this. This undermines Uganda's motivation to actually find the guy because they can say it's up to the ICC to do that. The US, which was not a member, actually saw this as a positive development. We thought it gave the international community some standing to get involved in the north, it gave us standing to provide non-lethal military assistance to the UPDF, which was trying to find him.[90]

Several European diplomats visited the prosecutor to express concern about the investigation's likely impact on the Ugandan peace process. At the root of the divergence between the United States and these European governments were differing calculations about the prospects for a negotiated solution to the LRA conflict. Most involved US diplomats believed that negotiations with the LRA had little promise and favored aggressive steps to confront Kony; their European and Canadian counterparts tended to be more sanguine about the prospects for negotiations and worried that the ICC's involvement might aggravate the conflict. Events on the ground reinforced their fears. A few weeks after the announcement of the referral, LRA forces killed more than 200 civilians at a refugee camp in northern Uganda, the worst single incident on Ugandan soil in almost a decade.[91]

As the investigations got underway, Moreno-Ocampo selected lead lawyers. He named Christine Chung, a former American federal prosecutor, to lead the Uganda investigation. Chung was one of the first lawyers the prosecutor had hired. A former federal prosecutor in New York, she had contacted the prosecutor about working at the court even before he was formally named. Her selection to lead the Uganda case afforded her the opportunity to comment on the US relationship with the court. "I'm voting with my feet," she told the *Wall Street Journal*. "The idea that the court is going to be prosecuting American soldiers trivializes the whole process."[92] To lead the Congo investigation, Moreno-Ocampo selected Serge Brammertz, a former Belgian prosecutor with good contacts throughout Europe.

As the ICC began its work in Uganda and Congo, court officials emphasized to diplomats their political sensitivity and their desire to work with, rather than undercut, the fragile political processes in those countries. In Uganda, the government became an important partner in the investigation. ICC officials coordinated their overall approach with senior ministers. For its part, the government turned over huge quantities of information on LRA crimes, including intercepts of radio and satellite phone communications. "We gave them excerpts, we gave them everything we had," said Mirjam Blaak, Uganda's ambassador to The Hague. "People from the military came [to The Hague] to hand over evidence." On the ground, the Ugandan armed forces provided security as the ICC teams conducted their initial visits to the still volatile north.[93]

In Congo, the political environment was even more delicate. After several years of intense conflict, the international community had helped broker a peace agreement between the war's major factions, signed in South Africa in April 2002.[94] The next year, a fragile transitional government formally took power, headed by Joseph Kabila. In theory, the Kabila government was the legitimate governing authority throughout the vast country. It had the backing of the UN peacekeeping force in the country and international donors. In reality, Kabila's government was a weak patchwork of different political movements and militia groups.[95] In early 2004, on the eve of formal ICC involvement, the stitches began to fray. Dissidents in Congo's eastern Kivu provinces broke with the government, and new fighting produced waves of displacement as civilians sought safety. The violence led to renewed tension between Congo and Rwanda, which exercised a strong influence in eastern Congo.[96]

Involved national diplomats and UN officials struggled to tamp down the violence and keep the peace accords alive. Throughout the east, the Congolese government's authority was paper thin. "Parallel chains of command persist in the army as well as in the administration as the former belligerents compete for resources and power," one independent analysis concluded.[97] In this environment of renewed political and military tension, the ICC chose to focus its investigation not on the Kivus, but on the northeastern province of Ituri. Crimes committed there had been well documented, and the Ituri conflict was also somewhat separable from the violence in the Kivus, which directly implicated the national peace agreement. The researcher Phil Clark has argued that focusing on Ituri allowed the court to keep itself as distant as possible from the more sensitive political struggle: "Of the various conflicts in the DRC, that in Ituri is the most isolated from the political arena in Kinshasa. In particular, there is less clear evidence to connect President Kabila to atrocities committed in Ituri.... Therefore, investigations and prosecutions in Ituri display the least capacity to destabilize the current government."[98]

In certain communications with the diplomatic community, ICC officials apparently acknowledged their desire not to interfere with the political transition. When ICC deputy prosecutor Serge Brammertz visited the US embassy in Congo, he left American officials convinced that the ICC would be targeting militia leaders who had not joined the unity government and remained outside the peace process. An embassy cable to Washington reported:

> Brammertz said the ICC plans to conduct its work within the wider context of the peace process and will need to strike the right balance of ending criminal impunity while not jeopardizing the transition. In particular, he hopes that ICC's initial investigations, which will focus on abuses committed by actors outside the transition, such as the Ituri armed groups, will help bring the transitional government closer together.[99]

Prosecution officials maintain that the Ituri investigation resulted entirely from an assessment of where the gravest crimes in Congo were occurring rather than political expediency. But they also acknowledged that Ituri's distance from the more sensitive political questions in Congo facilitated their work, and they did not hesitate to emphasize that in communications with concerned states.[100] Brammertz's comments mirrored an approach that the prosecutor himself would often use: simultaneously insisting on the court's independence from political considerations and emphasizing the political benefits its work could generate.

A New Pragmatism

The court's first investigations—done collaboratively with national governments—were not controversial internationally. Internally, the activity and sense of purpose boosted court morale. The frictions inherent in building the institution had taken a toll, and court president Philippe Kirsch confided to a diplomat that for the first year he had often "wonder[ed] why he agreed to join the ICC as President. It lacked work, its political prospects were poor, and bureaucratic infighting among the Registry, Chambers and OTP was rampant. Now, he says, things are better."[101]

The court had improved political prospects in part because states elected to sideline certain contentious issues. The Rome Statute had established the court's basic jurisdiction and rules, but several important tasks had been left for later. Of these outstanding issues, the most contentious by far was whether the court's members should define the crime of aggression. At the Rome Conference, influential court supporters, including the United Kingdom and France, had helped push aggression to the sidelines. Of the major powers supporting the court, only Germany had showed much enthusiasm for defining the crime.

The major-power aversion to specificity on aggression was not complicated. Unlike the other categories of crimes the ICC can prosecute, aggression goes directly to the reasons that states fight rather than their means of doing so. In that sense, it raised highly sensitive questions, particularly for major powers capable of and inclined to intervention abroad. Does any use of force without international legal authorization constitute aggression? If so, would the US-led invasion of Iraq qualify? Would NATO's intervention in Kosovo?

Because the major powers—and particularly the United States—were the ones most likely to use military force abroad, they watched the post-Rome Conference maneuvering on the issue closely. The arguments followed a predictable pattern: the permanent Security Council members insisted that only the Council could determine when aggression had occurred. They argued that the UN Charter made the Council the sole authority on the issue. A strong majority of states rejected that view and maintained that other bodies could also decide on whether an act of aggression had occurred. It was clear to many delegations that the P5 would be perfectly content to leave aggression undefined—and therefore unprosecuted. One delegate recalled that the P5 and their allies "delayed and delayed and delayed."[102] As the post-Rome Preparatory Commission met, the diplomats tasked with working on aggression realized that no consensus was possible.

When it began meeting, the ASP busied itself with electing judges and with the budgetary and technical steps necessary to make the court operational. "[A]ggression was allocated minimal meeting time within the framework of the Assembly."[103] Instead of grappling with the issue itself, the ASP passed responsibility for the thorny question to a new "special working group"—open to all states—that began meeting at Princeton University in June 2004. The working group's chairman was Liechtenstein's ambassador to the United Nations, Christian Wenaweser. For the next several years, Wenaweser and his staff organized and presided over occasional meetings on aggression on Princeton's campus. He made a calculated decision to keep discussions at a technical level as much as possible. "It seemed advisable to steer away, at least initially, from the questions that made aggression such a politically loaded topic."[104]

The failure of the court's members to define aggression before the institution became operational was a disappointment to many states, including the Arab countries, which had hoped Israel might be called to account for its annexation of Palestinian land. During the meetings of the Preparatory Commission, several Arab states submitted a definition of aggression that included no reference to the Security Council and which included in the definition "any military occupation...or any annexation by the use of the force."[105] But other observers of the court breathed a sigh of relief. Aggression, they were convinced, was still too explosive for the court to touch.[106]

So too was the question of alleged abuses by coalition forces in Iraq. By the spring of 2004, American abuses at the Abu Ghraib prison in Iraq had become a global scandal. The British government also faced new allegations about possible abuses by their forces. In early 2004, British authorities began investigating the suspicious deaths of several Iraqis in British custody.[107] Amnesty International identified multiple cases of civilian deaths and criticized the British government for conducting inquiries "shrouded in secrecy."[108] The mounting evidence that the forces of leading powers had committed war crimes put international organization officials in a difficult spot. In a carefully worded report, the UN's top human rights official conceded that the abuse of prisoners might constitute war crimes but also insisted that "everyone accepts the good intentions of the coalition governments."[109] For their part, the prosecutor and other court officials said nothing. Prosecution officials continued an internal review of allegations regarding Iraq, but with little sign that a full investigation was likely.

The swirling controversy over American abuses in Iraq did prompt a notable shift in Washington's relationship with the court. In 2002 and 2003, the United States had insisted that the UN Security Council include a broad immunity provision in resolutions reauthorizing existing peacekeeping missions.[110] Those immunity clauses were deeply unpopular with Security Council members that had joined the ICC, but for two years Washington got its way. When the issue arose again in the spring of 2004, however, the environment had changed. UN Secretary General Kofi Annan said an immunity resolution "would discredit the Council and the United Nations that stands for rule of law and the primacy of the rule of law."[111] Even states sympathetic to Washington's aversion to the ICC signaled that a new resolution would not be welcome.

After several weeks of consultations with other states on the Security Council, Washington let the issue drop. The perception that limiting the ICC's investigative power amounted to an attack on the international rule of law had introduced the first significant crack in the Bush administration's multifaceted campaign to marginalize the court. The administration was beginning to realize that the diplomatic effort required to fully marginalize the court might not be worth the effort.[112]

If the court's leading diplomatic opponent was beginning to adjust to new realities, court officials had the impression that a new, and less welcome, pragmatism was affecting the court's backers. The near euphoria that had prevailed at the end of the Rome Conference was fast dissipating. Daryl Robinson, a Canadian who worked in the prosecutor's office, traveled often in 2004 to help the court establish the official links with states whose cooperation it would need. He noted a change in the approach of even these supportive states:

> The ICC was benefiting from this very deep commitment of individuals who were the advisors to the state in all these different countries. But then the personnel rotated. And there was a change in attitude: the ICC was no longer this darling new creation. The ICC is just a fact, it's just another factor. There are new people who are just managing the ICC file. By the time I was there we were dealing with people they're managing the ICC file, minimizing their state's obligations and trying to maximize their own interests. It was a little disappointing.[113]

The "spirit of Rome"—the product of the intense 1998 negotiating experience—had been replaced by more normal political processes. For many supportive states, the ICC was now less a moral and ideological cause than just another international organization. For court members, and particularly the larger members, a critical part of managing their relationship with the court was controlling the growth in its budget. By the middle of 2004, the court was expanding quickly, and the larger member states kept a watchful eye on the balance sheet. The recent precedent of the Yugoslavia tribunal, the budget of which had ballooned to more than $100 million annually, loomed large.

Chaired by the court's largest funder, Germany, the budget committee met in August 2004 and expressed concern about possible fragmentation and duplication within the court. It endorsed the prosecutor's strategy of "conduct[ing] focused investigations to support a small number of selected charges against the most senior leaders," an approach it hoped would avoid "the resource-intensive investigatory approaches that had been employed by the ad hoc tribunals."[114] But the committee also gently chided the prosecutor for duplicating structures that existed in other parts of the court. The careful scrutiny was a reminder that any ambitions the court might harbor would have to contend with financial realities.

Pressure on Sudan

By early 2004, the violence in the Darfur region of Sudan had become a leading international issue. After rebel groups attacked police and military units in 2003, the Khartoum government responded with a brutal counterinsurgency campaign that resulted in thousands of deaths and a major wave of displacement. In February, UN experts reported that nearly 100,000 Darfurians had spilled across the Sudanese border into Chad and that 750,000 more were displaced within Sudan.[115] In May, Human Rights Watch accused the Sudanese government of massive ethnic cleansing.[116] That same month, the UN Security Council insisted, without providing any specifics, "that those responsible be held accountable."[117]

Meanwhile, a highly effective advocacy movement, operating mostly from the United States, ensured that the issue stayed on the agenda of policymakers. In July 2004, the US Congress passed a resolution declaring the crisis a genocide.[118] Two months later, US Secretary of State Colin Powell told a US Senate committee that he agreed with that assessment, a step that no other major diplomatic figure had taken. Almost immediately, President Bush himself concurred and asked for a full UN investigation.[119] The next month, the Security Council authorized a high-level commission of inquiry to examine reports of atrocities in the region and "identify the perpetrators of such violations with a view to ensuring that those responsible are held accountable."[120] By that point, the United Nations estimated that thousands had been killed and that 200,000 residents of Darfur had fled to Chad.[121]

For all the international attention it was receiving, however, the Darfur situation was not on the prosecutor's radar screen. Because Sudan was not an ICC member and because Sudanese citizens were carrying out the abuses, the court lacked jurisdiction. The only route to a court investigation was a UN Security Council referral, which appeared politically impossible. Lacking a route to jurisdiction, and consumed with its Congo and Uganda investigations, the prosecutor's office was on the sidelines of the expanding crisis. In July 2004, Sudan's foreign minister met with Moreno-Ocampo, but only in the context of the Uganda investigation; the foreign minister assured the prosecutor that Sudanese support for the LRA had ceased several years before and pledged to work together with Uganda to defeat Kony's forces.[122] The minister did not suggest that Sudan would give the court jurisdiction over its own internal violence, and the prosecutor did not ask.[123]

Washington held the key to an ICC role in Sudan, and its aversion to the court appeared to still be strong. In the fall of 2004, during presidential debates, President Bush sought to cast his opponent, Senator John Kerry, as overly deferential to global opinion. The president presented his opposition to the ICC as evidence of willingness to take unpopular stands to defend US interests:

> This is a body based in The Hague where unaccountable judges and prosecutors could pull our troops, our diplomats up for trial. And I wouldn't join it. And I understand that in certain capitals around the world that that wasn't a popular move. But it's the right move, not to join a foreign court that could—where our people could be prosecuted.[124]

After Bush won reelection in November, the same US Congress that had been so outspoken on Darfur sought to broaden aid restrictions on states that did not sign ICC immunity agreements. In December, US diplomats at the United Nations opposed European-proposed language in a Security Council resolution endorsing an ICC role in Burundi, whose government was considering seeking the court's assistance. The US ambassador to the UN urged European states not to use the Council to advance recognition of the court.[125]

Statements like these obscured a subtle shift, however. By early 2005, the young court looked very different from the institution that leading US opponents had depicted. Far from leaping at the chance to confront the United States and its allies, the court's top officials had shown no interest in pursuing investigations that implicated the superpower. The court had instead focused its efforts on African conflicts where the United States and other leading powers had few objections to investigations. Even the way it pursued those cases had signaled accommodation; the prosecutor had relied on referrals rather than his own power to initiate an investigation. In short, the ICC appeared to be working in ways broadly consistent with American interests. The stage was set for a remarkable change in the relationship between the superpower and the court.

5

Breakthrough (2005–2008)

A MAJOR BREAKTHROUGH between the court and the United States—in part engineered by Britain and France—ended the US campaign to marginalize the institution, placing it on much more secure ground. Several other major powers also became more receptive to the court's work. Japan became a member—and the court's largest funder. If the conceptual opposition to the court was yielding, the question of whether powerful states would back the institution in practice became acute. The court's early investigations yielded a series of arrest warrants that forced states to decide how they would integrate the demands of international justice into their foreign policies.

The End of Marginalization

In early January 2005, a group of investigators, lawyers, and forensic experts at the United Nations was hurriedly sifting through voluminous material they had collected on atrocities in the Darfur region of Sudan. Appointed by UN Secretary General Kofi Annan, the UN Commission of Inquiry faced a tight deadline to submit its report. On multiple trips to the region, the commission's small staff had interviewed hundreds of refugees, aid workers, human rights monitors, and others in Sudan and neighboring countries.[1]

Diplomats at the United Nations kept a close eye on the commission's work, anticipating that it would document widespread atrocities and call for international prosecutions. The French and British ambassadors quietly canvassed their Security Council colleagues about what many assumed was impossible: referring Sudan to the ICC. These diplomats hoped that a referral might give the international community another tool to mitigate the Sudan violence. If Sudanese leaders knew the court was watching, perhaps they would rein in the militia groups wreaking havoc in Darfur and more seriously consider a negotiated solution. At the very least, the court could offer some justice to the victims.

Paris and London saw an added benefit in a Security Council referral: strengthening the ICC. In 2002 and 2003, the United States had used the Council to limit the court's jurisdiction through broad immunity resolutions. ICC members on the Council complained—but ultimately acquiesced. Now, the two P5 members who had joined the court wanted to use the Council to empower the institution. A senior British diplomat worried that the ICC would be damaged if it were not allowed to address the crisis in Darfur. "[I]f the Council had not supported that [referral] resolution the signal it would send to the ICC would be very bad," he recalled. "I was very conscious that the failure to do it would have reverberated badly with the court."[2]

That these major powers were acting, at least in part, out of concern for the ICC's institutional health was an important development for the court. British and French support for a referral suggested that the active American marginalization campaign—and the more passive approaches of Russia, India, and China—might face a diplomatic counteroffensive. To this point, the major European powers had been willing to confront the United States about the ICC as a matter of principle; the push for a Darfur referral suggested that they might do so in specific situations as well.

As he counted potential votes, France's UN ambassador, Jean-Marc de la Sablière, was encouraged that the Council at that time included nine ICC members, and that neither Russia nor China appeared inclined to block a referral resolution. That made Washington the key. With its veto power, the United States could prevent a referral on its own. But as the French knew well, the Bush administration had been outspoken in condemning atrocities in Darfur.[3] "Our team here at the [United Nations] mission came to the conclusion that we could push the Americans on this issue," de la Sablière recalled.[4]

The French and British campaign benefited from good timing. The UN commission report was slated to appear as the Council considered another important aspect of Sudan policy: the possible dispatch of peacekeepers to monitor a peace agreement between north and south Sudan. The United States had helped shepherd the north-south peace negotiations and strongly supported sending peacekeepers. De la Sablière worked to link the issues. "Deliberations in the Security Council made clear that States were prepared to withhold their votes for a peacekeeping operation," a US diplomat has written, "until there was agreement on a referral to the International Criminal Court."[5]

As important, de la Sablière sought to cast the choice on an ICC referral as one between impunity and justice. "We wanted to put the Americans in a position where they would have to oppose something reasonable—and endorse impunity. We wanted the choice to be framed that way for them."[6] The strategy was effective. The US ambassador to the United Nations at the time, former senator John Danforth, warned the State Department that the issue of Darfur and the ICC might become a diplomatic "trainwreck."[7]

In late January 2005, the Commission of Inquiry's report went public. It called on the Council to refer the violence in Darfur to the ICC. "The Security Council's referral would be fully warranted, for indisputably the situation of Darfur constitutes a threat to the peace," the report concluded. "The prosecution by the ICC of persons allegedly responsible for the most serious crimes in Darfur would no doubt contribute to the restoration of peace in that region."[8] More than simply recommending an ICC referral, the report cast doubt on other international judicial options, including establishing a new ad hoc tribunal, expanding the jurisdiction of an existing tribunal, or creating hybrid mechanisms within the Sudanese legal system.[9]

Activists quickly amplified the message that an ICC role was essential. In so doing, they attempted a combination of rhetorical carrots and sticks. In an open letter to Condoleezza Rice, Human Rights Watch's executive director praised the administration's Sudan policy, noting that the United States had declared the violence there to be genocide long before others. US policy, he wrote, has helped "galvanize attention and action to stop violence against civilians." Allowing a referral, the letter insisted, would continue this pattern of moral leadership. "We hope that the United States will...prioritize[e] its commitment to the people of Darfur over its opposition to the ICC."[10] Others took a sharper tone. Writing in the *New York Times*, scholar and activist Samantha Power noted that a key figure in Sudan's violence opposed the involvement of the ICC and asked pointedly whether President Bush wanted to be "on the side of someone his administration considers a killer."[11]

Calls for the ICC to get involved also came from more unexpected quarters. Jack Goldsmith, a former Bush administration Defense and Justice Department official, advocated an ICC referral in a January *Washington Post* op-ed. His reasoning was simple: the United States had never objected to a court that took instructions from the UN Security Council; indeed, that had been the court Washington wanted. Goldsmith argued that supporting a Sudan referral could advance that policy. "The Darfur case allows the United States to argue that Security Council referrals are the *only* valid route to ICC prosecutions and that countries that are not parties to the ICC (such as the United States) remain immune from ICC control in the absence of such a referral." He acknowledged that such a position would invite a negative response:

> Critics would decry this approach as a double standard for Security Council members, who can protect themselves by vetoing a referral. But this double standard is woven into the fabric of international politics and is the relatively small price the international system pays for the political accountability and support that only the big powers, acting through the Security Council, can provide.[12]

In essence, Goldsmith was arguing for major-power control of the court. He urged the administration not to view pressure for a Council referral as a threat but as an opportunity to informally merge the court into the system of major-power privilege that the Security Council represented. His view had not yet prevailed in the administration. To avert the diplomatic embarrassment that would come with blocking a referral, the Bush administration advocated the creation of an ad hoc tribunal based in Africa.[13] Pierre Prosper, the administration's point person on war crimes issues, produced a concept paper recommending that the facilities of the UN tribunal created for Rwanda be used for Sudan trials. The paper suggested that a regional court would be more efficient and cost-effective, and that it would minimize the impression that Western states were judging Africans.[14]

Working from this script, US diplomats in several African countries sought to gin up support for the proposed tribunal.[15] Most of their interlocutors proved skeptical. Many African countries were ICC members and (at that point) they did not share American skepticism about the institution. Before the United States had developed any significant support for the proposed African tribunal, the British and French-led push for a Security Council referral on Darfur gathered momentum. The American dilemma was now acute. Certain voices in the administration, including John Bolton, advocated a veto of the referral.[16] Anything else, they insisted, would effectively give the ICC a US stamp of approval and fatally undercut the effort to marginalize it.

At several points, Secretary of State Condoleezza Rice discussed the issue with President Bush. She opposed vetoing a referral and recalled that the president shared her discomfort with allowing Sudanese leaders to escape accountability. "It was this dilemma of not wanting to send the wrong signal on Sudan," she said.[17] State Department legal adviser John Bellinger has a similar recollection. "The president was more concerned about the atrocities in Sudan than he was about the ICC. That was his specific decision. If there are no other ways to achieve accountability for the genocide in Sudan, then we don't have any problem abstaining."[18]

Bellinger also recalled that the court's uncontroversial early activities had eased concerns in Washington. "In 2005, hardliners in both Congress and the administration were still in high dudgeon about the court, so it helped that Ocampo had not actually done anything threatening to us."[19] After several conversations, Rice and Bush agreed that the United States would abstain on a referral resolution. An aversion to shielding Sudanese leaders had overwhelmed the strategy of marginalizing the court. As Rebecca Hamilton has written, "legally and politically, the first state in history to invoke the Genocide Convention could hardly veto [a] resolution designed to punish the perpetrators."[20]

On March 31, 2005, the Security Council voted to refer the situation in Sudan to the ICC.[21] Eleven of the Council's fifteen members—including nonmembers Russia and Japan—supported the resolution. France's de la Sablière applauded what he described as "a very positive step in the consolidation of the International Criminal Court." The United States, China, Brazil, and Algeria abstained. The US ambassador to the United Nations reiterated standard American objections to the court, but said "it is important that the international community speaks with one voice in order to help promote effective accountability." China insisted that it harbored "major reservations" about an ICC role in Sudan, which it feared would complicate diplomatic efforts to resolve the conflict. China's ambassador did not explain his government's choice to abstain rather than veto.[22]

Council members who belonged to the ICC had their own frustrations with the referral. Several expressed discomfort at the conditions the United States had insisted upon in exchange for its acquiescence.[23] Specifically, the United States negotiated language ensuring that the referral would not create jurisdiction over any citizens of nonmember states in Sudan (other than Sudanese, of course). At Washington's insistence, the resolution also included a reference to the Article 98 agreements US diplomats had negotiated with dozens of states. Finally, the resolution provided that no UN funds would go to the ICC as a result of the referral.[24]

These were not minor issues. The exclusion of ICC jurisdiction over nonmember state nationals in Sudan created an important precedent. The Rome Statute permitted the Security Council to refer "situations" to the court and did not appear to contemplate the Council tailoring referrals to exclude certain individuals. If the Council could refer the situation in Sudan but exclude the behavior of nonmember state nationals in Sudan, why could it not ask the court to investigate specific individuals? And if it could refer specific individuals only, what would be left of the court's independence? The limitation of jurisdiction in the resolution opened the door for the Council to quite specifically direct the court.[25] The prohibition on UN funding was also controversial, and in tension with the Rome Statute, which called for UN funding when the Council referred cases.[26] In their statements after the vote most ICC members on the Council expressed deep discomfort at these conditions. Brazil, a court member, refused to vote for the resolution. "The referral should not be approved at any cost," that country's ambassador insisted.[27]

More broadly, the Security Council action opened up the possibility that certain major powers—through the vehicle of the Council—would have a dramatic influence on the court's docket. By the summer of 2005, the prosecutor's office had expanded from a handful of staff to more than one hundred. But the court's resources were still quite limited, and member states, particularly the largest funders, watched growth in the court's budget hawkishly.[28] The Darfur referral obliged the prosecutor to shift resources significantly as he geared up for a major new investigation. That dynamic highlighted an important reality: a court responding to Security Council referrals (particularly without any additional UN funding) would have limited resources to initiate investigations the Security Council members did *not* favor, and that dynamic might help the Council indirectly manage the court's docket.

No one at the ICC was in the mood to quibble with the resolution's defects. Court officials were surprised and delighted by the referral, which seemed in one stroke to move the institution to the center of international conflict resolution efforts. A Security Council willing to refer cases could place violence and atrocities in nonmember states within the court's reach. Cooperation between the institutions also raised the possibility that the Council's expansive powers—including, ultimately, the right to impose sanctions and authorize the use of force—might be deployed to enforce arrest warrants and pressure recalcitrant states into cooperation. "Darfur was like a different dimension," recalled Moreno-Ocampo. "Suddenly we were connected with the Security Council.... It was a totally different game."[29]

The Sudan referral also appeared to transform the relationship between the superpower and the court. "We knew then that there was at least the possibility to go towards a relationship of benign neglect [from the United States], which was always our goal," said one senior court official.[30] In fact, the relationship soon moved beyond benign neglect to modest support. This accommodation involved sometimes subtle maneuvers. In the course of its investigation, the UN commission of inquiry had collected copious evidence related to crimes in Darfur. After the Security Council referral, the prosecutor's office dispatched an investigator to the UN's Geneva offices to recover the documents. He returned with more than thirty boxes loaded into his vehicle. As ICC officials sorted through the material, they discovered a sealed envelope from the US government. Months before, Washington had provided intelligence to the UN commission, not contemplating that it would be transferred to the ICC.

The prosecutor and his staff chose to leave the envelope sealed. They called the US embassy in The Hague and invited American personnel to collect it.[31] Two American diplomats recovered the envelope and met briefly with the prosecutor, marking the first time US diplomats had visited the court's headquarters. The prosecutor's gesture was well received:

> Rather than using the information that wasn't intended to be used in this way, [they were saying] we want to do the right thing. That was a big deal. Luis earned a lot of points with people in Washington when he did that. As far as I know that was the first official meeting between US government people and the prosecutor.[32]

Not long after that handover, US officials suggested that they might actively support the court's investigation in Sudan. Doing so required navigating obstacles created by the American Servicemembers' Protection Act, which prohibited any direct US support to the court. The Act included an exception that made permissible support for specific investigations, and Bush administration officials were ready to use that opening.[33] Difficult as the Darfur referral decision had been, the administration now wanted the investigations to produce results. According to Condoleezza Rice, British foreign minister Jack Straw asked whether the United States might signal publicly its willingness to assist with the investigation.

> I said it depends a bit on what "assist" means. Would we share information and intelligence? Will we go pick [indictees] up and deliver [them] to the court? No. Will we help facilitate what the court wants to carry out? Yes, we would do that. I pretty much made that call and told the president that I wanted to make that call and he didn't really object.[34]

American support for the Darfur investigation was a potential boon for the court. The US intelligence services had material—including communications intercepts and satellite imagery—that few other countries could offer the court. Even if these resources were provided on the condition that they not be used in court, they could be invaluable as court investigators hunted for evidence that could be. The Rome Statute clearly contemplated the possibility of states providing such "lead evidence." It permitted the prosecutor "not to disclose, at any stage of the proceedings, documents or information that the Prosecutor obtains on the condition of confidentiality and solely for the purpose of generating new evidence."[35]

Access to US intelligence was tempting for the court, but it also created the possibility that the court would become dependent on it. Some ICC officials believed that the international tribunal for Yugoslavia, in particular, had become overly reliant on classified material from major NATO states. One former ICC official described the ICTY and other ad hoc tribunals as "absolutely addicted to Western intelligence." These officials wanted to be cautious about the intelligence relationship, particularly given American ambivalence about the court. Court officials understood that while a steady flow of intelligence might aid investigations, it could also be used to guide the court toward certain prosecutions and away from others.[36] "It's always presented as 'we're going to help you.' But it's a way to orient your investigation. You get huge intelligence files on the person this one country wants to have indicted. It's so tempting for prosecutors and then we can't force our investigators to look at something else."[37] Mindful of this risk, the prosecutor's office did not approach the United States with specific requests for intelligence on Sudan. "That's a trap the prosecutor didn't fall into at all. He never used [US intelligence material] and never asked for it. He even had to refuse it."[38] Even as the US campaign to marginalize the court effectively ended, the specter of informal US control over the institution appeared.

Monster Hunts

As the Darfur referral raised the prospect of a new and more fruitful relationship between the ICC and key states, the prosecutor was preparing to seek his first arrest warrants. That next phase in the court's operations implicated a critical question about the court: Who would ensure that the individuals it sought actually appeared for trial? The prosecutor's first targets—militia commanders in Uganda and Congo—had little support in the international community. But the court soon discovered that the resources and will to arrest even outcasts were often in short supply.

During 2004 and early 2005, court teams had made multiple trips to Uganda. The ICC investigators there cast a wide net, meeting with groups of victims, government officials, foreign diplomats, aid workers, and community leaders.[39] For the most part, the court officials operated in a supportive environment. With the court's focus on the Lord's Resistance Army, Ugandan officials eagerly offered their help. Foreign embassies in Uganda also tried to assist. Diplomats shared information about the situation in the north with the investigators.[40] Although some civil society groups and local religious groups raised concerns about the inquiry, by early 2005, investigators had accumulated enough material to support indictments.[41]

In early strategy documents, the prosecutor had announced his intention to focus on those individuals who bore the greatest responsibility for crimes. Moreno-Ocampo had no intention of starting with lower-level offenders; he wanted the big fish and he wanted them first. In Uganda, his first targets were the leadership of the Lord's Resistance Army, including Joseph Kony himself, his deputy Vincent Otti, and three other senior commanders. Citing eyewitness accounts and radio intercepts, the prosecutor accused Kony of war crimes, enslavement, and rape. He documented a list of brutal assaults by Kony's forces on villages and camps sheltering displaced persons. In all, the prosecutor accused Kony of thirty-three war crimes and crimes against humanity.[42]

In July 2005, the ICC judges assigned to the case issued the arrest warrants. Because the prosecutor had requested that the warrants remain confidential, there was no public announcement. Senior Ugandan officials received word, but the panel of judges had to specifically approve other disclosures. From the court's perspective, sealed warrants had several advantages. They helped minimize any danger of retaliation against witnesses and victim's organizations. They also allowed the Ugandan government a period to adjust to the new reality and to let the tentative diplomatic initiative led by Ugandan minister Betty Bigombe play out. Only a few weeks before the warrants were issued, Bigombe remained hopeful about the chances for a negotiated settlement with the LRA. During this period, she reportedly spoke regularly to Kony and his deputies via satellite phone.[43] Public arrest warrants would almost certainly have shattered the initiative, and prosecution officials preferred not to be blamed for undermining negotiations they expected would fail of their own accord.

Sealed arrest warrants also maximized the admittedly small chance that LRA leaders might be caught off their guard. In the days after the judges issued the arrest warrants, they gradually broadened the "circle of trust," authorizing disclosure of the warrants to a select group, including senior UN officials, the United States, the United Kingdom, and France. The secret was hard to keep, however, and rumors of the arrest warrants leaked.[44] An incautious UN official even referred to them publicly.[45] In October 2005, the court finally made the warrants public. Moreno-Ocampo announced the arrest warrants at a press conference in The Hague during which he highlighted LRA crimes, emphasizing the abduction and sexual abuse of children.[46] UN Secretary General Kofi Annan declared that the warrants "send a powerful signal around the world that those responsible for such crimes will be held accountable for their actions."[47] Hopes for the court were running high; less than three years after opening its doors, the ICC was naming names.

The Uganda indictments were a milestone, but they also risked exposing the court's impotence. Even as the ICC prepared cells for its first prisoners, Kony issued a defiant statement and pledged that he would never surrender.[48] Instead, he invited the prosecutor to his jungle headquarters to discuss the matter (the prosecutor did not respond).[49] A deadlier message arrived a few weeks after the warrants became public: six foreign aid workers were killed by LRA forces, forcing aid agencies to cut back their operations in the region. Most observers interpreted the attack as a form of retaliation.[50] Kony's precise whereabouts remained a mystery.

The court, heavily dependent for support from states, now faced the question of how to enforce the arrest warrants it had issued. The prosecutor had emphasized that Uganda and neighboring states in which the LRA operated had the primary responsibility for apprehending the leaders. Rhetorically, at least, the states took that responsibility seriously. Sudanese officials announced their intention to capture Kony if he crossed into Sudanese territory.[51] Congolese and Ugandan authorities discussed creating a joint force to pursue LRA members.[52] But assigning responsibility to the cluster of states that had manifestly failed to capture or contain Kony—and several of whom had supported him at various points—was clearly inadequate. "How can the ICC charge Uganda to arrest Joseph Kony when they have failed for the last 19 years?" asked Betty Bigombe.[53] ICC officials hoped that they might be able to broker closer cooperation between the regional states affected directly by the LRA. Court officials met quietly with security officials from Uganda, Congo, and Sudan, but their ability to induce coordinated military action was limited.

Nor was it clear that major powers would step forward with their own diplomatic, military, and intelligence resources. There were some promising signs that the United States might back a more aggressive effort. Kony's pretensions to be serving God outraged George W. Bush. "How can this guy call himself a soldier of the Lord," Bush reportedly fumed at one point. "He's just a murderer."[54] In 2001, the United States had placed Kony's organization on a terrorist list, and the Pentagon was beefing up Ugandan military capabilities.[55] But Washington showed no readiness to participate directly in arrest operations.

The ICC warrants may have helped galvanize one multinational effort to snare the LRA leadership. In late 2005, diplomats and UN officials in the region learned that several units of the LRA had crossed into the northeast corner of the Democratic Republic of Congo and were sheltering in the vast Garamba National Park.[56] The UN peacekeeping force in Congo, working with the Congolese armed forces, deployed units to cut off the LRA fighters. In January 2006, apparently with some intelligence support from the United States and other Western powers, several dozen Guatemalan commandos serving with the UN mission raided a site in Garamba where senior LRA officials were thought to be based. The operation turned into a disaster; eight Guatemalans were killed, possibly from friendly fire. If Kony or his deputies were present during the clash, they apparently escaped unharmed.

After the incident, ICC officials spoke with senior British, South African, and French diplomats about using their special forces, intelligence resources, and airlift capabilities to help mount a more effective arrest operation. For the most part, however, the conversations did not lead to concrete plans. The major powers were willing to make modest investments in the regional effort to seize LRA leaders, but they were not willing to risk their own forces. Nor did the ICC establish its own dedicated arrest unit, a step that both the international tribunals for the former Yugoslavia and Rwanda ultimately took. In the ad hoc tribunals, these cells included "trackers," individuals whose primary job was to develop information on the whereabouts of those indicted and to facilitate planning for arrests. In a few cases, arrest cell personnel engaged directly with intermediaries to help secure arrests.

Moreno-Ocampo never felt comfortable establishing an analogous unit within the ICC. The prosecutor may have worried that states would see an arrest unit as overreach. The burden of enforcing arrest warrants remained squarely with states, most of whom failed to demonstrate a robust, sustained commitment to arresting indictees. When ICC president Philippe Kirsch addressed the Assembly of States Parties in late 2006, he reminded them of their obligations. "Our experience over the past years has reinforced the importance of cooperation," Kirsch said. "The Court does not have the power to arrest [indictees]. That is the responsibility of States and other actors. Without arrests, there can be no trials."[57]

Paths Not Taken

Events in 2005 and 2006 had propelled the ICC from theory into practice. The Darfur referral established the critical precedent of Security Council referral while the Uganda arrest warrants forced the court and states to grapple with how to enforce arrest warrants. Haltingly and sometimes messily, the court was in action. But many states, particularly leading powers, were at least as interested in understanding where the court would *refrain* from action. The Rome Statute accorded the prosecutor significant discretion as to which situations to investigate. By 2006, evidence suggested that he would use it to reassure powerful states.

In February 2006, Moreno-Ocampo publicly closed his file on alleged abuses by coalition forces in Iraq; there would be no full ICC investigation. That decision was not a surprise, but the prosecutor's explanation provided insight into the office's emerging standards for determining when abuses were grave enough to warrant court action. Moreno-Ocampo explained that while it appeared British forces had committed several war crimes in Iraq, there was no large-scale pattern of crimes. The isolated incidents that had occurred, the prosecutor concluded, were not grave or widespread enough to merit a full investigation. Moreno-Ocampo also noted that British authorities appeared to be investigating the accusations themselves.[58]

The prosecutor ended his Iraq investigation just as the conflict in that country reached a fever pitch. Insurgent groups, a mix of disaffected Baath party supporters and extremist fighters from around the Muslim world, were waging a campaign against coalition and Iraqi government forces. One clear element of the insurgent strategy was setting Iraq's Sunnis and Shiites against each other. In late 2005, forces affiliated with Abu Musab al-Zarqawi launched a series of attacks on Shia civilians that killed hundreds.[59] Iraq was turning toward full-scale civil war. As they responded, coalition forces continued to inflict civilian casualties, although commanders insisted that they were taking all possible precautions.

The ICC, an institution designed expressly to address mass atrocities, was on the sidelines of the Iraq imbroglio. Some observers saw marked political expediency in the prosecutor's decision not to pursue any cases there. William Schabas, a leading academic expert on the court, insisted that the prosecutor should have assessed the gravity of the alleged crimes by British forces in the light of the broader, bloody context. "Even if it is admitted that willful killing attributable to British forces only concerns 15 or 20 victims, surely that that this results from an aggressive war that has brought the deaths of hundreds

of thousands of Iraqi civilians is germane to the gravity determination."[60] For
Schabas, the prosecutor's choice to close the Iraq investigation was particularly unsettling because it coincided with the decision to charge a Congolese
warlord with recruitment of child soldiers, a crime arguably less grave than
willful killing. Schabas's view of the Iraq conflict—and of the prosecutor's
responsibilities—was far from universally accepted. Few other court scholars
argued that the prosecutor had an obligation to consider the Iraq war's origins
in determining whether the specific crimes over which he had jurisdiction
were serious enough to merit a full investigation. However, it was apparent by
2006 that the question of how to rank various situations was a critical one for
the court, and that the malleable concept of "gravity" provided the prosecutor
wide discretion in doing so.[61]

For a brief moment, it appeared the ICC might get much broader jurisdic-
tion in Iraq. In 2005, an Iraqi minister announced his intention to sign the
Rome Statute.[62] The statement created diplomatic shockwaves. Iraq's deputy
ambassador to the United Nations at the time, Feisal Istrabadi, recalled get-
ting two quick phone calls when the news broke. The first was from Jordan's
Prince Zeid, a prominent court supporter serving as president of the ICC
Assembly of State Parties. He asked excitedly whether the reports were true.
Istrabadi confessed that he did not know. Half an hour later, US ambassador
Anne Patterson called and asked the same question, with a tone of "grave concern." That alarm by the United States had an immediate effect; other senior
Iraqi officials quickly clarified that the human rights minister had no authority to sign the Rome Statute. When Istrabadi brought up the issue with Iraq's
foreign minister, he was told that the Americans "would have a fit" if Iraq
joined the court.[63] It appears that US pressure helped steer the Iraqi authorities away from a move that might have produced an ICC investigation. No
other major powers—even those who had vigorously opposed the Iraq war—
pushed publicly or privately for an ICC role in Iraq.

As important, there is no evidence that court officials at any point intervened to encourage Iraq's ratification of the statute. Nor did court officials
publicly or privately ask the Iraqi government to submit a declaration, permitted under the Rome Statute, giving the court jurisdiction even absent a
decision to join. According to one former ICC official, the prosecutor was
likely relieved not to have to consider the situation in Iraq any more than
he did. "I have no doubt there would have been enormous political pressure
against opening that investigation."[64] This unwillingness to seek out a role
for the court in Iraq contrasted sharply with the prosecutor's active cam-
paigns for referrals in Congo and Uganda. In both those cases, the prosecutor

had identified the situations as priorities for the court and negotiated with national leaders to arrange referrals.

Officials in the prosecutor's office saw the situations as fundamentally distinct. Congo and Uganda were court members and so the court already had broad jurisdiction. The prosecutor was not seeking jurisdiction in those cases, he was asking a government that already accepted the court's jurisdiction to trigger and cooperate with an investigation. Prosecution officials believed that "campaigning" for membership or jurisdiction in the territory of non-members like Iraq, by contrast, went beyond the office's mandate. "It's different to have jurisdiction and then get support [for an investigation] than to seek jurisdiction," Moreno-Ocampo said. "That's for advocates, not for me. I was not the world prosecutor. I was the state-party prosecutor."[65]

As with the decision not to open an investigation based on alleged coalition abuses, the prosecutor's choice not to seek out an Iraq referral was defensible. But it was a choice: there was nothing in the Rome Statute that precluded the prosecutor from campaigning for jurisdiction in Iraq or other places where his reach was limited. An alternative reality was possible: states might have faced a prosecutor who routinely called for jurisdiction over situations involving large-scale atrocities. By interpreting the office's role narrowly, prosecution officials were strictly limiting the ways they would deploy the court's moral authority.

As he closed his file on Iraq, the prosecutor kept mostly silent about the conflict in Afghanistan. That country had joined the ICC in 2004, giving the court broad jurisdiction over crimes committed on its territory. As the conflict there escalated, so did civilian casualties. Human Rights Watch put civilian deaths at more than 1,500 in 2005.[66] The toll more than doubled in 2006 as US and NATO forces battled resurgent Taliban forces.[67] Researchers documented nearly 200 bomb attacks in Afghanistan, more than 80 of which were carried out by the Taliban and directed mainly at civilians.[68] A rocket attack in Kunar province killed and injured scores of schoolchildren, car bombings struck markets, suicide attacks targeted funerals. Within OTP, officials maintained a file on Afghan violence, but they made no move toward a full investigation (figure 5.1).

The prosecutor was more interested in the situation in Colombia, where years of violence between government forces, leftist rebels, drug traffickers, and right-wing paramilitary groups had left thousands dead. Because Colombia joined the ICC in 2002, the court had jurisdiction over certain crimes committed on its territory.[69] The conflict there was in a particularly dynamic phase as the prosecutor began operating. With strong backing and

Battle Deaths in Iraq, Afghanistan, Uganda and Congo (2003–2006)

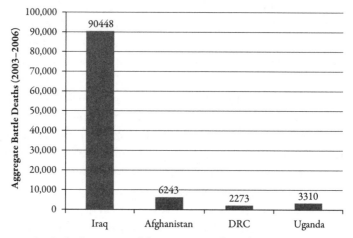

FIGURE 5.1 Battle deaths in Iraq, Afghanistan, Uganda, and Congo: 2003–2006.

Source note: Battle deaths are a highly imperfect metric for crimes that might fall under the jurisdiction of the court because many battle deaths do not constitute crimes. Battle deaths are employed here because of the absence of reliable data on potential crimes and because they provide a gauge of the intensity and scale of these conflicts, all of which have included significant violations of international criminal law. This illustration draws primarily on the Peace Research Institute Oslo (PRIO) Battle Deaths Dataset, Version 3.0, released in October 2009. PRIO's best estimate is used here for the Iraq, Afghanistan, and Uganda conflicts. Supplemental data for years 2003 and 2004 of the Congo conflict was drawn from the Uppsala Conflict Data Program (UCDP) Conflict Encyclopedia. UCDP uses the same definition for battle deaths and armed conflict, but also provides information for "non-state conflict" where both parties of a conflict dyad are non-state actors. This allowed the causalities from seven non-state conflict dyads (including FAPC-FNI, Hema-Lendu, and FNI-UPC) to be included in battle-death calculations for the conflict. The PRIO dataset is found at http://www.prio.no/Data/Armed-Conflict/Battle-Deaths/The-Battle-Deaths-Dataset-version-30/. Explanations explaining coding decisions for each conflict and year are found at http://www.prio.no/Global/upload/CSCW/Data/PRIObd3.0_documentation.pdf. The UCDP interactive Conflict Encyclopedia is found at http://www.ucdp.uu.se/gpdatabase/search.php.

significant aid from the United States, the government of Alvaro Uribe was engaged in a broad crackdown on FARC rebels. In 2003, the Bush administration dispatched hundreds of US troops and advisors to bolster the government effort.[70]

Civilian deaths and injuries in Colombia reached their highest levels in more than a decade just as the ICC became operational. Most estimates concluded that more than a thousand civilians were killed in 2002. Civilian casualties declined to about 600 each in 2003 and 2004 but remained significantly higher than average for the conflict. Local elections in the fall of 2003 were marred by multiple assassinations, likely committed by both left- and right-wing groups. While the grinding violence often escaped media attention, some atrocities were spectacular; in June 2004, for example, FARC rebels bound and killed more than thirty cocoa farmers who the rebels believed had supported right-wing paramilitary groups.[71] If there was substantial evidence of relevant crimes, the Colombian government's ability to investigate and commitment to prosecuting those responsible was in doubt. Even as it used newly aggressive tactics against the FARC, the government offered thousands of paramilitaries pardons and amnesty from prosecution or extradition, in exchange for their weapons.[72]

Citing the amnesties and pardons as evidence the Colombian government would not punish perpetrators for grave crimes, several leading human rights groups advocated ICC involvement. "Tens of thousands of crimes are being committed on a monthly basis," said one leading activist in 2005. "An ICC investigation is the only hope that there will be justice against those who commit crimes against humanity."[73] In October 2005, a human rights researcher wrote "Colombia suffers today, as it has for decades, from extremely high rates of impunity in cases involving violations of human rights and international humanitarian law...armed groups believe that they can ignore Colombian and international law without having to fear punishment."[74] In 2006, the prosecutor's office announced tersely that it had opened a preliminary inquiry, but there was no sign that it was preparing a formal investigation.[75] Instead, the prosecutor sent discreet requests for information to the government and monitored the Colombian government's own attempts to administer justice.

In all these situations—Iraq, Afghanistan, and Colombia—there were legitimate legal and practical obstacles to full ICC investigations. But there was also an emerging pattern: the court had not opened a full investigation anywhere the major powers had combat forces deployed, or even where they had strong interests. The court's caution was registering in the corridors of power. In June 2006, the *Wall Street Journal* ran a front-page story headlined "US Warms to Hague Tribunal." In the article, an unnamed administration official noted that the ICC prosecutor "seems to be going to great lengths to avoid stirring up the ire of the United States" and detailed the cooperation with the court that the United States was contemplating.[76] The next morning, State Department legal adviser John Bellinger found a copy of the article in his in-box, with a scrawled note from Condoleezza Rice. "John—what have you been saying?"[77] Bellinger knew that he had to be cautious about moving too quickly toward the court, but he was confident that Rice broadly backed the more friendly US policy.

Arrests and Complications

By early 2006, the court had calmed major-power anxieties about the institution and established a much more productive relationship with the United States, in particular. However, the ICC had failed to achieve another key goal: securing custody of an indictee. The unexecuted LRA indictments had established a worrisome precedent. As Philippe Kirsch reminded the court's members, without suspects in custody, the court could not start trials; there was no provision in the Rome Statute for *in absentia* proceedings. In early 2006, however, the court's drought ended. The breakthrough came not in Uganda, but in the Democratic Republic of Congo.

Since 2001, Thomas Lubanga had led one of several militia groups operating in the Ituri region of northeastern Congo. Ethnic tension had by 2002 turned Ituri into one of the country's most violent regions. Human Rights Watch researchers estimated that at least 5,000 civilians were killed in the region between July 2002 and March 2003. Lubanga's Union of Congolese Patriots (UPC) drew its strength from the Hema ethnic group, but it had also established links with powerful outsiders, including the Ugandan and Rwandan militaries.[78]

Lubanga's relationship with Congo's weak central government was contentious, and he remained outside the reconciliation process that had begun in 2002. Like most militia commanders operating in the region, Lubanga appears to have been responsible for serious crimes against civilians and recruitment of child soldiers. According to news reports, youngsters carrying Kalashnikovs served on his personal security detail.[79] Lubanga's downfall was sparked not by his abuses of civilians, however, but by an attack on UN peacekeepers in February 2005 that killed nine Bangladeshis. That attack prompted a broad crackdown by UN forces against the main militia groups in the region. Under pressure to do its part, the Congolese government arrested Lubanga, who had by then moved to Kinshasa to establish his UPC as a national political party.

Lubanga's arrest by the central government presented the ICC prosecutor with an important opportunity. From the start of the court's Congo investigation, Lubanga had been a target, but evidence linking him directly to murders, rape, and expulsions was weak. ICC investigators did not yet have witness testimony, communications intercepts, or documentary evidence that showed him ordering violent crimes. The developing legal case was much more solid on the charge of recruiting child soldiers. Nervous that Lubanga might be released by the Congolese authorities, Moreno-Ocampo decided to pursue an arrest warrant on that basis.[80] The pre-trial chamber issued the warrant in February 2006, and it was quickly transmitted to Kinshasa.

On March 17, 2006, Lubanga was escorted under guard to a French military aircraft, which flew directly to The Hague. The warlord reportedly wept as the plane left Congo.[81] When the aircraft landed hours later in The Hague, the court had its first prisoner. Lubanga was ferried from the airport to a brand new detention facility and received the full complement of rights the court gives to defendants. ICC officials ensured that Lubanga was handled carefully, even solicitously. He occupied a spacious cell with cable television, a private bathroom, and well-stocked kitchen.[82]

Moreno-Ocampo portrayed the Lubanga arrest as a historic turning point. "For 100 years, a permanent international criminal court was a dream," he said, "This dream is becoming a reality." He emphasized the political benefits of judicial intervention, describing the ICC investigation as "our contribution to building a stable democracy in Congo."[83] The ICC's unique challenge, the prosecutor wrote a few weeks later, "is to function within a worldwide criminal justice system without a world state."[84] The Lubanga arrest combined with even more dramatic developments that spring to suggest that such a global system might indeed be coming online. On March 11, in a prison cell only a few miles away from the ICC's headquarters, Slobodan Milošević died in the custody of the international tribunal for the former Yugoslavia. The former Yugoslav president had been suffering from high blood pressure and apparently died in his sleep from a heart attack.[85] Milošević's death cheated victims of a verdict, but it reminded the world that a former kingmaker had been brought low by an international court.

A few weeks later, another former head of state, Liberia's Charles Taylor, was arrested. Taylor had overthrown an autocratic government in 1990, fought a bloody civil war to secure his control over the country, and then helped orchestrate brutal violence in neighboring Sierra Leone. Indicted by a special court in Sierra Leone supported by the United Nations, Taylor lived quietly in Nigeria until his dramatic arrest on the Nigeria-Cameroon border in March 2006.[86] Even as it reinforced the principle that heads-of-state were not immune from prosecution, the Taylor arrest provided another small opportunity for rapprochement between the United States and the ICC. The Special Court for Sierra Leone and the Liberian government decided that a trial of Taylor in the region might be too destabilizing, and they explored whether the ICC's underutilized premises in The Hague might be available. State Department legal adviser John Bellinger called ICC president Philippe Kirsch to let him know that the United States had no objection to holding Taylor's trial at the ICC.[87]

The Taylor and Milošević prosecutions represented notable victories for the international criminal justice movement. "Despots are no longer assured of spending their golden years in quiet retirement," declared Human Rights Watch.[88] But they were victories of a particular sort. In both cases, the dictators' days in court came *after* key international players had determined that their usefulness to the political process had ended. Milošević's crackdown in Kosovo convinced Western leaders that he would be a source of continuing instability in the region rather than a useful intermediary. By the time he was indicted, Taylor had become an international pariah no longer in control of most of his own country. In both cases, the international prosecutions generated short-term complications, but they also meshed with the broader convictions of powerful states that leadership change was essential.

Khartoum Turns Hostile

The major powers were at a very different stage in their relationship with Sudan's regime. The Security Council had referred the matter to the court, but complex diplomacy continued between the United Nations, key outside powers, and the regime of Omar al-Bashir, which showed few signs of losing its grip on power. While the major Western powers had taken several bilateral and multilateral steps to increase pressure on Khartoum, none of them were actively pursuing regime change. They oscillated between confrontational and conciliatory language as they sought to balance their political, security, and human rights concerns. Moscow and Beijing showed even less inclination to ostracize the regime.[89]

The Security Council referral set in motion an investigative process that could not easily adjust to these shifting political winds. Even had the prosecutor wanted to hitch his investigative strategy to major-power diplomacy, it would have been difficult to track the diplomatic gyrations. In June 2005, the prosecutor initiated a formal investigation of the violence in Darfur.[90] Senior ICC officials, although not the prosecutor himself, traveled to Khartoum to explore whether the government would cooperate with the inquiry. The government had reacted harshly to the Security Council referral, but initial meetings with regime representatives were surprisingly cordial. ICC representatives first wanted to assess Sudan's internal judicial processes to understand whether the country was capable itself of investigating atrocities in Darfur. The government obliged by arranging meetings with members of the judiciary, the justice ministry, and other relevant officials. Sudanese officials even hosted an ICC delegation for a boat cruise on the Nile.[91] According to the prosecutor, one Sudanese official attempted a more direct approach, pushing $15,000 in cash across the table during a meeting with a court representative (he declined the offering).[92]

Behind the hospitality lay the clear possibility of outright confrontation between the court and the Sudanese government. Even as they offered cooperation, several senior Sudanese officials hinted that the ICC's investigation could push the country into even more serious turmoil. Their arguments seemed designed to make a war-weary West think twice about confronting Sudan's leaders. "Sudan is a very dangerous place," one official told a prominent Western journalist. "Your Somalia would be a picnic if Sudan degenerates into chaos. It would draw in the elements you fear most. It would require an influx of U.S. troops just like Afghanistan."[93]

To the surprise of some observers, the ICC did not publicly ask Khartoum to allow investigators into the contested Darfur region. In briefings to the Security Council, the prosecutor explained that he could not conduct investigations there because he had no means to ensure the safety of witnesses.[94] Instead, ICC investigators gathered information primarily through interviews of refugee populations in neighboring Chad, reports from aid agencies and others operating in Darfur, and even quiet interviews with select regime officials outside of Sudan. This strategy of investigating crimes committed in Darfur without sending investigators to the region may have postponed a full breakdown of relations with the Sudanese government, but it also invited criticism. Louise Arbour, the former ICTY prosecutor then serving as the UN's top human rights official, chastised the prosecutor for not insisting on an ICC presence in Darfur. She argued that the very presence of court investigators could have an important deterrent effect.[95]

The breakdown in relations with Khartoum came soon enough. By mid-2006, the ICC had narrowed its investigation to several incidents during which government-backed forces attacked civilian populations. Prosecutors focused on the responsibility of two figures in particular: Ahmed Haroun, a senior government minister, and Ali Kushayb, the leader of a pro-government militia group. As the ICC focus became clear, the regime's cooperation sputtered, and then ended entirely. Officials in Khartoum stopped responding to ICC requests for information and stalled on requests to interview senior government officials.

With Khartoum increasingly hostile, major powers were divided about the advisability of the looming indictments. The prosecutor's office received multiple calls from embassies with gentle suggestions about how to proceed. Advice from the key powers was often contradictory. A few Western diplomats expressed concern about the impact on negotiations and wanted to know whether the process could be stopped. Others had no problem with the indictments proceeding. Sometimes, there was uncertainty within governments. ICC officials recalled that one US diplomat advised prosecution officials to aim for lower-level officials; a few hours later, a different American official suggested aiming for senior regime officials.[96] The confusing signals from major-power diplomats reflected an important reality for the prosecutor: in many cases, key major powers were uncertain about what they wanted from the court.

In February 2007, the prosecutor sought indictments against Haroun and Ali Kushayb. His request described in painful detail how the men had funded, organized, and authorized attacks on the civilian population in Darfur. The evidence included accounts of the day Haroun flew by helicopter to Darfur, incited the *janjaweed* to treat Darfuri villagers as "booty" and then returned to Khartoum. A few hours later, several villages were in flames and dozens of civilians were dead. The prosecutor provided information that Ali Kushayb, for his part, had "personally inspected a group of naked women before they were raped by men in military uniform."[97] Sudanese officials rejected the charges and issued threats against anyone who attempted to arrest an indictee.[98]

In April, when the court formally issued arrest warrants for the two, the Sudanese foreign ministry announced that it would no longer cooperate with the court and would not surrender the two men. "We had extended our cooperation with the ICC for some time, but now the situation is completely different. It's not even a question of cooperation any more, it's a question that they want to try Sudanese citizens, which is absolutely nonsensical."[99] As Khartoum's language became more hostile, the prosecutor began insisting that the impasse represented a fundamental challenge to the court's authority. In Congo and Uganda, court officials had effectively been partners with the regimes in power. In Sudan, the ICC was directly confronting a sovereign government. As it did so, key capitals had to consider whether the ICC's battle would become their own.

Peace, Justice, and Diplomacy

As that confrontation developed, indications of how major powers might balance the ICC's credibility against other imperatives appeared in Uganda. In mid-2006, the on-again, off-again negotiations between the Ugandan government and the Lord's Resistance Army took a promising turn. From their camps in eastern Congo, LRA officials spoke periodically with Ugandan government representatives via satellite phone. They also called in to Ugandan radio stations to make their case to the people directly. Both publicly and privately, LRA officials insisted that they were ready to negotiate. The Ugandan government, for its part, was disappointed that the ICC indictments had not produced greater international support against Kony. "Our original idea was to get more cooperation from countries, from states parties basically," said Mirjam Blaak. "That never actually materialized."[100] While the Ugandan leadership was divided about the value of negotiations, President Museveni ultimately authorized his officials to pursue the opening with Kony.

As diplomatic efforts accelerated, the ICC-led campaign to isolate, ostracize, and apprehend Kony and his senior commanders came under pressure. In November 2006, senior UN official Jan Egeland met Joseph Kony near the border between Uganda and Congo. (Egeland alerted the ICC prosecutor in advance of the meeting.) It was the first such contact between a high-level UN official and Kony in years. During the brief encounter, Kony apparently told Egeland that he wanted the ICC warrants lifted as a condition for entering into formal talks. The Hague appeared to be weighing heavily on Kony's mind. In the bush, he reportedly discussed details of the court's processes with his deputies.[101]

Senior Ugandan officials signaled a willingness to negotiate the arrest warrants. "The people of northern Uganda have suffered enough. We should give peace talks a chance," said a presidential spokesperson.[102] Ugandan officials considered whether they could try Kony domestically and challenge the ICC's ability to hear the case.[103] The hopeful diplomacy placed the court and the prosecutor in a precarious position. Moreno-Ocampo did not want to appear as the primary obstacle to negotiations, but he and other court officials felt compelled to defend the court's arrest warrants. When Museveni told LRA leaders that he would guarantee their safety if they entered negotiations, a court spokesperson responded frostily. "It's the government of Uganda that referred the situation to the ICC in December 2003. They are now under obligation and made a commitment."[104]

Behind closed doors, court officials seethed about the weakness of the Ugandan commitment. One journalist noted, "Court officials are privately furious, not only because they risk seeing their historic first case reduced to farce, but because they launched the inquiry at the request of the Ugandan government, which is now accusing the ICC of neo-colonialism."[105] The former prosecutor of the Yugoslav tribunal, Richard Goldstone, warned that the court faced a real risk of being turned into a political instrument:

> I just don't accept that Museveni has any right to use the international
> criminal court like this. If you have a system of international justice

you've got to follow through on it. If in some cases that's going to make peace negotiations difficult that may be the price that has to be paid. The international community must keep a firm line and say are we going to have a better world because of the international court or not.[106]

The international community's line was anything but firm. The push for peace seemed to trump the search for justice. With financial and diplomatic support from the Nordic countries and Canada, formal negotiations between the Ugandan government and the LRA began in July 2006. The talks took place in Juba, the capital of southern Sudan. Sudanese officials facilitated the arrival of a large LRA delegation and helped transfer food, cash, and supplies to it. A video emerged of a southern Sudanese diplomat handing Kony cash. Officials shrugged off criticism from human rights groups. "Peace has to be negotiated," said Sudanese vice president Riek Machar.[107] Representatives from the United States and the European Union, among others, arrived in Juba to monitor the talks.

Once the negotiations began, the prosecutor opted to say little. Uganda's Mirjam Blaak saw that reticence as constructive. "If the court had been hammering on us and saying that what we were doing was illegal, that would have complicated matters and there would have been less confidence in the process."[108] To the prosecutor's dismay, however, many international diplomats involved in the Ugandan peace process appeared willing to work around the arrest warrants. In May 2006, South African president Thabo Mbeki called the warrants "a genuine problem."[109] Other observers, including the United States and key EU countries, were more reticent but were open to mechanisms for suspending or avoiding the warrants to achieve an agreement. The likely mechanism would have been a Security Council resolution referencing Article 16 of the Rome Statute, which permits that body to freeze ICC processes in the interests of international peace and security. In early 2007, a draft agreement circulated among the negotiators in Juba that included a call for an Article 16 resolution. The US and European officials monitoring the talks initialed the document.[110]

The court was experiencing the flip side of the reality that had produced a *rapprochement* with the United States: major powers with complex interests had difficulty making the court a priority. Just as John Bolton had struggled to keep President Bush focused on American antipathy to the court, European and other officials proved willing to risk the court's credibility to advance other diplomatic goals. In the end, major-power foreign ministries did not have to face that choice at the highest levels; the Juba peace talks floundered and then, after one last gasp, collapsed in 2008. The draft agreements calling for an Article 16 deferral were never signed. But for the court, the Juba process was an ominous sign that even supportive states might not back the institution when it mattered most.

Frustrated by the fickle commitment of states, the prosecutor delivered a scathing speech at a Nuremberg conference on international justice in May 2007. He complained that the court faced incessant—and, to his mind, unfair—calls to accommodate itself to political realities. "We also hear officials of States Parties calling for amnesties, the granting of immunities and other ways to avoid prosecutions, supposedly in the name of peace." The prosecutor insisted that "there can be *no* political compromise on legality and accountability" and he laid down a daunting challenge for states: "Dealing with the new legal reality is not easy. It needs political commitment; it needs hard and costly operational decisions: arresting criminals in the context of ongoing conflicts is a difficult endeavor. . . . *If States Parties do not actively support the Court, in this area as in others, then they are actively undermining it.*"[111]

Part of the System

Even as the practical complexities of applying a global criminal justice system were becoming apparent, the ICC continued to integrate itself into the global architecture. It attracted dozens of new member states and established linkages with key intergovernmental organizations. The process of international acceptance was incomplete however. The court made only limited progress in attracting major powers that had opted to stay outside the system.

Powerful Western states that had joined the court worked with the still potent civil society movement to encourage large-scale ratification of the Rome Statute. Germany and the United Kingdom, in particular, routinely encouraged nonmember states to join the ICC. Along with other supportive states, notably Canada and Australia, they helped organize and fund workshops to help wavering states sort through the complications of becoming a court member.[112] By the end of 2005, 100 states had ratified the Rome Statute, including several regional powers. Kenya ratified in March 2005, and Mexico joined in October 2005. In 2006, another four states joined, although none of them were powerful states (the new members were Chad, Comoros, Montenegro, and St. Kitts and Nevis).

In certain corners of the world, nonmember countries faced intense pressure to join. By 2006, the Czech Republic was the only member of the European Union that was not also a court member. Despite prodding from the prime minister, a coalition of skeptics in the Czech parliament several times held up the required legislation. As the Czech Republic prepared to take its turn as EU president, however, the situation became untenable. The government came under strong pressure from other EU members to ratify. In 2008, the parliament finally acquiesced.[113]

As more and more states joined the ICC, court officials also established links with other elements of the international system. Most important, the court developed a working relationship with the United Nations. Because the ICC was not formally part of the UN system, a detailed working relationship was vital, particularly when investigations took place in countries with large UN peacekeeping missions. In 2004, a cooperation agreement between the two institutions came into force.[114] Two years later, the court signed a broad agreement on cooperation with the European Union as well.[115]

The court and its supporters had less success encouraging larger powers to join. The EU's efforts to encourage universal ICC membership reflected that trend. In formal agreements with many states, the EU included an "ICC clause," which would encourage the state in question to move toward ICC membership. However, the EU did not insist on these clauses in agreements with most major powers.[116] The overall pattern of ICC membership suggested that larger powers were less likely to join the court than smaller ones, and that populous states with large militaries were particularly hesitant (figures 5.2 and 5.3).

The continued unwillingness of the United States, India, Russia, and China to join the court was a key element in this broader trend. The US approach to the court had become more pragmatic, but no influential voices on the American political spectrum advocated membership. Russia, which signed the Rome Statute in 2000, showed no signs of being prepared to ratify. When court president Philippe Kirsch visited Moscow in 2004, he was told that the technical obstacles to ratification were minor, but that the final decision was in the hands of Vladimir Putin.[117] Most observers believed that the Kremlin saw little benefit to joining the court and exposing Russian commanders and politicians to possible prosecution. While the court had refrained from launching an investigation of Russian conduct in Georgia, that conflict was a reminder of the complications that granting the court jurisdiction might entail.

Average Population Size

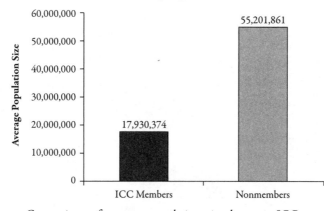

FIGURE 5.2 Comparison of average population size between ICC members and nonmembers

Source: Population data for this analysis drawn from World Bank World Development Indicators for 2012, last updated July 2, 2013. The average population size of nonmembers was 55,201,861, while the average population size of members was 17,987,781.

China also remained firmly on the outside. Chinese diplomats politely ignored the urgings of European states, including the United Kingdom, that they consider joining. Kirsch and several other court officials attended a Beijing conference in 2003 but met with low-level government officials only.[118] At the conference, Chinese legal experts and academics expressed concern about the court's broad scope of jurisdiction, threats to China's sovereignty, and complications reconciling domestic laws with the Rome Statute.[119]

Russian and Chinese misgivings never rose to the level of alarm that US officials had expressed, and neither Moscow nor Beijing engaged in a diplomatic campaign comparable to that launched by the Bush administration. Instead, they opted to watch the court closely. Both countries sent observers to the court's public briefings and to the Assembly of States Parties meetings. Their diplomats in The Hague remained in contact with the prosecutor's office. On the Security Council, they agreed to the referral of Darfur while expressing continuing reservations about the court.

The world's largest democracy, India, also appeared intent on remaining outside the court. Indian officials continued to express serious misgivings about the court's design and its impact on national sovereignty. Media commentary on the court was often hostile as well.[120] Philippe Kirsch visited Delhi in August 2005 and urged the country to join. "India, as one of the

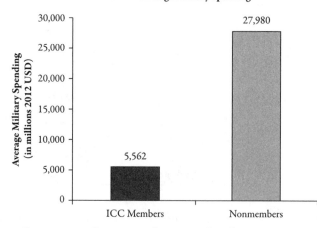

FIGURE 5.3 Comparison of average military spending between ICC members and nonmembers

Source: Military spending data for this analysis drawn from the Stockholm International Peace Research Institute (SIPRI) Military Expenditure Database. SIPRI data is based on open sources, including an annual questionnaire. The average military spending for all ICC member countries with figures provided by the SIPRI is $5,562.47 in 2012 USD, while the average for all nonmember countries is $27,980.00. SIPRI military spending data is missing for 57 UN member states. Those states for which data is absent are mostly smaller states, but include Cuba, Iran, Myanmar, Nepal, and Sudan. The database is available at http://www.sipri.org/research/armaments/milex/milex_database.

world's largest democracies, can help develop international law against mass crimes," he told an audience. Kirsch noted that the court had few members in Asia and suggested that India could help bridge that gap.[121] But senior Indian officials privately conceded that membership was unlikely and that the potential for hostilities with Pakistan and militants in Kashmir made accepting the court's jurisdiction impossible.

Japan offered much more fertile ground. At the Rome negotiations, the Japanese delegation had echoed certain US concerns about the court and had attempted to position itself as an interlocutor between the United States and court backers. After Rome, the Japanese government opted to observe the court in action before joining. But court officials, state backers of the court, and the advocacy community believed Japan would eventually join, and they made courting the country a priority. Officials in Tokyo received frequent visits from ICC advocates and other diplomats, mostly from Europe. Because of similarities between the German and Japanese legal systems, German advice proved particularly helpful in considering the changes that would be required to Japanese domestic legislation.[122]

Within the Japanese government, foreign ministry officials were usually the most vocal advocates of membership. The pressure from European countries and activist groups strengthened their hand. One Japanese official said, "I used the many visits from different delegations to try to leverage domestic and political support on the issue." In discussions with other government actors, ministry officials sought to characterize ICC membership as essential to maintaining Japan's broader international profile:

> One of the strongest points that we could make was that the ICC was very consistent with Japan's push for a rules-based international order and for the development of international humanitarian law. We tried to argue that it was inconceivable that Japan would not take part in this and we were able to make that case.[123]

The pull of the ICC was a substantial factor, but alliance politics also loomed large. Japan was hesitant to embrace the ICC while the United States, its closest military ally, remained hostile to it. As the US position mellowed in 2004–2005, Japan became more flexible. Research by Kersten Lukner suggests that Japanese diplomats watched closely the US reaction to Mexico's accession to gauge the likely impact on the bilateral relationship. "Tokyo appears to have deliberately delayed decision-making regarding its ICC membership in order to circumvent confrontation with the US, until Washington finally scaled back hostilities towards the Court."[124]

By mid-2006, Japanese officials felt reassured on that front and signaled their intention to join. Kirsch hailed the move. "It is clear that once Japan is within the system, it will lead other states in Asia to participate in the system." By joining, he maintained, the country "will be in a much better position to influence the shaping and the future of the court."[125] Japan formally acceded to the Rome Statute in October 2007. Financially, Japan's accession was a fillip for the court; the court apportioned the new member annual dues of more than $20 million in 2008, and Japan displaced Germany as the largest funder.[126] Court officials at several levels recall that Japanese diplomats wasted no time seeking to convert their new status into job placements for Japanese nationals. A veteran Japanese diplomat—one without any legal training—was elected as a judge as soon as a vacancy appeared.[127]

Japan's accession was a major boost for the court. For the prosecutor's office, however, the question of whether states formally joined the court often mattered much less than what they were willing to do when the court asked for help. The court's first years in operation demonstrated clearly that membership did not imply commitment, and that important support could sometimes come from nonmembers.

Court members often failed to complete the legislative work that membership entailed. By the end of 2006, only a few dozen court members had passed domestic legislation needed to ensure cooperation with the court. Less than half of the court's members had ratified the agreement giving diplomatic privileges and immunities to ICC officials. The record was even worse when it came to additional agreements the court sought covering information sharing with the court, relocation of witnesses, and enforcement of sentences. Philippe Kirsch reported in December 2006 that just one state had signed such an agreement.[128] Interest in the annual meetings of court member states appeared to decline as well. After full attendance in 2003, ten states missed the 2004 meeting, and seventeen skipped the 2005 session.[129]

The failure of many states to complete detailed cooperation agreements with the court did not mean that they would necessarily ignore specific requests. In fact, the record of states in responding to these requests was mixed and highly dependent on the context. Members that had failed to pass necessary supporting legislation sometimes proved receptive when asked to provide ICC investigators with access to a particular witness or to use their territory for an interview. Even states that had not joined the court sometimes responded when the prosecutor's office asked for assistance. As the Sudan investigation proceeded, for example, several nonmember Arab states allowed investigators to interview Sudanese officials on their soil. For the court's investigators, this kind of concrete cooperation was often more important than formal membership.[130]

What was emerging, in short, was an *ad hoc* rather than routinized system of state cooperation with and support for the court. The Rome Statute imposed few clear obligations on court members, and most states were taking full advantage of that flexibility. Nonmembers—who had no formal obligations—felt free to ignore the court, but they also realized that cooperation might sometimes serve their interests. This pattern of interaction with states was decidedly convenient for major powers. Large states with resources the court would often need benefited most from a flexible pattern of state support.

"A Moment in History"

As the court's confrontation with Sudan developed, the question of how key states would balance the ICC's interests with their own became acute. Khartoum signaled its defiance of the outstanding arrest warrants by elevating Ahmed Haroun to a ministerial post (perversely, for humanitarian affairs). A few weeks later, Haroun was asked to chair a high-level commission of inquiry that would examine human rights abuses. ICC officials blasted the moves. "He is like the fox being in charge of the chickens," said Moreno-Ocampo.[131] The other indictee, alleged *janjaweed* leader Ali Kushayb, had been placed in government custody on charges unrelated to abuses in Darfur. But the government rejected calls to send him to The Hague and, in September 2007, released him. Khartoum also punished several Sudanese journalists who had visited the ICC, accusing them of "commit[ing] an act that was contrary to the foundations of national identity."[132]

As Sudan's defiance intensified, the prosecutor suggested that implementation of the arrest warrants was essential to ending the conflict. "[Haroun] has to be removed, arrested, and sent to the Hague," he told a Canadian audience. "The system has to be dismantled. Otherwise, we are watching a new Rwanda."[133] At the United Nations, he warned that "there can be no political solution, no security solution, and no humanitarian solution as long as the alleged war criminals remain free in the Sudan."[134] The prosecutor even chastised the UN Secretary General for omitting justice issues in his reports on Darfur. Some key court backers echoed his sense of urgency. Jonathan Fanton of the influential MacArthur Foundation, which provided early financial backing for the court and the advocacy campaign surrounding it, warned that "unless the arrest warrants are enforced, the court will not succeed, and a moment in history to create a more just world will be lost."[135]

Fanton's words of warning represented one possible interpretation of the court's first few years in operation. It was apparent by the end of the court's fifth year that the de facto reconciliation with the superpower, the Security Council's partial embrace, and the court's growing international acceptance did not yet mean that power and justice had linked arms. The prospect that the court would be essentially toothless remained very real. Fanton and other court supporters suggested that absent a dramatic shift in state behavior, that condition could become permanent, and the court might slide toward irrelevance.

A more sanguine perspective was possible. The ICC had become part of the international community's architecture very quickly and had proved resistant to animosity from several leading powers. On Sudan, the British and French had helped engineer a Security Council referral. In so doing, they had helped shift the US position on the court. Japan, once skeptical, had become a member. The court had secured technical cooperation on certain initiatives from nonmembers. Five years into its operational life, the court's survival was no longer in doubt. In June 2008, the court commissioned a contest for the design of a new headquarters building large enough to accommodate its still growing staff.

Yet as they planned for the future, court officials still wondered whether time and global political dynamics were working in their favor. Was the surprising willingness of even skeptical powers to work with the court evidence that the institution was pulling major powers into its orbit? Or was some other dynamic at work?

Power Plays (2008–2013)

FIVE YEARS AFTER its opening, the political environment in which the ICC was operating had improved considerably. In important ways, skeptical major powers had accommodated themselves to the court's existence. This more permissive environment alleviated some of the pressure on the court, but it did not guarantee its effectiveness. The major powers, even those who were court members, demonstrated only limited interest in backing the court's warrants diplomatically and militarily. Through the Security Council and less formal mechanisms, moreover, these states exercised significant influence on the court's docket. For the most part, the court avoided challenging this influence, and the perception grew that powerful states had devised means of controlling the institution.

Setbacks and Success in Congo

Not all the ICC's problems were the product of lackluster state support; the court itself had stumbled on several occasions. Missteps were particularly evident in its Congo investigation. The court's first indictee—Ituri warlord Thomas Lubanga—was seen by many observers as a target of opportunity who had been charged only with the relatively minor crime of recruiting child soldiers.[1] Worse, the trial of the militia commander had not begun eighteen months after his arrival in The Hague. The most significant roadblock was a dispute over evidence. ICC staff had received copious material from UN officials in Congo on the understanding that the evidence would not be used at trial or shared with other parts of the court. Because of these confidentiality arrangements, the prosecutor refused to turn over certain evidence to the judges and defense lawyers even after repeated requests.

Finally, the judges supervising the case announced the dismissal of the charges and ordered Lubanga's release. "The trial process has been ruptured to such a degree that it is now impossible to piece together...a fair trial," one judge wrote.[2] The prosecutor eventually won a reprieve from the court's appeals chamber, but only after the UN had agreed to waive confidentiality of many documents.[3] After a delay of several months, the court proceedings restarted, but the incident was a traumatic beginning to the court's inaugural trial.

The dispute in the Lubanga case had important implications for the relationship between the court and those states with large intelligence services. The judges' interpretation of the court's statute and rules restricted the prosecutor's ability to gather evidence on a confidential basis. That, in turn, decreased the likelihood that states would offer the prosecutor intelligence, which they almost always provided on the condition of confidentiality. In the months after the Lubanga ruling, the prosecutor himself privately warned officials from several major states not to provide anything they were not willing to have shared with the judges.[4] Prosecution officials had already signaled their wariness about becoming overly dependent on intelligence from major states. The judges' decisions in the Lubanga litigation made intelligence cooperation with major powers significantly more complex.

In spite of these complications, the Congo investigation continued and even acquired some momentum. The first months of 2008 proved to be active ones, with an arrest in February and the release of a separate warrant soon after. In February, the court took custody of Mathieu Ngudjolo Chui, another key player in the bloody Ituri conflict. Ngudjolo had trained as a nurse and worked for a period as a medical assistant with the Red Cross. By mid-2002, however, he had taken command of a militia movement in Ituri.[5] In February 2003, his forces assaulted the village of Bogoro, which had been under the control of Thomas Lubanga's rival UPC militia. Most of its inhabitants belonged to the ethnic group from which the UPC drew its strength. Once the town fell, Ngudjolo's soldiers—some of them children—allegedly killed indiscriminately. "They were injuries caused by spears, machetes, bullets," one witness reported. "At one point I came across a two-year-old child who was dead. He had been hacked with machetes."[6] As many as 200 people died in the attack, almost all unarmed civilians.

Like other militia commanders in the region, Ngudjolo had a murky and shifting relationship with the country's weak central government. In 2003, he was briefly in government custody but was then released and cleared of charges. In 2006, he struck a deal with the government and was even made a colonel in the national armed forces. He told a journalist who interviewed him at the time that he did not fear international prosecution. "I cannot fear international justice because for what can I be arrested? I have created a political movement."[7] He headed to Congo's capital for training and full integration into the national armed forces. His deal with the government did not protect him for long. The ICC issued a sealed arrest warrant for Ngudjolo in 2007, and in February 2008 Congolese authorities arrested him and handed him over to the court.[8] Like Lubanga, Ngudjolo was accused of using child soldiers, but he also faced charges based on other war crimes and crimes against humanity.[9]

In April 2008, the court made public another arrest warrant—issued under seal in 2006—for an even more consequential figure. Bosco Ntaganda, a militia commander operating out of eastern Congo, had emerged as a powerful and often brutal force in the region. With apparent backing from Rwanda, his forces had become a significant obstacle to effective government control in the region.[10] Human rights organizations had documented ethnic killings, torture, and rape committed by his forces and these groups loudly condemned his attacks on UN troops in early 2004.[11] Ntaganda's ICC charges included recruitment of child soldiers, murder, rape, and sexual slavery.[12]

An even more dramatic development followed Lubanga's arrest and the release of Ntaganda's arrest warrant. On May 24, 2008, Belgian police arrived at a home near Brussels where senior Congolese politician Jean-Pierre Bemba was staying. For several years, Bemba had led a well-armed militia group, the Movement for the Liberation of Congo (MLC), that had fought in Congo and, for a period, in neighboring Central African Republic. As Congo's transitional government formed in 2003, Bemba became one of four vice-presidents, but he remained a formidable rival to President Joseph Kabila. He contested the July 2006 national elections and won more than 40 percent of the vote.[13] In 2007, after clashes between his security detail and government forces, he left Congo for Europe, claiming that the regime was persecuting him. As Bemba enjoyed European medical care and conversed with senior European politicians, the ICC concluded an investigation of crimes his forces committed in the Central African Republic in 2002 and 2003.[14] The Belgian authorities moved speedily as soon as the court transmitted the arrest warrant.[15]

The Ntaganda investigation and the Bemba arrest suggested the court's increased willingness and ability to pursue figures with high political and military profiles in the Congo. The smooth cooperation with the Belgian authorities, moreover, provided an example of how state cooperation could make the court effective. But a broader pattern of caution by the prosecutor remained. The arrest warrant for Bemba was issued only after he had lost national elections to Kabila. Moreover, the ICC had still not pursued any senior figures close to the president, although allegations of official involvement in abuses circulated widely.[16] Nor had the court pursued allegations that

the Rwandan government, which enjoyed strong American and British support, was funding rebel groups in Congo. The court's selection of cases convinced some observers that the court had trimmed its investigations to suit
regional and international political realities.[17]

Prosecution officials were keenly aware of the perception that they were
doing the bidding of Kabila and, more broadly, the Western countries backing his government. They maintained that the office was simply following
the evidence and its own procedures. The Bemba investigation moved slowly
not because of the elections, they insisted, but because the Central African
Republic had not decided whether it wanted to pursue a case against Bemba
on its own (a decision that likely would have made the case inadmissible on
complementarity grounds). As for prosecutions of regime officials or those of
outside states, the obstacle was evidence, not politics. For many court officials,
outside observers were frustratingly quick to assume political motives.[18]

Up the Ladder in Sudan

Outside of central Africa—and certain international law faculties—the developments in the ICC's Congo investigation received relatively little attention.
Violence in Congo had become chronic rather than spectacular, and international attention had waned. The media and the diplomatic world were much
more interested in the court's next moves in Sudan. The prosecutor continued
to call for the arrests of Ahmed Haroun and Ali Kushayb, but he also suggested that other Sudanese officials might be in the court's crosshairs. He told
the Security Council he would investigate "who bears the greatest responsibility for ongoing attacks against civilians, who is maintaining [Haroun] in a
position to commit crimes and who gives him instructions."[19] That language
pointed toward the top of the Sudanese regime and very likely to President
Omar al-Bashir.

As he signaled his intentions, Moreno-Ocampo consulted widely with
concerned diplomats and particularly with the permanent Security Council
powers. His regular briefings to the Council in New York provided easy
opportunities to exchange views, and these conversations made clear that
diplomats did not relish the idea of turning President Bashir into an international fugitive. Some said so directly. In early 2008, the prosecutor met
US special envoy to Sudan Richard Williamson at a dinner sponsored by
the MacArthur Foundation. US officials had met with the prosecutor several times since 2005, but the relationship was still tenuous. The event host,
MacArthur president Jonathan Fanton, arranged for the diplomat and the

prosecutor to meet discreetly before the dinner.[20] In the course of the conversation, the prosecutor suggested to Williamson, without saying so explicitly, that he would pursue Bashir. The American diplomat was blunt in response:

> I told him it would be a bad idea—that an arrest warrant wouldn't be productive. I told him not to go after the top. It limits the options of how we can move forward. He said, "my job's easier than yours. I'm like a train moving down the track and I just follow the evidence." That's how he characterized it. I said "I'm afraid you might hurt the institution you are trying to build." We agreed to disagree.[21]

Not all exchanges were as straightforward. Conversations between the prosecutor and government officials—particularly those of ICC members—were sometimes stilted. The prosecutor often spoke to diplomats in political terms he thought they would appreciate and understand and tried to emphasize the ways in which the court's investigations could mesh with their own policy goals. Instead of suggesting politicization, one former prosecution official argued that Moreno-Ocampo's approach actually reflected an unwillingness to engage with states on legal determinations; because he considered these topics off limits, the prosecutor moved the conversation with diplomats to their terrain. The official argued that Moreno-Ocampo's approach differed markedly in this respect from that of several ad hoc tribunal prosecutors:

> [Other international] prosecutors would come to capitals and see legal advisors and ask "what do you think?" and talk about details of the law. He doesn't think this is necessary, what's necessary is for states to act upon judicial decisions. When he speaks outside the court, he doesn't think he has to be speaking like a lawyer.[22]

This style of discourse produced occasional confusion. Several major-power diplomats recalled being surprised by the prosecutor's willingness to speak in political terms. For his part, the prosecutor believed he was simply generating support for the court by speaking to diplomats in their own terms:

> I asked diplomats to support justice....Because many diplomats didn't expect prosecutors to request that kind of assistance, some might have perceived me as making political requests or comments. No one can say that I asked for instructions or offered political negotiations, but I probably did open myself to charges of talking about non-judicial

matters. I did it because I was trying to implement my mandate and get the cooperation that I needed.[23]

Even if they believed he might be open to persuasion, national diplomats were usually careful to avoid the appearance of overtly guiding the prosecutor (Williamson's bluntness was unusual). Instead, the prosecutor's state interlocutors tended to raise questions and concerns that hinted at a preference rather than stating one directly. In early 2008, the prosecutor and his advisers fielded many questions and expressions of unease about the likely impact of a Bashir indictment. In one form or another, every P5 member communicated concern about the move.[24]

Moreno-Ocampo showed no sign of being daunted by the negative reaction. In June 2008, he dropped an even clearer hint that Bashir was his next target, telling the Security Council that the violence in Darfur "has required the sustained mobilization of the entire Sudanese state apparatus." He compared the Sudanese regime to Nazi Germany.[25] His scathing report, and subsequent indications that he was prepared to move against Bashir, set off alarm bells at the United Nations, in foreign ministries, and with humanitarian organizations working in Sudan. The UN Secretary-General convened a meeting with Security Council members to discuss the safety of UN personnel in the country. UN officials worried that an attack that had killed several peacekeepers in early July might foreshadow a broader government campaign against the international presence.[26] US diplomats in The Hague described the prosecutor's coming move against Bashir as "a high stakes gamble—not only for the ICC but for global politics."[27]

On July 14, 2008, Moreno-Ocampo played his hand. He announced that he was seeking an arrest warrant against the Sudanese president for genocide, crimes against humanity, and war crimes. He accused Bashir of masterminding a policy aimed at the destruction of several ethnic groups in Darfur and stressed the massive scale of the government campaign: "2.7 million people have been forcibly expelled from their homes," the prosecutor reported. He described how survivors of initial attacks were driven into the desert, where they were "killed or left to die."[28]

Anticipating the ICC move, the United Nations had withdrawn nonessential staff from Sudan, and most embassies in Khartoum beefed up their security.[29] The reaction in Sudan was vitriolic, but mostly peaceful. Government officials labeled the prosecutor a "terrorist" and the ICC the "European Court of Injustice."[30] A choreographed rally in Khartoum denounced the court, the United Nations, and the United States.[31] In the refugee camps sheltering many of the conflict's victims, there was satisfaction, and sometimes jubilation. "This decision will mark the end of Darfur crisis," one hopeful Darfuri refugee told a journalist. "It stops the killing and horrible crimes against the people."[32]

Behind the scenes, the prosecutor's request set in motion several weeks of active diplomacy. States had not dissuaded him from seeking an arrest warrant against Bashir, but they had a window of time in which to try to manage the outcome of his announcement. In previous cases, the court's judges had taken several months to review requested arrest warrants, and that expected limbo period allowed major players to consider how to integrate the ICC into their diplomacy.

Publicly and in Security Council gatherings, Chinese and Russian diplomats warned that the prosecutor's move could threaten the fragile progress in Darfur.[33] Backed by much of the African Union and the Arab League, they argued that the prosecutor was interfering recklessly with the diplomatic process. There was significant regional and international support for a Security Council move to quash the Bashir indictment process through the Rome Statute's Article 16 mechanism.[34] The leading Western powers shared this disquiet about pursuing Bashir, but they did not criticize the prosecutor's move. In public, they insisted that the judicial process should proceed independently.

More quietly, however, French and British diplomats explored a package deal with Sudan. If Khartoum would surrender Haroun and Kushayb to the court and allow free movement for UN peacekeepers, they suggested, then perhaps Paris and London could support an Article 16 resolution deferring the Bashir investigation. The notion was simple: use the prosecutor's announcement as leverage to achieve policy concessions the international community wanted. French diplomats reportedly circulated a working paper to Sudanese officials outlining the possible deal.[35] Britain's point person on Africa at the time, Mark Malloch Brown, acknowledged that he had doubts about the strength of the case against Bashir but denied that he was in favor of aborting the judicial proceeding or that London and Paris ever decided to support a deferral resolution. "Any discussions were highly tentative—I wasn't in a position to offer it and the Sudanese weren't sure they wanted to accept it." Yet Malloch Brown insisted that the deferral possibility should have been part of the diplomatic mix:

> The French and I both felt that Article 16 was there for a purpose. It was a one year delaying tactic—it doesn't stop justice, it just delays it.

I felt very strongly in that sense that it needed to be part of our toolkit in terms of trying to get better behavior from the Sudanese. Do I plead guilty to believing that Article 16 is a tool to be used politically and that the authors of the ICC had always understood it to be that? Yes.[36]

The European gambit did not go over well in Washington. In late July 2008, British and French diplomats at the United Nations inserted a neutral reference to the African Union's deferral request in a draft Security Council resolution on Darfur. US officials pushed the British, in vain, to remove the language. Rebuffed, the United States abstained from the vote and signaled its displeasure publicly. The reference to a deferral, the US ambassador insisted, "would send the wrong signal to Sudanese President Al-Bashir and undermine efforts to bring him and others to justice."[37] The British ambassador acknowledged that position but maintained that London "will not stand in the way of a Security Council discussion of whether there is a case for invoking Article 16."[38]

The episode was an odd reversal from the Council fights in 2002–2004, when the United States, in the face of European opposition, had insisted on a broad application of Article 16 to immunize the nationals of non-ICC members. In the days after the July 2008 disagreement, the three Western powers sought to reestablish a united front. In private meetings, French officials insisted to their American counterparts that no "deal" had yet been offered and elaborated on their thinking:

Let's say we suspend [the ICC investigation] for 12 months, with a review every three or four months. We could use that review to ensure that they keep doing what they said they would. This would help us achieve our ends and also preserve our prerogatives with the ICC....If they don't cooperate, we end the suspension and the ICC goes into action....We are not saying now that a suspension is in order, simply that events could develop in a way that suspending ICC action could be in everyone's best interest.[39]

A few weeks later, likely because of leaks by US officials, the British press got wind of the European discussions with Sudan regarding an Article 16 deferral. The coverage was not kind. In a September 2008 *Observer* article, human rights activists described the policy as "a shocking moral abdication on Britain's part."[40] Former ICTY prosecutor and UN human rights official Louise Arbour insisted that a Council deferral would marginalize the court: "To use a deferral for mere political convenience...would undermine the fledgling court. There is little hope for the promotion of the rule of law internationally if the most powerful international body makes it subservient to the rule of political expediency."[41] Policymakers had trouble deflecting that kind of legalist criticism. British official Mark Malloch Brown struggled to reframe the policy as a defense of the court:

> This is not about handing a defeat to the court in its early life. But Khartoum has interpreted the indictment against Bashir as a measure that pits Sudan against the Western world. A great deal is at stake; not just Darfur but the peace process in southern Sudan. We have to keep hold of the strategic intentions of the ICC, which we share—to end impunity and increase security in Darfur.[42]

Malloch Brown recalled being irritated by the media leaks, and the publicity helped undercut whatever support existed in his government for negotiations on deferring the Bashir indictment. "My own colleagues viewed being absolutely 100 percent on the right side of these human rights issues meant that I had no support in government even if I'd wanted to do an Article 16."[43]

That reluctance to be seen as negotiating away an international indictment persisted in Washington as well. As the annual UN General Assembly meetings approached, senior US policymakers discussed how to respond to an Article 16 push. Echoing the approach of human rights activists in 2005, special envoy Richard Williamson framed the issue for the president as whether the United States wanted to protect a man it had already condemned repeatedly. He recalled telling the president: "[T]here are some people here who are going to say this is bad because we'll be supporting the ICC. You were the first world leader to stand up and call it genocide. The question is do you want to help get a *genocidaire* off the hook." At that point, according to Williamson, "[The debate] was over."[44] In fact, there is no evidence that anyone in the administration was arguing for a deferral.[45]

Moreno-Ocampo was relieved that the deferral bid had foundered. When he encountered US war crimes ambassador Clint Williamson in the hallways of the United Nations, he enveloped the American in a bear hug.[46] The failure of the most serious attempt to defer a specific court investigation on political grounds underlined how diplomats, activists, and the media could deploy the institution's formidable normative power. Western politicians in particular had great difficulty defending the choice to sideline the court through a

Security Council deferral. There might have been a strong strategic and even moral case for doing so, but it had trouble competing with the powerful narrative of accountability.

The prosecutor had other reasons to be pleased with Washington's position. In the last months of 2008, the United States supported an offensive by Uganda and Congo against the Lord's Resistance Army. After President Bush personally approved, the new US Africa Command provided Ugandan officers with satellite phones, intelligence, and fuel to help mount the offensive, code-named Operation Lightning Thunder.[47] Launched at daybreak on December 14, the helicopter strike against Kony's suspected headquarters just missed its target. The LRA leader apparently disappeared into the jungle hours before the helicopters struck. In the weeks that followed, the LRA lashed out against villagers near the border between Congo and Uganda, killing at least 600 civilians.[48]

The Ugandan operation put pressure on the LRA, but it also highlighted the difficulty of conducting effective operations with only limited support from major military powers. Even with US funds, logistical support, and intelligence, Ugandan forces struggled. According to a detailed account of the raid, the Ugandans launched the airstrike before the helicopter-borne commando team was in the area, leaving the LRA a critical opportunity to escape. The near-miss did not produce a Western willingness to engage more directly. "[T]here seems to be very little appetite in Western capitals for fully owning such an operation at this time," one analysis concluded.[49]

Triple Crisis

By the latter half of 2008, three separate conflicts began that, taken together, offered insight into the prosecutor's criteria for launching investigations (see table 6.1). In December 2007, a disputed presidential election in Kenya sparked a rapid descent into internal violence. Outraged at apparent election fraud, supporters of the opposition political movement rioted in several cities. Within hours, the political controversy had ignited ethnic violence that resulted in the deaths of several hundred people and raised the specter of a civil war. Police and security forces were often passive or complicit as mobs attacked members of other ethnic groups. For several weeks, regional and international luminaries attempted to broker a power-sharing arrangement. Former UN Secretary General Kofi Annan emerged as the lead negotiator, and he succeeded in patching together a compromise in early 2008.[50] An international commission of inquiry investigated the violence and handed

Table 6.1 Comparison of Russia–Georgia, Gaza, and Kenya

Episode	Dates	Estimated Death Toll	ICC Jurisdiction
Kenya election violence	Dec. 30, 2007–Feb. 28, 2008	1,133–1,220[a]	Jurisdiction over Kenyan territory and nationals
Russia-Georgia war	Aug. 7–15, 2008	850[b]	Jurisdiction over Georgian territory and nationals
Gaza war	Dec. 27, 2008–Jan. 18, 2009	1,387–1,417[c]	Palestinian Authority submitted declaration attempting to grant ICC jurisdiction

[a] ICC Pre-Trial Chamber II, "Decision Pursuant to Article 15 of the Rome Statute on the Authorization of an Investigation into the Situation in the Republic of Kenya," ICC-01/09, p. 54, para. 131 (March 31, 2010), http://www.icc-cpi.int/iccdocs/doc/doc854287.pdf.

[b] Report of the Independent International Fact-Finding Mission on the Conflict in Georgia, vol. 1, p. 5, September 2009, http://www.ceiig.ch/pdf/IIFFMCG_Volume_I.pdf.

[c] The UN Fact Finding Mission on the Gaza Conflict reports that it drew figures from the field research of several nongovernmental groups. The UN report notes that authorities in Gaza reported 1,444 deaths and the Israeli authorities reported 1,166 deaths. Report of the United Nations Fact Finding Mission on the Gaza Conflict ("Goldstone Report") A/HRC/12/48, presented to the 12th Session of the Human Rights Council, para. 30, p. 17, September 25, 2009, http://www2.ohchr.org/english/bodies/hrcouncil/docs/12session/A-HRC-12-48.pdf.

Annan a list of alleged perpetrators as debate continued over how the individuals would be prosecuted, and by whom.

Then, in August 2008, long simmering tension between Russia and Georgia escalated into direct conflict. A series of tit-for-tat incidents in the disputed territory of South Ossetia produced large-scale Georgian military action. Local militia groups that opposed Georgian control, supported by a swelling Russian force, responded and eventually pushed back the Georgian military. By August 12, Russian forces and allied militias had entered Georgia proper, where they occupied several cities near the disputed border and then turned menacingly toward the capital of Tbilisi. Alarmed international mediators helped broker an end to the conflict, and most fighting concluded by August 15.[51]

Both Russian and Georgian officials claimed the other side had perpetrated atrocities. Objective analyses found that close to a thousand people were killed in the fighting, many of them civilians. After an exhaustive study of the conflict, Human Rights Watch concluded that the fighting "took a terrible toll on civilians, killing hundreds, displacing tens of thousands, and causing extensive damage to civilian property." Its investigators identified multiple examples of indiscriminate shelling by both sides and Georgian abuses of Ossetian prisoners. Some of the worst abuses, including murders and rapes, were committed by Ossetian militias operating in conjunction with Russian forces.[52]

Several months later, new fighting erupted in a dispute with a much longer pedigree. On December 27, 2008, Israeli warplanes struck a series of targets in the Gaza strip, including buildings and offices used by Hamas. The stated purposed of the operation was to "eliminate the weapons and the infrastructure that Hamas had used to launch attacks against Israeli civilians on thousands of occasions, and to prevent those attacks from recurring."[53] As the action continued, international criticism grew. The UN's top human rights official, former ICC judge Navi Pillay, condemned what she described as "Israel's disproportionate use of force."[54] An Israeli artillery strike that killed multiple Palestinian civilians, she said a week later, "appears to have all the elements of war crimes."[55] Leaders from France, Brazil, Indonesia, Russia, and China echoed that criticism. After three weeks, Israel ended the operation. The Israeli prime minister acknowledged that the operation had resulted in civilian casualties, although he placed the ultimate blame on Hamas.[56]

In all three situations, it appeared possible that the court could have space to investigate. Georgia had joined the court in 2003, giving it jurisdiction over crimes committed by Georgians as well as those committed on Georgian territory by noncitizens. The only violence that might be beyond the court's reach would be acts committed by non-Georgians on territory not clearly belonging to Georgia. Kenya had joined the court in 2005, and the jurisdictional picture there was even simpler because Kenyan nationals had committed all the alleged abuses on Kenyan territory. The jurisdictional question was most complex in Gaza. Israel had never joined the court. Along with the United States, Israel signed the Rome Statute in late 2000 but indicated that it would not ratify. When the Bush administration "unsigned" the statute a few years later, Israel followed suit.[57] Israel's decision not to join meant the court could not exercise jurisdiction solely on the basis of Israeli nationality. But there were other possible avenues. Some Israelis had dual nationality, including with ICC member states such as Australia and the United Kingdom. The question of Palestinian statehood and international recognition of Palestinian territory created the potential for ICC jurisdiction over Israeli actions. Almost 100 states recognized, in some form at least, a Palestinian state, and the Palestinian Authority had emerged as a quasi-government of the West Bank and Gaza Strip (although it lost effective control of Gaza to the Hamas movement in 2007).

On January 21, 2009, a day after most Israeli forces withdrew from Gaza, the Palestinian Authority's justice minister, Ali Khashan, flew to The Hague. He met with the prosecutor and then formally filed a declaration purporting to give the court jurisdiction to investigate crimes committed on Palestinian territory.[58] The Palestinians employed Article 12(3) of the Rome Statute, which permitted nonmember states to give the court jurisdiction over crimes on their territory.[59] The gambit put the prosecutor in a delicate position: he had to consider the fraught question of whether Palestine constituted a "state" for the purposes of the Rome Statute. The Palestinian move—and the prosecutor's willingness to even consider its jurisdictional declaration—created alarm in Israel and in Washington. Israeli politicians and government lawyers were accustomed to being outnumbered and ostracized in international organizations, and the legalistic turn in international relations worried them. The concerns increased in 2004, when the International Court of Justice had decided (in a nonbinding decision) that Israel's construction of a security wall violated international law.[60] Israeli officials had long worried that the ICC machinery would also turn in their direction. That now appeared possible.

The Prosecutor and His Critics

The Palestinian declaration opened the prosecutor to intense scrutiny. By the time it arrived, however, Moreno-Ocampo had already become a controversial figure in certain quarters. His decision to pursue Sudan's Bashir produced sharp criticism from a variety of African leaders. The prosecutor's African critics seized on the fact that all active ICC investigations were in African countries. Jean Ping, the chairman of the African Union, was particularly outspoken. "We think there is a problem with ICC targeting only Africans, as if Africa has been a place to experiment with their ideas," Ping said. "The law should apply to everyone and not only the weak."[61] In July 2009, the African Union decided that its members (even ICC member states) had no legal obligation to arrest Bashir.[62] William Pace, leader of the NGO coalition that had been instrumental in the ICC's creation, described the African backlash as "the most serious threat to the ICC" since the end of active American opposition.[63]

That the prosecutor was *persona non grata* with certain African leaders was not a surprise. The attacks on his performance in the Western media and by certain court supporters were more unexpected. Dissatisfaction with the prosecutor erupted publicly in mid-2008 when the *Guardian* newspaper described (with significant exaggeration) a "growing clamour to remove" Moreno-Ocampo because of management and other failings.[64] A few months later, two well-known Africa researchers published a long critique of the prosecutor in the journal *World Affairs*. They charged Moreno-Ocampo with badly mismanaging the prosecutor's office. More careful oversight, they suggested, would have avoided the long delays in the Lubanga trial. In their account, the authors relied on several unnamed individuals who had left the prosecutor's office disenchanted. A recurring theme in their critiques was the prosecutor's alleged love of the limelight:

> The Prosecutor had the opportunity to draw upon the accumulated expertise of existing international tribunals and some of the world's finest lawyers and investigators. This asset was rapidly squandered. Increasingly, Moreno Ocampo's staff found it difficult to agree with their own Prosecutor, whose penchant for publicity and extravagant claims rather than fine detail was the polar opposite of their own work ethic.[65]

That particular criticism extended to the prosecutor's most ambitious case. In late 2008, a former ICC senior trial attorney, Andrew Cayley, wrote an article questioning the prosecutor's decision to seek genocide charges against Sudan's president. While the article focused mainly on whether the violence in Darfur met the legal definition of genocide, its author left little doubt that he saw the genocide charge as another example of the prosecutor seeking publicity at the expense of building a strong case. "The ICC and its prosecutor would do well to remember that facts ultimately drive any criminal case," Cayley warned.[66]

To the complaints about the prosecutor's professionalism and management style was added a hint of scandal. In early 2005, members of the prosecutor's staff had learned of allegations that the prosecutor had pressured a South African journalist into having sexual relations. One prosecution office staff member recorded a phone call with the alleged victim and then alerted the court's judges. Eventually, several judges reviewed the allegations and determined that they were "manifestly unfounded."[67] No criminal charges were ever filed. But the incident continued to roil the court. The prosecutor fired the staff member who had publicized the accusation. That employee then sued the ICC for wrongful dismissal, and in July 2008 an international administrative tribunal awarded him monetary damages. In its decision, that tribunal criticized the prosecutor for having participated directly in the dismissal of the official.[68]

Given the variety of complaints against the prosecutor, it is striking that major powers most skeptical of the court made no apparent effort to attack his credibility or to use his professional and personal travails to cast doubt on the court. Given the strongly expressed US concerns about the prosecutor's discretion, the Bush administration's decision not to engage in or encourage criticism was notable. US officials were aware of the complaints but said nothing about them in public. That choice reflected a calculation that the prosecutor had in fact carried out his mandate with remarkable caution. "Luis was doing a credible job," said former State Department legal advisor John Bellinger. "I don't recall any 'hardliners' at the Justice or Defense departments using these allegations to urge us at State to complain about Luis, perhaps because he wasn't doing anything to attract their ire."[69] As one member of Moreno-Ocampo's staff wrote in his defense, "[t]he Prosecutor's strict observance of boundaries is what accounts, in no small part, for the Bush administration's abandonment, over time, of its categorical opposition to support for the court's work."[70]

The Obama Era

Even as his critics became increasingly vocal, the prosecutor could take some encouragement from the changed American political landscape. The election of Barack Obama as president promised a new chapter in relations between the United States and the court. In contrast to the 2004 race, the 2008 campaign featured little discussion of the ICC itself. But there was every reason to expect that an Obama administration would be much friendlier to the court. The Bush administration's alienation of other states on the ICC and the Kyoto Protocol, in particular, had been a staple of Democratic foreign policy criticism.[71]

As the new administration took shape, individuals supportive of the court moved into key positions. Yale University law professor Harold Koh, a champion of international human rights, became the State Department's legal adviser; legal scholar Anne-Marie Slaughter, also a court supporter, was appointed director of policy planning at the State Department; Stephen Rapp, a former chief prosecutor at the UN-backed Sierra Leone tribunal, was selected as the administration's point person on war crimes issues; and anti-genocide activist Samantha Power, who had strongly advocated an ICC role in Sudan, took a position on the National Security Council responsible for coordinating multilateral affairs, including international justice issues. Koh, Rapp, and Power had all known the prosecutor for several years. As law school dean, Koh had invited Moreno-Ocampo to several conferences, and the prosecutor had attended Power's wedding in 2008. One official who worked in both the Bush and Obama administrations described the new team as an "ICC glee club."[72]

Upon taking office, the Obama administration convened a series of meetings to review the US relationship with the court and to examine ways in which cooperation could be improved. For some US officials, that process shed light on how much the US position toward the court had already evolved. Clint Williamson, the US war crimes ambassador in the second Bush administration, recalled that several government officials were surprised to learn that he had met with the prosecutor on several occasions since 2007. The meetings had often taken place over dinner, occasionally at the prosecutor's apartment in The Hague, but never at the ICC or at the State Department. The decision to pursue these informal contacts did not pass through the often cumbersome interagency process. "We were able to establish a good, below-the-radar-screen working relationship," Williamson recalls. "Had there been more interagency consultation in advance, these kinds of contacts would have been much harder."[73]

The change in administration brought those interactions into the daylight and engaged the US government as a whole with the court in a new way. An interagency working group on the ICC began to meet in mid-2009. For the first time, the prosecutor and other court officials were invited to meetings at the White House and State Department, albeit with little publicity. At the United Nations, Susan Rice met with Christian Wenaweser, president of the Assembly of States Parties, to discuss US policy toward the court. ICC president Sang-Hyun Song, who had replaced Philippe Kirsch, also met with senior US officials and praised what he described as "a change of attitude" in Washington.[74]

In public, the new administration was cautious but managed to send several positive signals. During a trip to Africa early in her tenure, Secretary of State Hillary Clinton expressed "regret" that the United States had not joined the court. "I think we could have worked out some of the challenges that are raised concerning our membership," she told an audience in Kenya.[75] Shortly thereafter, her point person on war crimes issues, Stephen Rapp, announced that the United States would participate as an observer in the next meeting of court members, a step the Bush administration had never taken.[76]

Even with key officials convinced of the court's value and compatibility with US interests, the administration faced significant obstacles to placing American resources and political influence at its disposal. Existing legislation prohibited the United States from offering direct material support to the court in most situations. Many career Defense and State Department officials remained skeptical about the court. According to one administration official, the large US delegation that attended the meeting of ICC members in late 2009—interpreted by some observers as a dramatic show of support—actually signaled the diversity of views in the US government.[77]

The court still had limited support on Capitol Hill, and the possibility of asking the Senate to ratify the Rome Statute was quickly dismissed. Instead, the administration considered more routine ways of backing the court, including facilitating witness interviews and providing in-kind assistance to certain investigations. Officials also considered whether the United States could provide more intelligence, but soon realized that the Lubanga litigation—which had greatly restricted the prosecutor's ability to ensure that information remained confidential—imposed significant limitations.[78]

What the prosecutor wanted most from the new administration was assistance in tightening the noose on Sudan's Bashir. On March 4, 2009, the court's judges issued the arrest warrant that the prosecutor had sought. While they rebuffed the prosecutor on the genocide charge, the judges granted a warrant for crimes against humanity and war crimes. That move sparked a dramatic Sudanese reaction: the government expelled more than a dozen aid agencies working in Darfur, aggravating the humanitarian situation in the region.[79] UN officials and national diplomats scrambled to respond. President Obama's new special envoy to Sudan, former Air Force general Scott Gration, spent much of his first several weeks on the job negotiating the return of key aid groups.[80]

For Western diplomats working on the broader peace process in Sudan, the arrest warrants produced a different kind of complication: whether and how to interact with a government led by an ICC indictee. For weeks, Obama administration officials argued over whether US diplomats could meet with Bashir and what they should do if they encountered him at diplomatic functions. The administration ultimately compromised; meetings with the Sudanese president should only take place if they were essential to cement a peace deal or prevent a humanitarian crisis.[81] Other major Western powers also determined that their diplomats should avoid meeting with Bashir unless essential.[82] Although they had acquiesced to the referral, Russia and China showed no interest in isolating Bashir. Both governments sent envoys to meet with Bashir personally in 2009. Chinese premier Wen Jiabao reportedly had a friendly meeting with the Sudanese leader at a conference in Egypt.[83]

Western diplomats were willing to shun Bashir but, to the prosecutor's annoyance, they showed little interest in pushing him from power or engineering his arrest. As the weeks passed after the arrest warrant, the prosecutor became increasingly vocal about the unwillingness of national diplomats—particularly those from member states—to back up their professed commitment to the court with action. In late 2008, Moreno-Ocampo complained to American diplomats at the UN that the European Union was "doing nothing" to pursue Bashir. The prosecutor tried his hand at political analysis, advising the Americans that China would abandon Bashir so long as their oil interests were protected.[84]

A few months later, the prosecutor began to go public with his frustration. He chided the United Kingdom in particular for what he termed a "complex agenda" in Sudan that was preventing it from isolating Bashir. "What's the advantage for UK to be tough with Sudan when they have so much else on the agenda?" he asked. "If China, the US, the UK and Europe acted together, we would stop him."[85] In the absence of support for arrests in Sudan, the prosecutor occasionally resorted to public bravado. He revealed publicly that there had been discussions, in December 2007, of intercepting a plane scheduled to carry the indicted Ahmed Haroun to the pilgrimage in Saudi Arabia (at the last moment, Haroun chose not to board the flight). It is not clear how concrete plans to intercept the plane were, but Moreno-Ocampo cited that incident several times in discussing Bashir. "We believe that as soon as Bashir travels in international airspace he could be arrested," he told *Newsweek*. "We would try to organize that, yes. We did it once, we'd try to do it again."[86] The comments raised the eyebrows of several major-power diplomats, who doubted any such operation was being contemplated. In a cable to Washington, the senior US diplomat in Khartoum acknowledged that "public concerns that Bashir might be apprehended and turned over to the ICC...are grossly exaggerated."[87]

In the months after the arrest warrant, in fact, Bashir made a point of traveling. He was cautious at first, crossing the border to neighboring Eritrea and Egypt. Since neither of these countries were ICC members, they had no treaty obligation to arrest persons indicted by the court. Nor had the Security Council created an obligation for them. In referring Sudan to the court, the Council had only "urged" other states to cooperate with the court. In late March 2009, Bashir struck a more dramatic blow at the international arrest warrant. He was feted at an Arab League summit in Qatar, which UN

Secretary General Ban Ki-moon attended as an observer. The assembled Arab leaders expressed their solidarity with Bashir and warned that the arrest warrant could destabilize the region.[88]

Even worse for the court was the African Union's July 2009 resolution criticizing the conduct of the prosecutor and the court's impact in Sudan. The decision chastised the Council for failing to consider a deferral resolution and warned of the indictment's impact on Sudan's "delicate peace processes."[89] The African Union move provoked ire in the human rights community, and a few African governments distanced themselves from the decision. But the complications it created for the court were undeniable; the leading regional organization in Africa had declared that its member states—even ICC members—were not obliged to honor the court's arrest warrants. The court itself was ill-equipped to counter Bashir's diplomatic offensive and the broader African backlash. When the Sudanese president traveled to ICC member states or met with their diplomats, the court could protest and alert the Security Council, but it had few other levers to pull.

The Western powers intermittently tried to restrain Bashir's peregrinations. A few weeks after the arrest warrant was issued, the US embassy in Egypt asked Egyptian officials not to meet with Bashir. "Welcoming Bashir in Egypt so soon after the ICC decision sends a bad signal," the ambassador's talking points emphasized.[90] With broad European support, Denmark made clear that Bashir would be arrested if he attended the December 2009 Copenhagen climate change conference. That same year, Turkey invited Bashir to attend the Organization of the Islamic Conference summit in Istanbul. Under heavy EU pressure, Turkish leaders encouraged Bashir not to attend, and he canceled the trip.[91] Yet the Sudanese president still traveled widely (table 6.2).

It was difficult for even engaged governments to maintain effective pressure. Corralling Bashir implied routinely sending demarches and interceding with governments that might otherwise welcome the Sudanese leader. That effort was often too much for even major-power foreign ministries. The European major powers—Britain, France, and Germany—were most ideologically inclined to support the court, but they often struggled to respond quickly to Bashir's moves. Nor were they willing to link compliance with the ICC arrest warrant to development aid or other forms of leverage. Japan and Brazil occasionally expressed their concern to states that welcomed Bashir, but not consistently or with the implication that there would be consequences. For their part, Russia and China had no interest in the matter. None of these

Table 6.2 Selected Post-Arrest Warrant Travels by Omar al-Bashir

Date	Country	ICC status
3/23/2009	Eritrea	Signatory, but not a state party (signed Rome Statute but has not ratified)
3/25/2009	Egypt	Signatory, but not a state party
3/26/2009	Libya	Not a state party
4/1/2009	Saudi Arabia	Not a state party
2/3/2010	Qatar	Not a state party
7/22/2010	Chad	State Party
8/27/2010	Kenya	State Party
5/7/2011	Djibouti	State Party
6/19/2011	Malaysia	Not a state party
6/28/2011	China	Not a state party
8/8/2011	Chad	State Party
10/14/2011	Malawi	State Party
1/7/2012	Libya	Not a state party
3/29/2012	Iraq	Not a state party
5/23/2012	Eritrea	Signatory, but not a state party
7/15/2012	Ethiopia	Not a state party
7/31/2012	Qatar	Not a state party
8/30/2012	Iran	Not a state party
8/31/2012	Ethiopia	Not a state party
9/16/2012	Egypt	Signatory, but not a state party
9/24/2012	Ethiopia	Not a state party
11/5/2012	Saudi Arabia	Not a state party
2/16/2013	Chad	State Party
4/12/2013	South Sudan	Not a state party
5/24/2013	Ethiopia	Not a state party

Source: Compiled from news accounts.

major powers were willing to impose economic or other costs on states that allowed Bashir on their territory.

For the Obama administration as well, the effort to quarantine Bashir sometimes succumbed to other priorities. Securing a peace agreement in Darfur and engineering the peaceful independence of South Sudan both involved delicate negotiations with Khartoum. In the context of this complex diplomacy, key US officials viewed the arrest warrant as an impediment. The

US special envoy to Sudan, Scott Gration, did not disguise his preference for putting justice on the back burner:

> Right now, we are working very hard in Darfur and in the south to put into place those things that are required to save lives and make a brighter future. That doesn't mean that we're not interested in accountability and justice. Those things will come when the time is right…[t]hat's why we're continuing to talk with the government of Khartoum, the Government of Sudan. That's why we continue to negotiate with them to be able to save lives, to be able to bring peace, and then when the time is right, we'll ensure that there's accountability and justice in accordance with the international systems.[92]

Gration's insistence that justice could wait directly contradicted the prosecutor's repeated insistence that no lasting peace was possible in Sudan without accountability. The special envoy's view was contested within the administration, particularly by UN ambassador Susan Rice. She consistently argued for a more confrontational approach to Bashir and locked horns with Gration on several occasions, including over how to respond to Bashir's reelection as president in April 2010. In important respects, however, Gration's view prevailed.[93]

Prosecutorial Discretion

While the prosecutor was berating key member states for their passivity on Sudan, he was also considering what new investigations to launch. Of the three crises that developed in late 2008—Russia–Georgia, the Gaza war, and the Kenya election violence—the prosecutor pursued Kenya most actively. But he approached even that investigation cautiously, waiting for almost a year before making his move. During that period, a high-level international commission investigated the violence and produced a confidential list of individuals most responsible for the violence. The commission recommended that the ICC investigate if domestic institutions proved incapable of doing so. In July 2009, the lead international mediator, former UN Secretary General Kofi Annan, decided that the Kenyan authorities were not serious about investigating the violence and transmitted to the prosecutor the sealed envelope containing names of the leading suspects.[94]

In late 2009, the prosecutor finally sought authority from the judges to open a formal investigation. In so doing, the prosecutor for the first time used his *proprio motu* authority to initiate an investigation not referred by a state or by the UN Security Council. He did so, however, as part of a carefully negotiated process and with strong backing from the international community's lead mediator and the major powers most concerned about the situation in Kenya. Internationally, the Kenya inquiry was as uncontroversial a use of the controversial *proprio motu* power as could be designed.

There was more discord about the wisdom of a Kenya investigation among the ICC judges who reviewed the matter than among major powers. A judicial panel gave the prosecutor authority to open the investigation in March 2010, but one judge, Hans-Peter Kaul of Germany, vigorously dissented. He argued that the violence in Kenya did not meet the threshold that should be required for crimes against humanity. More broadly, he worried that the court might spread itself too thin if it did not police the line between serious crimes and crimes of concern to the international community as a whole. He warned that eroding that distinction

> would broaden the scope of possible ICC intervention almost indefinitely. This might turn the ICC, which is fully dependent on State cooperation, in[to] a hopelessly overstretched, inefficient international court, with related risks for its standing and credibility. Taken into consideration the limited financial and material means of the institution, it might be unable to tackle all the situations which could fall under its jurisdiction with the consequence that the selection of the situations under actual investigation might be quite arbitrary.[95]

Rather than being arbitrary, the prosecutor's decisions about which situations to investigate continued to follow a pattern: avoiding confrontation and entanglement with major powers. The prosecutor was willing to investigate crimes committed in Kenya but not those committed in the course of the Russia–Georgia conflict. There was no lack of evidence in the latter. The Russians reportedly provided the court with material purporting to document the crimes of Georgia's leaders. Residents of South Ossetia flooded the court with complaints about the conduct of Georgian forces, most of which were delivered to the court by the Russian embassy.[96] For its part, Georgia submitted files on alleged atrocities by Russian forces and pro-Russian Ossetian militia groups.[97] In March 2010, Moreno-Ocampo's chief of staff visited Moscow and Tbilisi to discuss the investigation.[98] That trip was the high point of ICC engagement, however. The prosecutor's office updated its file but made no move toward a full investigation.

On Palestine, the prosecutor also moved carefully. He invited legal analyses on whether the court would have jurisdiction and insisted that a decision would take time. "I am still listening," he told *Al-Hayat* in September 2009. "It is a very important decision and I cannot decide without being completely certain."[99] That threshold—complete certainty—was unattainable, and it is not clear why the prosecutor insisted on it. If the prosecutor had initiated a Palestine investigation on the basis of the January 2009 referral, his decision would have been reviewed by a panel of judges, who would be better equipped to answer the legal question of whether Palestine was a state.

The publication in September of the Goldstone Report, commissioned by the UN's Human Rights Council, increased pressure on the prosecutor to act. The blistering review accused Israel of deliberately attacking civilian infrastructure in Gaza, abusing detainees, using Palestinians as human shields, and arbitrarily depriving wounded civilians of medical care. These and other violations, it argued, created individual criminal responsibility. The report's authors insisted that Israel had not shown itself capable of investigating abuses on its own and concluded that the violations "fall within the subject-matter jurisdiction of the International Criminal Court."[100]

As the prosecutor faced questions on the pace of his Gaza deliberations, US and Israeli officials met quietly to consider the Israeli response to the Goldstone report. In New York, US ambassador to the UN Susan Rice privately emphasized to Israeli president Shimon Peres the US "commitment not to allow the issue to move from the Security Council to the International Criminal Court."[101] In Tel Aviv, US and Israeli officials discussed the ICC inquiry on several occasions. Israeli officials plied their American counterparts for advice on whether to contact the prosecutor directly. The Israelis wanted more than guidance, however. They wanted direct American political pressure on the court. During a February 2010 meeting in Tel Aviv, the senior Israeli military lawyer, Avichai Mandelblit, pressed US officials to make public their opposition to an ICC investigation:

> Mandelblit said the [Israeli government] was troubled that the ICC issue was not yet off the table and that it appeared to be a political decision for Ocampo, with much pressure coming from the Arab League for the ICC to deal with Western countries rather than "just Africa."...[another Israeli official] noted that the ICC was the most dangerous issue for Israel and wondered whether the U.S. could simply state publicly its position that the ICC has no jurisdiction over Israel regarding the Gaza operation.[102]

The United States did not oblige with a public statement about the court's jurisdiction. In private, however, senior administration officials made clear to the prosecutor that they saw little value in "criminalizing the world's longest running and most intractable regional dispute," as one administration official put it.[103] They urged him not to take any steps that would set the court on a path toward a full investigation. In these conversations, American officials often purported to be looking out for the institution's best interests. A Palestine investigation, they suggested, might be too much political weight for the institution to bear. They made clear that proceeding with the case would be a major blow to the institution.[104]

Israel did not rely entirely on these US interventions. In late 2009, Israeli officials established direct contact with the prosecutor. During several quiet meetings in The Hague, including a dinner at the Israeli ambassador's residence, the Israelis pressed Moreno-Ocampo to determine quickly that Palestine was not a state and that the court could therefore not accept its grant of jurisdiction.[105] The prosecutor hesitated; he was attracted to the argument that Palestine had enough attributes of statehood to make its declaration legitimate. He also wondered whether he should simply refer the question of Palestine's status to the court's Assembly of States Parties for a decision. That possibility alarmed the Israelis; they knew the ASP would likely support Palestine's right to confer jurisdiction. Facing powerful pressure from multiple directions, the prosecutor temporized.

While Israeli officials fretted about ICC scrutiny, the major Western powers had concerns of their own about potential investigations. With violence in Afghanistan on the rise, the prosecutor's office had sent a letter to the Afghan government and to key NATO states seeking additional information. The frequent attacks on civilians in Afghanistan were undeniable. The United Nations reported more than 2,400 civilian deaths in 2009, the highest total since the Taliban regime fell in 2001.[106] August and September were particularly deadly months. On August 25, suspected Taliban elements detonated a truck bomb in the eastern city of Kandahar, killing nearly fifty civilians and displacing dozens of families.[107] Meanwhile, coalition airstrikes continued to take a toll on civilians. A September strike by German warplanes reportedly killed more than ninety villagers, many of whom had rushed to gather fuel from a disabled tanker truck.[108]

Neither the Kabul government nor the leading NATO states had any desire to encourage an ICC role. When the prosecutor mentioned the request to Afghanistan's ambassador, the envoy at first denied that Afghanistan was a member of the court (he later explained to the prosecutor that he had not realized his country had joined the Rome Statute).[109] The prosecutor's office also received calls from several NATO states, including Germany, expressing concern about any investigation there. For all their rhetoric in other contexts about the importance of justice to lasting peace, major Western states saw no place for international investigations in Afghanistan. According to ICC officials, there were no substantive replies to their requests from the Afghan government or from any NATO states.[110] NATO's silence sent an important signal about the preferences of these states, but it also created a significant evidentiary problem for the court. To open a formal investigation on its own, the prosecutor would have to convince a panel of judges that there was a "reasonable basis" to believe relevant crimes had been committed. Absent active cooperation by the Afghan authorities and NATO forces, the prosecutor might have difficulty meeting that threshold.[111]

The prosecutor's silence on Afghanistan bolstered a trend of cautious behavior on the opening of investigations and the expansion of the court's jurisdiction. Confronted with a vacuum of official information, for example, the prosecutor might have chosen a vigorous public strategy of seeking cooperation. Instead, he limited himself to occasional private requests and put no pressure on involved states. That approach contrasted sharply with his willingness to publicly chastise states for their failure to enforce existing arrest warrants.

The court also stayed quiet about one of the bloodiest episodes to occur during its first decade of operation. In 2009, the government of Sri Lanka launched a military offensive to end a brutal, decades-long insurgency in that country's north. In the final offensive, government forces committed widespread abuses. Experts estimated that the civilian death toll ran as high as 40,000.[112] Because Sri Lanka was not a court member, the court lacked jurisdiction to investigate. Consistent with its past practice, the prosecutor and other officials made no statements encouraging involved states or the Security Council to give it jurisdiction.

The prosecutor's approach suggested a sharp differentiation between the court's strategic positioning and its tactical operations. Once the prosecutor had been clearly accorded jurisdiction, he was willing to defy major-power pressure regarding who he investigated and when he sought indictments, as the Bashir indictment demonstrated. In bureaucratic terms, the prosecutor fiercely defended his office's autonomy. When several states in 2009 sought to activate a court oversight mechanism that could investigate prosecution officials, Moreno-Ocampo warned that it posed "an undue risk" of interference with his prosecutorial independence.[113] The prosecutor also did not hesitate to chide even major powers for their lack of energy in backing the court's decisions. But he was much more cautious about involving the court in new situations, even when he had the jurisdiction he needed.

"A Wobbly Bicycle"

Since 2002, the potentially explosive question of whether and how the court would prosecute the crime of aggression had been mostly contained. Periodic meetings of expert-level officials took place at Princeton University beginning in 2004.[114] With little public attention, the participants inched toward a draft definition of aggression. But a high-level "review conference" scheduled for 2010—the first chance for ICC members to consider changes to the Rome Statute—promised to revive the debate. A number of states, backed by some activist groups, insisted that the ICC would not be fully functional until it could prosecute aggression. The debate on the issue that took place in 2010 was in many respects the completion of the Rome Conference. Unlike the 1998 conference, however, the 2010 negotiations featured vigorous and mostly cohesive efforts by the permanent Security Council members to limit the court's reach.

For Paris and London, the Obama administration's decision to participate as an observer in meetings of court members was welcome, and particularly on the aggression issue. In the last year of the Bush administration, French officials had unsuccessfully pressed their American counterparts to engage with the court's processes enough to help defend what they saw as the Security Council's prerogative to identify acts of aggression. France, a senior official warned, "is beginning to feel isolated due to the hostility against the [Security Council] and is unsure if a satisfactory result is possible."[115] The Obama administration's decision to attend the review conference as an observer made it easier for the P5 members to coordinate their efforts and concentrate their diplomatic strength.

There were some tactical differences between the P5. The British and French, who had been participating in the expert-level meetings on aggression, were ready to acquiesce to the emerging definition of aggression, whereas the United States, Russia, and China remained skeptical. But the P5 were united in their desire to give the Security Council exclusive power to trigger aggression prosecutions by the court. In defending that position, the P5 argued repeatedly that the UN Charter accorded the Council exclusive power to determine when an act of aggression had occurred.

The P5 sometimes cast their position as an effort to protect the ICC from "politicization." Aggression, they suggested, was too explosive for a weak institution still finding its feet. US State Department legal adviser Harold Koh sounded that theme in a March 2010 speech. "We are concerned that adopting a definition of aggression at this point in the court's history could divert the ICC from its core mission, and potentially politicize and weaken this young institution," he told the American Society of International Law. "If you think of the Court as a wobbly bicycle that is finally starting to move forward, is this frankly more weight than the bicycle can bear?"[116] Koh's concern for the court's stability echoed the administration's approach on Palestine; US officials were becoming adept at framing efforts to guide the court as expressions of concern for its well-being.

Koh's view was shared by a significant number of ICC advocates and supporters. Former ICTY prosecutor Richard Goldstone wrote, "[T]he issues that would arise from dealing with allegations of aggression would give ammunition to critics who claim it is a politicized institution."[117] A coalition of nongovernmental organizations argued similarly:

> [A]ggression—crime based on acts committed against a state—raises fundamentally political considerations about a state's initial decision to resort to the use of force.... For obvious reasons, the ICC strives to present itself as an effective judicial body that is independent of political concerns. Amending the Rome Statute now to grant the Court jurisdiction over aggression will exacerbate the challenges the ICC already faces in fending off attacks about its perceived politicization.[118]

These voices rarely acknowledged that there were real differences over what the court's core mission should be. Prioritizing the prosecution of war crimes, crimes against humanity, and genocide over aggression was itself a choice that many states did not accept. The Nuremberg-era conception of aggression as the foundational international crime still resonated, particularly in the Arab World and with the Non-Aligned Movement. Certain major players such as Germany and Brazil also supported defining the crime (in 1998, Germany had been instrumental in keeping aggression in the Rome Statute). For many, the US-led Iraq war made the case for criminalizing aggression: the US decision to invade began a chain of calamities, including radicalization and insurgency, that ultimately took the lives of more than 100,000 people, many of them civilians. Even if US and coalition forces did not deliberately target civilians, their unauthorized military action set in motion conflict, insurgency, and radicalization that would.

On this view, choosing not to pursue aggression was itself politicizing the court—and mostly to benefit those states with large militaries likely to use force without clear international authorization. A criminal approach to conflict that focused on deliberate targeting of civilians—and excluded unauthorized uses of force—was a system that worked decidedly to the major powers' benefit. Those states in possession of trained, technologically advanced militaries had little need to terrorize civilians. (When they had found it essential to do so, as during the Second World War, they had ensured that postwar justice did not cover their activities.)

As diplomats from around the world arrived in Kampala, Uganda for the review conference in May 2010, the outcome was very much in doubt. In opening statements, dozens of envoys stressed the importance of prosecuting the crime. Brazil's envoy insisted that "fully integrating this crime into the Rome Statute remains a crucial step toward a more stable, democratic and just world order."[119] If activating aggression was the conference's ostensible focus, the thinly veiled agenda of many states was rebuffing the permanent Security Council members. As had been the case at the Rome Conference, the privileges accorded those powerful states loomed large. Most states in Kampala would not accept an outcome that left the court wholly dependent on Security Council approval to prosecute crimes of aggression.

Unlike at the Rome Conference, however, the P5 maintained a mostly unified front, and their combined diplomatic weight proved formidable. After two weeks, the delegates emerged with a complex package that left the P5 satisfied, if not pleased. The agreed amendments excluded nonmember states from prosecution entirely, even if the alleged act of aggression occurred against an ICC member state. "No U.S. national can be prosecuted for aggression while the U.S. is not a signatory," Harold Koh reported as the conference closed.[120] All ICC member states were given the option of opting out of jurisdiction for aggression crimes. Even in cases where the court had jurisdiction, the prosecutor was required to wait six months for Security Council action before initiating any aggression prosecution on his own. For added measure, delegates agreed that the aggression amendments would not come into force until 2017, at the earliest.[121] The P5 did not get everything they wanted, but they secured their essential goal. "The P5 got what really mattered to them," one small-state diplomat said, "but others prevailed a bit on their principles."

Full Speed on Libya

In December 2010, a lone act of protest in Tunisia sparked a large-scale political movement. The "Arab Spring" unrest quickly crossed borders. Demonstrations followed in Algeria, where security forces battled protesters.

A month later, the unrest spread to Libya. Particularly loud protests broke out in the western city of Benghazi. On February 17, hundreds of protesters took to the streets of Libya's capital, Tripoli, and burned government buildings. Security forces fired on the protesters, killing several. Within days, the uprising lurched toward full civil war, with opposition forces concentrated in Benghazi. The Muammar Gaddafi regime pledged to crush the rebel forces, and many observers worried that large-scale massacres were possible.

Libya was not an ICC member state, and Gaddafi himself had in fact emerged as one of the court's most outspoken critics. In the months before the uprisings began, Gaddafi had railed against the ICC indictments in Sudan, which he labeled "official terrorism."[122] His extreme animosity was, in part, a product of Libya's idiosyncratic foreign policy, but it also reflected a broader Arab distrust of the court. Jordan was the only Arab state that had joined the court. If the ICC was to play a role in the unrest associated with the Arab Spring, it would have to be via the UN Security Council.

As the violence escalated in Libya, the Security Council met hurriedly to craft a response. Gaddafi's relative isolation, the defection of a number of senior Libyan diplomats, and the Arab League's condemnation of the regime produced an unusual dynamic on the Council: Russia and China were willing to contemplate measures against a government facing internal opposition. With strong support from Germany, British and French diplomats drafted a resolution imposing an arms embargo and targeted sanctions, and referring the violence to the ICC. The referral proved to be the most contentious element of the draft, and several Council diplomats expected it to drop out before passage. "Our strategy was to aim high and see what we could get," recalled German ambassador Peter Wittig.[123] India and the African states on the Council advocated a staggered approach that would prioritize an arms embargo and other steps before referring the matter to the ICC. Indian ambassador Hardeep Singh Puri had instructions from his capital to oppose any ICC reference in the resolution. Recognizing that Council support for some reference to the ICC was substantial, he suggested instead that the resolution include only the *threat* of a referral.[124]

As the Saturday negotiations continued, the language referring Libya to the ICC showed surprising sticking power. To help persuade holdouts, European diplomats approached Libya's own UN ambassador—who had distanced himself from the Gaddafi regime—to see if he could build support for a referral. He wrote a letter to the Council president endorsing the idea, and French officials ensured that it was circulated quickly to all Council members.[125] The letter helped tip the balance, although China's ambassador

delayed negotiations for several hours while he awaited final word from
Beijing. Finally, in the evening, he received instructions to vote yes.[126] "We
were surprised that we got away with this bold move," said German ambassador Wittig.

On February 26, 2011, the Council unanimously approved a resolution
imposing an arms embargo on Libya, enacting targeted financial sanctions
against its leaders, and referring the violence there to the ICC.[127] Western
leaders immediately sought to convert the referral into leverage on the regime.
British officials reportedly made concerted efforts to contact senior Libyan
officials and warn them of the consequences of a continued crackdown.
"People working for this regime should remember that international justice
has a long reach and a long memory," said Prime Minister David Cameron.[128]
In early March, President Obama reportedly communicated with senior
regime officials to warn them against attacking civilians.[129] That message was
aired in public as well. "I want to send a very clear message to those who are
around Colonel Gaddafi," he said during an Oval Office appearance. "It is
their choice to make, how they operate moving forward, and they will be held
accountable for whatever violence continues to take place there."[130]

Some Western officials were surprised, however, by just how fast that legal
reckoning came. The prosecutor moved with unprecedented speed to open a
formal investigation. When the Security Council referred Sudan to the court,
the prosecutor deliberated for more than two months before opening a full
investigation. On Libya, he waited less than a week.[131] The absence of national
proceedings speeded up the process, since the prosecutor did not have to assess
the genuineness of those investigations. But it is also clear that the prosecutor
hoped to demonstrate that the court could be effective in a fast-moving political crisis. He hurriedly assembled a team of investigators that began gathering
evidence from a variety of public sources, electronic records, and confidential
interviews. The slew of Libyan officials defecting provided the prosecutor's
office with a valuable insight into the regime's inner workings.[132]

At the urging of the British and French governments, the Security Council
soon turned from sanctions and judicial intervention to direct military means.
As Gaddafi's forces moved toward the rebel stronghold of Benghazi, Western
leaders worried that a rout and massacre were imminent.[133] On March 17, with
five members abstaining, the Council authorized "all necessary means" to
defend civilians.[134] Within hours of that resolution, French warplanes flew
the mission's first combat sorties, and cruise missiles from US warships struck
Libyan air defense and radar installations. Even as the court investigated, key
NATO states were in active combat against Gaddafi's forces.

For a brief moment, power and justice appeared to be working toward one purpose: the enforcement of international law protecting civilians. But as Gaddafi clung to power, an operation that Western leaders had hoped would quickly tip the balance against the regime turned into a protracted and controversial campaign. Fissures began to emerge within the Western coalition. In the United States, congressional critics and some academics questioned the military campaign's legal basis.[135] Meanwhile, rumors swirled that senior regime officials, even Gaddafi himself, were exploring exit strategies. Italy's prime minister floated the idea of arranging safe haven for Gaddafi and other senior Libyan officials. The United States signaled that it would not obstruct the move, even though it might place the men beyond the court's reach.[136] A British official suggested that Gaddafi's fate "has to be a process for the Libyan people."[137] The continued discussions of exit strategies for regime leaders worried activists. "Justice cannot be turned on and off depending on the needs of the moment," Human Rights Watch warned.[138]

The prosecutor's investigation was moving at breakneck speed. In early May, he flew from The Hague to brief the Security Council on his progress. He reported that his team had collected evidence that the regime planned the crackdown on opponents well in advance and recruited mercenaries from abroad for assistance. He announced his intention to bring charges against three individuals responsible for crimes against humanity. None too subtly, he linked the coming indictments to the Council's stated goal of protecting civilians. "Arresting those who ordered the commission of crimes," he insisted, "will contribute to the protection of civilians in Libya because it will deter ongoing crimes." He then urged the Council members to prepare the groundwork for seizing those indicted:

> Arrests cannot be successfully conducted without serious planning and preparation, which takes time. The international community should take steps now to assist on such practical planning. As UN Secretary-General Ban Ki-moon reflected in Kampala, "now we have the ICC, permanent, increasingly powerful, casting a long shadow. There is no going back."[139]

Not all the diplomats the prosecutor was addressing shared that sentiment. Some US officials, in particular, had become concerned about the pace of the ICC investigation and the possibility that it might interfere with diplomatic efforts. Facing criticism at home, the Obama administration was keeping a close eye on all possible diplomatic avenues, including a mediation effort by the African Union, led by Mauritanian president Abdel Aziz.[140] In this context, State Department legal adviser Harold Koh and National Security Council senior director Samantha Power reached out to the prosecutor's office to discuss how the court's strategy was meshing with diplomatic and military efforts.

"We in the U.S. government were interested in knowing the prosecutor's plans and thinking so we could leverage whatever timing he had in mind to try to use it to get Gaddafi to leave or surrender," Power said. She recalled the conversation as a "brainstorming session" during which she and Koh exchanged ideas with the prosecutor, particularly about the timing of indictments and whether they should be public or sealed.[141] "The prosecutor has a mission but what he does can also have broader strategic impact," Koh said of the conversation. "We didn't so much want to give him guidance as to help him avoid potholes."[142] Other officials familiar with the call remembered a more pointed message: that the United States was concerned public indictments might become a diplomatic obstacle.[143] According to officials in the court, the prosecutor himself viewed the call as a form of pressure. "He clearly perceived it as [the United States] trying to stop him or interfere with his decision."[144]

Whether or not pressure was intended, Moreno-Ocampo plunged ahead. On May 16, he announced that he was seeking arrest warrants for Muammar Gaddafi, his son Saif, and the regime's intelligence chief, al-Senussi. "The evidence shows that Muammar Gaddafi, personally, ordered attacks on unarmed Libyan civilians," he said at a press conference in The Hague. "His forces attacked Libyan civilians in their homes and in the public space, repressed demonstrations with live ammunition, used heavy artillery against participants in funeral processions, and placed snipers to kill those leaving mosques after the prayers."[145] The prosecutor reported that his office had received cooperation from high-level Libyan officials and that his team was almost ready for trial.

Yet the prosecutor's tone regarding international involvement in arrests had changed markedly in the weeks since he briefed the Security Council. "My office has not requested the intervention of international forces to implement the arrest warrants," he insisted. "Should the court issue them and the three individuals remain in Libya, Libyan authorities have the primary responsibility to arrest them."[146] That more restrained language was not by chance. In his conversations with Western diplomats, the prosecutor had found little enthusiasm for deploying NATO resources to effect arrest operations. Any attempts to seize the Gaddafis or Al-Senussi would be risky and would highlight the presence of Western troops on the ground. The Security Council resolution authorizing military action had specifically precluded "occupa-tion," and the Western powers had all ruled out sending ground troops. It was an open secret that a small group of Western operatives were in Libya, but their presence was not officially acknowledged and their role was limited to advising rebel forces and guiding coalition air strikes.[147] In this environment, the Western powers leading the intervention had no interest in supporting arrest operations.

For the prosecutor, it was hard to avoid the conclusion that the Security Council had once again deployed the ICC without any commitment to ensuring its effectiveness. Those concerns grew as Gaddafi's regime crumbled. Muammar Gaddafi himself was captured and then killed by opposition fight-ers on October 20, 2011.[148] His son Saif evaded capture for a few weeks longer, but militia forces eventually caught up with him as he raced for the border with Niger. With Saif Gaddafi in custody, the prosecutor and other court officials scrambled to prepare for his transfer to The Hague. Court officials reminded the Libyan authorities of their international obligation—imposed via the Security Council—to cooperate with the arrest warrant. Libya's fragile new government was not convinced however. It faced strong pressure to try Saif at home.

For their part, the Western states that had engineered Gaddafi's defeat issued cautious and sometimes ambiguous statements. A US spokesperson insisted that the trial location was "a matter for the Libyan authorities and the Libyan people to decide."[149] European leaders generally emphasized that the ICC should have a role but did not demand that Libya hand over Saif. When Libya's former intelligence chief, al-Senussi was located, French officials sug-gested that they wanted to put Senussi on trial and did not mention sending him to The Hague.[150] Briefly a key element in the international response to Libya, the court now appeared peripheral. "The interests of the court and the interests of key states aligned for a moment," a former prosecution official said, "but the moment didn't last long."[151]

Control and Construction

For a number of the court's most committed supporters, the way key Security Council members handled the Libya referral added to a growing disquiet about how power politics and international justice were mixing. Not only had the Security Council referral of Libya included provisions limiting jurisdiction over non-ICC members and emphasizing that no UN funds were going to the court, but Council members had exhibited little

willingness to support the court in apprehending suspects. Those expressing concern included Christian Wenaweser, who served as president of the
court's Assembly of State Parties from 2008 through 2011. In a speech to
ICC members, he argued that the relationship between the court and the
Council required examination:

> We as States Parties will have to think about the relationship between
> the Security Council and the Court.... We have had two referrals of
> situations by the Council, one of them by consensus. This was essential
> in giving the Court the place it currently has. In the future, we thus no
> longer have to look at referrals from the point of view of acceptance of
> the Court—we have achieved that acceptance—but rather from the
> best interest of international criminal justice. This means in concrete
> terms a genuine commitment to ensure that justice is done, by provid-
> ing the necessary diplomatic and financial support.[152]

Off the dais, Wenaweser was more pointed. "Is the Security Council genu-
inely committed to making sure that there is no impunity or is this about
something else?"[153] That "something else" was political control. The willingness of powerful states to direct the court without committing to its success
was evident in several situations. The prosecutor's regular briefings to the
Council on Sudan included routine calls for a tougher stance toward the
regime that were routinely ignored.

Among the ICC membership, the perception that the Security Council
was instrumentalizing the court—referring situations with strict conditions
and then not providing financial or political support—had become widespread. In private meetings with ICC officials, non-major-power national
diplomats voiced concern that the court was coming under the control of the
Council. "If the Prosecutor cannot start proprio motu investigations due to
financial constraints but continues with [Security Council] referrals then the
independence of the ICC is at risk," one diplomat said.[154]

The increasingly apparent outer limits to major-power support did
not imply an inactive court. The prosecutor attempted new mechanisms
of generating support for the court, including by tapping public opinion.
Moreno-Ocampo collaborated extensively with activists making a film about
the Lord's Resistance Army and the hunt for Joseph Kony. The prosecutor
featured prominently in the resulting video, which became in Internet sensa-
tion. He defended the broader activist campaign of which the video was a
part. It had, he said, "mobilized the world."[155]

Meanwhile, the work of investigations and prosecutions continued. In late 2011, the court opened a new investigation in Cote d'Ivoire, where political violence had erupted the year before. After refusing to recognize the results of an election that his opponent had won, President Laurent Gbagbo was condemned by the UN Security Council. In April 2011, French troops and international peacekeepers pushed Gbagbo and his forces from power. The ICC then sought his arrest on charges that he had ordered violence against political opponents.[156] The new Ivorian government handed him to the court a few days later. In March 2012, the judges convicted Congolese warlord Thomas Lubanga on charges of recruiting child soldiers—the court's first ever conviction. The trials of several other Congolese militia commanders continued. Meanwhile, prosecution officials inched forward with their cases against several Kenyan leaders for the 2008 election violence. The new and continuing cases were each complex in their own ways, with significant political implications for their respective states.

Yet this court activity appeared to be occurring within a major-power comfort zone. The prosecutor's long-awaited decision on Palestine—released in April 2012—strengthened the case that international political realities continued to shape the court's activities. More than three years after Palestine asked the court to investigate, the prosecutor decided that it was not his role to determine Palestine's legal status. The Rome Statute, he concluded, "provides no authority for the Office of the Prosecutor to adopt a method to define the term 'State.'"[157] That decision, which foreclosed the possibility that the prosecutor would open an investigation on his own authority, mostly relieved Israeli and American officials.

A few months later, Moreno-Ocampo completed his term as prosecutor and handed responsibility to Fatou Bensouda, his deputy since 2006. The handover came just as the court marked its first decade in operation. Bensouda had the strong support of the court's African members; in fact, the diplomats organizing the search for a successor had to restrain the African Union from endorsing her candidacy before the established consultation period had concluded.[158] The idea of an African prosecutor had appeal outside the continent. "In the course of the consultations that we held that there was a strong view across the regions it would be good to have an African as the next prosecutor," said Christian Wenaweser, the European diplomat who oversaw the search process.[159]

Formally, the court's members considered a final group of four candidates put forward by Wenaweser and his committee. But Bensouda quickly emerged as the prohibitive favorite. She secured the support of the United

Kingdom, France, Germany, and Japan. Although it still lacked a formal role, the United States watched the selection process closely and was pleased to see Bensouda's candidacy gather support. In large part, the degree of major-power comfort with Bensouda reflected the fact that for all her differences with Moreno-Ocampo in rhetoric and style, she represented continuity. She had been deeply involved in the creation of a prosecutorial strategy that these powers for the most part endorsed.[160]

In the wake of her election, Bensouda sometimes spoke in terms that suggested she might be more willing to challenge powerful states. She highlighted the role of smaller states in the court's work, speaking in terms that like-minded diplomats had often used during the negotiations that produced the Rome Statute to contrast their approach with that of larger powers. "International justice gives power of leadership to small and medium countries, to principled states, those who are determined to use the power of the law, not the power of arms, to protect their citizens and their territories," she said. She also warned against the idea that politicians should be able to direct the court. "We are a new tool, a judicial tool, not a tool in the hands of politicians who think they can decide when to plug or unplug us."[161]

In fact, the new prosecutor continued the mostly deferential strategic behavior that had characterized her predecessor's tenure. After a formal request by the national government, she opened a new investigation of alleged atrocities in Mali. It was the court's eighth formal investigation—and the eighth in Africa. In five of those cases, the national government in question had requested an ICC role, although sometimes prodded by the court. In two other cases, the Security Council had asked the court to investigate. Only in Kenya had the court acted on its own, and it did so with broad international support.

Elsewhere, caution prevailed. The court remained quiet on Afghanistan and the Russia–Georgia conflict. A prosecution official acknowledged that the involvement of major powers in those cases "loomed large."[162] The prosecutor's office continued monitoring Colombia, but there were no signs it was moving toward a full investigation. Bensouda also moved cautiously on Palestine, even though the jurisdictional picture had clarified significantly. Shortly before the new prosecutor was elected, the UN General Assembly voted overwhelmingly to accord Palestine the status of a non-member observer state.[163] The international community had said clearly that Palestine was a state, apparently resolving the key uncertainty that prevented the court from accepting the Palestinian Authority's 2009 grant of jurisdiction.

With the UN vote accomplished, the prosecutor's office might have simply reconsidered the previous jurisdictional grant, and initial comments by the prosecutor suggested she might do so. Soon, her tone changed and she suggested that Palestine would need to submit a new request. "The ball is now in the court of Palestine," she reportedly said.[164] By shifting the burden of action, the prosecutor allowed diplomatic processes to work. The United States used that space to make clear its opposition to further Palestinian action in The Hague. Palestinian negotiators, meanwhile, employed the prospect of additional action as leverage with the Israelis. With the court's full acquiescence, the possibility of an ICC investigation had become part of the political process. For some in the court, this deference to the political process was entirely appropriate. "If we wade into it without the support or enthusiasm of the states involved, it's not likely to succeed," former prosecution coordinator Alex Whiting said. "We're just sticking our nose into something where we're not likely to succeed." More broadly, he argued, the court was correct to chart a cautious course whenever the political environment was fraught:

> We operate in a political world and all the cases we do are highly politically charged and our institution is politically charged. You can't let those aspects govern your decisions but you can't be oblivious to them either. We're building an institution here. We're not a national justice ministry, which has tons of authority through years of operation and acceptance in society. They can throw their weight around. We have no weight. We're the Wizard of Oz behind the curtain. If we were purists about everything we did, we'd quickly run into trouble.[165]

The prosecutor's stance in turn allowed the reconciliation between the United States and the court to continue unimpeded. In March 2013, the indicted Congolese warlord Bosco Ntaganda appeared unexpectedly at the US embassy in Rwanda and requested transfer to the ICC. The rebel movement Ntaganda once led had fractured, and he had apparently decided that The Hague was his safest option. After several days of negotiations with the Rwandan government and the court, the US embassy facilitated Ntaganda's transfer to The Hague.[166] The Ntaganda affair represented the most direct US involvement with court proceedings. A week later, at the Obama administration's urging, the US Congress agreed to expand its "Rewards for Justice" program to individuals indicted by the ICC. Bensouda appeared in Washington with the US ambassador on global justice issues and praised the United States for its recent support. One analyst called their joint appearance a "lovefest."[167]

The next month, on the outskirts of The Hague, a group of dignitaries gathered on the edge of rolling dunes. Wearing construction helmets and white coats, they symbolically broke ground for the ICC's new, permanent headquarters. "This is a point of no return on the path of international criminal justice," one official said. The court's president told the audience of diplomats and observers, "By investing in the magnificent building that will rise here, you have sent a powerful message to the world that the ICC is a truly permanent institution, that international justice is here to stay, and that the age of impunity for the worst international crimes really will come to an end."[168] In the space of a decade, the court had moved from extreme fragility toward a much firmer place in the landscape of world politics. How much it had altered that landscape was less clear.

Conclusion

A CONSTRAINED COURT

THE INTERNATIONAL CRIMINAL Court represents one of the world's most elaborate experiments in enforcing legal restrictions on violence. By threatening the prosecution of individuals—including senior government and military officials—who commit or order crimes, it seeks to constrain the behavior of even powerful states. At the same time, the court's structure provides few formal avenues for these states to manage the institution. The degree of major-power control was a central issue during the negotiations that produced the Rome Statute, and many court supporters saw its relative independence as a key attribute. But that independence also posed a daunting challenge for the institution, which is heavily reliant on support from states, and particularly those with global reach.

As the preceding chapters have sought to document, the court's first decade has featured a mutual accommodation between the court and leading states. There is evidence that this has been an interactive process of signaling and response. State and court behavior have interacted and influenced each other in important ways. Understanding the dynamic between the ICC and major powers is critical both to assessing the particular trajectory of this institution and for gaining insight on how international organizations accommodate powerful states.

State Behavior

Major powers have adopted a variety of approaches to the court, and there is no uniform pattern of behavior. In developing policies toward the ICC, the group of states identified in this account as major powers—the permanent five Security Council members, Germany, Japan, India, and Brazil—have responded to unique mixtures of domestic political, foreign policy, and institutional interests and pressures. Yet a premise of this account has been that these states would share a concern: their lack of control over an institution that erodes sovereignty in unprecedented ways.

Chapter 1 outlined three theoretically grounded expectations for major-power behavior toward the court: marginalization, control, and acceptance. Marginalization would involve powerful states, even those that had joined the court, seeking to weaken an institution they could not control. Powerful states seeking to manage the court rather than systematically weaken it would be evidence of control behavior. Acceptance behavior, by contrast, allowed for the possibility that even skeptical major powers would eventually support the institution. Marginalization and control behavior would indicate that sovereignty concerns were dominating major-power behavior toward the court, while acceptance would likely indicate that other factors had superseded these concerns.

The Limits of Marginalization

The United States was the only major power to adopt a policy of active marginalization. Between 2001 and early 2005, it often sought to undermine the court through its public statements, to limit the court's reach through bilateral and multilateral instruments, and, at times, to discourage other states from joining and supporting the institution. The other skeptical major powers—Russia, China, India, and (at that point) Japan—mostly opted for a policy of passive marginalization. They offered the court no significant resources or backing but did not consistently challenge its legitimacy, seek to discourage other states from supporting the institution, or systematically attempt to limit its ability to act.

US global influence ensured that its marginalization campaign had a significant impact on the environment in which the court operated. For example, the United States succeeded in passing Security Council resolutions limiting ICC jurisdiction that many court members perceived as hostile. It negotiated bilateral immunity agreements, arguably in tension with the Rome Statute, through which dozens of court members committed not to send US citizens to the court. For court officials and supportive states, the US campaign was a significant concern. Yet this effort was short-lived. By early 2006, the United States had mostly abandoned the effort, and the failure of that campaign merits close analysis.

One element in that failure was the inability of the United States to induce other states to marginalize the court. The US strategy had difficulty competing with the narrative of accountability that the court's supporters—including both state and nonstate actors—deployed in its defense. Most US objections to the Rome Statute relied on unique American legal and institutional concerns and had limited traction beyond the United States. Those arguments that had potential broader appeal—principally the assertion that the court would interfere with domestic political choices—had little credibility coming from a country that had spearheaded previous international judicial interventions. The US inability to credibly advance the sovereignty objection made its opposition appear to be little more than an exercise in exceptionalism: the United States wanted international justice, but only if it could control how it would be applied. Other skeptical major powers, notably China, India, and Russia, might have more credibly advanced the sovereignty objection. They had been much less involved in previous international judicial interventions and more cautious about interference in the domestic affairs of states. Yet these states adopted a mostly passive approach to the court and did not mount such an effort.

The US inability to convince other states made its marginalization effort a lonely and unpopular one. Key civil society actors and some of the states that had most actively supported the court's creation complained loudly. Most important for this analysis, major powers who had joined the court worked in the opposite direction. The European Union encouraged ratification of the Rome Statute around the world. Brazil supported ratification in Latin America and beyond. More quietly, European diplomats worked to smooth the way for the Democratic Republic of Congo's 2004 referral of its internal violence to the court. That referral allowed the court to launch its first major investigation with the support of the state most directly involved.

Some major-power court members more directly countered the US marginalization effort. The European powers—Britain, France, and Germany—helped deflect pressure on smaller European states to sign immunity agreements. Meanwhile, these states opposed US efforts to enact broad annual exemptions from ICC jurisdiction at the Security Council. In 2004, in the wake of the Abu Ghraib scandal, they helped defeat the US effort to renew that exemption. These competing pushes made the ICC a significant irritant in US bilateral relations with several traditional allies.

The Sudan referral in March 2005 marked a decisive test for rival major-power efforts regarding the court. French and British diplomats worked quite deliberately to frame the question of a referral as one between accountability and impunity. The strategy worked well. At the highest level, US leaders elevated accountability in Sudan over objections to the ICC. In the wake of the referral itself, British officials helped push the superpower even farther by encouraging the United States to offer limited support for the court's investigation.

If the Sudan referral effectively ended the active US marginalization campaign, it also reflected a change in the more passive approaches of other states.

Despite expressing reservations about the court, China and Russia acquiesced to the referral. Six years later, and with reluctance, India voted for the referral of Libya to a court that Delhi had spurned. In all three cases, it appears that the perceived diplomatic and image cost of opposing a referral was deemed too high. The evidence of the court's first decade suggests that, even for the most powerful states, marginalization has been difficult to sustain.

Control Mechanisms

If marginalization proved unsustainable for even the most skeptical major powers, there is evidence that several major powers have instead attempted to control the court. These states have employed a variety of mechanisms, not all of which have been successful. Several of these mechanisms are discussed below. It is important to acknowledge, however, that the major powers have not all engaged in control behavior or used the same instruments. The P5 members have had readier access to the Security Council's levers of control than other major powers. Moreover, certain major powers have demonstrated a much greater willingness than others to exert informal pressure on the court.

Security Council Referrals

Twice, in the cases of Sudan and Libya, the UN Security Council has referred situations to the court, giving the ICC jurisdiction it otherwise lacked. Because these referrals constituted an endorsement of the ICC by the world's most powerful multilateral body, they were seen as milestones for the institution. Yet the referrals also became significant acts of control. In both Libya and Sudan, the court launched full investigations that consumed investigative resources. The referrals allowed the major-power dominated Security Council to shape the resource-constrained court's docket.

The specific form those referrals took accentuated that control. Primarily because of US insistence, the Council opposed the allocation of UN funds to support the resulting investigations. The Council also excluded categories of individuals from the referral; in both Libya and Sudan, the Council resolutions precluded jurisdiction over the nationals of other nonmember states in those countries. These were significant assertions of Security Council primacy that neither the prosecutor's office nor the judges have challenged.

Most important, the Council in no way committed itself to the success of the investigations it made possible. The Council resolutions included no enforcement mechanisms and imposed no binding obligations on nonmember states (other than the country subject to investigation). In practice, the

Council has shown itself incapable of or uninterested in enforcing the ICC arrest warrants that resulted from the investigations. The ICC prosecutor's periodic calls for diplomatic support from the Council have become routine, and they are routinely ignored.

Security Council Deferrals

The control behavior described in the first chapter anticipated that major powers would use both Security Council referrals and deferrals to manage the court. One of the most intriguing aspects of the court's first decade has been the Council's failure to use its deferral power in specific cases. In several situations, Council members considered that option. The P5 all appeared willing to consider a deferral of the ICC investigation in Uganda if necessary to achieve a peace agreement (the failure of those negotiations prevented high-level consideration of the issue). After the indictment of Sudanese president Omar al-Bashir in 2009, China, Russia, the United Kingdom, and France were all willing to consider a deferral of that case. In 2009, the Kenyan government briefly sought to generate support for a deferral as well.

In each of these cases, the push for a delay ultimately failed. The perception that a deferral would marginalize the court appears to have been a significant factor. That dynamic was most evident in the attempt to arrange a deferral of the Sudan investigation. Just as Britain and France had deployed the court's normative power to engineer a referral, Bush administration officials helped defeat the later deferral bid by insisting on the importance of accountability. Thus far, the court's normative power has effectively deactivated one key major-power instrument of control.

Informal Signaling

There is evidence that several major powers have regularly communicated their preferences on investigative strategy to court officials. For example, all the permanent Security Council members discouraged the prosecutor from indicting Sudan's president. Several leading NATO powers, including Germany, expressed concern about the court's preliminary enquiry into Afghanistan. In 2010, Chinese officials communicated to prosecution officials their discomfort with a court investigation of North Korean actions against South Korea. US officials clearly signaled their opposition to a full investigation in Palestine. During the Libya investigation, US officials expressed concern about the diplomatic impact of quick indictments. As is discussed below, these informal interventions have not always succeeded. In several situations, the prosecutor clearly ignored pressure from major powers. In other contexts, it appears that pressure has been more successful. Nor have all major powers engaged in this signaling. There is little evidence, for example, that Indian, Japanese, or Brazilian officials have attempted to steer the court in any significant way.

Diplomatic and Military Support

The court's dependence on state resources makes the selective provision of those resources a potentially powerful instrument of control. Russia, China, and India have done very little to support the court. The major European powers, by contrast, have generally sought to broaden support for the court. In the critical area of enforcing arrest warrants, however, even broadly supportive states have often abandoned the institution. Certain of the major powers—the United Kingdom, France, and the United States—have devoted some resources to encouraging or facilitating arrests in Uganda and Congo. Even these limited resources were unavailable to the court in other situations, however. There is little evidence that the Western powers offered support for arrests related to the Sudan or Libya investigations, for example. In general, major-power support has been inconsistent and has varied significantly depending on the political context.

Access to Intelligence

The ICC is highly dependent on information and evidence, some of which states possess. Particular types of intelligence—including satellite imagery and communications intercepts—are sometimes available only through major-power intelligence services. This reality raises the possibility that major-powers could use their access to information to direct the court. For several reasons, it appears that this dynamic has been muted. First, prosecution officials have been alert to the possibility and have sought to develop investigative strategies that do not rely heavily on access to national intelligence. Second, rulings by the court's judges have imposed obstacles to a steady flow of intelligence from states. In at least one situation, however, it does appear that major states have used their possession of key information to manage the court. The prosecutor sought information from NATO states on the Afghan conflict, material they were uniquely positioned to provide. Leading NATO states chose not to respond substantively to these court requests. As was the case with the Yugoslav war crimes tribunal, NATO states used the flow of intelligence to help avoid inconvenient international judicial scrutiny.

Rome Statute Amendment Process

One of the most successful examples of major-power control behavior occurred during the 2010 review conference that considered changes to the Rome Statute. On the critical question of whether and how the court could pursue aggression prosecutions, the P5 (joined by several other major powers) used their political weight to protect themselves and to limit the court's ability to pursue these cases. That outcome will help direct the court away from investigations that most threaten major-power freedom of action. This amendment process was particularly notable because it involved nonmember states decisively influencing a negotiating process in which only member states could formally participate.

Budget and Oversight

For major-power member states, larger budget assessments are the only way that the ICC system formally recognizes their status. Through the court's Assembly of States Parties (ASP), major-power member states might use the resulting financial leverage to exercise control over the institution. There is little evidence that this has happened. As with all international organizations, major powers have scrutinized the court budget to ensure that it does not expand too rapidly. But there is no evidence that states have attempted to use budget processes to directly or indirectly influence the investigative strategy of the court. Despite the concerns of the prosecutor, it also does not appear that ASP oversight of court personnel has been used in an effort to influence court strategy or investigations.

Judgeships

The Rome Statute does not accord larger states privileged access to judgeships. In practice, however, major powers that have joined the court have usually succeeded in obtaining and maintaining judgeships. These states have expended diplomatic resources to ensure the election of their candidates. The success of a Japanese candidate almost immediately after that country joined the court (and became its largest contributor) was particularly notable. The ICC has not yet developed a custom of major-power judgeships as established as the International Court of Justice's "P5 convention." France recently lost its hold on a judgeship. But it appears that most major-state members will have nationals on the ICC bench. Assessing whether judges have ruled in ways their home states might prefer—and therefore whether judgeships offer an element of control—is an important task, but one this study has not attempted.

Acts of Acceptance

There have been certain important moves toward acceptance of the court by major powers, notably Japan's decision to join the court, the US decision to end its marginalization campaign, and Chinese and Russian willingness to refer cases to the court through the Security Council. Key court member states such as Britain, France, and Germany worked to oppose the American marginalization campaign. But these discrete acts have not yet produced acceptance behavior as described in the first chapter: the overall pattern of major-power support to the court remains highly inconsistent. To this point, there is little evidence that these states are willing to consistently deploy their resources to support the court.

Court Behavior

The first chapter argued that the court's own behavior could be important in determining the institution's trajectory and establishing relations with major powers. In assessing court behavior, this account has focused on the figure of the prosecutor, who is the engine of court activity and enjoys significant discretion in that role. Chapter 1 outlined several possible behaviors that the court's prosecutor might adopt toward these states. The first of these was an entirely apolitical approach in which the preferences of major powers would play no part in prosecutorial decisions. A second approach allowed for limited consideration of geopolitical realities in order to ensure that an investigation would be feasible. A strategic approach was a third possibility. In this scenario, building support with powerful states would be a factor in selecting situations and cases to investigate. Finally, there was the (unlikely) possibility that the prosecutor's office would essentially take direction from major powers.

The prosecutor has several functions, and distinguishing between two of these is particularly important in assessing the prosecutor's behavior. One key responsibility is determining whether and when to request or initiate a formal court investigation (the "initiation" function). Once an investigation has commenced, the prosecutor then has a second broad responsibility: creating an investigative strategy, selecting individuals to prosecute, and determining the method and timing of arrest warrants (the "investigation" function). In performing these two functions, the prosecutor has demonstrated quite distinct approaches to the major powers, both rhetorically and substantively.

Volume and Tone

It was argued at the outset that court officials had significant potential to use the institution's moral authority to influence states and potentially enhance the institution's autonomy. The record thus far reveals a bifurcated approach to encouraging cooperation and support from states. In performing their investigation function, court officials have become increasingly loud. The prosecutor has quite directly challenged member states—including major powers—for their perceived failures. The prosecutor's criticism of the United Kingdom regarding Sudan is a notable example of this approach. Regular briefings to the Security Council have also provided opportunities to prod these powerful states to action.

In the court's initiation function, however, the prosecutor has been remarkably quiet. Faced with information deficits regarding potential investigations, most notably Afghanistan, the prosecutor has chosen not to challenge major powers. The prosecutor and other court officials have also not sought to expand the court's jurisdiction. Faced with evidence of large-scale crimes in nonmember states, notably Iraq, Syria, and Sri Lanka, the prosecutor has said little about whether states or the Security Council should give the court jurisdiction. Prosecution officials insist that doing so would be impermissibly "political." That interpretation is understandable but not at all inevitable. In selecting this strategy, court officials have limited their ability to deploy the court's moral authority. Major states do not face a prosecutor actively (and, in some cases, embarrassingly) calling attention to situations where the court lacks jurisdiction.

A quiet approach has also prevailed in other respects. Neither the prosecutor nor other court officials have challenged the way in which the Security Council has referred situations to the court. As discussed in chapter 4, the court has ample cause for complaint about the restrictions the Council has included in its referrals. Particularly in its initiation function, the court has not used its voice to challenge major powers.

A Strategic Approach to Initiating Investigations

That pattern of deference is also evident in the prosecutor's critical decisions about where to start full investigations. There is strong circumstantial evidence that the court has used its discretion in opening investigations to avoid entanglement with major powers and to reassure them about the court's intentions. The prosecutor's signals to the United States on Iraq in 2003 were early evidence of this trend. His choice of Congo and Uganda as the first investigations—and his efforts to secure referrals from those countries—bolstered the perception that the court would focus on internal violence by nonstate actors and seek to work with national governments.

By the time the United States, Russia, and China faced the choice of whether to effectively legitimize the court through a Security Council referral, therefore, they had reassuring indications of how the court would use its discretion. It is highly unlikely that these states would have permitted a referral if the court had adopted a more aggressive stance initially. In this sense, court and major-power behavior interacted and reinforced each other; deferential signals from the court resulted in a significant concession by skeptical major powers.

Evidence that the court prefers to avoid situations involving major powers has continued to mount. The clearest example of this tendency is Afghanistan. The court has broad jurisdiction there but has decided not to open a formal investigation despite high levels of violence, often involving civilians. Other exercises of the court's prosecutorial discretion also evidence this pattern. The prosecutor declined to conduct a full investigation in Iraq. The court has not opened a full investigation in Colombia, a close US ally that has hosted US troops and advisers. Even as he opened an investigation in Kenya, the prosecutor opted not to pursue a full investigation of the Russia-Georgia conflict. The prosecutor temporized on Palestine's referral and ultimately decided that he did not have the authority to accept the referral.

There is no "smoking gun" evidence that the prosecutor has made these choices because of perceived major-power preferences or out of a desire to avoid entanglement with them. There are plausible nonpolitical arguments against investigations in each of these cases. Because the prosecutor has only infrequently explained a decision not to open an investigation, moreover, there is little documentary evidence to assess. But the overall pattern strongly suggests that the prosecutor's office has, to this point, used its discretion on where to open investigations strategically.

Independence in Conducting Investigations

The strategic orientation outlined above does not imply that the prosecutor has taken instructions from major powers. Indeed, there is ample evidence of the prosecutor being willing to rebuff pressure from powerful states. He has been most willing to do so, however, once he has launched a formal investigation. In this investigative role, the prosecutor sought an arrest warrant for Sudan's president despite the concerns of most powerful states. In Libya, the prosecutor pursued quick arrest warrants against senior regime officials despite American concerns. It is notable that the clearest examples of the prosecutor's willingness to proceed in the face of major-power opposition have occurred in situations where the major powers had already affirmatively given the court jurisdiction through Security Council referrals. Having received the blessing of key powers, the prosecutor has been resistant to then take direction from those states on how to conduct the investigation or when to seek indictments.

Certain observers have argued that the prosecution's behavior in specific investigations does suggest a strategic approach. Specifically, there have been suggestions that the prosecutor has avoided seeking arrest warrants against regime officials and allies in Uganda and the Democratic Republic of Congo essentially on political grounds. These claims are difficult to substantiate, however, and the evidence is much less clear than during the initiation phase.

The combination of major-power control behavior and the prosecutor's strategic approach on investigations has yielded a court that is independent but constrained in important respects. The ICC is still a young institution, and its future trajectory may change significantly. There is no formal impediment to the court taking a more assertive position vis-à-vis the major powers. There is evidence that certain other supranational courts, particularly in Europe, have become bolder with time. Indeed, it is possible to see the court's cautious and restrained first decade as an essential first phase of institution building. But there are also reasons to expect that the ICC will remain constrained. The investigation of senior officials for the use of armed force creates sensitivity that other international court proceedings do not. Major powers will likely continue to have a shared interest in the court staying away from situations involving other major powers. Moreover, the court's early years have created a path from which it may not be easy to deviate. The court's second prosecutor has emerged from within the institution and was involved in many of the choices the first prosecutor made. Given this background, she may be disinclined to chart a dramatically different course.

Implications

From a theoretical perspective, the evidence that the ICC has been significantly constrained by major-power interests broadly reinforces existing scholarship documenting the ways in which strong states can informally control international organizations.[1] The evidence of the court's first decade does not disturb the broad insight that international organizations often serve as vehicles for major-power influence. Some diplomats and many activists conceived of the court as an instrument that might significantly alter international political realities. A decade later, there is little evidence that this has occurred. Instead, the court has, for the most part, become an instrument in the toolkit of major powers responding to instability and violence in weaker states.

This reality should not obscure the power of the ideals and norms that underlie the institution. There is important evidence supporting the "norm cascade" that constructivist scholars have identified in the area of international justice. The failure of the US-led marginalization campaign and other efforts to delay or defer court processes on political grounds signal that even major powers are limited in their ability to challenge frontally justice processes that have begun. Rather than translating into a clear victory for the ICC, however, that inability may have instead opened space for less obvious mechanisms of control. The ICC's first decade suggests that the norm cascade is real, but that there are still powerful obstacles to the flow of impartial international justice.

The particular mechanisms of major-power control in the case of the ICC suggest several avenues for further research. The interaction between the court and the Security Council is a central element of the ICC's story thus far. Those ICC members serving on the Council have to balance their competing interests in the international architecture, and that effort may be important for understanding how states deal with "nested" institutional relationships.[2] For non-ICC members on the Security Council, another conceptual issue arises: the ability of states to influence an organization to which they do not belong. This phenomenon appears not only in interactions between the Council and the court but also with respect to certain other control mechanisms.

The actions of the prosecutor's office also have potentially important theoretical implications. As has been noted, scholarship on international organizations has paid relatively little attention to the decision-making of the officials who run these organizations. To the extent international organizations are accorded significant autonomy, this becomes an increasingly important area of study. The prosecutor's strategic use of his discretion offers insight into how informal pressure can influence international officials. It also offers some evidence that these officials may anticipate the preferences of key actors and seek to act on them.

From a policy and advocacy perspective, the court's first decade produces a complex picture. Assuming that the pattern of political constraint holds, what are the implications for the ICC and the broader project of international justice? Supportive states and civil society actors have invested considerable time and resources in the court. The legalist perspective that they have often championed demands that legal considerations trump political ones. That orientation has difficulty accepting the outcome of a politically constrained court. From this perspective, evidence that political power is even indirectly influencing the court's work should be damaging to the institution.

There are signs that the court has already begun to experience that damage. The backlash in many African capitals after President Bashir's indictment marked the beginning of an ongoing challenge to the court's legitimacy. An important element of the African critique is a belief that the prosecutor has acted to shield powerful non-African states from scrutiny.[3] For the moment, however, the disquiet of these states with the court's constraints has not coalesced into pressure that would force changes either to the ICC's formal structure or to the application of its discretion.

It will not be surprising if the world is willing to tolerate an international justice system constrained by major-power interests. As chapters 2 and 3 attempted to document, other significant international justice initiatives have been influenced and constrained by political considerations. Instead of being denounced for their defects and limitations, these instruments were mostly celebrated and, in fact, served as the inspiration for the ICC. Double standards are deeply rooted in existing global governance structures, and the new court appears more likely to reflect those than to alter them.

In this sense, the ICC's experience may also be instructive for the broader project of reforming existing institutions and designing new ones. The post–Second World War international architecture faces increasing pressure for reform, often in the direction of more equitable treatment of states and the abandonment of major-power privilege.[4] The court's first decade suggests that it may be possible to design international institutions around power—but not to escape it.

Notes

INTRODUCTION

1. ICC Office of the Prosecutor, Press Conference on Libya, May 16, 2011, http://www.icc-cpi.int/en_menus/icc/structure%20of%20the%20court/office%20of%20the%20prosecutor/reports%20and%20statements/statement/Pages/statement%20icc%20prosecutor%20press%20conference%20on%20libya%2016%20may%202011.aspx.

2. Beth A. Simmons and Allison Danner, "Credible Commitments and the International Criminal Court," *International Organization* 64, no. 2 (2010): 226.

3. Kathryn Sikkink has argued that other national prosecutions of political and military leaders, primarily in Latin America, were an important bridge between the Nuremberg experience and the post-Cold War tribunals. See Kathryn Sikkink, *The Justice Cascade: How Human Rights Prosecutions Are Changing World Politics*, The Norton Series in World Politics (New York: W. W. Norton & Company, 2011).

4. UN Diplomatic Conference of Plenipotentiaries on the Establishment of an International Criminal Court, Rome, 15 June–17 July 1998, Official Records, vol. 2, p. 129, http://untreaty.un.org/cod/icc/rome/proceedings/E/Rome%20Proceedings_v2_e.pdf.

5. Press Release, Secretary-General, "Secretary-General Says Establishment of International Criminal Court is Major Step in March Towards Universal Human Rights, Rule of Law," U.N. Press Release L/2890 (July 18/20, 1998), http://www.un.org/News/Press/docs/1998/19980720.l2890.html.

6. UN Diplomatic Conference of Plenipotentiaries, 67.

7. Ibid., 74.

8. Ibid., 83.

9. Judith N. Shklar, *Legalism* (Cambridge, MA: Harvard University Press, 1964), 110.

10. Luis Moreno-Ocampo, "Statement Made at the Ceremony for the Solemn Undertaking of the Chief Prosecutor of the ICC," June 16, 2003, http://www.icc-cpi.int/nr/rdonlyres/d7572226-264a-4b6b-85e3-2673648b4896/143585/030616_moreno_ocampo_english.pdf. Moreno-Ocampo was quoting and endorsing an earlier comment by court president Philippe Kirsch.

11. Barbara Koremenos, Charles Lipson, and Duncan Snidal, "The Rational Design of International Institutions," *International Organization* 55, no. 4 (2001): 762. (Noting that "states rarely allow international institutions to become significant autonomous actors.")

12. Precisely defining a group of major powers is not easy. This account considers the five permanent members of the Security Council (the United States, the United Kingdom, France, China, and Russia) to be major powers. All have substantial armed forces, sizeable nuclear arsenals, and global interests. The four leading contenders for permanent Security Council seats (Japan, Germany, Brazil, and India) are also treated as major powers, largely as a consequence of their economic power.

13. Kenneth W. Abbott and Duncan Snidal, "Why States Act through Formal International Organizations," *Journal of Conflict Resolution* 42, no. 1 (1998): 3–32.

14. Theodor Meron, "Judicial Independence and Impartiality in International Criminal Tribunals," *American Journal of International Law* 99, no. 2 (2005): 359–69.

15. There are three routes to ICJ jurisdiction: a state can agree in advance to broad ICJ jurisdiction; treaties may specify that the court has jurisdiction; or states can conclude special agreements conferring jurisdiction. See International Court of Justice, "Basis of the Court's Jurisdiction," http://www.icj-cij.org/jurisdiction/index.php?p1=5&p2=1&p3=2.

16. Mia Swart, "[Review] Ruth Mackenzie, Kate Malleson, Penny Martin, and Philippe Sands QC (eds.), *Selecting International Judges: Principle, Process, and Politics*," *Leiden Journal of International Law* 24, no. 3 (2011): 789–92.

17. See Petros C. Mavroidis, "Remedies in the WTO Legal System: Between a Rock and a Hard Place," *European Journal of International Law* 11, no. 4 (2000): 763–813. He notes that "the effectiveness of countermeasures depends on the relative economic importance of the party adopting them" (807).

18. Erik Voeten, "International Judicial Independence," in *Interdisciplinary Perspectives on International Law and International Relations: The State of the Art*, ed. Jeffrey L. Dunoff and Mark A. Pollack (Cambridge: Cambridge University Press, 2012), 421, 428.

19. This study can best be categorized as an interpretive case study, which Jack Levy defines as a project that "aim[s] to explain/interpret a single case as an end in itself rather than to develop broader theoretical generalizations." Jack S. Levy, "Qualitative Methods in International Relations," in *Millennial Reflections on International Studies*, ed. Michael Brecher and Frank P. Harvey (Ann Arbor: University of Michigan Press, 2002). For a good discussion of collaboration between diplomatic history and international relations theory, see Colin Elman and Miriam Fendius Elman, "Diplomatic History and International Relations Theory: Respecting Difference and Crossing Boundaries," *International Security* 22, no. 1 (1997): 5–21.

20. For a discussion of strategies regarding elite interview strategies generally, see Joel D. Aberbach and Bert A. Rockman, "Conducting and Coding Elite

Interviews," *PS: Political Science and Politics* 35, no. 4 (2002): 673–76. See also Jaber F. Gubrium and James A. Holstein, *Handbook of Interview Research: Context and Method* (Thousand Oaks, CA: Sage Publications, 2002).

CHAPTER 1

1. John J. Mearsheimer, "The False Promise of International Institutions," *International Security* 19, no. 3 (1994): 5–49. Jack L. Goldsmith and Eric A. Posner, *The Limits of International Law* (New York: Oxford University Press, 2006).

2. Eric A. Posner and John C. Yoo, "Judicial Independence in International Tribunals," *California Law Review* 93, no. 1 (2005): 1–74.

3. Eric A. Posner, "The Decline of the International Court of Justice," University of Chicago Law School, John M. Olin Law & Economics Working Paper Series, 2004.

4. Kenneth W. Abbott and Duncan Snidal, "Why States Act through Formal International Organizations," *Journal of Conflict Resolution* 42, no. 1 (1998): 16, 18–19.

5. Jacob Katz Cogan, "Competition and Control in International Adjudication," *Virginia Journal of International Law* 48, no. 2 (2008): 415.

6. Karen J. Alter, "Agents or Trustees? International Courts in their Political Context," *European Journal of International Relations* 14, no. 1 (2008): 55.

7. Christopher Rudolph, "Power, Interests, and International Institutions: Regime Complexes and the ICC." Paper presented at the ISA Annual Convention, April 3–6, 2013. San Francisco, CA.

8. Randall W. Stone, *Controlling Institutions: International Organizations and the World Economy* (Cambridge: Cambridge University Press, 2011), 15.

9. Cogan, "Competition and Control in International Adjudication," 411.

10. See Laurence R. Helfer, "Exiting Treaties," *Virginia Law Review* 91, no. 7 (2005): 1579.

11. See Laurence R. Helfer and Anne-Marie Slaughter, "Why States Create International Tribunals: A Response to Professors Posner and Yoo," *California Law Review* 93, no. 3 (2005): 899–956. W. Michael Reisman, *Systems of Control in International Adjudication and Arbitration: Breakdown and Repair* (Durham, NC: Duke University Press, 1992).

12. Laurence R. Helfer, "Why States Create International Tribunals: A Theory of Constrained Independence," in *Conferences on New Political Economy* (Tübingen, Germany: Mohr Siebeck, 2006). See also Beth A. Simmons and Allison Danner, "Credible Commitments and the International Criminal Court," *International Organization* 64, no. 2 (Spring 2010): 225–56.

13. See Kathryn Sikkink, *The Justice Cascade: How Human Rights Prosecutions Are Changing World Politics*, 1st ed. (New York: W. W. Norton & Co., 2011).

14. Edith M. Lederer, "War Crimes Prosecutor Vows to Win Trust," Associated Press, April 23, 2003.

15. Michael N. Barnett and Martha Finnemore, *Rules for the World: International Organizations in Global Politics* (Ithaca, NY: Cornell University Press, 2004), 23.

16. Louise Arbour, "The Need for an Independent and Effective Prosecutor in the Permanent International Criminal Court," *Windsor Yearbook of Access to Justice* 17 (1999): 213.

17. Rome Statute on an International Criminal Court [hereinafter Rome Statute], Preamble, July 17, 1998, UN Doc. A/CONF. 183/9, 2187 U.N.T.S. 90, http://untreaty.un.org/cod/icc/statute/romefra.htm.

18. Alter, "Agents or Trustees? International Courts in their Political Context," 46.

19. See in particular Clifford J. Carrubba, Matthew Gabel, and Charles Hankla, "Judicial Behavior under Political Constraints: Evidence from the European Court of Justice," *American Political Science Review* 102, no. 4 (2008): 435–52. For a subtle analysis in the context of a different European court, see Erik Voeten, "The Impartiality of International Judges: Evidence from the European Court of Human Rights," *American Political Science Review* 102, no. 4 (2008): 417–33. See also Ruth Mackenzie and Philippe Sands, "International Courts and Tribunals and the Independence of the International Judge," *Harvard International Law Journal* 44 (2003): 271–85.

20. Luc Côté, "Reflections on the Exercise of Prosecutorial Discretion in International Criminal Law," *Journal of International Criminal Justice* 3, no. 1 (2005): 162–86. Matthew Brubacher, "Prosecutorial Discretion within the International Criminal Court," *Journal of International Criminal Justice* 2, no. 1 (2004): 71–95. Allison Marston Danner, "Navigating Law and Politics: The Prosecutor of the International Criminal Court and the Independent Counsel," *Stanford Law Review* 55, no. 5 (2003): 1633–65.

CHAPTER 2

1. Richard Bessel, *Germany 1945: From War to Peace* (New York: HarperCollins, 2009), 3, 6, 96–97. Joseph E. Persico, *Nuremberg: Infamy on Trial* (New York: Penguin Books, 1994), 39.

2. Norbert Ehrenfreund, *The Nuremberg Legacy: How the Nazi War Crimes Trials Changed the Course of History* (New York: Palgrave Macmillan, 2007).

3. Gary Jonathan Bass, *Stay the Hand of Vengeance: The Politics of War Crimes Tribunals* (Princeton, NJ: Princeton University Press, 2000), 182.

4. Ibid., 160.

5. Ibid., 154.

6. Ehrenfreund, *The Nuremberg Legacy*, 7–10.

7. Madoka Futamura, *War Crimes Tribunals and Transitional Justice: The Tokyo Trial and the Nuremburg Legacy* (London: Routledge, 2008), 45.

8. Charter of the International Military Tribunal—Annex to the Agreement for the Prosecution and Punishment of the Major War Criminals of the European Axis

("London Agreement"), U.S.-Fr.-U.K.-U.S.S.R., Aug. 8, 1945, 59 Stat. 1544, 82 U.N.T.S. 279, http://www.unhcr.org/refworld/docid/3ae6b39614.html.

9. Justice Robert H. Jackson, Opening Statement before the Nuremberg International Military Tribunal (November 21, 1945) "Trial of the Major War Criminals before the International Military Tribunal, Nuremberg, 14 November 1945–1 October 1946" (Nuremberg, Germany: Secretariat of the International Military Tribunal under the jurisdiction of the Allied Control Authority for Germany, 1947), 2:154, http://www.loc.gov/rr/frd/Military_Law/pdf/NT_Vol-II.pdf.

10. For more on the decision to not prosecute the Japanese emperor, see Herbert P. Bix, *Hirohito and the Making of Modern Japan*, 1st ed. (New York: HarperCollins, 2000), 582–85; and Yoriko Otomo, "The Decision Not to Prosecute the Emperor," in *Beyond Victor's Justice? The Tokyo War Crimes Trial Revisited*, ed. Yuki Tanaka, Tim McCormack, and Gerry Simpson (Leiden: Martinus Nijhoff Publishers, 2011). For more on American and Japanese joint efforts to keep evidence incriminating the emperor out of the trial of General Hideki Tojo, see Robert Harvey, *American Shogun: A Tale of Two Cultures* (Woodstock, NY: Overlook Press, 2006), 375, 377.

11. Foreign Relations of the United States, 1947, Vol. 6, "Japan: Occupation and Control of Japan," Aide Mémoire from the British Embassy to the Department of State, Ref: 302/34/47, Washington, Oct. 9, 1947, para. 2(c), p. 305.

12. Kevin Jon Heller, *The Nuremberg Military Tribunals and the Origins of International Criminal Law* (Oxford: Oxford University Press, 2011), 22.

13. "Trials of War Criminals before the Nuernberg Military Tribunals under Control Council Law No. 10 ("Green Series"), October 1946 to April 1949" (Washington, DC: U.S. Government Printing Office), http://www.loc.gov/rr/frd/Military_Law/NTs_war-criminals.html.

14. David Luban, *Legal Modernism* (Ann Arbor: University of Michigan Press, 1994), 336.

15. Versailles Peace Treaty, part VII, art. 227, June 28, 1919, 13 A.J.I.L. Supp. 151, 385, http://avalon.law.yale.edu/subject_menus/versailles_menu.asp.

16. These initiatives are succinctly described in a 1949 report; see UN Secretary-General, "Historical Survey of the Question of International Criminal Jurisdiction—Memorandum Submitted by the Secretary-General," 1949, A/CN.4/7Rev.1, http://untreaty.un.org/ilc/documentation/english/a_cn4_7_rev1.pdf.

17. Charter of the International Military Tribunal—Annex to the Agreement for the Prosecution and Punishment of the Major War Criminals of the European Axis ("London Agreement"), art. 6(c), U.S.-Fr.-U.K.-U.S.S.R., Aug. 8, 1945, 59 Stat. 1544, 82 U.N.T.S. 279, http://www.unhcr.org/refworld/docid/3ae6b39614.html.

18. Whitney R. Harris, "Justice Jackson at Nuremberg," *International Lawyer* 20, no. 3 (1986): 867.

19. See indictment in Trial of the Major War Criminals before the International Military Tribunal. Nuremberg ("Blue Series"), Nov. 14, 1945 to Oct. 1, 1946, vol. I,

count III(C)(2), p. 54, http://www.loc.gov/rr/frd/Military_Law/pdf/NT_Vol-I. pdf. The indictment indicates that 11,000 Polish prisoners of war were killed in the Katyn Forest near Smolensk in September 1941.

20. Bradley F. Smith, *Reaching Judgment at Nuremberg* (New York: Basic Books, 1977), 299.

21. Quoted in Robert E. Conot, *Justice at Nuremberg*, 1st ed. (New York: Harper & Row, 1983), 68. Letter from Robert Jackson to Harry S. Truman, Oct. 12, 1945, p. 4, Harry S. Truman Presidential Museum & Library, http://www.trumanlibrary. org/whistlestop/study_collections/nuremberg/documents/index.php?pagenumber= 4&documentid=7-2&documentdate=1945-10-12&studycollectionid=nuremberg &groupid=.

22. Karl Doenitz Judgment (Oct. 1, 1946, International Military Tribunal), http:// avalon.law.yale.edu/imt/juddoeni.asp. For an account of the sentences, see also Whitney R. Harris, *Tyranny on Trial: The Trial of the Major German War Criminals at the End of World War II at Nuremberg, Germany, 1945-1946* (Dallas: Southern Methodist University Press, 1999), 478–81.

23. Corfu Channel (U.K. v. Alb.), 1949 I.C.J., http://www.icj-cij.org/docket/index. php?p1=3&p2=3&k=cd&case=1.

24. Foreign Relations of the United States, 1946, Vol. 1, "General, the United Nations," IO Files: US/A/C.6/25, United States Delegation Working Paper, New York, November 14, 1946, Proposal Regarding Draft Resolution on Codification of International Law, "Discussion," 540.

25. Benjamin B. Ferencz, *An International Criminal Court, a Step Toward World Peace: A Documentary History and Analysis*, 2 vols. (London: Oceana Publications, 1980), 2:6–7. Citing resolutions adopted by the UN General Assembly during the second part of its first session, from Oct. 23 to Dec. 15, 1946, resolutions 94 and 95, reproduced in Ferencz, 127.

26. UN General Assembly, *Prevention and Punishment of the Crime of Genocide*, December 9, 1948, A/RES/260, available at: http://www.refworld.org/ docid/3b00f0873.html.

27. Foreign Relations of the United States, 1948, Vol. 1, Part 1, "General, the United Nations," IO Files: US (P)/A/343 United States Delegation Position Paper, Paris, December 6, 1948, Report of the Sixth Committee on the Draft Convention on Genocide, Section 2, para. 3, 299. In supporting the provision, a US official foreshadowed the concept of complementarity that would be so central in the eventual ICC. "Jurisdiction of the international tribunal in any case shall be subject to a finding by the tribunal that the State in which the crime was committed had failed to take appropriate measures to bring to trial persons who, in the judgment of the court, should have been brought to trial." UNSG 1949 memo, note 16 above, 39.

28. A. H. Feller, "We Move, Slowly, Toward World Law," *New York Times*, June 5, 1949, SM10.

29. Ehrenfreund, *The Nuremberg Legacy*, 35.

30. Susanne Karstedt, "The Nuremberg Tribunal and German Society: International Justice and Local Judgment in Post-Conflict Reconstruction," in *The Legacy of Nuremberg: Civilising Influence or Institutionalised Vengeance?*, ed. David A. McCormack and Timothy L. H. Blumenthal, International Humanitarian Law Series (Leiden: Martinus Nijhoff Publishers, 2008), 26–28.

31. "World Crime Court Opposed by Briton," *New York Times*, August 3, 1951, 4.

32. "U.N. Powers Split on Crime Tribunal: France Backs World Court for Genocide and Aggression—Impractical, Britain Says," *New York Times*, November 8, 1952, 4.

33. U.N. GAOR, 7th Sess., 1st phase plen. mtg. U.N. Doc. A/2186 and Add. 1 (Sept. 16, 1952), reproduced in Ferencz, *An International Criminal Court, a Step Toward World Peace*, 2:379.

34. U.N. GAOR, 7th Sess. (Nov. 12, 1952), reproduced in Ferencz, *An International Criminal Court, a Step Toward World Peace*, 2:409.

35. U.N. GAOR, 7th Sess., 1st phase plen. mtg. U.N. Doc. A/2186 and Add. 1 (Sept. 16, 1952), reproduced in Ferencz, *An International Criminal Court, a Step Toward World Peace*, 2:367–68.

36. Draft Statute for an International Criminal Court, Chapter III, art. 26, in Annex to Report of the 1953 Committee on International Criminal Jurisdiction, 27 July to 20 August 1953, UN General Assembly Official Records: Ninth Session, Supplement No. 12 (A/2645), reproduced in Ferencz, *An International Criminal Court, a Step Toward World Peace*, 2:455.

37. Marlies Glasius, *The International Criminal Court: A Global Civil Society Achievement*, Routledge Advances in International Relations and Global Politics (London: Routledge, 2006), 8–9. Richard A. Falk, "Nuremberg and Vietnam," *New York Times*, December 27, 1970, 165. Bertrand Russell, *War Crimes in Vietnam* (London: George Allen & Unwin Ltd., 1967), 125–27, 130.

38. M. Cherif Bassiouni and Daniel H. Derby, "Final Report on the Establishment of an International Criminal Court for the Implementation of the Apartheid Convention and Other Relevant International Instruments (Symposium on the Future of Human Rights)," *Hofstra Law Review* 9, no. 2 (1981): 525–27.

39. See Ferencz, *An International Criminal Court, a Step Toward World Peace*.

40. Benjamin B. Ferencz, *A Common Sense Guide to World Peace* (New York: Oceana Publications, 1985), xi.

41. See Jeff McMahan, "Just Cause for War," *Ethics & International Affairs* 19, no. 3 (2005): 1–21. J. Bryan Hehir, "Just War Theory in a Post-Cold War World," *Journal of Religious Ethics* 20, no. 2 (1992): 237–57.

42. Geneva Convention Relative to the Protection of Civilian Persons in Time of War (Fourth Geneva Convention), Aug. 12, 1949, 6 U.S.T. 3516, 75 U.N.T.S. 287, http://www.unhcr.org/refworld/docid/3ae6b36d2.html.

43. Israel Shenker, "U.N. Struggling with Perennial and Elusive Problem: Defining Aggression," *New York Times*, December 9, 1971, 14.

44. G.A. Res. 3314 (XXIX), Annex (Dec. 14, 1974), http://www.un.org/documents/ga/res/29/ares29.htm.

45. Paul Hofmann, "Debate on Terror Postponed by U.N.: Recommended by Committee U.S., Canada Seek Law Assembly to Take Up Issue at '75 Session—Definition of Aggression Approved," *New York Times*, December 15, 1974. Julius Stone, *Conflict through Consensus: United Nations Approaches to Aggression* (Baltimore: Johns Hopkins University Press, 1977), 1–3. Stone references UN documents A/C.6/SR 1477, p. 6 (British remarks); A/C.6/SR 1480, p. 15 (Soviet remarks); A/C.6/SR 1475, p. 8 (Chinese remarks).

46. See, e.g., Julius Stone, "Hopes and Loopholes in the 1974 Definition of Aggression." *American Journal of International Law* 71, no. 2 (1977): 224–46; Louis Sohn, "The Definition of Aggression," *Virginia Law Review* 45 (1959): 697.

47. Michael Dobbs, "Bosnia Crystallizes U.S. Post-Cold War Role; As Two Administrations Wavered, the Need for U.S. Leadership Became Clear," *Washington Post*, December 3, 1995, A1. Robin Wright, "When No One is Prepared to Say 'No' to Aggression: Bosnia: The Failure to Halt Ethnic Strife is Having a Deep and Destructive Impact on the Post-Cold War World. Goodby Desert Storm Principles," *Los Angeles Times*, May 23, 1993, 1. Martha Brill Olcott, "Bosnia May Become First Post-Cold War Fatality," *Dayton (OH) Daily News*, September 25, 1993.

48. See, e.g., Michael Matheson, *Council Unbound: The Growth of UN Decision Making on Conflict and Postconflict Issues after the Cold War* (Washington, DC: US Institute of Peace Press, 2006); David L. Bosco, *Five to Rule Them All: The UN Security Council and the Making of the Modern World* (New York: Oxford, 2009), 163–83.

49. See, e.g., Jane Perlez, "No Unity on Balkans at Europe Summit," *New York Times*, December 7, 1994, A12; Ian Traynor, David Hearst, and Yigal Chazan, "US and Russia at Odds as Serbs Batter Gorazde," *Guardian*, April 22, 1994, 20.

50. S.C. Res. 780, U.N. Doc. S/RES/780 (Oct. 6, 1992).

51. David Scheffer, *All the Missing Souls: A Personal History of the War Crimes Tribunals* (Princeton, NJ: Princeton University Press, 2012), 18.

52. S.C. Res. 808, ¶ 1, U.N. Doc. S/RES/808 (Feb. 22, 1993).

53. S.C. Res. 955, U.N. Doc. S/RES/955 (Nov. 8, 1994).

54. See, e.g., Richard Goldstone, "Justice as a Tool for Peace-making: Truth Commissions and International Criminal Tribunals," *N.Y.U. Journal of International Law and Politics* 28 (1995): 485; Theodor Meron, "The Case for War Crimes Trials in Yugoslavia," *Foreign Affairs* 72, no. 3 (1993): 122–35.

55. S.C. provisional verbatim record, 3175th mtg. at 11, U.N. Doc. S/PV.3175 (Feb. 22, 1993).

56. Author interview with David Scheffer.

57. John Hagan, *Justice in the Balkans: Prosecuting War Crimes in the Hague Tribunal* (Chicago: University of Chicago Press, 2003), 55–56.

58. Richard J. Goldstone, *For Humanity: Reflections of a War Crimes Investigator* (New Haven, CT: Yale University Press, 2000), 84.

59. Hagan, *Justice in the Balkans*, 71.

60. Jane Perlez, "Serb Lawyer Vows Not to Cooperate with War Crimes Tribunal," *New York Times*, March 6, 1996, A11. William Drozdiak, "War Crimes Tribunal Arraigns 1st Suspect; Bosnian Serb Pleads Not Guilty to Charges That He Killed Muslims at Detention Camp," *Washington Post*, April 27, 1995, A31. Dean E. Murphy, "Serb General Indicted by U.N. Tribunal," *Los Angeles Times*, March 2, 1996, 1.

61. 3453rd Meeting of the UN Security Council, UN Document S/PV.3453 (Nov. 8, 1994).

62. Victor Peskin, *International Justice in Rwanda and the Balkans: Virtual Trials and the Struggle for State Cooperation* (Cambridge: Cambridge University Press, 2008), 151.

63. Alison Des Forges, quoted in Human Rights Watch, "Prosecutorial Incompetence Frees Rwandan Genocide Suspect; Rights Group Deplores Failings at International Criminal Tribunal for Rwanda," news release, November 9, 1999, http://www.hrw.org/news/1999/11/08/prosecutorial-incompetence-frees-rwandan-genocide-suspect.

64. Human Rights Watch documented hundreds of indiscriminate killings committed by the Rwandan Patriotic Front (RPF) as the forces advanced into Rwanda in mid-July 1994. See "Human Rights Watch World Report 1995" (New York, 1995), paras. 3, 4 "The New Government of Rwanda" http://www.hrw.org/reports/1995/WR95/AFRICA-08.htm#P397_139563. See also Alison Des Forges, "Leave None to Tell the Story" (Human Rights Watch, 1999). Section on RPF available at: http://www.hrw.org/legacy/reports/1999/rwanda/Geno1-3-03.htm#P86_35545. Allegations of RPF killings of civilians resurfaced again in 1997; see "Attacked by All Sides: Civilians and the War in Eastern Zaire" (Human Rights Watch, 1997), http://www.hrw.org/legacy/reports/1997/zaire2/zaire0397web.pdf. An August 1997 report released by the United Nations Human Rights Field Operation in Rwanda also detailed RPF abuses in May and June 1997. For more, see Human Rights Watch, "Human Rights Watch and the FIDH [International Federation of Human Rights Leagues] Demand End to Killings of Civilians by Rwandan Soldiers," news release, Aug. 14, 1997, http://www.hrw.org/news/1997/08/13/human-rights-watch-and-fidh-demand-end-killings-civilians-rwandan-soldiers.

65. "Soros Foundations Network 2001 Report" (Open Society Foundations), 102, http://www.soros.org/sites/default/files/a_complete_9.pdf. "Soros Foundations Network 2002 Report" (Open Society Foundations), 170, http://www.soros.org/sites/default/files/a_complete_report_0.pdf. MacArthur Foundation, "MacArthur Announces $1.5 Million in Grants Related to International Criminal Court," news release, Nov. 15, 2002, http://www.macfound.org/

press/press-releases/the-macarthur-foundation-announces-15-million-in-grants-related-to-international-criminal-court/. MacArthur Foundation, "Strengthening the International Criminal Court," news release, Jan. 30, 2004, http://www.macfound.org/press/press-releases/macarthur-provides-more-than-17-million-in-support-of-the-international-criminal-court-january-30-2004/.

66. The discussion on the court's likely deterrent effect is extensive and varied. See David L. Bosco, "The International Criminal Court and Crime Prevention: Byproduct or Conscious Goal?" *Michigan State University College of Law Journal of International Law* 19, no. 2 (2011): 163. For canvassing and assessing the various studies on the ICC's preventive impact, see James F. Alexander, "The International Criminal Court and the Prevention of Atrocities: Predicting the Court's Impact," *Villanova Law Review* 54, no. 1 (2009): 1–56; Julian Ku and Jide Nzelibe, "Do International Criminal Tribunals Deter or Exacerbate Humanitarian Atrocities?" *Washington University Law Review* 84, no. 4 (2006): 777–833; Payam Akhavan, "Beyond Impunity: Can International Criminal Justice Prevent Future Atrocities?" *American Journal of International Law* 95, no. 1 (2001): 7–31. Michael L. Smidt, "The International Criminal Court: An Effective Means of Deterrence?" *Military Law Review* 167 (2001): 156–240. David Wippman, "Atrocities, Deterrence, and the Limits of International Justice," *Fordham International Law Journal* 23 (1999): 473–88.

67. "The Quest for International Justice" (Amnesty International, 1995), 11, http://www.amnesty.org/en/library/asset/IOR40/004/1995/en/4a11dc12-eb48-11dd-8c1f-275b8445d07d/ior400041995en.pdf.

68. Draft Statute for an International Criminal Court, adopted by the UN International Law Commission, 46th session, 1994, and submitted to the General Assembly, http://untreaty.un.org/ilc/texts/instruments/english/draft%20articles/7_4_1994.pdf.

69. Philippe Kirsch and John T. Holmes, "The Birth of the International Criminal Court," in *The International Criminal Court*, ed. Olympia Bekou and Robert Cryer (Aldershot, England: Ashgate/Dartmouth, 2004), 8.

70. See Mitja Mertens, "The International Criminal Court: A European Success Story," *EU Diplomacy Papers* (2011), http://www.coleurope.eu/website/study/eu-international-relations-and-diplomacy-studies/research-activities/eu-diplomacy. Glasius, *The International Criminal Court*, 42.

71. Author interview with John Washburn.

72. Statement by H. E. Ambassador Chen Shiqiu, Sixth Committee of the UN General Assembly (Oct. 30, 1995), http://www.iccnow.org/documents/China1PrepCmt30Oct95.pdf.

73. Statement by the Representative of the United Kingdom, Sixth Committee of the UN General Assembly (Nov. 2, 1995), http://www.iccnow.org/documents/UK1PrepCmt2Nov95.pdf.

74. "Role of Security Council in Triggering Prosecution Discussed in Preparatory Committee for International Criminal Court" (Apr. 4, 1996), http://www. iccnow.org/documents/RoleofSC4Apr96.pdf.

75. U.S. Mission to the UN, "Agenda Item 142: Establishment of an International Criminal Court," news release 182, November 1, 1995, http://www.state.gov/documents/organization/65827.pdf.

76. Christopher Keith Hall, "The First Two Sessions of the UN Preparatory Committee on the Establishment of an International Criminal Court," *American Journal of International Law* 91, no. 1 (1997): 182.

77. "Bosnia War Crimes Prosecutor Points Finger at France," Agence France-Presse, December 13, 1997. Christian Spillmann, "Paris Denies Inaction on Bosnian War Criminals," Agence France Presse, December 14, 1997. "French FM Meets Prosecutor Amid Row over Bosnian War Criminals," Agence France Presse, December 15, 1997. "France Determined Bosnian War Criminals Will Not Escape: Jospin," Agence France-Presse, December 16, 1997. "UN Prosecutor to Hold Talks in Paris," Agence France-Presse, May 4, 1999. "General Morillon to be First French Soldier to Testify at ICTY," Agence France-Press, June 15, 1999. International Criminal Tribunal for the former Yugoslavia, "Statement by the Prosecutor Louise Arbour Following Her Meeting with the French Minister of Foreign Affairs, Mr. Hubert Vedrine," news release, December 15, 1997, http://www.icty.org/sid/7429/en.

78. World Federalist Movement, "Views of the World Federalist Movement on the Establishment of a Permanent International Criminal Court," news release, March 25, 1996, http://www.iccnow.org/documents/1PrepCmtViewsonICCWFM.pdf.

79. Author interview with Roger Clark.

80. Ronen Steinke, *The Politics of International Criminal Justice: German Perspectives from Nuremberg to the Hague* (Oxford: Hart Publishing, 2012), 104, 106.

81. Human Rights Watch, "Commentary for the Preparatory Commission on the Establishment of a Permanent International Criminal Court," March 1996, http://www.iccnow.org/documents/1PrepCmtCommentaryHRW.pdf.

82. G.A. Res. 50/46, UN Doc A/50/49 (Dec. 18, 1995).

83. Fanny Benedetti and John L. Washburn, "Drafting the International Criminal Court Treaty: Two Years to Rome and an Afterword on the Rome Diplomatic Conference," *Global Governance* 5, no. 1 (1999): 3.

84. Michael Dobbs, "U.S. Appoints Envoy on Bosnia War Crimes," *Washington Post*, May 21, 1997.

85. See John M. Goshko, "Britain Differs on U.N. Court; Proposed Tribunal's Power, Reach at Issue," *Washington Post*, December 12, 1997, A51.

86. Author interview with Gilbert Bitti.

87. Author interview with Béatrice le Frapper du Hellen.

88. Scheffer, *All the Missing Souls*, 177–78.

89. Author interview with Gilbert Bitti.

90. Author interview with former US diplomat.

91. Author interview with William Lietzau.

92. M. Cherif Bassiouni, "Preface to the Second Edition," in *Commentary on the Rome Statute of the International Criminal Court: Observers' Notes, Article by Article*, ed. Otto Triffterer (Munich, Germany: Verlag C. H. Beck oHG, Hart Publishing, and Nomos, 2008), xxv.

93. United Nations, "Secretary-General Says Establishment of International Criminal Court is Major Step in March towards Universal Human Rights, Rule of Law," news release, L/ROM/23, July 20, 1998 (remarks from July 18, 1998), http://www.un.org/News/Press/docs/1998/19980720.l2890.html.

94. Farhan Haq, "Alliances Cut through North-South Divide," *Terra Viva*, June 22, 1998, http://www.ips.org/icc/tv2206.htm.

95. Author interview with Hans Peter Kaul.

96. For analyses of this trend, see P. J. Simmons, "Learning to Live with NGOs," *Foreign Policy*, no. 112 (Autumn 1998): 82–96. See also David Rieff, "Civil Society and the Future of the Nation-State: The False Dawn of Civil Society," *Nation* 268, no. 7 (1999): 11–16.

97. Philippe Kirsch and John T. Holmes, "The Birth of the International Criminal Court: The 1998 Rome Conference," *Canadian Yearbook of International Law* 36 (1998): 13.

98. Gary T. Dempsey, "Reasonable Doubt: The Case Against the Proposed International Criminal Court" (Washington, DC: Cato Institute, July 16, 1998), http://www.cato.org/pubs/pas/pa-311es.html. Karl K. Schonberg, "The General's Diplomacy: U.S. Military Influence in the Treaty Process, 1992–2000," *Seton Hall Journal of Diplomacy and International Affairs* 68, no. 3 (2002): 79.

99. Barbara Crossette, "Helms Vows to Make War on U.N. Court," *New York Times*, March 27, 1998.

100. James Rubin, U.S. Department of State, news briefing, June 15, 1998, http://usembassy-israel.org.il/publish/press/state/archive/1998/june/sd1616.htm.

101. Ramesh Jaura and Alison Dickens, "US Speak More Softly," *Terra Viva*, July 16, 1998, http://www.ips.org/icc/tv1607.htm.

102. Author interview with member of the US negotiating team.

103. Michael J. Struett, *The Politics of Constructing the International Criminal Court: NGOs, Discourse, and Agency*, 1st ed. (New York: Palgrave Macmillan, 2008), 117–18.

104. Jaura and Dickens, "US Speak More Softly."

105. "India Blasts Special Treatment for Security Council," *Terra Viva*, June 17, 1998, http://www.ips.org/icc/tv1706.htm.

106. See *The International Criminal Court—The Making of the Rome Statute: Issues, Negotiations, Results*, ed. Roy S. Lee, Project on International Courts and Tribunals (The Hague: Kluwer Law International, 1999).

107. Author interview with Prince Zeid.

108. Philippe Kirsch, "The Development of the Rome Statute," in *The International Criminal Court—The Making of the Rome Statute: Issues, Negotiations, Results*, ed. Roy S. Lee, Project on International Courts and Tribunals (The Hague, Boston: Kluwer Law International, 1999), 453.

109. Author interview with Philippe Kirsch. See also Cedric Ryngaert, "The International Criminal Court and Universal Jurisdiction: A Fraught Relationship?" *New Criminal Law Review: An International and Interdisciplinary Journal* 12, no. 4 (2009): 499. For a selection of views on jurisdiction expressed by state delegations, see UN Diplomatic Conference of Plenipotentiaries on the Establishment of an International Criminal Court, Rome, 15 June–17 July 1998, Official Records, vol. 2, Summary records of the plenary meetings and of the meetings of the Committee of the Whole, pp. 183–191, http://untreaty.un.org/cod/icc/rome/proceedings/E/Rome%20Proceedings_v2_e.pdf.

110. See "War Crimes Tribunal is a Go," *Toronto Star*, July 18, 1998.

111. Author interview with Richard Dicker.

112. Author interview with major-power diplomats.

113. Scheffer, *All the Missing Souls*, 220.

114. Author interview with Philippe Kirsch. Scheffer, *All the Missing Souls*, 220–22.

115. Statement by William R. Pace, Coalition for the International Criminal Court, 10 Years' Celebration of the Adoption of the Rome Statute, Peace Palace-The Hague (July 3, 2008).

116. Author interview with John Washburn, Convener for the American Non-Governmental Organizations Coalition for the International Criminal Court (AMICC).

117. Kirsch and Holmes, "The Birth of the International Criminal Court: The 1998 Rome Conference," 37.

CHAPTER 3

1. For more detail on unsuccessful proposals to include terrorism, drug trafficking, and mercenaries in the court's jurisdiction, see Kai Ambos and Otto Triffterer, *Commentary on the Rome Statute of the International Criminal Court*, 2nd ed. (Munich, Germany: Verlag C. H. Beck oHG, Hart Publishing, and Nomos, 2008), 130–32. David J. Scheffer, "Staying the Course with the International Criminal Court," *Cornell International Law Journal* 35, no. 1 (2002): 50 n. 7, pp. 73–74, 83. For accounts of discussions in Rome on including these crimes, see UN Diplomatic Conference of Plenipotentiaries on the Establishment of an International Criminal Court, Rome, 15 June–17 July 1998, Official Records, vol. 2, Summary records of the plenary meetings and of the meetings of the Committee of the Whole, 6th meeting (June 18, 1998), pp. 171–172, http://untreaty.un.org/cod/icc/rome/proceedings/E/Rome%20Proceedings_v2_e.pdf.

2. Rome Statute of the International Criminal Court ("Rome Statute") art. 6, July 17, 1998, UN Doc. A/CONF. 183/9, 2187 U.N.T.S. 90, http://untreaty.un.org/cod/icc/statute/romefra.htm.

3. Ibid., art. 7.

4. Ambos and Triffterer, *Commentary on the Rome Statute of the International Criminal Court*, 228, 229.

5. Ibid., 369.

6. Ibid., 410–13.

7. Rome Statute, arts. 7(1)(g), 7(2)(f), 8(2)(e)(vi), July 17, 1998, UN Doc. A/CONF. 183/9, 2187 U.N.T.S. 90, http://untreaty.un.org/cod/icc/statute/romefra.htm.

8. Ibid., art. 42(1).

9. Ibid., art. 46.

10. Ibid., arts. 36(8)(a)(i–iii).

11. Ibid., art. 15(1).

12. Ibid., art. 15(3–5).

13. Ibid., arts. 12(2)(a–b) respectively provide for this jurisdiction.

14. For a summary of the discussions over jurisdiction, see Philippe Kirsch and John T. Holmes, "The Rome Conference on an International Criminal Court: The Negotiating Process," *American Journal of International Law* 93, no. 1 (1999): 4. For additional detail, see Ambos and Triffterer, *Commentary on the Rome Statute of the International Criminal Court*, 539–61. For very detailed accounts of these discussions, see UN Diplomatic Conference of Plenipotentiaries on the Establishment of an International Criminal Court, Rome, 15 June–17 July 1998, Official Records, vol. 2, Summary records of the plenary meetings and of the meetings of the Committee of the Whole, 7th, 8th, and 9th meetings (June 19 and June 22, 1998), pp. 182–199, http://untreaty.un.org/cod/icc/rome/proceedings/E/Rome%20Proceedings_v2_e.pdf. These discussions on preconditions to exercise of jurisdiction and temporal jurisdiction refer to drafts of arts. 6, 7, 8, and 9, pp. 22–24.

15. Rome Statute, arts. 17–19, July 17, 1998, UN Doc. A/CONF. 183/9, 2187 U.N.T.S. 90, http://untreaty.un.org/cod/icc/statute/romefra.htm.

16. Rome Statute, art. 87(7).

17. William Pace, "A Victory for Peace," *International Criminal Court Monitor*, June 2002, 1, http://www.iccnow.org/documents/monitor21.200106.english.pdf.

18. James Bone, "War Crimes Court Pits United States against the World," *Times* (London), April 11, 2002, 19.

19. Thomas W. Lippman, "America Avoids the Stand; Why the U.S. Objects to a World Criminal Court," *Washington Post*, July 26, 1998, C1.

20. Ruth Wedgwood, "Fiddling in Rome: America and the International Criminal Court," *Foreign Affairs* 77, no. 6 (1998): 20.

21. "A Historic Vote for Justice," *Japan Times*, July 20, 1998.

22. "Nothing Gained by America's Global Tantrum," *Canberra Times*, July 21, 1998, A9.

23. "Canada Shines on World Stage," *Toronto Star*, July 21, 1998, A14.

24. Rupert Cornwell, "US Rebuffed as International War-Crimes Court is Backed," *Independent* (London), July 19, 1998, 17. John Hooper and Ian Black, "Self-Interest Brings Court into Contempt; Cynicism and Special Pleading are Marring Attempts to Create World Justice," *Guardian* (London), July 15, 1998, 17.

25. David Scheffer, *All the Missing Souls: A Personal History of the War Crimes Tribunals* (Princeton, NJ: Princeton University Press, 2012), 229–31.

26. David Scheffer, U.S. Department of State briefing, July 31, 1998, http://www.amicc.org/docs/Scheffer7_31_98.pdf.

27. David J. Scheffer, Remarks to the UN General Assembly, Oct. 21, 1998, David J. Scheffer, "The U.S. Perspective on the ICC," in *The United States and the International Criminal Court: National Security and International Law*, ed. Carl Kaysen and Sarah B. Sewall (Lanham, MD: Rowman & Littlefield Publishers, 2000), 116.

28. David J. Scheffer, Remarks to the UN General Assembly, Oct. 21, 1998.

29. Mike Trickey, "Canada, U.S. at Odds over World Court," *Gazette* (Montreal), June 12, 2000, A10.

30. Press Release, Secretary-General, Secretary-General Urges "Like-Minded" States to Ratify Statute of International Criminal Court, U.N. Press Release SG/SM/6686 (Sept. 1, 1998), http://www.un.org/news/Press/docs/1998/19980901.sgsm6686.html.

31. Author interview with Judge Philippe Kirsch.

32. Ibid.

33. Russian Federation, Proposal submitted to the Preparatory Commission for the International Criminal Court by the Russian Federation on the definition of the crime of aggression, U.N. Doc. PCNICC/1999/DP.12 (July 29, 1999), http://www.un.org/Docs/journal/asp/ws.asp?m=PCNICC/1999/DP.12.

34. David Connett, John Hooper, and Peter Beaumont, "Pinochet Arrested in London," *Guardian* (London), October 17, 1998, http://www.guardian.co.uk/world/1998/oct/18/pinochet.chile.

35. To the extent the case against Pinochet was built on crimes against Spanish nationals in Chile, it can be seen as an example not of universal jurisdiction but passive personality jurisdiction. However, the Spanish case was expanded to include non-Spanish nationals. See Juan E. Mendez, "National Reconciliation, Transnational Justice, and the International Criminal Court," *Ethics & International Affairs* 15, no. 1 (2001): 25–44.

36. See Ian Brownlie, *Principles of Public International Law* (New York: Oxford University Press, 1990): 304–5; Kenneth C. Randall, "Universal Jurisdiction under International Law," *Texas Law Review* 66 (1990): 785–841.

37. Eduardo Gallardo, "Arrest of Former Dictator Rattles Chile's Democratic Transition," Associated Press, October 22, 1998.

38. Jeremy Rabkin, interview by Phil Ponce, *News Hour with Jim Lehrer*, Public Broadcasting System (PBS), December 2, 1998, http://www.pbs.org/newshour/bb/latin_america/july-dec98/pinochet_12-2.html.

39. John R. Bolton, "Courting Danger: What's Wrong with the International Criminal Court," *National Interest*, no. 54 (Winter 1998/1999): 60–71.

40. For Bolton's perspective on the legitimacy of the court and prosecutor, see John R. Bolton, "The Risks and Weaknesses of the International Criminal Court from America's Perspective," *Law and Contemporary Problems* 64, no. 1 (2001): 169. John R. Bolton, "American Justice and the International Criminal Court," *DISAM (Defense Institute of Security Assistance Management) Journal of International Security Assistance Management* 26, no. 2 (2003): 28. For a discussion on concerns regarding lack of limits to ICC jurisdiction, see Bolton, "The Risks and Weaknesses of the International Criminal Court from America's Perspective," 169–71. Bolton, "American Justice and the International Criminal Court." For concerns about the prosecutor's political motivations, see John R. Bolton, *Surrender Is Not an Option: Defending America at the United Nations* (New York: Threshold Editions, 2007), 85. For a description of efforts to secure more than one hundred bilateral agreements ensuring no Americans, even private non-military citizens, would be surrendered to the ICC, see ibid., 85–87. Bolton, "American Justice and the International Criminal Court," 28–30.

41. Slobodan Lekic, "Arrests of War Crimes Suspects Seen as Key to Peace in Bosnia," Associated Press, May 23, 1997.

42. William Drozdiak, "NATO Chiefs Block Call for Pursuit of War Criminals," *Washington Post*, June 13, 1997, A36.

43. Theodor Meron, "Answering for War Crimes: Lessons from the Balkans," *Foreign Affairs* 76, no. 1 (1997): 8.

44. Chris Hedges, "NATO Troops Kill a Serbian Suspect in War Atrocities," *New York Times*, July 11, 1997, A1.

45. Ben Macintyre, "Prosecutor Says French Harbour War Criminals in Bosnia," *Times* (London), December 15, 1997.

46. Charles Trueheart, "France Splits with Court over Bosnia; Generals Won't Testify in War Crimes Cases," *Washington Post*, December 16, 1997, A22.

47. John Hagan, *Justice in the Balkans: Prosecuting War Crimes in the Hague Tribunal* (Chicago: University of Chicago Press, 2003), 105–7.

48. Charles Trueheart, "Bosnian Serb Wanted for Genocide Arrested; War Crimes Tribunal Charges General Led Massacre of Muslims," *Washington Post*, December 3, 1998, A1.

49. Hagan, *Justice in the Balkans*, 110–12.

50. Paul Knox, "Canadian Judge's Bokl Move Hailed," *Globe and Mail*, January 19, 1999, A9.

51. Scheffer, *All the Missing Souls*, 259.

52. Hagan, *Justice in the Balkans*, 115–17.

53. Wesley Clark, *Waging Modern War* (New York: Public Affairs, 2001), 160.

54. Scheffer, *All the Missing Souls*, 262–64.

55. Janet Wilson, "Prosecutor Arbour on Verge of Indicting Milosevic," *Los Angeles Times*, May 27, 1999, A1. Joy Copley and Chris Stephen, "Milosevic Indicted for War Crimes," *Scotsman* (Edinburgh), May 27, 1999, 1. Hagan, *Justice in the Balkans*, 121.

56. Author interview with Louise Arbour.

57. Hagan, *Justice in the Balkans*, 121. Hagan cites Ed Vulliamy and Patrick Wintour, "War in the Balkans: Hawks Smell a Tyrant's Blood: NATO's New Confidence Suggests That the Neck of Slobodan Milosevic, the Butcher of Belgrade, May Itself Now Be on the Block," *Observer* (London), May 30, 1999, 15.

58. Scheffer, *All the Missing Souls*, 278.

59. Hagan, *Justice in the Balkans*, 122.

60. Steven Lee Myers, "Chinese Embassy Bombing: A Wide Net of Blame," *New York Times*, April 17, 2000, A1. Richard Boudreaux and John-Thor Dahlburg, "Crisis in Yugoslavia: NATO Planes Hit Chinese Embassy in Belgrade; 2 Die," *Los Angeles Times*, May 8, 1999, 1.

61. "Civilian Deaths in the NATO Air Campaign" (Human Rights Watch, 2000), 5, http://www.hrw.org/sites/default/files/reports/natbm002.pdf.

62. Scheffer, *All the Missing Souls*, 279.

63. Carla Del Ponte, *Madame Prosecutor: Confrontations with Humanity's Worst Criminals and the Culture of Impunity: A Memoir* (New York: Other Press, 2009), 60 (emphasis added).

64. U.N. Security Council, 55th Sess. 4150th mtg. at 3, U.N. Doc. S/PV.4150 (June 2, 2000), http://www.un.org/ga/search/view_doc.asp?symbol=S/PV.4150. See also International Criminal Tribunal for the former Yugoslavia, "Prosecutor's Report on the NATO Bombing Campaign," news release, June 13, 2000, http://www.icty.org/sid/7846.

65. For reference to the interview, see Jon Holbrook, "World Court is a Creature of Politics rather than Justice," *The Times*, September 26, 2000.

66. Lisa Fitterman, "NATO and the Rule of Law: Legal Experts Say Milosevic Has a Case When He Takes Allies to Court," *The Gazette* (Montreal), May 9, 1999, B3.

67. See, for example, Robert Skidelsky and Michael Ignatieff, "Is Military Intervention over Kosovo Justified?" *Prospect* (London), May 3-4, June 20, 1999, http://www.prospectmagazine.co.uk/magazine/military-intervention-kosovo-justified/.

68. Serbia filed the cases on April 29, 1999. See Legality of Use of Force (Serb. v. Belg., Can., Fra., Ger., It., Neth., Port., U.K.) 1999 I.C.J. (April 29) (application). Legality of Use of Force (Yugo. v. Spain, U.S.) 1999 I.C.J. (April 29) (application).

69. See, for example, "Press Conference with (Russian) State Duma Speaker Sergey Baburin and Vice Chairman of the State Duma Defense Committee Alexei Arbatov on Kosovo," *Official Kremlin International News Broadcast*, July 6, 1999; and Igor Ivanov, "Russia in the Changing World: The President and the Foreign

Ministry Will Seek to Build a Multipolar World," *Ngezavisimaya Gazeta*, June 25, 1999, 1, via Official Kremlin International News Broadcast.

70. For a good description of Milošević's downfall and Western pressure, see "Milosevic in the Hague: What it Means for Yugoslavia and the Region," in *Balkans Briefing* (Belgrade/Brussels: International Crisis Group, July 6, 2001), http://www.crisisgroup.org/~/media/Files/europe/Serbia%2016. For detail on European economic pressure to turn over Milošević, see British Broadcasting Corporation (BBC), "Aid Linked to Milosevic Removal," October 8, 1999, http://news.bbc.co.uk/2/hi/europe/469228.stm. See also BBC, "Milosevic Extradition Unlocks Aid Coffers," June 29, 2001, http://news.bbc.co.uk/2/hi/europe/1413144.stm.

71. Kofi Annan's remarks to the Preparatory Commission for the International Criminal Court, "Preparatory Committee—3—1st Meeting (AM)" news release L/2907, February 16, 1999, http://www.un.org/News/Press/docs/1999/19990216.l2907.html.

72. Stan Lehman, "Judge Who Sought Pinochet Extradition Calls for Ratification of Treaty Creating War Crimes Court," Associated Press, September 23, 2000.

73. Associated Press, "Pope Backs Global Human Rights," December 13, 1999, http://www.apnewsarchive.com/1999/Pope-Backs-Global-Human-Rights/id-3bffc9291a490c4a4cebcc5c0b2c786d.

74. Joe Lauria, "Canada Launches Campaign for Global War Crimes Court," *Ottawa Citizen*, September 14, 2000.

75. Michael J. Struett, *The Politics of Constructing the International Criminal Court: NGOs, Discourse, and Agency*, 1st ed. (New York: Palgrave Macmillan, 2008), 136–42.

76. For accounts of these events, see "Human Rights Watch World Report 2000" (New York: Human Rights Watch), "International Criminal Court," para. 17, under "The Role of the NGO Coalition (CICC)," http://www.hrw.org/legacy/wr2k/Issues-09.htm. "Human Rights Watch World Report 2001" (New York: Human Rights Watch), "International Justice: International Criminal Court," under "The Work of Nongovernmental Organizations," http://www.hrw.org/legacy/wr2k1/special/icc.html#icc. Ibid., "International Justice: International Criminal Court," under "International Criminal Court Campaign Developments," http://www.hrw.org/legacy/wr2k2/internationaljustice.html#International%20Criminal%20Court.

77. For a selection of studies exploring patterns in signing and ratification of the International Criminal Court, see Eric Neumayer, "A New Moral Hazard? Military Intervention, Peacekeeping and Ratification of the International Criminal Court," *Journal of Peace Research* 46, no. 5 (2009): 659–70. Terrence L. Chapman and Stephen Chaudoin, "Ratification Patterns and the International Criminal Court," *International Studies Quarterly* (2012). Beth A. Simmons and Allison Danner, "Credible Commitments and the International Criminal Court," *International Organization* 64, no. 2 (2010): 225–56. Frederic Megret, "Why

Would States Want to Join the ICC? A Theoretical Exploration Based on the Legal Nature of Complementarity," in *Complementary Views on Complementarity*, ed. Gerben Kor Jann Kleffner (The Hague: T. M. C. Asser Press, 2005). Jay Goodliffe and Darren Hawkins, "A Funny Thing Happened on the Way to Rome: Explaining International Criminal Court Negotiations," *Journal of Politics* 71, no. 3 (2009): 977–97. Sara McLaughlin Mitchell and Emilia Justyna Powell, *Domestic Law Goes Global: Legal Traditions and International Courts* (Cambridge: Cambridge University Press, 2011).

78. Coalition for an International Criminal Court, "Brazil Formally Joins Supporters of the International Criminal Court: More Ratifications Expected before July 1st Entry into Force," news release, June 20, 2002, http://www.iccnow.org/documents/pressrelease20020620.pdf.

79. "South Africa Calls for International Crime Court," *Panafrican News Agency*, November 28, 2000.

80. Article 18 of the Vienna Convention on the Law of Treaties provides that a signatory to a treaty is "obliged to refrain from acts which would defeat the object and purpose of a treaty." The United States has not ratified the VCLT, but its provisions are generally agreed to have become customary international law. Scheffer, *All the Missing Souls*, 234–35, 43–47.

81. Robert S. McNamara and Benjamin B. Ferencz, "For Clinton's Last Act," *New York Times*, December 12, 2000, A33.

82. Author interview with Eric Schwartz.

83. Scheffer, *All the Missing Souls*, 241.

84. Author interview with David Scheffer.

85. John R. Bolton, "Unsign That Treaty," *Washington Post*, January 4, 2001, A21.

86. American Servicemembers' Protection Act of 2000, 22 U.S.C. § 2008(a) (2002).

87. Rademaker recalls negotiating directly with a young Justice Department lawyer named John Yoo about the bill's provisions. Yoo was concerned that the draft bill represented an encroachment on the executive branch's ability to manage foreign policy. At their first meeting, both Rademaker and Yoo pulled out copies of the U.S. Constitution and announced their intent to defend its provisions on the control of US foreign policy. Author interview with Stephen Rademaker.

88. Author interview with Stephen Rademaker.

89. For analysis of US policy and concerns with an international court's jurisdiction regarding American citizens, see Diane F. Orentlicher, "Unilateral Multilateralism: United States Policy toward the International Criminal Court," *Cornell International Law Journal* 36 (2004): 418–22. For a look at US sovereignty concerns with European policies and global governance institutions, see Jeremy Rabkin, "Is EU Policy Eroding the Sovereignty of Non-Member States?" *Chicago Journal of International Law* 1, no. 2 (2000): 273–90. For a discussion of how these concerns relate specifically to the ICC, see ibid., 277–80. For further discussion on these issues, see related articles within that journal issue, stemming

from an April 2000 conference organized by the American Enterprise Institute "Trends in Global Governance: Do They Threaten American Sovereignty?" See, for example, Paul B. Stephan, "International Governance and American Democracy," *Chicago Journal of International Law* 1, no. 2 (2000): 237–56. Joel Richard Paul, "Is Global Governance Safe for Democracy?," *Chicago Journal of International Law* 1, no. 2 (2000): 263–71. John R. Bolton, "Should We Take Global Governance Seriously?," *Chicago Journal of International Law* 1, no. 2 (2000): 205–21.

90. Jane Mayer, *The Dark Side: The Inside Story of How the War on Terror Turned into a War on American Ideals* (New York: Doubleday, 2008), 129.

91. Military Technical Agreement between the International Security Assistance Force and the Interim Administration of Afghanistan, January 4, 2002, http://webarchive.nationalarchives.gov.uk/+/http://www.operations.mod.uk/isafmta.pdf.

92. See, for example, Colum Lynch, "European Countries Cut Deal to Protect Afghan Peacekeepers," *Washington Post*, June 20, 2002, A15.

93. Author interview with David Tolbert.

94. Neil Tweedie and Joshua Rozenberg, "New International Criminal Court Set Up: UN Ratifies its Ground-Breaking Treaty for Global Justice, Despite Being Snubbed by America and China," *Daily Telegraph* (London), April 12, 2002, 16.

95. Marc Grossman, "American Foreign Policy and the International Criminal Court" (remarks to the Center for Strategic and International Studies, Washington, DC, May 6, 2002), http://2001-2009.state.gov/p/us/rm/9949.htm.

96. Thomas Ricks, "US Signs Treaty on War Crimes Tribunal," *Washington Post*, January 1, 2001, A1.

97. Bolton, *Surrender Is Not an Option*, 85.

98. Author interview with Lincoln Bloomfield.

99. Author interview with Elizabeth Jones.

100. Serge Schmemann, "U.S. Links Peacekeeping to Immunity from New Court," *New York Times*, June 19, 2002, 3.

101. John Ibbitson, "Canada Condemns World Court Compromise," *Globe and Mail* (Toronto), July 13, 2002, A11. Warren Hoge, "Bosnia Veto by the U.S. is Condemned by Britain," *New York Times*, July 2, 2002, A8.

102. Afghanistan acceded to the Rome Statute on February 10, 2003. That year the United States provided Afghanistan with $404.6 million total in military assistance and $56.7 million in economic assistance, according to the US Overseas Loans & Grants [Greenbook], Prepared by USAID Economic Analysis and Data Services. Statistics available at http://gbk.eads.usaidallnet.gov/data/detailed.html.

103. Alison Des Forges, "Leave None to Tell the Story" (Human Rights Watch, 1999), "Numbers" and "The Rwandan Patriotic Front," http://www.hrw.org/legacy/

reports/1999/rwanda/Geno15-8-03.htm#P713_229872. Gérard Prunier, *Africa's World War: Congo, the Rwandan Genocide, and the Making of a Continental Catastrophe* (Oxford: Oxford University Press, 2009), 15–16. "Rwanda: Reports of Killings and Abductions by the Rwandese Patriotic Army, April-August 1994" (Amnesty International, 1994), http://www.amnesty.org/en/library/info/AFR47/016/1994/en.

104. "Great Lakes: IRIN Weekly Round-Up, 5/26/97: Genocide Survivors Protest against ICTR Prosecutor," *Integrated Regional Information Network*, May 26, 1997, http://www.africa.upenn.edu/Hornet/irin_52697.html. Chris Simpson, "UN Criminal Tribunal Chief Banned from Rwanda," *Inter-Press Service*, November 27, 1999, http://www.ipsnews.net/1999/11/rights-un-criminal-tribunal-chief-banned-from-rwanda/.

105. Victor Peskin, *International Justice in Rwanda and the Balkans: Virtual Trials and the Struggle for State Cooperation* (Cambridge: Cambridge University Press, 2008), 172.

106. Ibid., 186.

107. International Criminal Tribunal for Rwanda, "Prosecutor Outlines Future Plans," news release ICTR/INFO-9-2-254, December 13, 2000, http://www.unictr.org/tabid/155/Default.aspx?id=362.

108. "Letter dated 26 July 2002 from the President of the International Criminal Tribunal for the Prosecution of Persons Responsible for Genocide and Other Serious Violations of International Humanitarian Law Committed in the Territory of Rwanda and Rwandan Citizens Responsible for Genocide and Other Such Violations Committed in the Territory of Neighbouring States between 1 January and 31 December 1994 addressed to the President of the Security Council" July 29, 2002, UN Doc. S/2002/847, http://www.un.org/Docs/journal/asp/ws.asp?m=S/2002/847.

109. Del Ponte, *Madame Prosecutor*, 225.

110. See David A. Kaye, "Justice Beyond The Hague: Supporting the Prosecution of International Crimes in National Courts" (New York: Council on Foreign Relations, 2011), Council Special Report No. 61, p. 17. For voluntary and UN assessed US contributions to the tribunals from 1999 to 2002, see "Part 6: Legal Developments" sections of yearly "United States Participation in the United Nations: Report by the Secretary of State to the Congress" reports issued by the U.S. Department of State Bureau of International Organization Affairs, at http://www.state.gov/p/io/rls/rpt/index.htm. For UN assessed US contributions for each tribunal, see "Assessment of Member States' Contributions for the Financing of the International Criminal Tribunal for the Prosecution of Persons Responsible for Serious Violations of International Humanitarian Law Committed in the Territory of the Former Yugoslavia since 1991 from 1 January 1994 to 31 December 2003" (New York: UN Secretariat, 2003), pages 10, 14, 18, 22, 26, 30, 34, 38, 42, 46,

http://www.un.org/ga/search/view_doc.asp?symbol=ST/ADM/SER.B/476. "Assessment of the contributions of Member States for the financing of the International Criminal Tribunal for the Prosecution of Persons Responsible for Genocide and Other Serious Violations of International Humanitarian Law Committed in the Territory of Rwanda and Rwandan Citizens Responsible for Genocide and Other Such Violations Committed in the Territory of Neighbouring States between 1 January and 31 December 1994, for the period up to 31 October 1995 through 31 December 2003" (New York: UN Secretariat, 2003), pp. 8, 12, 16, 20, 24, 28, 32, http://www.un.org/ga/search/view_doc.asp?symbol=ST/ADM/SER.B/477. ICTY and ICTR reports available at http://www.un.org/en/ga/contributions/tribunals.shtml.

111. Rome Statute, art. 126(1), July 17, 1998, UN Doc. A/CONF. 183/9, 2187 U.N.T.S. 90, http://untreaty.un.org/cod/icc/statute/romefra.htm.

112. A. S. Muller, "Setting Up the International Criminal Court: Not One Moment but a Series of Moments," *International Organizations Law Review* 1, no. 1 (2004): 189–96.

113. Author interview with Sam Muller. See also ibid., 192; and Zsolt Hetesy, "Completing the Work of the Preparatory Commission: The Making of the Basic Principles of the Headquarters Agreement," *Fordham International Law Journal* (2002): 629.

114. Author interview with Sam Muller.

CHAPTER 4

1. "Remarks to the 10th Mountain Division at Fort Drum, New York, July 19, 2002," in *Public Papers of the Presidents of the United States: George W. Bush (2002, Book II)*, http://www.gpo.gov/fdsys/pkg/PPP-2002-book2/pdf/PPP-02-book2-doc-pg1270.pdf.

2. For a description of the campaign, see Bolton, *Surrender Is Not an Option*, 85–86. See also David Scheffer, "Article 98(2) of the Rome Statute: America's Original Intent," *Journal of International Criminal Justice* 3, no. 2 (2005): 333–53.

3. S.C. Res. 1422, para. 2, U.N. Doc. S/RES/1422 (July 12, 2002), http://www.un.org/Docs/journal/asp/ws.asp?m=S/RES/1422.

4. United States Central Command details the roles of countries that have participated in military operations in Afghanistan since 2001. For accounts of force deployments and activities, see "About CENTCOM: Coalition Countries," http://www.centcom.mil/coalition-countries.

5. Dick Cheney, "Remarks by the Vice President to the Veterans of Foreign Wars 103rd National Convention" (speech, Nashville, TN, August 26, 2002), http://georgewbush-whitehouse.archives.gov/news/releases/2002/08/20020826.html.

6. Scott Peterson, "Chance for Chechen Peace Wanes; Thursday, Russian Officials Vowed to 'Wipe Out' Commanders of Chechnya's Resistance," *Christian Science Monitor*, November 1, 2002, 6.

7. Thom Shanker and Seth Mydans, "Rumsfeld Says Threat of War over Kashmir is Receding," *New York Times*, June 14, 2002, 17. "Back from the Edge on Kashmir," *New York Times*, June 12, 2002, 28.

8. Elizabeth Becker, "On World Court, U.S. Focus Shifts to Shielding Officials," *New York Times*, September 7, 2002, A4.

9. Dexter Filkins, "Flaws in U.S. Air War Left Hundreds of Civilians Dead," *New York Times*, July 21, 2002, 1. Carlotta Gall and Eric Schmitt, "Shocked Afghans Criticize U.S. Strike; Toll Is Some 40 Dead and 100 Wounded," *New York Times*, July 3, 2002, A3.

10. Memorandum from Michael Wood (August 15, 2002), published as part of the Chilcot Inquiry, http://www.iraqinquiry.org.uk/media/43499/doc_2010_01_26_11_02_28_403.pdf.

11. Researchers with the Peace Research Institute Oslo (PRIO), Uppsala Conflict Data Program, and the Department of Peace and Conflict Research at Uppsala University find that 2003 marked the year with the fewest active conflicts since the 1970s. For more, see Lotta Harbom, Erik Melander, and Peter Wallensteen, "Dyadic Dimensions of Armed Conflict, 1946–2007," *Journal of Peace Research* 45, no. 5 (2008): 697. For more on the declining battle deaths and other patterns, see also Bethany Lacina and Nils Petter Gleditsch, "Monitoring Trends in Global Combat: A New Dataset of Battle Deaths," *European Journal of Population / Revue Européenne de Démographie* 21, no. 2/3 (2005): 145–66. Bethany Lacina, Nils Petter Gleditsch, and Bruce Russett, "The Declining Risk of Death in Battle," *International Studies Quarterly* 50, no. 3 (2006): 673–74. Monty G. Marshall and Ted Robert Gurr, "Peace and Conflict 2005" (College Park: University of Maryland Center for International Development and Conflict Management, 2005), 11–12, http://www.systemicpeace.org/PC2005.pdf.

12. See Iulia Motoc, "Report on the Situation of Human Rights in the Democratic Republic of the Congo, Submitted by the Special Rapporteur," March 10, 2004, Commission on Human Rights, 60th Sess., U.N. Doc. E/CN.4/2004/34 http://www.unhchr.ch/Huridocda/Huridoca.nsf/0/e17f022df5c7829dc1256e98003806 63/$FILE/G0411748.pdf.

13. Agence France-Presse, "New Rebel Group Seizes West Sudan Town," February 26, 2003.

14. Chris Stephen, "International Criminal Court to Open in Face of US Opposition; Hopes Are High for the New International Criminal Court Despite US Hostility," *Irish Times* (Dublin), March 8, 2003, 13. Chris Stephen, "Jury Is Out on Future of Hague War Crimes Court," *Scotland on Sunday* (Edinburgh), March 9, 2003, 27.

15. Author interview with Jozias van Aarsten.

16. Author interview with Valentin Zellweger.

17. Author interview with Judge Song.

18. Author interview with Sam Muller.

19. Rome Statute, arts. 36(4)(b), 36(5), 36(6)(a), 36(7) 36(8)(a), July 17, 1998, UN Doc. A/CONF. 183/9, 2187 U.N.T.S. 90, http://untreaty.un.org/cod/icc/statute/romefra.htm.

20. ICC Assembly of States Parties Resolution ICC-ASP/1/Res.3, para. 3(b) (September 9, 2002), http://untreaty.un.org/cod/icc/elections/texts/electionofjudges%28e%29.pdf.

21. See Mia Swart, "[Review] Ruth Mackenzie, Kate Malleson, Penny Martin, and Philippe Sands QC (eds.), *Selecting International Judges: Principle, Process, and Politics*," *Leiden Journal of International Law* 24, no. 3 (2011): 789–92. Ruth Mackenzie et al., *Selecting International Judges: Principle, Process, and Politics* (Oxford: Oxford University Press, 2010).

22. Mackenzie et al., *Selecting International Judges*, 122–24.

23. "Election of the judges of the International Criminal Court, First election (first resumed session of the Assembly of States Parties, held from 3 to 7 February 2003) Results," United Nations, http://untreaty.un.org/cod/icc/asp/aspfra.htm.

24. Author interview with Philippe Kirsch.

25. Author interview with Sam Muller.

26. Author interview with Christian Wenaweser.

27. Author interviews with Prince Zeid, Hans Peter-Kaul, and Silvia Fernandez.

28. "New Hero," *Newsweek*, December 25, 1994, http://www.thedailybeast.com/newsweek/1994/12/25/new-hero.html.

29. Patt Morrison, "Luis Moreno-Ocampo; 1st Prosecutor," *Los Angeles Times*, November 19, 2011, A17.

30. Author interview with Hans-Peter Kaul.

31. Author interview with US diplomats.

32. David Scheffer, *All the Missing Souls: A Personal History of the War Crimes Tribunals* (Princeton, NJ: Princeton University Press, 2012).

33. Author interview with national diplomat. Other diplomats involved in the process, including Prince Zeid himself, do not recall the previous US support for Moreno-Ocampo as a factor.

34. Author interview with Bruno Cathala.

35. International Criminal Court Public Information Office, "Press-Kit: Inaugural Ceremony: Swearing-in of the Judges of the ICC" (March 11, 2003), http://www.iccnow.org/documents/ICCPressKit200303Eng.pdf.

36. Commissioner for External Relations Chris Patten, "Inauguration of the International Criminal Court" (Brussels, Belgium: European Commission, March 11, 2003), http://europa.eu/rapid/pressReleasesAction.do?reference=IP/03/354&format=HTML&aged=0&language=EN&guiLanguage=en.

37. Statement by HRH Prince Zeid Ra'ad Zeid Al-Hussein, President of the Assembly of States Parties to the Rome Statute of the International Criminal

Court at the Inaugural Meeting of Judges of the International Criminal Court, March 11, 2003, http://www.icc-cpi.int/NR/rdonlyres/6D0FE045-1D39-4CD3-BA77-B9517380EC18/144080/Statement_by_HRH_Prince_Zeid_Ra_EN.pdf. Joshua Rozenberg, "Global Court Opens Despite US Fears: International Justice Gets a Permanent Home with 18 Judges at the Hague," *Daily Telegraph* (London), March 12, 2003, 18.

38. BBC Summary of World Broadcasts documented an Al-Jazeera TV screen caption, in Arabic, reading, "A number of people were injured in the Al-Dawrah area of Baghdad after bombardment," at 1021 GMT, March 20, 2003. See "Al-Jazeera Reports Iraqis Injured in Bombing," BBC Summary of World Broadcasts, via Lexis Nexis.

39. Steven Edwards, "War Crimes Case Planned Against U.S: Washington Says Groups' Bid Proves ICC a Political Tool," *National Post*, April 15, 2003, A14. Tosin Sulaiman, "Group Investigating Whether U.S., British Troops Committed War Crimes," *Knight Ridder Tribune Business News*, April 24, 2003. Steven Edwards, "Try U.S., Britain for Bombings in Iraq, War Crimes Court Urged," *Ottawa Citizen*, January 27, 2004, A9.

40. Steven Edwards, "War Crimes Case Planned Against U.S.: Washington Says Groups' Bid Proves ICC a Political Tool," *National Post* (Toronto), April 15, 2003, A14. "Investigation Into Possible UK War Crimes in Iraq; UK Attorney, U.S. Colleagues Granting Media Interviews," *U.S. Newswire*, April 11, 2003. "Coalition Forces to be Investigated for War Crimes in Iraq," *U.S. Newswire*, January 26, 2004. Steven Edwards, "Try U.S., Britain for Bombings in Iraq, War Crimes Court Urged," *Ottawa Citizen* (Toronto), January 27, 2004, A9. Steven Edwards, "Jurists Will Investigate Suspected War Crimes," *Vancouver Sun*, January 27, 2004, A9.

41. "Sudanese Legal Experts Call for Prosecution of Bush, Blair over Iraq War," *BBC Monitoring Middle East—Political*, April 14, 2003, citing text of report in English by Sudanese newspaper *Khartoum Monitor* website on April 12, referencing a memorandum provided to the UN country representative in Khartoum and published by *Al-Wifaq* daily newspaper, No. 1850, on page 5.

42. Author interview with private lawyer. The memorandum recommended that Iraq consider giving the court jurisdiction by invoking Article 12(3) of the Rome Statute rather than by ratifying the statute. An Article 12(3) declaration has immediate effect while a ratification does not come into effect for sixty days.

43. Helena Smith, "Greeks Accuse Blair of War Crimes in Iraq: Athens Lawyers; Hague Case Names PM, Straw and Hoon," *Guardian* (London), July 29, 2003, 11. Ambrose Evans-Pritchard, "Blair Accused by Greeks of Crimes against Humanity," *Daily Telegraph* (London), July 29, 2003, 12.

44. For a synopsis of communications and complaints received immediately by the ICC that did not fall within the court's jurisdiction, see International Criminal Court Office of the Prosecutor, "Communications Received by the Office of the Prosecutor of the ICC," news release 009.2003-EN, July

16,   2003,   http://www.icc-cpi.int/NR/rdonlyres/9B5B8D79-C9C2-4515-9
06E-125113CE6064/277680/16_july__english1.pdf.

45. Author interview with Luis Moreno-Ocampo.

46. Author interviews with Luis Moreno-Ocampo and General John Altenburg.

47. "Election of the Prosecutor, Statement by Mr. Moreno Ocampo, April 22, 2003,"
http://www.icc-cpi.int/Menus/ICC/Structure+of+the+Court/Office+of+
the+Prosecutor/Reports+and+Statements/Press+Releases/Press+
Releases+2003/.

48. Colum Lynch, "US Confronts EU on War Crimes Court; Immunity Pact Issue
Threatens Relations," *Washington Post*, June 10, 2003, A17.

49. Dan Bilefsky, "Bushes on Trial? Belgium Is Sweating Out Its Own War-Crimes
Law," *Wall Street Journal*, March 28, 2003, A11.

50. Donald Rumsfeld, *Known and Unknown: A Memoir* (New York: Sentinel,
2011). 599.

51. Glenn Frankel, "Belgian War Crimes Law Undone by Its Global Reach; Cases
Against Political Figures Sparked Crises," *Washington Post*, September 30, 2003,
A1. Ambrose Evans-Pritchard, "US threatens to pull NATO HQ out of Belgium,"
Daily Telegraph (London), June 13, 2003, 15. Roland Watson, "Rumsfeld's Threat
to Belgium over War Crimes Law," *Times* (London), June 13, 2003, 20.

52. Lynda Hurst, "Belgium Reins in War-Crime Law; U.S. Threats Finally Sink
'Universal Jurisdiction' Suits Anti-War Activists Used Court to Sue American
Leaders," *Toronto Star*, June 29, 2003, F4. Ian Black, "Belgium Gives in to
US on War Crimes Law," *Guardian* (London), June 24, 2003, 13. Ambrose
Evans-Pritchard, "Belgium Restricts War Crimes Law," *Daily Telegraph* (London),
June 24, 2003, 14.

53. "ICC: A Cautious Beginning with Mixed Signals from the Prosecutor," July 15,
2003, http://www.cablegatesearch.net/cable.php?id=03THEHAGUE1806&q=
assure%20designed%20icc.

54. See International Criminal Court, Office of the Prosecutor, First Public Hearing of
the Office of the Prosecutor, June 17-18, 2003, http://www.icc-cpi.int/en_menus/
icc/structure%20of%20the%20court/office%20of%20the%20prosecutor/net-
work%20with%20partners/public%20hearings/Pages/first%20public%20hear-
ing.aspx.

55. Author interview with Luis Moreno-Ocampo.

56. Author interview with Luis Moreno-Ocampo.

57. Howard W. French, "Mobutu Sese Seko, 66, Longtime Dictator of Zaire,"
New York Times, September 8, 1997, http://partners.nytimes.com/library/
world/090897obit-mobutu.html. John Pomfret, "Rwandans Led Revolt in
Congo," *Washington Post*, July 9, 1997, A1, http://www.washingtonpost.com/
wp-srv/inatl/longterm/congo/stories/070997.htm.

58. "Congo Crisis: Military Intervention in Ituri" (Nairobi, New York,
Brussels: International Crisis Group, 2003), i, http://www.crisisgroup.org/~/

media/Files/africa/central-africa/dr-congo/Congo%20Crisis%20Military%20 Intervention%20in%20Ituri.

59. UN Integrated Regional Information Networks, "Congo-Kinshasa; Interview with UN Under-Secretary for Peacekeeping Operations" (June 5, 2003).

60. Author interview with former ICC officials.

61. For accounts of visits with international dignitaries, see 2003 and 2004 ICC press releases, http://www.icc-cpi.int/en_menus/icc/press%20and%20media/ press%20releases/Pages/index.aspx.

62. The first diplomatic briefing of the ICC took place February 12, 2004. Records of subsequent diplomatic briefings at http://www.icc-cpi.int/en_menus/icc/ reports%20on%20activities/court%20reports%20and%20statements/Pages/ index.aspx.

63. Author interview with European diplomat.

64. Author interview with European diplomat.

65. Author interview with former ICC official.

66. Author interview with David Kaye.

67. Philippe Kirsch, "Statement by Judge Philippe Kirsch, President of the International Criminal Court, at the Inaugural Meeting of the Judges," March 11, 2003, http:// www.icc-cpi.int/NR/rdonlyres/48D76A79-7315-49C2-A16F-86D7CFAAE721/ 143846/PK_20030311_En.pdf.

68. Author interview with Philippe Kirsch.

69. Virginia Morris and Michael P. Scharf, *The International Criminal Tribunal for Rwanda*, 2 vols., vol. 1 (Irvington-on-Hudson, NY: Transnational Publishers, 1998), 380–81, 383. U.N. Secretary-General, *Report of the Secretary-General Pursuant to Paragraph 2 of Security Council Resolution 808 (1993)*, ¶ 87 (p. 22), U.N. Doc. S/25704 (May 3, 1993), http://www.un.org/Docs/journal/asp/ ws.asp?m=S/25704. U.N. Secretary-General, *Report of the Secretary-General, Financing of the International Criminal Tribunal for the Prosecution of Persons Responsible for Genocide and Other Serious Violations of International Humanitarian Law Committed in the Territory of Rwanda and Rwandan Citizens Responsible for Genocide and Other Such Violations Committed in the Territory of Neighbouring States between 1 January and 31 December 1994*, ¶ 33, U.N. Doc. A/C.5/51/29/Add.1 (May 12, 1997), http://www.un.org/Docs/journal/asp/ ws.asp?m=A/C.5/51/29/Add.1.

70. Author interview with former ICC official.

71. Author interview with former ICC official.

72. The office had several names before finally acquiring JCCD.

73. Author interview with Luis Moreno-Ocampo.

74. Author interview with former ICC officials.

75. Author interview with Paul Siels.

76. See, e.g., Anthony Vinci, "The Strategic Use of Fear by the Lord's Resistance Army," *Small Wars & Insurgencies* 16, no. 3 (2005): 360–81.

77. "Tracking down Uganda's Rebels, BBC News," May 10, 2002, http://news.bbc. co.uk/2/hi/africa/1980333.stm; "Beginnings in Uganda," Enough Project, http:// www.enoughproject.org/conflicts/lra/beginnings-in-uganda#Iron.

78. For context on Uganda's political landscape and those of its neighbors in 2003, see Ted Dagne and Maureen Farrell, "Africa's Great Lakes Region: Current Conditions in Burundi, Democratic Republic of the Congo, Rwanda, and Uganda" (Washington, DC: Congressional Research Service, 2003), http://fpc. state.gov/documents/organization/26016.pdf. For a synopsis of Uganda political changes and international support in the late 1990s, see James C. McKinley, "After a String of Dictators, Ugandans Get to Vote Again," *New York Times*, May 10, 1996, A3. See also Alan Zarembo, "Museveni Juggles Ugandan Democracy: President Says Western Donors Shouldn't Tell Africans How They Should Be Running Their Affairs," *Globe and Mail* (Toronto), May 13, 1996. Oliver Furley and James Katalikawe, "Constitutional Reform in Uganda: The New Approach," *African Affairs* 96, no. 383 (1997): 243–60. For an in-depth look at these issues, see Ellen Hauser, "Donors and Democracy in Uganda: An Analysis of the Role of Western Donors in Democratization Efforts in Uganda" (Ph.D., University of Wisconsin-Madison, 1997).

79. See joint presidential declaration of principles and Clinton's remarks: "Communique: Entebbe [Uganda] Summit for Peace and Prosperity: Joint Declaration of Principles, March 25, 1998," in *Public Papers of the Presidents of the United States: William J. Clinton (1998, Book I)*, 434–38, http://www.gpo.gov/ fdsys/pkg/PPP-1998-book1/pdf/PPP-98-book1-doc-pg434.pdf. "Remarks at the Entebbe Summit for Peace and Prosperity, March 25, 1998," in *Public Papers of the Presidents of the United States: William J. Clinton (1998, Book I)*, 438–39, http:// www.gpo.gov/fdsys/pkg/PPP-1998-book1/pdf/PPP-98-book1-doc-pg438.pdf.

80. World Bank World Development Indicators Data on Uganda's Gross National Income (GNI) and Net Bilateral Aid Flows from Germany, Japan, United Kingdom, and United States, http://databank.worldbank.org/ddp/home. do?Step=12&id=4&CNO=2.

81. International Criminal Court Article 98 Agreement, U.S.-Uganda, June 12, 2003, T.I.A.S. 03-1023, http://www.state.gov/documents/organization/152670.pdf.

82. Author interview with Luis Moreno-Ocampo.

83. "ICC Warrants Not Stopping Peace Search—Expert," *Monitor*, October 27, 2007, http://allafrica.com/stories/200710280004.html.

84. Author interview with Mirjam Blaak; see also Payam Akhavan, "The Lord's Resistance Army Case: Uganda's Submission of the First State Referral to the International Criminal Court," *American Journal of International Law* 99, no. 2 (2005): 403–21; Sarah M. H. Nouwen and Wouter G. Werner, "Doing Justice to the Political: The International Criminal Court in Uganda and Sudan," *European Journal of International Law* 21, no. 4 (2010): 941–65.

85. Author interview with Darryl Robinson.

86. Arthur Max, "International Criminal Court Gets Its First Case: Against Rebels in Uganda," *Associated Press*, January 29, 2004.

87. Luis Moreno-Ocampo, "Letter from ICC Prosecutor to President Philippe Kirsch" (The Hague, June 17, 2004), http://www.icc-cpi.int/iccdocs/doc/doc271808.PDF.

88. Author interview with Jimmy Kolker.

89. Author interviews with former ICC officials. For a brief description of Congo referral, see Benjamin N. Schiff, *Building the International Criminal Court* (Cambridge: Cambridge University Press, 2008), 212–13. For a description of domestic political dynamics in Congo that also shaped Kabila's incentives for referring the situation to the ICC, see William W. Burke-White, "Complementarity in Practice: The International Criminal Court as Part of a System of Multi-level Global Governance in the Democratic Republic of Congo," *Leiden Journal of International Law* 18, no. 3 (2005): 563–68.

90. Author interview with Ambassador Jimmy Kolker. For more on US assistance, see Carter Dougherty, "U.S. Aids Uganda Against Rebels: Support Seen as Payback for Stance on Iraq," *Washington Times*, October 24, 2003, A18. "Bush Joins War against Kony's LRA," *The East African*, October 27, 2003. "US Aid for Fight against Lord's Resistance Army," *UN Integrated Regional Information Networks*, October 28, 2003.

91. Office of the Prosecutor International Criminal Court, "Statement by the Prosecutor Related to Crimes Committed in Barlonya Camp in Uganda," http://www.icc-cpi.int/NR/rdonlyres/47964D88-93C8-4E71-9119-4DA540E-F5EE2/143705/PIDSOTP0022004EN2.pdf. John Donnelly, "Up to 192 Killed in Uganda as Rebels Torch Civilian Camp," *Boston Globe*, February 23, 2004. Geoffrey Muleme, "Rebels Kill 192 in Uganda; Many Burned Alive in Huts during Refugee Camp Slaughter," *Chicago Sun-Times*, February 23, 2004, 33.

92. Jess Bravin, "International Criminal Court Picks U.S. Lawyer to Lead First Case," *Wall Street Journal*, January 30, 2004, A10.

93. Human Rights Watch, "Courting History: The Landmark International Criminal Court's First Years" (2008), 57–58, http://www.hrw.org/sites/default/files/reports/icc0708webwcover.pdf.

94. Inter-Congolese Dialogue: Political Negotiations on the Peace Process and on Transition in the DRC: Global and Inclusive Agreement on Transition in the Democratic Republic of the Congo, Dec. 16, 2002, http://www.ucdp.uu.se/gpdatabase/peace/DRC%2020021216.pdf.

95. Burke-White, "Complementarity in Practice," 562–63.

96. "Violence in the East Endangers Stability of Kinshasa's Transitional Government," *SouthScan* (London), March 8, 2004. "DRCongo: Former Rebels Reportedly Threaten to Withdraw from Institutions," *BBC Summary of World Broadcasts*, February 25, 2004, citing report translated from French broadcast by Congolese Radio Bukavu, at 0430 GMT, February 25, 2004. For

additional context, see discussion by Alison Des Forges in Human Rights Watch, "Democratic Republic of Congo—Rwanda Conflict: A Human Rights Watch Backgrounder," December 5, 2004, http://www.hrw.org/news/2004/12/04/democratic-republic-congo-rwanda-conflict.

97. "The Congo's Transition Is Failing: Crisis in the Kivus" (Brussels, Nairobi: International Crisis Group, 2005), i, http://www.crisisgroup.org/~/media/Files/africa/central-africa/dr-congo/The%20Congos%20Transition%20Is%20Failing%20Crisis%20in%20the%20Kivus.pdf.

98. Phil Clark, "Law, Politics and Pragmatism: The ICC and Case Selection in Uganda and the Democratic Republic of Congo," in *Courting Conflict? Justice, Peace and the ICC in Africa*, ed. Nicholas Waddell and Phil Clark (London: Royal African Society, 2008), http://www.royalafricansociety.org/images/stories/courting%20conflict%20-%20ojustice%2C%20peace%20and%20the%20icc%20in%20africa.pdf.

99. "ICC Gearing up to Start Congo Investigation," August 4, 2004, http://cablegatesearch.net/cable.php?id=04KINSHASA1476&q=congo%20gearing%20icc%20start%20to%20up.

100. Author interview with former ICC officials.

101. "ICC: Getting Down to Business?" July 27, 2004, http://cablegatesearch.net/cable.php?id=04THEHAGUE1885&q=business%20down%20getting%20icc%20to.

102. Author interview with Roger Clark.

103. *The Princeton Process on the Crime of Aggression: Materials of the Special Working Group on the Crime of Aggression, 2003–2009*, ed. Stefan Barriga, Wolfgang Danspeckgruber, and Christian Wenaweser (Boulder, CO: Lynne Rienner Publishers), ix.

104. Ibid.

105. Preparatory Commission for the International Criminal Court, *Proposal submitted by Bahrain, Iraq, Lebanon, the Libyan Arab Jamahiriya, Oman, the Sudan, the Syrian Arab Republic and Yemen*, U.N. Doc. PCNICC/1999/DP.11 (February 26, 1999), http://untreaty.un.org/cod/icc/documents/aggression/english/1999.dp11.pdf.

106. See Sean D. Murphy, "Aggression, Legitimacy and the International Criminal Court," *European Journal of International Law* 20, no. 4 (2009): 1147–56. Theodor Meron, "Defining Aggression for the International Criminal Court," *Suffolk Transnational Law Review* 25, no. 1 (2001): 1–15.

107. Marie Woolf, "Iraq in Crisis: CPS [Crown Prosecution Service] Considers Charges over Death of Iraqi," *Independent* (London), May 27, 2004, 4.

108. Rory McCarthy, "Amnesty Details Killing of Civilians by British Soldiers," *Guardian* (London), May 11, 2004, 5.

109. Warren Hoge, "U.N. Rights Chief Says Prison Abuse May Be War Crime," *New York Times*, June 5, 2004, A6.

110. In formal terms, these immunity provisions were actually uses of the Security Council's power to defer ICC investigations (provided to the Council under Article 16 of the Rome Statute). Because Article 16 only permitted deferrals of up to twelve months, the United States sought to renew on an annual basis the broad exemption for those serving with UN-authorized missions.

111. "Daily Press Briefing by the Office of the Spokesman for the Secretary-General [Stéphane Dujarric, Associate Spokesman]," http://www.un.org/News/briefings/docs/2004/db061704.doc.htm. Warren Hoge, "Annan Rebukes U.S. for Move to Give Its Troops Immunity," *New York Times*, June 18, 2004, A10.

112. Author interviews with former Bush administration officials.

113. Author interview with Daryl Robinson.

114. "Report of the Committee on Budget and Finance" (The Hague: International Criminal Court Assembly of States Parties, August 13, 2004).

115. UN Information Service, "Eight UN Human Rights Experts Gravely Concerned about Reported Widespread Abuses in Darfur, Sudan" (Statement issued in Geneva on March 26, 2004; press release AFR/873, HR/CN/1065 issued March 29, 2004), http://www.un.org/News/Press/docs/2004/afr873.doc.htm.

116. Human Rights Watch and Julie Flint, "Darfur Destroyed: Ethnic Cleansing by Government and Militia Forces in Western Sudan" (May 2004), http://www.hrw.org/sites/default/files/reports/sudan0504full.pdf.

117. S.C. Pres. Statement 2004/18, U.N. Doc. S/PRST/2004/18 (May 25, 2004), http://www.un.org/ga/search/view_doc.asp?symbol=S/PRST/2004/18.

118. S. Con. Res. 99, H.Con.Res. 467, 108th Cong. (2004) Declaring Genocide in Darfur, Sudan, http://www.gpo.gov/fdsys/pkg/BILLS-108sconres99es/pdf/BILLS-108sconres99es.pdf.

119. Jim VandeHei, "In Break with U.N., Bush Calls Sudan Killings Genocide," *Washington Post*, June 2, 2005.

120. S.C. Res. 1564, para. 12, U.N. Doc. S/RES/1564 (Sept. 18, 2004), http://www.un.org/docs/sc/unsc_resolutions04.html.

121. "New Significant Outflow of Sudanese Refugees into Chad," UN High Commissioner for Refugees, August 17, 2004, http://www.unhcr.org/cgi-bin/texis/vtx/search?page=search&docid=412206084&query=+sudan%20+chad%20+darfur.

122. Author interview with Luis Moreno-Ocampo.

123. Author interview with Luis Moreno-Ocampo.

124. "Presidential Debate in Coral Gables, Florida, September 30, 2004," in *Public Papers of the Presidents of the United States: George W. Bush (2004, Book II)*, p. 2263, http://www.gpo.gov/fdsys/pkg/PPP-2004-book2/pdf/PPP-2004-book2-doc-pg2248.pdf.

125. Colum Lynch, "Massacre Probe Concerns U.S.; Role of International Court in U.N. Investigation is Cited," *Washington Post*, December 2, 2004, A24.

CHAPTER 5

1. For a critical assessment of the commission's work, see Samuel Totten, "The UN International Commission of Inquiry on Darfur: New and Disturbing Findings," *Genocide Studies and Prevention* 4, no. 3 (2009): 354–78.

2. Author interview with senior British diplomat.

3. Rebecca Hamilton, *Fighting for Darfur: Public Action and the Struggle to Stop Genocide* (New York: Palgrave Macmillan, 2011), 100–103. Nicholas D. Kristof, "If This Is Not Genocide, What Is?" *International Herald Tribune*, June 17, 2004, 9. Nicholas D. Kristof, "Dare We Call It Genocide?" *New York Times*, June 16, 2004, A21. Nicholas D. Kristof, "The West Stands by While Genocide Unfolds," *International Herald Tribune*, June 1, 2004, 6. Marc Lacey, "White House Reconsiders Its Policy on Crisis in Sudan," *New York Times*, June 12, 2004, A3. Samantha Power and John Prendergast, "Break Through to Darfur: Combine Leverage, Internationalism and Aid to Stop the Killing in Sudan," *Los Angeles Times*, June 2, 2004, B13.

4. Author interview with Jean-Marc de la Sablière.

5. Nicholas Rostow, "U.N. Realities," in *Looking to the Future: Essays on International Law in Honor of W. Michael Reisman*, ed. Mahnoush H. Arsanjani et al. (Boston: Martinus Nijhoff Publishers, 2010), 1021.

6. Author interview with Jean-Marc de la Sablière.

7. See the now-unclassified cable from US Ambassador to the UN John Danforth, "Peace and Accountability: A Way Forward," January 7, 2005. Released by National Security Archive, http://www.gwu.edu/~nsarchiv/NSAEBB/NSAEBB335/Document4.PDF.

8. "Report of the International Commission of Inquiry on Darfur to the United Nations Secretary-General Pursuant to Security Council Resolution 1564 of 18 September 2004" (Geneva, January 25, 2005), art. 584, p. 148, http://www.un.org/news/dh/sudan/com_inq_darfur.pdf.

9. Ibid., arts. 573–82, pp. 146–48.

10. Elise Keppler, "Grave Crimes: Darfur and the International Criminal Court" published by Human Rights Watch and *The World Today*, a publication of Chatham House (UK), January 2, 2005, http://www.hrw.org/news/2005/01/01/grave-crimes-darfur-and-international-criminal-court. "U.S.: ICC Best Chance for Justice in Darfur: U.S. Should Support or Abstain from a Security Council Referral of Darfur to the International Criminal Court," Human Rights Watch open letter to Condoleezza Rice, January 22, 2005, http://www.hrw.org/news/2005/01/21/us-icc-best-chance-justice-darfur. "U.N.: Security Council Must Act on Darfur," Letter to Select UN Security Council Members from Human Rights Watch, March 18, 2005, http://www.hrw.org/news/2005/03/17/un-security-council-must-act-darfur.

11. Samantha Power, "Court of First Resort," *New York Times*, February 10, 2005, A23.

12. Jack Goldsmith, "Support War Crimes Trials for Darfur," *Washington Post*, January 24, 2005, A15.

13. John P. Cerone, "Dynamic Equilibrium: The Evolution of US Attitudes toward International Criminal Courts and Tribunals," *European Journal of International Law* 18, no. 2 (2007): 289.

14. Hamilton, *Fighting for Darfur*, 61–62.

15. Ibid., 61. Cerone, "Dynamic Equilibrium," 291. See also the now-unclassified cable from US Assistant Secretary of State Kim Holmes, "Gaining African Support for Sudan Action in the UNSC," January 30, 2005. Released by National Security Archive, http://www.gwu.edu/~nsarchiv/NSAEBB/NSAEBB335/Document6.PDF.

16. Author interview with Bush administration officials.

17. Author interview with Condoleezza Rice.

18. Author interview with John Bellinger.

19. Author email communication with John Bellinger.

20. Hamilton, *Fighting for Darfur*, 68.

21. S.C. Res. 1593, U.N. Doc. S/RES/1593 (March 31, 2005).

22. "Statement by French Ambassador De la Sablière after the Vote of Resolution 1593," http://www.iccnow.org/documents/France_Darfur1593_Press31Mar05.pdf. United States Mission to the United Nations, Explanation of Vote by Ambassador Anne W. Patterson, Acting U.S. Representative to the United Nations, on the Sudan Accountability Resolution, in the Security Council, March 31, 2005. For the vote tally and remarks by Patterson, then Chinese representative Wang Guangya, then De la Sablière, respectively, among other comments following the vote, see UN Security Council, 60th year, 5158th mtg. pp. 2–4, 5, 8–9, U.N. Doc. S/PV.5158 (March 31, 2005).

23. See remarks by César Mayoral (Argentina), Jean-Marc de la Sablière (France), and Augustine Mahiga (Tanzania) immediately following vote, UN Security Council, 60th year, 5158th mtg. pp. 7–9, U.N. Doc. S/PV.5158 (March 31, 2005).

24. S.C. Res. 1593, art. 6, preamble, U.N. Doc. S/RES/1593 (March 31, 2005).

25. For a discussion of this point, see Robert Cryer, "Sudan, Resolution 1593, and International Criminal Justice," *Leiden Journal of International Law* 19, no. 1 (2006): 195–222.

26. Rome Statute, art. 115(b), July 17, 1998, UN Doc. A/CONF. 183/9, 2187 U.N.T.S. 90, http://untreaty.un.org/cod/icc/statute/romefra.htm. S.C. Res. 1593, para. 7, U.N. Doc. S/RES/1593 (March 31, 2005).

27. U.N. SCOR, 60th Year, 5158th mtg. p. 11, U.N. Doc. S/PV.5158 (March 31, 2005), http://www.un.org/ga/search/view_doc.asp?symbol=S/PV.5158.

28. International Criminal Court Assembly of States Parties, 4th Sess. "Report of the Committee on Budget and Finance on the Work of Its Fourth Session," pp. 12–13, art. 42, ICC-ASP/4/2 (April 15, 2005), http://www.icc-cpi.int/iccdocs/asp_docs/library/asp/ICC-ASP-4-2_English.pdf.

29. Author interview with Luis Moreno-Ocampo.

30. Author interview with former ICC official.

31. Author interview with Luis Moreno-Ocampo.

32. Author interview with David Kaye.

33. In late 2005, US Assistant Secretary of State for Bureau of African Affairs Jendayi Frazer told a congressional committee that Deputy Secretary of State Robert Zoellick had said, "[I]f we were asked by the ICC for our help, we would try to make sure that this gets pursued fully." See *Sudan: Losing Ground on Peace? Hearing before the Subcomm. on Africa, Global Human Rights & International Operations, of the H. Comm. on International Relations*, 109th Cong. p. 54 (November 1, 2005) (statement of Assistant Secretary of State for Bureau of African Affairs Jendayi Frazer), http://commdocs.house.gov/committees/intl-rel/hfa24374.000/hfa24374_0f.htm.

34. Author interviews with Condoleezza Rice, Jack Straw.

35. Rome Statute, art. 54(e), July 17, 1998, UN Doc. A/CONF. 183/9, 2187 U.N.T.S. 90, http://untreaty.un.org/cod/icc/statute/romefra.htm. S.C. Res. 1593, para. 7, U.N. Doc. S/RES/1593 (March 31, 2005), http://www.un.org/Docs/journal/asp/ws.asp?m=S/RES/1593.

36. Author interview with Béatrice Le Fraper du Hellen.

37. Author interview with former ICC official.

38. Author interview with former ICC official.

39. "ICC Team Here to Investigate War Crimes in North," *New Vision* (Kampala), August 27, 2004. "Uganda: International Criminal Court Team Arrives to Prepare LRA War Probe," *UN Integrated Regional Information Networks* (Nairobi), August 26, 2004. "UN War Crimes Team to Probe Atrocities in Northern Ugandan War," Agence France-Presse, August 25, 2004.

40. Author interviews with ICC officials.

41. Despite the Ugandan government's support for the ICC investigation at this time, local Ugandan civil society groups expressed concerns about renewed LRA violence. In mid-March 2005 a group of Acholi religious leaders visited The Hague in an effort to dissuade the pursuit of arrest warrants. For more, see Frank Nyakairu (and agencies), "Uganda: Government Insists on ICC Trial for Kony," *Daily Monitor* (Kampala), March 19, 2005. Blake Lambert, "Tribe Opposes Court Role," *Washington Times*, March 31, 2005, A13. "Uganda: Acholi Leaders in the Hague to Meet ICC Over LRA Probe," *UN Integrated Regional Information Networks* (Nairobi), March 16, 2005. "Uganda: ICC Threats Might Mar Peace Talks, Church Says," *New Vision* (Kampala), February 14, 2005.

42. See Office of the Prosecutor of the International Criminal Court and Pre-Trial Chamber II, "Warrant of Arrest for Joseph Kony Issued on 8 July 2005 as Amended on 27 September 2005" pp. 12–19, ICC-02/04–01/05 (September 27, 2005), http://www.icc-cpi.int/iccdocs/doc/doc97185.PDF.

43. "Uganda: Waiting for Elusive Peace in the War Ravaged North," *UN Integrated Regional Information Networks* (Nairobi), June 9, 2005, http://www.irinnews.org/fr/Report/54852/UGANDA-Waiting-for-elusive-pe ace-in-the-war-ravaged-north.

44. "International Court Issues Warrants for Uganda Rebel Leaders: Report" Agence France-Presse, June 11, 2006. Marc Perelman, "International Court Criticized for Uganda Intervention," *Forward* (New York), April 1, 2005.

45. "International Court Preparing First Arrest Warrant for Ugandan Suspects," Associated Press, February 8, 2005. "UN Criminal Court to Target Uganda Rebels, DR Congo Militia," Agence France-Presse, February 8, 2005.

46. Luis Moreno-Ocampo, "Press Conference on the Uganda Arrest Warrants," news release, ICC-OTP-20051014–109, October 14, 2005, http://www. icc-cpi.int/en_menus/icc/press%20and%20media/press%20releases/2005/ Pages/press%20conference%20on%20the%20uganda%20arrest%20warrants. aspx. See Moreno-Ocampo's remarks on the LRA treatment of children in his speech, p. 5, http://www.icc-cpi.int/NR/rdonlyres/2919856F-03E0-403F-A1A8- D61D4F350A20/277305/Uganda_LMO_Speech_141020091.pdf.

47. Press Release, Secretary-General, Secretary-General Welcomes Arrest Warrants, First from International Criminal Court, as "Powerful Signal Around World," U.N. Press Release SG/SM/10167, L/3095 (Oct. 14, 2005), http://www.un.org/ News/Press/docs/2005/sgsm10167.doc.htm.

48. "Uganda: Drop Cases against Me, Kony Tells World Court," *Monitor* (Kampala), May 25, 2006. "Uganda: Rebel Leader Rejects Amnesty Offer as America, UN Insist on Arrests," *Monitor* (Kampala), July 7, 2006. "Uganda: LRA's Otti Vows to Kill ICC Captors," *Monitor* (Kampala), October 13, 2006.

49. "Uganda: Kony Will Eventually Face Trial, Says ICC Prosecutor," *UN Integrated Regional Information Networks* (Nairobi), July 7, 2006.

50. Riazat Butt, "Briton Killed as Uganda Rebels Attack Tourists," *Guardian* (London), November 9, 2005, 6. David Blair, "Rebels Murder British Aid Man," *Daily Telegraph* (London), November 8, 2005, 17.

51. Anthony Deutsch, "ICC Prosecutor Says Sudan will Assist in Arrest of LRA Leader Kony," Associated Press, October 13, 2005.

52. "Democratic Republic of Congo, Uganda, to Work Together to Find LRA Rebels: UN," Agence France-Presse, October 19, 2005. Cathy Majtenyi, "Uganda Joins Forces with the Democratic Republic of Congo to Find Ugandan Rebels in DRC," *Voice of America,* via *U.S. Fed News,* October 20, 2005.

53. Frank Nyakairu, "Peace Talks with LRA Face Collapse," *Daily Monitor* (Kampala), October 9, 2005.

54. Scott Johnson, "Hard Target: The Hunt for Africa's Last Warlord," *Newsweek,* May 25, 2009. See also Mica Rosenberg, "Doubts Still Shroud UN Peacekeeper Deaths in Congo," Reuters, November 15, 2006, http://uk.reuters.com/ article/2006/11/15/uk-guatemala-congo-idUKN1543499920061115.

55. See "U.S. Aids Uganda against Rebels," *Washington Times*, October 23, 2003.

56. Gus Selassie, "Deputy Leader of Ugandan Rebel Movement Reported to be Seeking Asylum in DRCongo," *World Markets Analysis*, September 26, 2005. Chris Ochowun, "Kony Flees into Congo," *The New Vision*, via BBC Monitoring Newsfile, November 5, 2005. Edmund Sanders, "Ruthless Rebels of Uganda Appear to be Losing Steam; The Lord's Resistance Army is Running Short of Fighters and Bullets. Hopes for Peace Grow," *Los Angeles Times*, October 10, 2005. Blake Lambert, "Ugandan Rebel Push Threatens Neighbors; The LRA Crossed into Congo, Opening a New Front in the Conflict," *The Christian Science Monitor*, October 7, 2005.

57. "President of ICC Delivers Second Annual Report to UN General Assembly— Need for International Cooperation Stressed," Coalition for the International Criminal Court, October 9, 2006.

58. Luis Moreno-Ocampo (untitled statement), pp. 8–9, February 9, 2006, http:// www.icc-cpi.int/NR/rdonlyres/04D143C8-19FB-466C-AB77-4CDB2 FDEBEF7/143682/OTP_letter_to_senders_re_Iraq_9_February_2006.pdf.

59. Anthony Loyd and Ali Hamdani, "Baghdad's Worst Day of Slaughter," *Times* (London), September 15, 2005, 39. Ellen Knickmeyer and Naseer Nouri, "Insurgents Kill 160 in Baghdad; Toll from Day-Long Wave of Attacks Is Largest in Iraqi Capital since Invasion," *Washington Post*, September 15, 2005, A1. Edward Wong, "Scores Killed in Iraq as Two Mosques Are Hit; Attacks in North Follow Baghdad Carnage," *International Herald Tribune*, November 19, 2005, 5.

60. William A. Schabas, "Prosecutorial Discretion v. Judicial Activism at the International Criminal Court," *Journal of International Criminal Justice* 6, no. 4 (2008): 748.

61. For more analysis on the gravity determinant in the prosecutor's choice of cases, see Susana SáCouto and Katherine Cleary, "The Gravity Threshold of the International Criminal Court," *American University International Law Review* 23, no. 5 (2008): 807–54. Margaret M. deGuzman, "Gravity and the Legitimacy of the International Criminal Court," *Fordham International Law Journal* 32, no. 5 (2009): 1400–65. Ray Murphy, "Gravity Issues and the International Criminal Court," *Criminal Law Forum* 17, no. 3-4 (2006): 281–315.

62. "Iraq Plans to Sign up to International Criminal Court," Agence France-Presse, February 17, 2005.

63. Author interview with Ambassador Feisal Istrabadi.

64. Author interview with former ICC official.

65. Author interview with Luis Moreno-Ocampo.

66. The World Bank's World Development Indicators (WDI) figure for "battle-related deaths" in Afghanistan in 2005 is 1,271. Data is available at http://databank. worldbank.org/ddp/home.do?Step=12&id=4&CNO=2. The Peace Research Institute, Oslo (PRIO) Battle Deaths Data set, version 3.0, released October 2009, gives its best estimate for 2005 battle-related deaths in Afghanistan as 1,268.

Data is available at http://www.prio.no/CSCW/Datasets/Armed-Conflict/ Battle-Deaths/The-Battle-Deaths-Dataset-version-30/. Human Rights Watch notes, in its "World Report 2006: Events of 2005," that more than 1,500 Afghan civilians lost their lives in political violence (p. 222, http://www.hrw.org/sites/ default/files/reports/wr2006.pdf).

67. The World Bank's WDI figure for "battle-related deaths" in Afghanistan in 2006 is 3,167. Data is available at http://databank.worldbank.org/ddp/home. do?Step=12&id=4&CNO=2. The PRIO Battle Deaths Data set, version 3.0, released October 2009, gives its best estimate for 2005 battle-related deaths in Afghanistan as 3,154. Data is available at http://www.prio.no/CSCW/Datasets/ Armed-Conflict/Battle-Deaths/The-Battle-Deaths-Dataset-version-30/). Human Rights Watch estimated, in its "World Report 2007: Events of 2006," that more than 3,000 Afghans had lost their lives in 2006, more than 1,000 of them civilians (p. 238, http://www.hrw.org/legacy/wr2k7/wr2007master.pdf).

68. Human Rights Watch notes that the 189 bombings in 2006 killed almost 500 civilians, with 177 additional civilians killed in other violent attacks, at least 350 of which were conducted by insurgent forces. For additional detail on these attacks, see "Afghanistan: The Human Cost: The Consequences of Insurgent Attacks in Afghanistan," April 2007, Volume 19, No. 6(C), pp. 3–4, http://www.hrw.org/sites/ default/files/reports/afghanistan0407webwcover.pdf. For the reference to eighty suicide attacks that killed mostly civilians, see Human Rights Watch "World Report 2007: Events of 2006," p. 238, http://www.hrw.org/legacy/wr2k7/wr2007master.pdf.

69. In acceding to the Rome Statute, Colombia took advantage of Article 124, which allowed countries to be exempt from war crimes prosecutions for seven years (in Colombia's case, until 2009). However, the court retained jurisdiction over crimes against humanity and acts of genocide committed on Colombian territory.

70. Scott Wilson, "U.S. Moves Closer to Colombia's War; Involvement of Special Forces Could Trigger New Wave of Guerrilla Violence," *Washington Post*, February 7, 2003, A22. Karen DeYoung, "Bush Uses Exemption on Colombia Forces," *Washington Post*, February 22, 2003, A21.

71. See Kim Housego, "Wave of Slayings and Kidnappings Spreads Fear in Colombia Ahead of Local Elections across Nation," Associated Press, October 18, 2003. Juan Forero, "Colombia Massacre Raises Fear of a Rebel Offensive," *International Herald Tribune*, June 18, 2004, 4.

72. Juan Forero, "Rightist Militias in Colombia Offer to Disarm 3,000 of Their Fighters," *New York Times*, October 9, 2004, A5. "Documentos exclusivos: así se fraguó el acuerdo de paz con los 'paras,'" *Semana*, April 26, 2010.

73. "Colombia War Crimes Probe Urged," *BBC News*, June 29, 2005, http://news. bbc.co.uk/2/hi/americas/4633955.stm.

74. "Colombia—Serious Concern over Demobilization Process," Human Rights Watch, para. 3 (October 29, 2005), http://www.hrw.org/news/2005/10/28/ colombia-serious-concern-over-demobilization-process.

75. For more on the court's approach on Colombia, see Kai Ambos and Florian Huber, "The Colombian Peace Process and the Principle of Complementarity of the International Criminal Court: Is There Sufficient Willingness and Ability on the Part of the Colombian Authorities or Should the Prosecutor Open an Investigation Now?", Extended version of the Statement in the "Thematic session: Colombia, ICC OTP—NGO 19/20 October 2010, The Hague," *Georg-August-Universität Göttingen, Institute for Criminal Law and Justice Department of Foreign and International Criminal Law* (January 5, 2011), http://www.icc-cpi.int/NR/rdonlyres/2770C2C8-309A-408E-A41B-0E69F098F421/282850/civil1.pdf.

76. Jess Bravin, "U.S. Warms to Hague Tribunal; New Stance Reflects Desire to Use Court to Prosecute Darfur Crimes," *Wall Street Journal*, June 14, 2006, A4.

77. Author interview with John Bellinger.

78. See Anneke Van Woudenberg, "Ethnically Targeted Violence in Ituri," in *Challenges of Peace Implementation: The UN Mission in the Democratic Republic of the Congo*, ed. Mark Malan and Joao Gomes Porto (Pretoria, South Africa: Institute for Security Studies, 2004). David Pallister, "UN Names Forces in Struggle for Congo Gold Fields," *Guardian* (London), December 4, 2003, 1.

79. Anthony Deutsch, "Congolese Rebel Leader Extradited to International Criminal Court," Associated Press, March 18, 2006.

80. Interview with ICC officials.

81. "Profile: DR Congo militia leader Thomas Lubanga," *BBC News* (July 10, 2012), http://www.bbc.co.uk/news/world-africa-17358799.

82. Damiano Beltrano, "Life in the World's First Global Jail," *InterDependent* (United Nations Association of the United States), Fall 2009.

83. Luis Moreno-Ocampo, "Press Conference in Relation with the Surrender to the Court of Mr. Thomas Lubanga Dyilo," March 18, 2006, http://www.icc-cpi.int/NR/rdonlyres/4760D87D-750C-4BFD-9CD0-1AE171DFC553/143842/LMO_20060318_En1.pdf.

84. Luis Moreno-Ocampo, "A Global Web of Justice is Up and Running: The International Criminal Court," *International Herald Tribune*, June 12, 2006, 8.

85. "Milosevic Found Dead in His Cell," *BBC News*, March 11, 2006, http://news.bbc.co.uk/2/hi/europe/4796470.stm.

86. Craig Timberg, "Liberia's Taylor Found and Arrested," *Washington Post*, March 30, 2006, A16.

87. Author interviews with John Bellinger and Philippe Kirsch.

88. Reed Brody, "Milosevic, Saddam, Taylor. Who's Next? Bringing Tyrants to Justice," *International Herald Tribune*, April 1, 2006, 6.

89. Danna Harman, "How China's Support of Sudan Shields a Regime Called 'Genocidal,'" *Christian Science Monitor*, June 26, 2007, 1.

90. Luis Moreno-Ocampo, "The Prosecutor of the ICC Opens Investigation in Darfur," news release ICC-OTP-0606–104, June 6, 2005, http://www.icc-cpi.int/en_menus/icc/press%20and%20media/press%20releases/2005/Pages/

the%20prosecutor%20of%20the%20icc%20opens%20investigation%20in%20 darfur.aspx.

91. Author interview with former ICC officials.

92. Author interview with Luis Moreno-Ocampo.

93. Elizabeth Rubin, "If Not Peace, Then Justice," *New York Times Magazine*, April 2, 2006, 42–46.

94. See Office of the Prosecutor, "Third Report of the Prosecutor of the International Criminal Court to the UN Security Council Pursuant to UNSCR 1593 (2005)," June 14, 2006.

95. "Observations of the United Nations High Commissioner for Human Rights invited in Application of Rule 103 of the Rules of Procedure and Evidence," ICC-02/05, October 10, 2006, http://www.icc-cpi.int/iccdocs/doc/doc259768. pdf.

96. Author interview with former ICC officials.

97. Luis Moreno-Ocampo, "International Criminal Court Prosecutor Opening Remarks on the Situation in Darfur," news release ICC-OTP-20070227–208, February 27, 2007, http://www.icc-cpi.int/en_menus/icc/situations%20 and%20cases/situations/situation%20icc%200205/press%20releases/Pages/ prosecutor%20opening%20remarks.aspx. Office of the Prosecutor and Pre-Trial Chamber I, "Warrant of Arrest for Ali Kushayb." ICC-02/05–01/07 (April 27, 2007), http://www.icc-cpi.int/iccdocs/doc/doc279858.PDF.

98. Mohamed Osman, "Sudan Rejects ICC War-Crime Allegations Against Two Sudanese," Associated Press, February 27, 2007. "Sudanese Minister Named by ICC Says Prosecutor's Case "Weak,'" *Akhir Lahzah* newspaper article translated by BBC Monitoring Middle East, February 28, 2007, citing excerpt of interview with Sudanese Minister of State for Humanitarian Affairs Ahmed Haroun, published on the website of Sudanese newspaper *Akhir Lahzah* on February 28. See also "Sudanese Minister Threatens Action against International Court Proponents." *Al-Hayat* newspaper article translated by BBC Monitoring Middle East, March 1, 2007, citing Al-Nur Ahmad al-Nur, "Khartoum Threatens to 'Slaughter' Those Who Try to Extradite Suspects to ICC from Khartoum," *Al-Hayat*, March 1, 2007.

99. Frank Nyakairu and news agencies, "Sudan Government Suspends Agreement on Kony on 20 March," *Daily Monitor* (Kampala), March 20, 2007.

100. Author interview with Mirjam Blaak.

101. Henry Mukasa, "Kony, Otti Study ICC Rules," *New Vision* (Kampala), November 21, 2006.

102. "M7 Rejects Kony Hunt," *New Vision* (Kampala), November 18, 2006.

103. See, for example, "Uganda: Historic ICC Arrest Warrants Evoke Praise, Concern," Inter Press Service, October 14, 2005; "Uganda: Amnesty Commission Opposes Warrant Arrests for LRA's Kony," *Daily Monitor* (Kampala), October 10, 2005; "Uganda: LRA Talks Over, Says Bigombe," *New Vision* (Kampala), October 10,

2005; "Uganda: ICC Indictments to Affect Northern Peace Efforts, Says Mediator," *UN Integrated Regional Information Networks* (Nairobi), October 10, 2005; "Uganda: Museveni Gives Kony Amnesty," *New Vision* (Kampala), July 4, 2006.

104. "Uganda 'Must Arrest' Rebel Leader," BBC News (May 18, 2006), http://news.bbc.co.uk/2/hi/africa/4992896.stm.

105. Chris McGreal, "Justice or Reconciliation?: African Search for Peace Throws Court into Crisis: Uganda Fears First Crucial Test for Tribunal Could Prolong Brutal 20-Year Civil War," *Guardian* (London), January 9, 2007, 14.

106. Ibid.

107. "South Sudan Launches Peace Talks," *Sudan Tribune* (Paris), June 8, 2006.

108. Author interview with Mirjam Blaak.

109. "South Africa's Mbeki Questions International Court's Move to Cite Ugandan Rebels," South African Press Association, June 2, 2006.

110. Author interview with Western official involved in Juba negotiations.

111. Address by Luis Moreno-Ocampo, "Building a Future on Peace and Justice," June 25, 2007, http://www.peace-justice-conference.info/download/speech%20moreno.pdf.

112. See, for example, January 25–26, 2005, Public Seminar "The International Criminal Court (ICC) and the New International Justice" in Bogota, Colombia, sponsored by Canada's Ministry of Foreign Affairs. March 16–18 "Regional Seminar on the ICC and Gender Justice," in Buenos Aires, Argentina, sponsored by the embassies of Canada and Germany in Buenos Aires. Coalition for an International Criminal Court archive of events for 2005, http://www.coalition-fortheicc.org/documents/CICC_ArchiveofEvents_2005.pdf. See also February 9, 2006, International Seminar "Prosecution of International Crimes in Colombia and the International Criminal Court," sponsored by the Canadian government. Coalition for an International Criminal Court archive of events for 2006, http://www.coalitionfortheicc.org/documents/CICC_ArchiveofEvents_2006.pdf.

113. See "Czech Lower House Recognizes International Criminal Court," Czech News Agency (CTK), October 29, 2008; "International Court for War Crimes Gets Snubbed by Czechs," *Prague Post*, April 18, 2007 (noting pressure to ratify).

114. Negotiated Relationship Agreement between the International Criminal Court and the United Nations, ICC-ASP/3/Res.1, adopted October 4, 2004, entered into force July 22, 2004, http://www.icc-cpi.int/NR/rdonlyres/916FC6A2-7846-4177-A5EA-5AA9B6D1E96C/0/ICCASP3Res1_English.pdf.

115. Agreement between the International Criminal Court and the European Union on Cooperation and Assistance, http://eur-lex.europa.eu/LexUriServ/site/en/oj/2006/l_115/l_11520060428en00500056.pdf.

116. See Mitja Mertens, "The International Criminal Court: A European Success Story?" EU Diplomacy Papers, January 2011, 15.

117. Author interview with Philippe Kirsch.

118. Ibid.

119. Yan Ling, "The Beijing Symposium on the Comparative Study of International Criminal Law and the Rome Statute," *Chinese Journal of International Law* 3, no. 1 (2004): 307.

120. Editorial in *The Hindu*, excerpted in "Editorial Roundup," Associated Press, April 14, 2005.

121. "ICC Judge Calls for India to Become Member of Court," *Citizens for Global Solutions* (January 4, 2006), http://archive2.globalsolutions.org/issues/international_criminal_court/learn/India.

122. Author interview with Japanese official.

123. Ibid.

124. Taku Tamaki, "Recasting 'Nuclear-Free Korean Peninsula' as a Sino-American Language for Co-ordination," *Japanese Journal of Political Science* 13, no. 1 (2012): 59–81.

125. Setsuko Kamiya, "Chief Justice of ICC Lauds Japan Pledge to Join Tribunal," *McClatchy—Tribune Business News*, December 7, 2006.

126. International Criminal Court Assembly of States Parties, 10th Sess. "Report of the Committee on Budget and Finance on the Work of Its Tenth Session," pp. 186–87, ICC-ASP/7/20 (April 2008), http://www.icc-cpi.int/iccdocs/asp_docs/B.pdf.

127. Fumiko Saiga was elected judge in January 2009; she passed away in April of that year and was replaced by another Japanese judge, Kuniko Ozaki, in a special election. See "Delivering on the Promise of a Fair, Effective and Independent Court: Election of ICC and ASP Officials: Judges: Fourth Election—2009," *Coalition for the International Criminal Court*, http://iccnow.org/?mod=electionjudges2009.

128. Philippe Kirsch, "Fifth Session of the Assembly of States Parties: Opening Remarks," pp. 3–4, November 23, 2006, http://www.icc-cpi.int/iccdocs/asp_docs/library/organs/presidency/PK_20061123_en.pdf.

129. International Criminal Court Assembly of States Parties, 5th Sess. "Report of the Bureau on Ratification and Implementation of the Rome Statute and on Participation in the Assembly of States Parties," ICC-ASP/5/26 (November 17, 2006), http://www.icc-cpi.int/iccdocs/asp_docs/library/asp/ICC-ASP-5-26_English.pdf.

130. Author interviews with former ICC officials.

131. UN News Centre, "Sudan Not Cooperating on Arrests of War Crimes Suspects, Says Prosecutor" (2007), http://www.un.org/apps/news/story.asp?NewsID=23625&Cr=sudan&Cr1=icc#.UZf4S8pQVjo.

132. "Sudan: Seven Journalists Charged for Attending World Criminal Court Training," *Akhir Lahzah* newspaper article translated by BBC Monitoring Middle East, October 11, 2007.

133. Olivia Ward, "Prosecutor Points the Finger of Guilt; International Criminal Court Counsel Frustrated in His Bid to Bring Sudanese Minister to the Hague," *Toronto Star*, September 9, 2007, A13.

134. UN News Centre, "UN Calls for More Offers of Troops, Specialist Units for Hybrid Force in Darfur," http://www.un.org/apps/news/story. asp?NewsID=23889&Cr=sudan&Cr1#.UEfGgaPoxqI.

135. Jonathan F. Fanton, "International Justice: Editorial: Mocking the Powerless and the Powerful (September 21, 2007)," *New York Times*, September 28, 2007, http:// www.nytimes.com/2007/09/28/opinion/lweb28darfur.html.

CHAPTER 6

1. Allegations and accounts, if not hard evidence, of worse misdeeds committed by Lubanga's UPC forces abounded. See Amnesty International, "DRC: On the Precipice: The Deepening Human Rights and Humanitarian Crisis in Ituri," p. 9, March 2003, http://www.amnesty.org/en/library/asset/AFR62/006/2003/ en/66d41fed-d731-11dd-b0cc-1f0860013475/afr620062003en.pdf. See also Human Rights Watch, "Chaos in Eastern Congo: U.N. Action Needed Now," Briefing Paper, p. 4, October 2002, http://www.hrw.org/sites/default/files/ reports/easterncongo-bck.pdf. Human Rights Watch, "Ituri: 'Covered in Blood': Ethnically Targeted Violence in Northeastern DR Congo," pp. 5, 19, 21–30, July 2003, http://www.hrw.org/sites/default/files/reports/DRC0703.pdf. For specific detail on Lubanga's recruitment of child soldiers, see "DRC: MONUC Denounces Recruitment of Child Soldiers by Lubanga's UPC/RP," *UN Integrated Regional Information Networks* (Nairobi), February 7, 2003. See also Benjamin N. Schiff, *Building the International Criminal Court* (Cambridge: Cambridge University Press, 2008), 220.

2. ICC Pre-Trial Chamber I, "Decision on the Consequences of Non-Disclosure of Exculpatory Materials Covered by Article 54(3)(e) Agreements and the Application to Stay the Prosecution of the Accused, Together with Certain Other Issues Raised at the Status Conference on 10 June 2008," para. 93, ICC-01/04–01/06–1401 (June 13, 2008), http://www.icc-cpi.int/iccdocs/doc/doc511249. pdf.

3. For an informed account of this incident by a senior UN official, see Larry D. Johnson, "The Lubanga Case and Cooperation between the UN and the ICC: Disclosure Obligation v. Confidentiality Obligation," *Journal of International Criminal Justice* 10, no. 4 (2012): 895 in particular. See also ICC Pre-Trial Chamber I, "Situation in the Democratic Republic of the Congo: In the Case of the Prosecutor v. Thomas Lubanga Dyilo: Reasons for Oral Decision Lifting the Stay of Proceedings," ICC-01/04–01/06–1644 (January 23, 2009), http://www.icc-cpi.int/iccdocs/JUDSUMM/JSV_ICC_0104_0106_1644.pdf.

4. Author interview with Luis Moreno-Ocampo.

5. His group was called "Front des nationalistes et intégrationnistes (FNI)," Front for National Integration. For a synopsis of the complex mix of ethnic and armed groups in Ituri in mid-2003, and a look at FNI, see Human Rights Watch,

"Ituri: 'Covered in Blood': Ethnically Targeted Violence in Northeastern DR Congo," pp. 14–16, July 2003, http://www.hrw.org/sites/default/files/reports/DRC0703.pdf. For more details of documented FNI crimes, see Human Rights Watch, "Seeking Justice: The Prosecution of Sexual Violence in the Congo War," pp. 18–19, March 2005, http://www.hrw.org/sites/default/files/reports/drc0305.pdf.

6. Emily Ponder, "Child Soldiers Allegedly Helped Pillage Bogoro: Witness Recounts How Child Soldiers Wielding Spears Looted Ituri Village," *Institute for War & Peace Reporting*, ACR Issue 248, February 26, 2010, http://iwpr.net/report-news/child-soldiers-allegedly-helped-pillage-bogoro.

7. Tristan McConnell, "A Congo Warlord—Arrested for Crimes against Humanity—Explains Himself," *Christian Science Monitor*, February 15, 2008, 20.

8. Marlise Simons, "Third Ex-Warlord Sent to U.N. Court," *New York Times*, February 8, 2008, 6.

9. ICC Office of the Prosecutor and Pre-Trial Chamber I, "Warrant of Arrest for Mathieu Ngudjolo Chui," paras. i-ix, ICC-01/04-02/07 (July 6, 2007), http://www.icc-cpi.int/iccdocs/doc/doc453054.PDF.

10. Human Rights Watch, "Killings in Kiwanja: The UN's Inability to Protect Civilians," p. 10, December 2008, http://www.hrw.org/sites/default/files/reports/drc1208web.pdf. International Crisis Group, "Scramble for the Congo: Anatomy of an Ugly War," p. 33, December 20, 2000, http://www.crisisgroup.org/~/media/files/africa/central-africa/dr-congo/scramble%20for%20the%20congo%20anatomy%20of%20an%20ugly%20war.pdf. International Crisis Group, "Congo: Four Priorities for Sustainable Peace in Ituri," pp. 3, 30, 32, May 13, 2008, http://www.crisisgroup.org/~/media/files/africa/central-africa/dr-congo/congo%20four%20priorities%20for%20sustainable%20peace%20in%20ituri.pdf.

11. Human Rights Watch, "Ituri: 'Covered in Blood': Ethnically Targeted Violence In Northeastern DR Congo," pp. 24–26, July 2003, http://www.hrw.org/sites/default/files/reports/DRC0703.pdf. "DRC: MONUC Chief Summons Militia Leader over Attacks," *UN Integrated Regional Information Networks* (Nairobi), January 23, 2004, http://www.irinnews.org/Report/48223/DRC-MONUC-chief-summons-militia-leader-over-attacks.

12. ICC Office of the Prosecutor and Pre-Trial Chamber I, "Warrant of Arrest" for Bosco Ntaganda (issued under seal), paras. i-iii, ICC-01/04-02/06 (August 22, 2006), http://www.icc-cpi.int/iccdocs/doc/doc305330.PDF.

13. For a description of the disputed first election in July and a chart of July election results by province and candidate, see International Crisis Group, "Securing Congo's Elections: Lessons from the Kinshasa Showdown," pp. 1–2, Annex B on p. 10, October 2, 2006, http://www.crisisgroup.org/~/media/Files/africa/central-africa/dr-congo/B042%20Securing%20Congos%20Elections%20Lessons%20from%20the%20Kinshasa%20Showdown.pdf. The chart in Annex

B indicates Bemba won 49 percent of the vote in Kinshasa, while Kabila won almost 15 percent of the vote in Kinshasa. For election results of both rounds of voting, see International Foundation for Electoral Systems (IFES), "DR Congo, Presidential Elections," Results of First Round (July 30, 2006) and Second Round (October 29, 2006), http://www.electionguide.org/results.php?ID=1208.

14. Despite the activities of Bemba and the MLC within Ituri in the early 2000s, Bemba's ICC case itself centered on crimes committed in neighboring Central African Republic. See ICC Office of the Prosecutor and Pre-Trial Chamber III, "Warrant of Arrest for Jean-Pierre Bemba Gombo," paras. 9, 12–16, 18–21, ICC-01/05-01/08 (May 23, 2008), http://www.icc-cpi.int/iccdocs/doc/doc504390.PDF. For an in-depth investigation of war crimes committed in the Central African Republic at this time, see Fédération internationale des ligues des droits de l'homme (FIDH) / International Federation for Human Rights, "War Crimes in the Central African Republic: 'When the Elephants Fight, the Grass Suffers,'" February 2003, http://www.fidh.org/IMG/pdf/FIDH_Report_WarCrimes_in_CAR_English_Feb2003.pdf. Documentation of crimes tied to Bemba's forces, and a case for his prosecution at the ICC, are described on pp. 21–35.

15. For accounts of Bemba's arrest, see "Congo Ex-rebel Chief Bemba Arrested," *Financial Times* (London), May 25, 2008. "Congo Ex-Official is Held in Belgium on War Crimes Charges," *New York Times*, May 25, 2008, A13. "Bemba Arrested for War Crimes," *Independent*, May 26, 2008, 20. For a closer look at the ICC investigation in CAR and the role of civil society groups, see Marlies Glasius, "Global Justice Meets Local Civil Society: The International Criminal Court's Investigation in the Central African Republic," *Alternatives: Global, Local, Political* 33, no. 4 (2008): 413–33. This piece provides historical and political context surrounding the opening of the ICC investigation (pp. 415–16).

16. See United Nations Organization Mission in the Democratic Republic of the Congo (MONUC) and Office of the United Nations High Commissioner for Human Rights, "The Human Rights Situation in the Democratic Republic of Congo (DRC) during the Period January to June 2007," paras. 1, 2, 5, 6, 38–42, pp. 2–3, 9, September 27, 2007, http://www.ohchr.org/Documents/Countries/UNHROBiannualReport01to062007.pdf. See also Amnesty International, "Democratic Republic of Congo: Torture and Killings by State Security Agents Still Endemic," October 2007, http://www.amnesty.org/en/library/asset/AFR62/012/2007/en/45cad2e8-d374-11dd-a329-2f46302a8cc6/afr620122007en.pdf.

17. Jonathan Graubart, "Rendering Global Criminal Law an Instrument of Power: Pragmatic Legalism and Global Tribunals," *Journal of Human Rights* 9, no. 4 (2010): 409–26. Phil Clark, "Law, Politics and Pragmatism: The ICC and Case Selection in Uganda and the Democratic Republic of Congo," in *Courting*

Conflict? Justice, Peace and the ICC in Africa, ed. Nicholas Waddell and Phil Clark (London: Royal African Society), 2008.

18. Author interviews with former ICC officials.

19. UN Security Council, 62nd year, 5789th mtg. p. 5, U.N. Doc. S/PV.5789 (Dec. 5, 2007), http://www.un.org/ga/search/view_doc.asp?symbol=S/PV.5789.

20. Author interview with Jonathan Fanton.

21. Author interview with Richard Williamson; account confirmed in interviews with former ICC prosecutor Luis Moreno-Ocampo.

22. Author interview with former ICC official.

23. Author interview with Luis Moreno-Ocampo.

24. Author interviews with former ICC officials.

25. UN Security Council, 63rd year, 5905th mtg, p. 4, U.N. Doc. S/PV.5905 (June 5, 2008), http://www.un.org/ga/search/view_doc.asp?symbol=S/PV.5905.

26. Record and official communiqué of this closed meeting: UN Security Council, 5934th mtg. U.N. Doc. S/PV.5905 (July 16, 2008), http://www.un.org/ga/search/view_doc.asp?symbol=S/PV.5934. Neil MacFarquhar, "Pursuit of Sudan's Leader Incites Debate," *New York Times*, July 12, 2008, A6. "Rights Group Fears Sudanese Backlash," *CNN.com*, July 15, 2008, http://www.cnn.com/2008/WORLD/africa/07/15/darfur.charges/index.html.

27. Cable from US Embassy in the Hague to Secretary of State, "ICC Prosecutor to File a New Application in Darfur Situation," July 14, 2008, http://www.cablegatesearch.net/search.php?q=high+stakes+gamble+ICC&qo=0&qc=0&qto=2010-02-28. Human rights advocates and analysts were divided on the implications of the move. See, for example, Julie Flint and Alex de Waal, "'This Prosecution Will Endanger the People We Wish to Defend in Sudan,'" *Observer* (London), July 13, 2008, 41. International Crisis Group, "New ICC Prosecution: Opportunities and Risks for Peace in Sudan," news release, July 14, 2008, http://www.crisisgroup.org/en/publication-type/media-releases/2008/new-icc-prosecution-opportunities-and-risks-for-peace-in-sudan.aspx. Human Rights Watch, "Darfur: ICC Moves against Sudan's Leader: Charges against al-Bashir a Major Step to Ending Impunity," news release, July 15, 2008, http://www.hrw.org/news/2008/07/14/darfur-icc-moves-against-sudan-s-leader.

28. ICC Office of the Prosecutor, "Prosecutor's Statement on the Prosecutor's Application for a Warrant of Arrest under Article 58 against Omar Hassan Ahmad al Bashir," p. 3, July 14, 2008, http://www.icc-cpi.int/iccdocs/asp_docs/library/organs/otp/ICC-OTP-ST20080714-ENG.pdf.

29. "UN to Withdraw Non-Critical Staff from Darfur," Canadian Broadcasting Corporation (CBC) News, July 14, 2008. "UN Airlifts Staff from Darfur as Tension Mounts: Indictment Could Lead to Violence," *Cape Argus* (Cape Town, South Africa), July 15, 2008.

30. "Sudan: Presidential Aide Terms ICC 'European Court of Injustice,'" Sudan TV, translated from Arabic by BBC Monitoring Middle East, July 13, 2008. Account

cites remarks made by Sudanese Presidential Aide Nafi Ali Nafi at a military ceremony in Omdurman, Sudan. Edmund Sanders and Maggie Farley, "To Sudan,
Court is Criminal," *Chicago Tribune*, July 12, 2008, 9. "Sudan to File Charges
against ICC Prosecutor, Report Says," *Sudan Tribune* (Paris), June 20, 2008.

31. For accounts of protests, see Associated Press and Reuters, "Sudan Says a Warrant
Holds Peril for Darfur: Thousands Backing Leader Rally in Capital," *International
Herald Tribune* (Paris), July 14, 2008. Lydia Polgreen and Neil MacFarquhar,
"Sudanese Protest War Crimes Case against President at Scripted Rally in
Capital," *New York Times*, July 14, 2008.

32. Katy Glassborow, "Darfuris' Mixed Feelings over Bashir Warrant: Some
Unhappy that Genocide Charges against Sudanese President Weren't Included in
Indictment," *Institute for War & Peace Reporting*, ACR Issue 207, April 29, 2009,
http://iwpr.net/report-news/darfuris-mixed-feelings-over-bashir-warrant.   For
more on the range of reactions from Darfuris, see "Bashir's Indictment 'Giant Step
for International Justice'—Darfur Rebels," *Sudan Tribune* (Paris), July 15, 2008.
Najum Mushtaq, "Sudan: ICC's Indictment of President Bashir Sparks Hope,
Fear," Inter Press Service, July 18, 2008. "Darfur Investigator Finds Refugees'
Voices in Tune with Sudan Indictment," Voice of America, July 18, 2008.

33. Stephen McDonell, "China Concerned by ICC's Sudan Arrest Plans," Australian
Broadcasting Corporation, July 15, 2008. Audra Ang, "China Concerned by
International Criminal Court's Move to Seek Arrest of Sudan's President,"
Associated Press, July 15, 2008. "Russian Envoy Says 'Concern' at UN over
Sudanese President Arrest Warrant," Interfax news agency report in Russian trans-
lated by BBC Worldwide Monitoring, July 15, 2008.

34. Simon Tisdall, "West Faces Clash with Africa on War Crime Indictment," *Guardian*
(London), February 17, 2008, 19. See also "African Union Asks Court to Halt Bashir
Warrant," *Daily Monitor* (Kampala), July 15, 2008. "AU Urges Court to Give Peace
Process a Chance in Darfur," Hirondelle News Agency, July 15, 2008. "Arab League
to Hold Emergency Meeting on Sudan-ICC Crisis," Deutsche Presse-Agentur, July
14, 2008. "Sudan Asks League to Set Urgent Meeting: Court Might Issue Warrant
for President," *International Herald Tribune* (Paris), July 14, 2008.

35. "Sudan: P-3 Discussions on Sudan-ICC Issues," *Daily Telegraph* (London),
February 4, 2011.

36. Author interview with Mark Malloch Brown.

37. UN Security Council, 63rd year, 5947th mtg, p. 8, U.N. Doc. S/PV.5947 (July 31,
2008), http://www.un.org/ga/search/view_doc.asp?symbol=S/PV.5947.

38. Ibid., p. 3.

39. Cable from American Embassy in Paris, "Sudan/Darfur: Exploring the Possibility
of Suspending an ICC Indictment to Improve Sudanese Behavior," August 6,
2008, http://wikileaks.org/cable/2008/08/08PARIS1519.html.

40. Alex Duval Smith, "Britain Blocks Prosecution of Sudan's Ruler: Human Rights
Groups Criticise Strategy on Darfur," *Observer* (London), September 14, 2008, 44.

41. Louise Arbour, "Justice v. Politics," *International Herald Tribune*, September 17, 2008, 6.

42. Smith, "Britain Blocks Prosecution of Sudan's Ruler: Human Rights Groups Criticise Strategy on Darfur," 44.

43. Author interview with Mark Malloch Brown.

44. Author interview with Ambassador Richard Williamson.

45. Author interview with Cameron Hudson.

46. Author interview with Clint Williamson.

47. Cable from US Embassy Kampala to Secretary of State, "Uganda: Continued U.S. Support For Anti-lra Efforts Critical," January 14, 2010, http://wikileaks.org/cable/2010/01/10KAMPALA23.html; see also Jeffrey Gettleman and Eric Schmitt, "U.S. Aided a Failed Plan to Rout Ugandan Rebels," *New York Times*, February 7, 2009, A1.

48. United Nations Organization Mission in the Democratic Republic of the Congo and Office of the High Commissioner for Human Rights, "Summary of Fact Finding Missions on Alleged Human Rights Violations Committed by the Lord's Resistance Army (LRA) in the Districts of Haut-Uélé and Bas-Uélé in Orientale Province of the Democratic Republic of Congo," paras. 52–55, pp. 15–16, December 2009, http://www2.ohchr.org/SPdocs/Countries/LRAReport_December2009_E.pdf. Human Rights Watch, "DR Congo: LRA Slaughters 620 in 'Christmas Massacres': Protection Urgently Needed as Killings Continue," January 17, 2009, http://www.hrw.org/news/2009/01/17/dr-congo-lra-slaughters-620-christmas-massacres.

49. Julia Spiegel and Noel Atama, "Finishing the Fight against the LRA," Enough Project report, May 12, 2009, http://www.enoughproject.org/files/lra_strategy_paper_051209.pdf.

50. For Annan's account of his involvement, see Kofi A. Annan and Nader Mousavizadeh, "The Fate of the Continent: Africa's Wars, Africa's Peace," in *Interventions: A Life in War and Peace* (New York: Penguin Press, 2012), 184–208. See also Roger Cohen, "How Kofi Annan Rescued Kenya," *New York Times Review of Books*, August 14, 2008.

51. Megan K. Stack, "Conflict in Caucasus: Ossetians Praise Russians; Blow to U.S. Foreign Policy; Russian Claims Appear Inflated; South Ossetia is Badly Damaged but Bears No Sign of a Genocide by Georgia. Residents Hail Moscow as a Savior," *Los Angeles Times*, August 18, 2008, A1. Kim Sengupta, "Judgement Day Dawns after Russia Pledges to Quit Georgia," *Independent* (London), August 18, 2008, 20. Steven Erlanger, "West is Struggling to Unite on Georgia: Russia Agrees to Withdraw, But NATO is Riven by How to Deal With the Crisis," *International Herald Tribune* (Paris), August 18, 2008, 1. Catherine Belton and Charles Clover, "West is United in Stand on Georgia," *Financial Times* (London), August 18, 2008, 1.

52. Human Rights Watch, "Up in Flames: Humanitarian Law Violations and Civilian Victims in the Conflict over South Ossetia," pp. 2, 6–11, January 2009, http://www.hrw.org/sites/default/files/reports/georgia0109web.pdf.

53. Israeli Defense Forces Operation Cast Lead report: "The Operation in Gaza 27 December 2008-18 January 2009: Factual and Legal Aspects," Section II, para. 16, p. 5, July 2009.

54. UN Office of the High Commissioner for Human Rights, "UN Human Rights Chief Expresses Her Grave Concern in the Escalating Violence in Gaza," news release, December 28, 2008, http://www.unhchr.ch/huricane/huricane.nsf/view01/F5307C1E012294F6C125752D005CD71F?opendocument.

55. Rory McCarthy, "UN Human Rights Chief Accuses Israel of War Crimes," *Guardian* (London), January 10, 2009, 6.

56. Israeli Prime Minister Olmert made this statement: "On behalf of the Government of Israel, I wish to convey my regret for the harming of uninvolved civilians, for the pain we caused them, for the suffering they and their families suffered as a result of the intolerable situation created by Hamas." Israel Ministry of Foreign Affairs, "The Operation in Gaza—Factual and Legal Aspects," http://mfa.gov.il/MFA/PressRoom/2009/Pages/Statement_PM_Ehud_Olmert_17-Jan-2009.aspx.

57. Dan Izenberg and Herb Keinon, "Israel Will Not Join International Criminal Court," *Jerusalem Post*, July 1, 2002, 1.

58. Palestinian National Authority, Ministry of Justice, Office of Minister, "Declaration Recognizing the Jurisdiction of the International Criminal Court," January 21, 2009, http://www.icc-cpi.int/NR/rdonlyres/74EEE201-0FED-4481-95D4-C8071087102C/279777/20090122PalestinianDeclaration2.pdf. Marlise Simons, "Palestinians Press International Court for Inquiry on Possible Gaza War Crimes," *New York Times*, February 11, 2009, 13. For additional context, see Alain Pellet, "The Palestinian Declaration and the Jurisdiction of the International Criminal Court," *Journal of International Criminal Justice* 8, no. 4 (2010): 981–99.

59. Article 12(3) provides "[i]f the acceptance of a State which is not a Party to this Statute is required…that State may, by declaration lodged with the Registrar, accept the exercise of jurisdiction by the Court with respect to the crime in question."

60. "Legal Consequences of the Construction of a Wall in the Occupied Palestinian Territory," International Court of Justice Advisory Opinion, July 9, 2004, http://www.icj-cij.org/docket/files/131/1671.pdf.

61. "AU Backs Sudan President in ICC Row," *Sudan Tribune* (Paris), February 3, 2009.

62. African Union Assembly, Decisions and Declarations reached by the Assembly of the African Union, July 1-3, 2009, Sirte, Libya, Assembly/AU/Dec.243–267 (XIII) Rev.1 Assembly/AU/Decl.1-5(XIII), para. 10, p. 2, http://www.au.int/en/sites/

default/files/ASSEMBLY_EN_1_3_JULY_2009_AUC_THIRTEENTH_
ORDINARY_SESSION_DECISIONS_DECLARATIONS_%20
MESSAGE_CONGRATULATIONS_MOTION_0.pdf.

63. Colum Lynch, "International Court under Unusual Fire: Africans Defend Sudan's Indicted Leader," *Washington Post*, June 30, 2009, A6.

64. David Pallister, "Growing Clamour to Remove the Hague Prosecutor Who Wants This Man Arrested: Move to Hold Sudan Leader over Darfur Sparks Outcry: Let the Judges Decide, Says Man at Eye of Storm," *Guardian* (London), August 18, 2008, 13. Mark Lattimer, "For All Bashir's Bravado, He is Marked as Damaged Goods: The Sudanese President Will Soon Find His Security Council Allies Can't Shield Him from the Impact of Being Cast as Global Pariah," *Guardian* (London), July 16, 2008, 16.

65. Julie Flint and Alex de Waal, "Case Closed: A Prosecutor Without Borders," *World Affairs* 171, no. 4 (2009): 23–38.

66. Andrew T. Cayley, "The Prosecutor's Strategy in Seeking the Arrest of Sudanese President Al Bashir on Charges of Genocide," *Journal of International Criminal Justice* 6, no. 5 (2008): 830.

67. William Schabas, *The International Criminal Court: A Commentary on the Rome Statute*, Oxford Commentaries on International Law (Oxford; New York: Oxford University Press, 2010), 612. See also International Labor Organization, 105th Session, Administrative Tribunal Judgment No. 2757, issued in Geneva, July 9, 2008, pp. 3–4, http://www.ilo.org/dyn/triblex/triblexmain.fullText?p_lang=fr&p_judgment_no=2757&p_language_code=EN.

68. International Labor Organization, 105th Session, Administrative Tribunal Judgment No. 2757, http://www.ilo.org/dyn/triblex/triblexmain.fullText?p_lang=fr&p_judgment_no=2757&p_language_code=EN.

69. Author interview with John Bellinger.

70. Christine Chung, "A Prosecutor Without Borders," *World Affairs* 172, no. 1 (2009): 104.

71. See, for example, Will Marshall, "The Blair Democrats: Ready for Battle," *Washington Post*, May 1, 2003, A27.

72. Author interview with former US government official.

73. Author interview with J. Clint Williamson.

74. Cable from US Mission to the United Nations to Secretary of State, "Amb. DiCarlo Meets with International Criminal Court President Song," May 19, 2009, http://wikileaks.org/cable/2009/05/09USUNNEWYORK519.html.

75. Ewen MacAskill, "U.S. May Face Down Fear of Prosecution and Join International War Crimes Court, Clinton Hints," *Guardian* (London), August 6, 2009, 17.

76. Tom Maliti, "Envoy Says US to Attend War Crimes Court Meeting," Associated Press, November 16, 2009.

77. Author interview with senior Obama administration official.

78. Author interview with US government official.

79. Guillaume Lavallee, "Beshir Lashes Out at West as Fears Mount for Darfur," *Agence France Presse*, March 5, 2009. Edith M. Lederer, "UN Warns 'Irrevocable Damage' in Darfur Expulsions," *Associated Press*, March 5, 2009. "Sudan Expulsions Could Spark Conflict-Aid Groups," *Reuters*, March 6, 2009.

80. Author interview with Scott Gration.

81. Author interview with US government officials.

82. Marlise Simons, "As a Wanted Man, Sudan's President Can't Escape His Diplomatic Isolation," *New York Times*, May 2, 2010, 8.

83. Chinese Ministry of Foreign Affairs, "Wen Jiabao Meets with Presidents of Seychelles, Tanzania, Sudan, the Republic of Congo, and Uganda," November 2006, http://www.fmprc.gov.cn/eng/wjdt/wshd/t279855.htm.

84. Cable from US Mission to the United Nations to US Secretary of State, "ICC'S Ocampo on Sudan: Go After Bashir's Money and Call for his Arrest; Reassure China," March 24, 2009, http://wikileaks.org/cable/2009/03/09USUNNEWYORK306.html.

85. Afua Hirsch, "Britain Failing to Make Bashir's Arrest a Priority, says ICC's Chief Prosecutor," *Guardian* (London), May 24, 2009.

86. Arlene Getz, "Rocking the Courtroom," *Newsweek*, March 30, 2009.

87. Cable from US Embassy Khartoum to Secretary of State, "President Bashir Rethinking Attendance At Arab League Summit," March 23, 2009, http://wikileaks.org/cable/2009/03/09KHARTOUM408.html.

88. Brian Murphy, "Sudan's Leader Arrives in Qatar; Arab League Allies Ignore ICC Warrant, Give Warm Welcome," *Washington Post*, March 30, 2009, A11. Andrew England, "League Rejects Warrant for Bashir," *FT.com* (2009).

89. Decisions and Declarations reached by the Assembly of the African Union, July 1-3, 2009, Sirte, Libya, Assembly/AU/Dec. 243–267 (XIII) Rev.1 Assembly/AU/Decl.1-5(XIII), para. 10, p. 2, http://www.au.int/en/sites/default/files/ASSEMBLY_EN_1_3_JULY_2009_AUC_THIRTEENTH_ORDINARY_SESSION_DECISIONS_DECLARATIONS_%20MESSAGE_CONGRATULATIONS_MOTION_0.pdf.

90. Cable from Secretary of State to American Embassy Cairo, "Demarche on Dealing with Sudanese President Bashir during His Visit to Cairo," March 24, 2009, http://wikileaks.org/cable/2009/03/09STATE28317.html.

91. "Sudan's Bashir to Miss OIC Summit after EU Objected," *Reuters*, November 8, 2009.

92. "Sudan: The Fifth Anniversary of the Comprehensive Peace Agreement," briefing by Scott Gration, Special Envoy for Sudan, Foreign Press Center, Washington, DC, January 11, 2010, http://fpc.state.gov/135047.htm.

93. Author interview with Scott Gration.

94. Jeffrey Gettleman, "Under Wraps, Kenya's Bill for Bloodshed Nears Payment," *New York Times*, July 16, 2009, 15.

95. Hans-Peter Kaul, "Dissenting Opinion of Judge Hans-Peter Kaul," in Pre-Trial Chamber II, "Decision Pursuant to Article 15 of the Rome Statute on the Authorization of an Investigation into the Situation in the Republic of Kenya," ICC-01/09–19-Corr 01–04-2010 (March 31, 2010), http://www.icc-cpi.int/iccdocs/doc/doc854562.pdf.

96. For news accounts, see "Materials on Events in 2008 Were Sent to the International Criminal Court," *Georgia Times*, August 8, 2011. "Russian Investigative Committee: Georgia Was Trying to Discredit Russian Army in August 2008 Conflict," Interfax, August 8, 2012. For a 2012 status report on the investigation, see ICC Office of the Prosecutor, "Report on Preliminary Examination Activities 2012," paras. 120–40 (November 2012), http://www.icc-cpi.int/iccdocs/otp/OTP2012ReportonPreliminaryExaminations22Nov2012.pdf.

97. Eka Janashia, "Georgian Government to Probe August 2008 War," *Central Asia-Caucasus Institute Analyst*, April 17, 2003, http://www.cacianalyst.org/publications/field-reports/item/12708-georgian-government-to-probe-august-2008-war.html.

98. Ministry of Foreign Affairs of the Russian Federation, "Visit to Russia by Representatives of the Office of the Prosecutor of the International Criminal Court," new release 285-10-03-2010, March 10, 2010, http://www.mid.ru/brp_4.nsf/0/DA277988EE244453C32576E3003F6D0F.

99. Raghida Durgham, "Ocampo Tells Al-Hayat: 'Al-Bashir is Still Hunted and Justice Will Be Done'," *Al-Hayat* (London), September 12, 2009.

100. Report of the United Nations Fact Finding Mission on the Gaza Conflict ("Goldstone Report") A/HRC/12/48, presented to the 12th Session of the Human Rights Council, para. 1966, p. 422, September 25, 2009, http://www2.ohchr.org/english/bodies/hrcouncil/docs/12session/A-HRC-12-48.pdf.

101. Cable from US Mission to the United Nations to Secretary of State, "Ambassador Rice's October 20 Meeting with Israeli President Peres," October 28, 2009, http://wikileaks.org/cable/2009/10/09TELAVIV2375.html.

102. Cable from US Embassy Tel Aviv to Secretary of State, http://www.cablegate-search.net/cable.php?id=10TELAVIV417&q=arab%20icc%20mandelblitIDF "Mag Mandelblit On IDF Investigations Into Operation Cast Lead," February 23, 2010, http://www.cablegatesearch.net/search.php?q=ICC+mandelblit+arab&qo=0&qc=0&qto=2010-02-28.

103. Author interview with senior Obama administration official.

104. Ibid.

105. Author interview with former ICC officials.

106. "Afghanistan: Annual Report 2009: Protection of Civilians in Armed Conflict," United Nations Assistance Mission in Afghanistan (UNAMA), Afghanistan Independent Human Rights Commission, 2010, 1, http://unama.unmissions.org/Portals/UNAMA/human%20rights/Protection%20of%20Civilian%202009%20report%20English.pdf.

107. United Nations Assistance Mission in Afghanistan, Statement by the Special Representative of the Secretary-General for Afghanistan, Kai Eide, August 26, 2009.

108. "After Afghan Strike, Charred Flesh and Burning Rage," Reuters, September 4, 2009.

109. Author interview with Luis Moreno-Ocampo.

110. Author interview with former ICC officials.

111. Ibid.

112. UN Secretary-General, *Report of the Secretary-General's Internal Review Panel on United Nations Action in Sri Lanka*, ¶ 34 (November 2012), http://www.un.org/News/dh/infocus/Sri_Lanka/The_Internal_Review_Panel_report_on_Sri_Lanka.pdf.

113. See Office of the Prosecutor, "Legal Memorandum on the IOM Mandate," November 19, 2010, http://iccforum.com/media/background/oversight/2010-11-19_OTP_Memorandum_on_IOM_Mandate_%28English%29.pdf.

114. See generally *The Princeton Process on the Crime of Aggression: Materials of the Special Working Group on the Crime of Aggression, 2003–2009*, ed. Stefan Barriga, Wolfgang Danspeckgruber, and Christian Wenaweser (Boulder, CO: Lynne Rienner Publishers, 2009).

115. Cable from American Embassy in France to Secretary of State, "S/WCI Amb Williamson's Meeting With French MFA Legal Advisor Belliard," January 23, 2008, http://wikileaks.org/cable/2008/01/08PARIS120.html.

116. Harold Koh, "The Obama Administration and International Law," speech to the American Society of International Law, March 25, 2010, http://www.state.gov/s/l/releases/remarks/139119.htm.

117. Richard Goldstone, "Prosecuting Aggression," *International Herald Tribune* (Paris), May 27, 2010, 7.

118. Open Society Foundations, "Open Society Justice Initiative Highlighting Complementarity and Outreach at ICC Review," news release, May 26, 2010, http://www.opensocietyfoundations.org/press-releases/open-society-justice-initiative-highlighting-complementarity-and-outreach-icc-review.

119. Statement from Brazilian representative to the Review Conference on the Rome Statute of the International Criminal Court (ICC) in Kampala, Uganda, May 31-June 11, 2010, http://www.iccnow.org/documents/ICC-RC-gendeba-Brazil-ENG.pdf.

120. Howard LaFranchi, "US Opposes ICC Bid to Make 'Aggression' a Crime under International Law," *Christian Science Monitor*, June 15, 2010.

121. See Rome Statute, arts. 8*bis* and 15*bis*.

122. "Libya's Gaddafi to Rein in Sudanese Rebel," Reuters, July 20, 2010.

123. Author interview with Peter Wittig.

124. Author interview with Hardeep Singh Puri.

125. Author interview with French official.

126. Author interviews with French, South African, and US diplomats.

127. S.C. Res. 1970, U.N. Doc. S/RES/1970 (February 26, 2011), http://www.un.org/Docs/journal/asp/ws.asp?m=s/res/1970%282011%29.

128. Nicholas Watt and James Meikle, "Libya Officials Bribed by Britain to Help Evacuate UK Citizens," *Guardian* (London), February 25, 2011. "Libya Unrest: Cameron Backs 'War Crimes' Investigation," BBC News, February 25, 2011, http://www.bbc.co.uk/news/uk-politics-12576985.

129. Scott Wilson and Joby Warrick, "Obama Appeals Directly to Top Libyan Officials," *Washington Post*, March 8, 2011, A8.

130. Jesse Lee, "President Obama to Those Conducting Violence in Libya: 'It is Their Choice…and They Will Be Held Accountable,'" *White House Blog*, March 7, 2011, http://www.whitehouse.gov/blog/2011/03/07/president-obama-those-conducting-violence-libya-it-their-choice-and-they-will-be-hel.

131. Luis Moreno-Ocampo, Decision Assigning the Situation in the Libyan Arab Jamahiriya to Pre-Trial Chamber I (ref: 2011/017/LMO/JCCD-rr), March 2, 2011, http://www.icc-cpi.int/iccdocs/doc/doc1032133.pdf.

132. Author interview with former ICC officials.

133. "Libyan Revolution on Road to Collapse: As Gadhafi Forces Ring Strategic City, Many Fear How Regime Will Treat 'Rats and Vermin,'" *Toronto Star*, March 16, 2011, A4. Ewen MacAskill, Simon Tisdall, and Nicholas Watt, "Middle East: US Backs No-Fly Zone over Libya but Rebels Fear Aid Will Come Too Late to Stop Gaddafi," *Guardian* (London), March 16, 2011, 18.

134. S.C. Res. 1973, U.N. Doc. S/RES/1973 (March 17, 2011), http://www.un.org/Docs/journal/asp/ws.asp?m=S/RES/1973%20%282011%29.

135. See, for example, Bruce Ackerman, "Legal Acrobatics, Illegal War," *New York Times*, June 21, 2011, A27. Rand Paul, "Obama's Unconstitutional Libyan War: By Not Consulting Congress, President has Violated War Powers Act," *Washington Times*, June 16, 2011, 1.

136. Julian Borger, Richard Norton-Taylor, and Paul Harris, "Diplomats Meet as Italy Plots Leader's Escape Route," *Guardian* (London), March 29, 2011, 1.

137. Roland Watson et al., "Gaddafi's Way Out: Rebel Saloon-Car Army Drives on Towards Sirte: Allies May Allow Dictator to Leave Libya International Coalition Split over Ceasefire," *Times* (London), March 29, 2011, 1, 5.

138. Human Rights Watch, "UN Security Council: Support ICC Probe on Libya: Prosecutor to Brief Council on Libya," news release, May 3, 2011, http://www.hrw.org/news/2011/05/03/un-security-council-support-icc-probe-libya.

139. ICC Office of the Prosecutor, "Statement to the United Nations Security Council on the Situation in the Libyan Arab Jamahiriya, pursuant to UNSCR 1970 (2011)," para. 27 (May 4, 2011), http://www.icc-cpi.int/en_menus/icc/structure%20of%20

the%20court/office%20of%20the%20prosecutor/reports%20and%20statements/
statement/Pages/statement%20to%20the%20united%20nations%20security%20
council%20on%20the%20situation%20in%20the%20libyan%20.aspx.

140. See African Union Peace and Security Council, "Report of the Chairperson of
the Commission on the Activities of the AU High Leven Ad Hoc Committee
on the Situation in Libya," April 26, 2011, http://www.au.int/en/sites/default/
files/275%20-%20Report%20on%20Libya%20_Eng%20_%20%283%29.pdf.

141. Author interview with Samantha Power.

142. Author interview with Harold Koh.

143. Author interview with US and other Western diplomats.

144. Author interview with former ICC official.

145. Luis Moreno-Ocampo, "Statement: ICC Prosecutor Press Conference on Libya,"
May 16, 2011, http://www.icc-cpi.int/en_menus/icc/structure%20of%20the%20
court/office%20of%20the%20prosecutor/reports%20and%20statements/state-
ment/Pages/statement%20icc%20prosecutor%20press%20conference%20
on%20libya%2016%20may%202011.aspx.

146. Ibid.

147. Damien McElroy et al., "Libya: Cameron Vows Support as Rebels Set Up
Government in Tripoli," *Times* (London), August 22, 2011. "Europeans Vow to
Send Officers to Help Rebels," *National Post* (Toronto), April 21, 2011, A16.

148. Kareem Fahim, Anthony Shadid, and Rick Gladstone, "Violent End to an Era as
Qaddafi Dies in Libya," *New York Times*, October 20, 2011.

149. Victoria Nuland, U.S. Department of State Daily Press Briefing, November 21,
2011, http://www.state.gov/r/pa/prs/dpb/2011/11/177605.htm.

150. Afua Hirsch, "Libya, France and ICC Compete for Custody of Gaddafi
Intelligence Chief: Gaddafi's Brother-in-Law and Spymaster Abdullah al-Senussi
Seized after Flying into Mauritania on False Passport," *Guardian* (London),
March 18, 2011. Christopher Stephen, "ICC Competes with Libya and France for
Senussi," Radio Netherlands Worldwide, March 19, 2012.

151. Author interview with former ICC official.

152. ICC Assembly of States Parties, 10th Sess. "Closing Remarks by Christian
Wenaweser as ASP President," p. 2 (December 2011), http://www.icc-cpi.int/
iccdocs/asp_docs/ASP10/Statements/ASP10-ST-PASP-CW-CLRemarks-
ENG.pdf.

153. Author interview with Christian Wenaweser.

154. Notes from "Friends of the ICC" session with Fatou Bensouda, provided by
national diplomat.

155. Anna Holligan, "Invisible Children's Kony Campaign Gets Support of ICC
Prosecutor," BBC News, March 8, 2012.

156. ICC Office of the Prosecutor and Pre-Trial Chamber III, "Warrant of Arrest for
Laurent Koudou Gbagbo," ICC-02/11 (November 23, 2011), http://www.icc-cpi.
int/iccdocs/doc/doc1276751.pdf.

157. ICC Office of the Prosecutor, "Situation in Palestine," para. 6, p. 2 (April 3, 2012), http://www.icc-cpi.int/NR/rdonlyres/C6162BBF-FEB9-4FAF-AFA9-836106 D2694A/284387/SituationinPalestine030412ENG.pdf.

158. African Union Executive Council, 19th Ordinary Sess. "Decision on African Candidatures for Posts within the International System," Doc. EX.CL/673(XIX) (June 23–28, 2011), http://www.au.int/en/sites/default/files/EX%20CL%20 Dec%20644-667%20%28XIX%29%20_E.pdf.

159. "Gambia's Bensouda Set to be Next ICC Prosecutor," Agence France-Presse, December 1, 2011.

160. Author interview with Harold Koh; European diplomats.

161. David Smith, "New Chief Prosecutor Defends International Criminal Court," *Guardian* (London), May 23, 2012.

162. Author interview with former ICC prosecution official.

163. G.A. Res 67/19, U.N. Doc. A/RES/67/19 (Nov. 29, 2012), http://www.un.org/ Depts/dhl/resguide/r67.shtml.

164. John V. Whitbeck, "Palestine and the ICC," *Palestine Chronicle*, April 6, 2013, http://palestinechronicle.com/palestine-and-the-icc/#.UYkvlkocMyc.

165. Interview with Alex Whiting.

166. See Jeffrey Gettleman, "Rebel Leader in Congo is Flown to the Hague," *New York Times*, March 22, 2013.

167. David Kaye, "America's Honeymoon with the ICC: Will Washington's Love for International Law Last?" *Foreign Affairs*, April 16, 2013.

168. Sang-Hyun Song, "Remarks at Groundbreaking Ceremony for ICC Permanent Premises," April 16, 2013, http://www.icc-cpi.int/en_menus/ icc/press%20and%20media/press%20releases/Documents/pr898/ Groundbreaking-Ceremony-ICC-President-Statement.pdf.

CONCLUSION

1. See, e.g., Randall Stone, *Controlling Institutions: International Organizations and the World Economy* (Cambridge: Cambridge University Press, 2011); Richard Steinberg, "In the Shadow of Law or Power? Consensus-based Bargaining and Outcomes in the GATT/WTO," *International Organization* 56, no. 2 (2002): 339-74.

2. See, e.g., Karen J. Alter and Sophie Meunier, "The Politics of International Regime Complexity," *Perspectives on Politics* 7, no. 1 (2009): 13–24.

3. See David Bosco, "Why is the International Criminal Court Picking Only on Africa?" *Washington Post*, March 29, 2013.

4. See G. John Ikenberry, *Liberal Leviathan: The Origins, Crisis, and Transformation of the American World Order* (Princeton, NJ: Princeton University Press, 2011).

Sources and Further Reading

BOOKS AND REPORTS

Afghanistan Independent Human Rights Commission. "Afghanistan: Annual Report 2009: Protection of Civilians in Armed Conflict." United Nations Assistance Mission in Afghanistan (UNAMA), 2010.

Ambos, Kai, and Florian Huber. "The Colombian Peace Process and the Principle of Complementarity of the International Criminal Court: Is There Sufficient Willingness and Ability on the Part of the Colombian Authorities or Should the Prosecutor Open an Investigation Now?" Extended version of the Statement in the "Thematic Session: Colombia, ICC OTP—NGO 19/20 October 2010, The Hague." Georg-August-Universität Göttingen, Institute for Criminal Law and Justice Department of Foreign and International Criminal Law (January 5, 2011).

Ambos, Kai, and Otto Triffterer. *Commentary on the Rome Statute of the International Criminal Court*. 2nd ed. Munich, Germany: Verlag C. H. Beck oHG, Hart Publishing, and Nomos, 2008.

Amnesty International. "Democratic Republic of Congo: Torture and Killings by State Security Agents Still Endemic," October 2007, http://www.amnesty.org/en/library/asset/AFR62/012/2007/en/45cad2e8-d374-11dd-a329-2f46302a8cc6/afr620122007en.pdf.

Amnesty International. "DRC: On the Precipice: The Deepening Human Rights and Humanitarian Crisis in Ituri," March 2003, http://www.amnesty.org/en/library/asset/AFR62/006/2003/en/66d41fed-d731-11dd-bocc-1f0860013475/afr620062003en.pdf.

Amnesty International. "The Quest for International Justice." 1995.

Amnesty International. "Rwanda: Reports of Killings and Abductions by the Rwandese Patriotic Army, April–August 1994." 1994.

Annan, Kofi A., and Nader Mousavizadeh. "The Fate of the Continent: Africa's Wars, Africa's Peace." In *Interventions: A Life in War and Peace*, 159–208. New York: Penguin Press, 2012.

Barnett, Michael N., and Martha Finnemore. *Rules for the World: International Organizations in Global Politics.* Ithaca, NY: Cornell University Press, 2004.

Bass, Gary Jonathan. *Stay the Hand of Vengeance: The Politics of War Crimes Tribunals.* Princeton, NJ: Princeton University Press, 2000.

Bassiouni, M. Cherif. "Preface to the Second Edition." In *Commentary on the Rome Statute of the International Criminal Court: Observers' Notes, Article by Article,* edited by Otto Triffterer, xli. Munich, Germany: Verlag C. H. Beck oHG, Hart Publishing, and Nomos, 2008.

"Beginnings in Uganda." Enough Project, http://www.enoughproject.org/conflicts/lra/beginnings-in-uganda#Iron.

Bessel, Richard. *Germany 1945: From War to Peace.* New York: HarperCollins, 2009.

Bix, Herbert P. *Hirohito and the Making of Modern Japan.* 1st ed. New York: HarperCollins, 2000.

Bolton, John R. *Surrender Is Not an Option: Defending America at the United Nations.* New York: Threshold Editions, 2007.

Cheney, Dick. "Remarks by the Vice President to the Veterans of Foreign Wars 103rd National Convention" (speech, Nashville, TN, August 26, 2002), http://georgewbush-whitehouse.archives.gov/news/releases/2002/08/20020826.html.

Chinese Ministry of Foreign Affairs. "Wen Jiabao Meets with Presidents of Seychelles, Tanzania, Sudan, the Republic of Congo, and Uganda," November 2006, http://www.fmprc.gov.cn/eng/wjdt/wshd/t279855.htm.

Clark, Phil. "Law, Politics and Pragmatism: The ICC and Case Selection in Uganda and the Democratic Republic of Congo." In *Courting Conflict? Justice, Peace and the ICC in Africa,* edited by Nicholas Waddell and Phil Clark. London: Royal African Society, 2008. http://www.royalafricansociety.org/images/stories/courting%20conflict%20-%20justice%2C%20peace%20and%20the%20icc%20in%20africa.pdf.

Coalition for an International Criminal Court. Archive of Events for 2005, http://www.coalitionfortheicc.org/documents/CICC_ArchiveofEvents_2005.pdf.

Coalition for an International Criminal Court. Archive of Events for 2006, http://www.coalitionfortheicc.org/documents/CICC_ArchiveofEvents_2006.pdf.

"Communique: Entebbe [Uganda] Summit for Peace and Prosperity: Joint Declaration of Principles, March 25, 1998." In *Public Papers of the Presidents of the United States: William J. Clinton (1998, Book I),* 434–38.

Conot, Robert E. *Justice at Nuremberg.* 1st ed. New York: Harper & Row, 1983.

Dagne, Ted, and Maureen Farrell. "Africa's Great Lakes Region: Current Conditions in Burundi, Democratic Republic of the Congo, Rwanda, and Uganda." Washington, DC: Congressional Research Service, 2003.

Danforth, John. "Peace and Accountability: A Way Forward." January 7, 2005. US Department of State cable released by National Security Archive, http://www.gwu.edu/~nsarchiv/NSAEBB/NSAEBB335/Document4.PDF.

Del Ponte, Carla. *Madame Prosecutor: Confrontations with Humanity's Worst Criminals and the Culture of Impunity: A Memoir.* New York: Other Press, 2009.

Dempsey, Gary T. "Reasonable Doubt: The Case against the Proposed International Criminal Court." Washington, DC: Cato Institute, July 16, 1998.

Des Forges, Alison. "Leave None to Tell the Story." Human Rights Watch, 1999.

Des Forges, Alison. Human Rights Watch, "Democratic Republic of Congo—Rwanda Conflict: A Human Rights Watch Backgrounder," December 5, 2004, http://www.hrw.org/news/2004/12/04/democratic-republic-congo-rwanda-conflict.

Ehrenfreund, Norbert. *The Nuremberg Legacy: How the Nazi War Crimes Trials Changed the Course of History*. New York: Palgrave Macmillan, 2007.

Fédération internationale des ligues des droits de l'homme (FIDH) / International Federation for Human Rights. "War Crimes in the Central African Republic: 'When the Elephants Fight, the Grass Suffers,'" February 2003, http://www.fidh.org/IMG/pdf/FIDH_Report_WarCrimes_in_CAR_English_Feb2003.pdf.

Ferencz, Benjamin B. *An International Criminal Court, a Step Toward World Peace: A Documentary History and Analysis*. 2 vols. London: Oceana Publications, 1980.

Foreign Relations of the United States. 1946, Vol. 1, "General, the United Nations," IO Files: US/A/C.6/25, United States Delegation Working Paper, New York, November 14, 1946, Proposal Regarding Draft Resolution on Codification of International Law, "Discussion," 540.

Foreign Relations of the United States. 1948, Vol. 1, Part 1, "General, the United Nations," IO Files: US (P)/A/343 United States Delegation Position Paper, Paris, December 6, 1948, Report of the Sixth Committee on the Draft Convention on Genocide, Section 2, para. 3, 299.

Futamura, Madoka. *War Crimes Tribunals and Transitional Justice: The Tokyo Trial and the Nuremburg Legacy*. London: Routledge, 2008.

Glasius, Marlies. *The International Criminal Court: A Global Civil Society Achievement*. Routledge Advances in International Relations and Global Politics. London: Routledge, 2006.

Goldsmith, Jack L., and Eric A. Posner. *The Limits of International Law*. New York: Oxford University Press, 2006.

Goldstone, Richard J. *For Humanity: Reflections of a War Crimes Investigator*. New Haven, CT: Yale University Press, 2000.

Grossman, Marc. "American Foreign Policy and the International Criminal Court" (remarks to the Center for Strategic and International Studies, Washington, DC, May 6, 2002), http://2001-2009.state.gov/p/us/rm/9949.htm.

Gubrium, Jaber F., and James A. Holstein. *Handbook of Interview Research: Context and Method*. Thousand Oaks, CA: Sage Publications, 2002.

Hagan, John. *Justice in the Balkans: Prosecuting War Crimes in the Hague Tribunal*. Chicago: University of Chicago Press, 2003.

Hamilton, Rebecca. *Fighting for Darfur: Public Action and the Struggle to Stop Genocide*. New York: Palgrave Macmillan, 2011.

Harris, Whitney R. *Tyranny on Trial: The Trial of the Major German War Criminals at the End of World War II at Nuremberg, Germany, 1945-1946*. Dallas, TX: Southern Methodist University Press, 1999.

Harvey, Robert. *American Shogun: A Tale of Two Cultures*. Woodstock, NY: Overlook Press, 2006.

Hauser, Ellen. "Donors and Democracy in Uganda: An Analysis of the Role of Western Donors in Democratization Efforts in Uganda." Ph.D., University of Wisconsin-Madison, 1997.

Helfer, Laurence R. "Why States Create International Tribunals: A Theory of Constrained Independence." In *Conferences on New Political Economy*, 253–76. Tübingen, Germany: Mohr Siebeck, 2006.

Heller, Kevin Jon. *The Nuremberg Military Tribunals and the Origins of International Criminal Law*. Oxford: Oxford University Press, 2011.

Holmes, Kim. "Gaining African Support for Sudan Action in the UNSC." January 30, 2005. US Department of State cable released by National Security Archive, http://www.gwu.edu/~nsarchiv/NSAEBB/NSAEBB335/Document6.PDF.

Human Rights Watch. "Afghanistan: The Human Cost: The Consequences of Insurgent Attacks in Afghanistan." April 2007, Volume 19, No. 6(C), http://www.hrw.org/sites/default/files/reports/afghanistan0407webwcover.pdf.

Human Rights Watch. "Attacked by all Sides: Civilians and the War in Eastern Zaire." 1997.

Human Rights Watch. "Chaos in Eastern Congo: U.N. Action Needed Now" Briefing Paper, October 2002, http://www.hrw.org/sites/default/files/reports/easterncongo-bck.pdf.

Human Rights Watch. "Civilian Deaths in the NATO Air Campaign." 2000.

Human Rights Watch. "Colombia—Serious Concern Over Demobilization Process," October 29, 2005, http://www.hrw.org/news/2005/10/28/colombia-serious-concern-over-demobilization-process.

Human Rights Watch. "Courting History: The Landmark International Criminal Court's First Years." 2008.

Human Rights Watch. "Darfur: ICC Moves against Sudan's Leader: Charges against al-Bashir a Major Step to Ending Impunity," news release, July 15, 2008, http://www.hrw.org/news/2008/07/14/darfur-icc-moves-against-sudan-s-leader.

Human Rights Watch. "DR Congo: LRA Slaughters 620 in 'Christmas Massacres': Protection Urgently Needed as Killings Continue," January 17, 2009, http://www.hrw.org/news/2009/01/17/dr-congo-lra-slaughters-620-christmas-massacres.

Human Rights Watch. "Human Rights Watch and the FIDH [International Federation of Human Rights Leagues] Demand End to Killings of Civilians by Rwandan Soldiers," news release, Aug. 14, 1997, http://www.hrw.org/news/1997/08/13/human-rights-watch-and-fidh-demand-end-killings-civilians-rwandan-soldiers.

Human Rights Watch. "Ituri: 'Covered in Blood': Ethnically Targeted Violence in Northeastern DR Congo," July 2003, http://www.hrw.org/sites/default/files/reports/DRC0703.pdf.

Human Rights Watch. "Killings in Kiwanja: The UN's Inability to Protect Civilians," December 2008, http://www.hrw.org/sites/default/files/reports/drc1208web.pdf.

Human Rights Watch. "Prosecutorial Incompetence Frees Rwandan Genocide Suspect; Rights Group Deplores Failings at International Criminal Tribunal for Rwanda," news release, Nov. 9, 1999, http://www.hrw.org/news/1999/11/08/prosecutorial-incompetence-frees-rwandan-genocide-suspect.

Human Rights Watch. "Seeking Justice: The Prosecution of Sexual Violence in the Congo War," March 2005, http://www.hrw.org/sites/default/files/reports/drc0305.pdf.

Human Rights Watch. "U.N.: Security Council Must Act on Darfur." Letter to Select UN Security Council Members, March 18, 2005, http://www.hrw.org/news/2005/03/17/un-security-council-must-act-darfur.

Human Rights Watch. "U.S.: ICC Best Chance for Justice in Darfur: U.S. Should Support or Abstain from a Security Council Referral of Darfur to the International Criminal Court." Open letter to Condoleezza Rice, January 22, 2005, http://www.hrw.org/news/2005/01/21/us-icc-best-chance-justice-darfur.

Human Rights Watch. "UN Security Council: Support ICC Probe on Libya: Prosecutor to Brief Council on Libya," news release, May 3, 2011, http://www.hrw.org/news/2011/05/03/un-security-council-support-icc-probe-libya.

Human Rights Watch. "Up in Flames: Humanitarian Law Violations and Civilian Victims in the Conflict over South Ossetia," pp. 2, 6–11, January 2009, http://www.hrw.org/sites/default/files/reports/georgia0109web.pdf.

Human Rights Watch. *World Report 1995.* New York, 1995.

Human Rights Watch. *World Report 2000.* New York, 2000.

Human Rights Watch. *World Report 2001.* New York, 2001.

Human Rights Watch. "World Report 2006: Events of 2005." http://www.hrw.org/sites/default/files/reports/wr2006.pdf.

Human Rights Watch. "World Report 2007: Events of 2006." http://www.hrw.org/legacy/wr2k7/wr2007master.pdf.

Human Rights Watch and Julie Flint. "Darfur Destroyed: Ethnic Cleansing by Government and Militia Forces in Western Sudan." 75, May 2004.

International Crisis Group. "Congo Crisis: Military Intervention in Ituri." Nairobi, New York, Brussels: International Crisis Group, 2003.

International Crisis Group. "Congo: Four Priorities for Sustainable Peace in Ituri," May 13, 2008, http://www.crisisgroup.org/~/media/files/africa/central-africa/dr-congo/congo%20four%20priorities%20for%20sustainable%20peace%20in%20ituri.pdf.

International Crisis Group. "The Congo's Transition is Failing: Crisis in the Kivus." Brussels, Nairobi: International Crisis Group, 2005.

International Crisis Group. "Milosevic in the Hague: What it Means for Yugoslavia and the Region." In *Balkans Briefing*. Belgrade/Brussels: International Crisis Group, July 6, 2001.

International Crisis Group. "New ICC Prosecution: Opportunities and Risks for Peace in Sudan," news release, July 14, 2008, http://www.crisisgroup.org/en/publication-type/media-releases/2008/new-icc-prosecution-opportunities-and-risks-for-peace-in-sudan.aspx.

International Crisis Group. "Scramble for the Congo: Anatomy of an Ugly War," December 20, 2000, http://www.crisisgroup.org/~/media/files/africa/central-africa/dr-congo/scramble%20for%20the%20congo%20anatomy%20of%20an%20ugly%20war.pdf.

International Crisis Group. "Securing Congo's Elections: Lessons from the Kinshasa Showdown," October 2, 2006, http://www.crisisgroup.org/~/media/Files/africa/central-africa/dr-congo/B042%20Securing%20Congos%20Elections%20Lessons%20from%20the%20Kinshasa%20Showdown.pdf.

International Foundation for Electoral Systems (IFES). "DR Congo, Presidential Elections," Results of First Round (July 30, 2006) and Second Round (October 29, 2006), http://www.electionguide.org/results.php?ID=1208.

Israeli Defense Forces Operation Cast Lead report. "The Operation in Gaza 27 December 2008–18 January 2009: Factual and Legal Aspects," July 2009, http://dover.idf.il/NR/rdonlyres/14998311-6477-422B-B5EE-50C2F1B31D03/0/FINALDRAFTwithclearance.pdf.

Karstedt, Susanne. "The Nuremberg Tribunal and German Society: International Justice and Local Judgment in Post-Conflict Reconstruction." In *The Legacy of Nuremberg: Civilising Influence or Institutionalised Vengeance?*, edited by David A. McCormack and Timothy L. H. Blumenthal, International Humanitarian Law Series, 13–35. Leiden: Martinus Nijhoff Publishers, 2008.

Kaye, David A. "Justice Beyond The Hague: Supporting the Prosecution of International Crimes in National Courts." New York: Council on Foreign Relations, 2011.

Kirsch, Philippe. "The Development of the Rome Statute." In *The International Criminal Court—The Making of the Rome Statute: Issues, Negotiations, Results*, edited by Roy S. Lee, Project on International Courts and Tribunals, 451–62. The Hague, Boston: Kluwer Law International, 1999.

Kirsch, Philippe, and John T. Holmes. "The Birth of the International Criminal Court." In *The International Criminal Court*, edited by Olympia Bekou and Robert Cryer, xxv. Aldershot, England: Ashgate/Dartmouth, 2004.

Koh, Harold. "The Obama Administration and International Law," speech to the American Society of International Law, March 25, 2010, http://www.state.gov/s/l/releases/remarks/139119.htm.

Letter from Robert Jackson to Harry S. Truman, Oct. 12, 1945, p. 4, Harry S. Truman Presidential Museum & Library, http://www.trumanlibrary.org/whistlestop/study_collections/nuremberg/documents/index.php?pagenumber=4&documentid=7-2&documentdate=1945-10-12&studycollectionid=nuremberg&groupid=.

Luban, David. *Legal Modernism.* Ann Arbor: University of Michigan Press, 1994.

Mackenzie, Ruth, Kate Malleson, Penny Martin, and Philippe Sands. *Selecting International Judges: Principle, Process, and Politics.* Oxford: Oxford University Press, 2010.

Marshall, Monty G., and Ted Robert Gurr. "Peace and Conflict 2005." College Park: University of Maryland Center for International Development and Conflict Management, 2005.

Mayer, Jane. *The Dark Side: The Inside Story of How The War on Terror Turned into a War on American Ideals.* New York: Doubleday, 2008.

Megret, Frederic. "Why Would States Want to Join the ICC? A Theoretical Exploration Based on the Legal Nature of Complementarity." In *Complementary Views on Complementarity,* edited by Gerben Kor Jann Kleffner. The Hague: T. M. C. Asser Press, 2005.

Ministry of Foreign Affairs of the Russian Federation. "Visit to Russia by Representatives of the Office of the Prosecutor of the International Criminal Court," news release 285-10-03-2010, March 10, 2010, http://www.mid.ru/brp_4.nsf/o/DA277988EE244453C32576E3003F6D0F.

Mitchell, Sara McLaughlin, and Emilia Justyna Powell. *Domestic Law Goes Global Legal Traditions and International Courts.* Cambridge: Cambridge University Press, 2011.

Morris, Virginia, and Michael P. Scharf. *The International Criminal Tribunal for Rwanda.* 2 vols. Vol. 1. Irvington-on-Hudson, NY: Transnational Publishers, 1998.

"A National Security Strategy for a New Century." William J. Clinton administration, Oct. 1, 1998.

Nuland, Victoria. U.S. Department of State Daily Press Briefing, November 21, 2011, http://www.state.gov/r/pa/prs/dpb/2011/11/177605.htm.

Otomo, Yoriko. "The Decision Not to Prosecute the Emperor." In *Beyond Victor's Justice? The Tokyo War Crimes Trial Revisited,* edited by Yuki Tanaka, Tim McCormack, and Gerry Simpson, 63–78. Leiden: Martinus Nijhoff Publishers, 2011.

Patten, Chris. "Inauguration of the International Criminal Court." Brussels, Belgium: European Commission, March 11, 2003.

Patterson, Anne W. "Explanation of Vote by Ambassador Anne W. Patterson, Acting U.S. Representative to the United Nations, on the Sudan Accountability Resolution, in the Security Council." March 31, 2005, http://archive.usun.state.gov/press_releases/20050331_055.html.

Persico, Joseph E. *Nuremberg: Infamy on Trial.* New York: Penguin Books, 1994.

Peskin, Victor. *International Justice in Rwanda and the Balkans: Virtual Trials and the Struggle for State Cooperation.* Cambridge: Cambridge University Press, 2008.

"Presidential Debate in Coral Gables, Florida, September 30, 2004." In *Public Papers of the Presidents of the United States: George W. Bush (2004, Book II),* 2248–71.

The Princeton Process on the Crime of Aggression: Materials of the Special Working Group on the Crime of Aggression, 2003–2009, edited by Stefan Barriga, Wolfgang Danspeckgruber, and Christian Wenaweser. Boulder, CO: Lynne Rienner Publishers, 2009.

Prunier, Gérard. *Africa's World War: Congo, the Rwandan Genocide, and the Making of a Continental Catastrophe*. Oxford: Oxford University Press, 2009.

Reisman, W. Michael. *Systems of Control in International Adjudication and Arbitration: Breakdown and Repair*. Durham, NC: Duke University Press, 1992.

"Remarks at the Entebbe Summit for Peace and Prosperity, March 25, 1998." In *Public Papers of the Presidents of the United States: William J. Clinton (1998, Book I)*, 438–39.

"Remarks to the 10th Mountain Division at Fort Drum, New York, July 19, 2002." In *Public Papers of the Presidents of the United States: George W. Bush (2002, Book II)*, 1270–74.

Report of the Independent International Fact-Finding Mission on the Conflict in Georgia. Vol. 1, September 2009, http://www.ceiig.ch/pdf/IIFFMCG_Volume_I.pdf.

"Report of the International Commission of Inquiry on Darfur to the United Nations Secretary-General Pursuant to Security Council Resolution 1564 of 18 September 2004." Geneva, January 25, 2005.

Report of the United Nations Fact Finding Mission on the Gaza Conflict ("Goldstone Report"). A/HRC/12/48, presented to the 12th Session of the Human Rights Council, September 25, 2009, http://www2.ohchr.org/english/bodies/hrcouncil/docs/12session/A-HRC-12-48.pdf.

Rostow, Nicholas. "U.N. Realities." In *Looking to the Future: Essays on International Law in Honor of W. Michael Reisman*, edited by Mahnoush H. Arsanjani, Jacob Katz Cogan, Robert D. Sloane, and Siegfried Wiessner. Leiden: Martinus Nijhoff Publishers, 2010.

Rubin, James. US Department of State news briefing, June 15, 1998, http://usembassy-israel.org.il/publish/press/state/archive/1998/june/sd1616.htm.

Rumsfeld, Donald. *Known and Unknown: A Memoir*. New York: Sentinel, 2011.

Russell, Bertrand. *War Crimes in Vietnam*. London: George Allen & Unwin Ltd., 1967.

Schabas, William. *The International Criminal Court: A Commentary on the Rome Statute*. Oxford Commentaries on International Law. Oxford: Oxford University Press, 2010.

Scheffer, David. *All the Missing Souls: A Personal History of the War Crimes Tribunals*. Princeton, NJ: Princeton University Press, 2012.

Scheffer, David J. U.S. Department of State briefing, July 31, 1998, http://www.amicc.org/docs/Scheffer7_31_98.pdf.

Scheffer, David J. "The U.S. Perspective on the ICC." In *The United States and the International Criminal Court: National Security and International Law*, edited by Carl Kaysen and Sarah B. Sewall, 115–18. Lanham, MD: Rowman & Littlefield Publishers, 2000.

Schiff, Benjamin N. *Building the International Criminal Court*. Cambridge: Cambridge University Press, 2008.

Shklar, Judith N. *Legalism*. Cambridge, MA: Harvard University Press, 1964.

Sikkink, Kathryn. *The Justice Cascade: How Human Rights Prosecutions Are Changing World Politics.* New York: W. W. Norton & Co., 2011.

Smith, Bradley F. *Reaching Judgment at Nuremberg.* New York: Basic Books, 1977.

"Soros Foundations Network 2001 Report." Open Society Foundations.

"Soros Foundations Network 2002 Report." Open Society Foundations.

Spiegel, Julia, and Noel Atama. "Finishing the Fight against the LRA," Enough Project report, May 12, 2009, http://www.enoughproject.org/files/lra_strategy_paper_051209.pdf.

Stone, Julius. *Conflict through Consensus: United Nations Approaches to Aggression.* Baltimore: Johns Hopkins University Press, 1977.

Stone, Randall W. *Controlling Institutions: International Organizations and the World Economy.* Cambridge: Cambridge University Press, 2011.

Struett, Michael J. *The Politics of Constructing the International Criminal Court: NGOs, Discourse, and Agency.* 1st ed. New York: Palgrave Macmillan, 2008.

Sudan: Losing Ground on Peace? Hearing before the Subcomm. on Africa, Global Human Rights & International Operations, of the H. Comm. on International Relations, 109th Cong. (November 1, 2005) (statement of Assistant Secretary of State for Bureau of African Affairs Jendayi Frazer), http://commdocs.house.gov/committees/intlrel/hfa24374.000/hfa24374_0f.htm.

"Sudan: The Fifth Anniversary of the Comprehensive Peace Agreement," briefing by Scott Gration, Special Envoy for Sudan, Foreign Press Center, Washington, DC, January 11, 2010, http://fpc.state.gov/135047.htm.

"Trial of the Major War Criminals before the International Military Tribunal, Nuremberg, 14 November 1945-October 1946." Nuremberg, Germany: Secretariat of the International Military Tribunal under the jurisdiction of the Allied Control Authority for Germany, 1947.

"Trials of War Criminals before the Nuernberg Military Tribunals under Control Council Law No. 10 ("Green Series"), October 1946 to April 1949." Washington, DC: U.S. Government Printing Office.

U.S. Mission to the UN, "Agenda Item 142: Establishment of an International Criminal Court," news release 182, November 1, 1995, http://www.state.gov/documents/organization/65827.pdf.

Van Woudenberg, Anneke. "Ethnically Targeted Violence in Ituri." In *Challenges of Peace Implementation: The UN Mission in the Democratic Republic of the Congo,* edited by Mark Malan and Joao Gomes Porto. Pretoria, South Africa: Institute for Security Studies, 2004.

Voeten, Erik. "International Judicial Independence." In *Interdisciplinary Perspectives on International Law and International Relations: The State of the Art,* edited by Jeffrey L. Dunoff and Mark A. Pollack, 421–44. Cambridge: Cambridge University Press, 2012.

Wood, Michael. Memorandum from August 15, 2002, published as part of the Chilcot Inquiry, http://www.iraqinquiry.org.uk/media/43499/doc_2010_01_26_11_02_28_403.pdf.

ARTICLES FROM NEWSPAPERS AND NEWS SERVICES

"African Union Asks Court to Halt Bashir Warrant." *Daily Monitor* (Kampala), July 15, 2008.

"Al-Jazeera Reports Iraqis Injured in Bombing." BBC Summary of World Broadcasts, 1021 GMT, March 20, 2003.

"Arab League to Hold Emergency Meeting on Sudan-ICC Crisis." Deutsche Presse-Agentur, July 14, 2008.

"AU Backs Sudan President in ICC Row." *Sudan Tribune* (Paris), February 3, 2009.

"AU Urges Court to Give Peace Process a Chance in Darfur." Hirondelle News Agency, July 15, 2008.

"Back from the Edge on Kashmir." *New York Times*, June 12, 2002, Section A; Column 1; Editorial Desk; p. 28.

"Bashir's Indictment 'Giant Step for International Justice'—Darfur Rebels." *Sudan Tribune* (Paris), July 15, 2008.

"Bemba Arrested for War Crimes." *Independent* (London), May 26, 2008, 20.

"Bosnia War Crimes Prosecutor Points Finger at France." Agence France-Presse, December 13, 1997.

"Bush Joins War against Kony's LRA." *East African*, October 27, 2003.

"Canada Shines on World Stage." *Toronto Star*, July 21, 1998, A14.

"Coalition Forces to be Investigated for War Crimes in Iraq." U.S. Newswire, January 26, 2004.

"Colombia War Crimes Probe Urged." BBC News (June 29, 2005). http://news.bbc.co.uk/2/hi/americas/4633955.stm.

"Congo Ex-Official Is Held in Belgium on War Crimes Charges." *New York Times*, May 25, 2008, A13.

"Congo Ex-rebel Chief Bemba Arrested." *Financial Times* (London), May 25, 2008, 20.

"Czech Lower House Recognizes International Criminal Court." Czech News Agency (CTK), October 29, 2008.

"Darfur Investigator Finds Refugees' Voices in Tune with Sudan Indictment." Voice of America, July 18, 2008.

"Delivering on the Promise of a Fair, Effective and Independent Court: Election of ICC and ASP Officials: Judges: Fourth Election—2009." In *Coalition for the International Criminal Court*. http://iccnow.org/?mod=electionjudges2009.

"Democratic Republic of Congo, Uganda, to Work Together to Find LRA Rebels: UN." Agence France-Presse, October 19, 2005.

"Documentos exclusivos: así se fraguó el acuerdo de paz con los 'paras'." *Semana*, April 26, 2010.

"DRC: MONUC Chief Summons Militia Leader over Attacks." UN Integrated Regional Information Networks (Nairobi), January 23, 2004.

"DRC: MONUC Denounces Recruitment of Child Soldiers by Lubanga's UPC/RP." UN Integrated Regional Information Networks (Nairobi), February 7, 2003.

"DRCongo: Former Rebels Reportedly Threaten to Withdraw From Institutions." BBC Summary of World Broadcasts, February 25 2004.

"Editorial Roundup." Associated Press, April 14, 2005.

"Europeans Vow to Send Officers to Help Rebels." *National Post* (Toronto), April 21, 2011, A16.

"France Determined Bosnian War Criminals Will Not Escape: Jospin." Agence France-Presse, December 16, 1997.

"Gambia's Bensouda Set to be Next ICC Prosecutor." Agence France-Presse, December 1, 2011.

"General Morillon to be First French Soldier to Testify at ICTY." Agence France-Press, June 15, 1999.

"Great Lakes: IRIN Weekly Round-Up, 5/26/97: Genocide survivors protest against ICTR prosecutor." Integrated Regional Information Network, May 26, 1997.

"ICC Judge Calls for India to Become Member of Court." *Citizens for Global Solutions* (January 4, 2006). http://archive2.globalsolutions.org/issues/international_criminal_court/learn/India.

"ICC Team Here to Investigate War Crimes in North." *New Vision* (Kampala), August 27, 2004.

"ICC Warrants Not Stopping Peace Search—Expert" *Monitor* (Kampala, Uganda), October 27, 2007, http://allafrica.com/stories/200710280004.html.

"India Blasts Special Treatment for Security Council." *Terra Viva*, June 17, 1998.

"International Court for War Crimes Gets Snubbed by Czechs." *Prague Post*, April 18, 2007.

"International Court Issues Warrants for Uganda Rebel Leaders: Report." Agence France-Presse, June 11, 2006.

"International Court Preparing First Arrest Warrant for Ugandan Suspects." Associated Press, February 8, 2005.

"Investigation into Possible UK War Crimes in Iraq; UK Attorney, U.S. Colleagues Granting Media Interviews." U.S. Newswire, April 11, 2003.

"Iraq Plans to Sign up to International Criminal Court." Agence France-Presse, February 17, 2005.

"Kenyan Civil Society Calls for Local Justice for Victims of Post-Poll Violence." KTN radio, via BBC Monitoring Africa, July 15, 2009.

"Libyan Revolution on Road to Collapse: As Gadhafi Forces Ring Strategic City, Many Fear How Regime Will Treat 'Rats and Vermin.'" *Toronto Star*, March 16, 2011, A4.

"Libya's Gaddafi to Rein in Sudanese Rebel." Reuters, July 20, 2010.

"Libya Unrest: Cameron Backs 'War Crimes' Investigation." BBC News, February 25, 2011.

"Materials on Events in 2008 Were Sent to the International Criminal Court." *Georgia Times*, August 8, 2011.

"M7 Rejects Kony Hunt." *New Vision* (Kampala), November 18, 2006.

"Milosevic Found Dead in His Cell." BBC News (March 11, 2006). http://news.bbc.co.uk/2/hi/europe/4796470.stm.

"New Hero." *Newsweek*, December 25, 1994.

"New Rebel Group Seizes West Sudan Town." Agence France-Presse, February 26, 2003.

"Pope Backs Global Human Rights." Associated Press, December 13, 1999.

"President of ICC Delivers Second Annual Report to UN General Assembly—Need for International Cooperation Stressed." Coalition for the International Criminal Court, October 9, 2006.

"Press Conference with (Russian) State Duma Speaker Sergey Baburin and Vice Chairman of the State Duma Defense Committee Alexei Arbatov on Kosovo." Official Kremlin International News Broadcast, July 6, 1999.

"Profile: DR Congo militia leader Thomas Lubanga." BBC News (July 10, 2012). http://www.bbc.co.uk/news/world-africa-17358799.

"Rights Group Fears Sudanese Backlash." CNN.com, July 15, 2008.

"Russian Envoy Says 'Concern' at UN over Sudanese President Arrest Warrant." Interfax news agency report in Russian translated by BBC Worldwide Monitoring, July 15, 2008.

"Russian Investigative Committee: Georgia was Trying to Discredit Russian Army in August 2008 Conflict." Interfax, August 8, 2012.

"Some Kenyan MPs Oppose ICC Trial of Post-Poll Violence Suspects." KTN radio, via BBC Monitoring Africa, July 15, 2009.

"South Africa Calls for International Crime Court." Panafrican News Agency, November 28, 2000.

"South Africa's Mbeki Questions International Court's Move to Cite Ugandan Rebels." South African Press Association, June 2, 2006.

"South Sudan Launches Peace Talks." *Sudan Tribune* (Paris), June 8, 2006.

"Sudan Asks League to Set Urgent Meeting: Court Might Issue Warrant for President." *International Herald Tribune* (Paris), July 14, 2008.

"Sudanese Legal Experts Call for Prosecution of Bush, Blair over Iraq War." BBC Monitoring Middle East—Political, April 14, 2003.

"Sudanese Minister Named by ICC Says Prosecutor's Case "Weak.' " *Akhir Lahzah* newspaper article translated by BBC Monitoring Middle East, February 28, 2007.

"Sudanese Minister Threatens Action against International Court Proponents." *Al-Hayat* newspaper article translated by BBC Monitoring Middle East, March 1, 2007.

"Sudan Expulsions Could Spark Conflict-Aid Groups," Reuters, March 6, 2009.

"Sudan: P-3 Discussions on Sudan-ICC Issues." *Daily Telegraph* (London), February 4, 2011.

"Sudan: Presidential Aide Terms ICC 'European Court of Injustice.'" Sudan TV, translated from Arabic by BBC Monitoring Middle East, July 13, 2008.

"Sudan Says a Warrant Holds Peril for Darfur: Thousands Backing Leader Rally in Capital." Associated Press and Reuters, *International Herald Tribune* (Paris), July 14, 2008.

"Sudan's Bashir to Miss OIC Summit after EU Objected." Reuters, November 8, 2009.

"Sudan: Seven Journalists Charged for Attending World Criminal Court Training." *Akhir Lahzah* newspaper article translated by BBC Monitoring Middle East, October 11, 2007.

"Sudan to File Charges against ICC Prosecutor, Report Says." *Sudan Tribune* (Paris), June 20, 2008.

"Tracking Down Uganda's Rebels." BBC, May 10, 2002, http://news.bbc.co.uk/2/hi/africa/1980333.stm.

"Uganda: Acholi Leaders in the Hague to Meet ICC over LRA Probe." UN Integrated Regional Information Networks (Nairobi), March 16, 2005.

"Uganda: Amnesty Commission Opposes Warrant Arrests for LRA's Kony." *Daily Monitor* (Kampala), October 10, 2005.

"Uganda: Drop Cases against Me, Kony Tells World Court." *Monitor* (Kampala), May 25, 2006.

"Uganda: Historic ICC Arrest Warrants Evoke Praise, Concern." Inter Press Service, October 14, 2005.

"Uganda: ICC Indictments to Affect Northern Peace Efforts, Says Mediator." UN Integrated Regional Information Networks (Nairobi), October 10, 2005.

"Uganda: ICC Threats Might Mar Peace Talks, Church Says." *New Vision* (Kampala), February 14, 2005.

"Uganda: International Criminal Court Team Arrives to Prepare LRA War Probe." UN Integrated Regional Information Networks (Nairobi), August 26, 2004.

"Uganda: LRA's Otti Vows to Kill ICC Captors." *Monitor* (Kampala), October 13, 2006.

"Uganda: LRA Talks Over, Says Bigombe." *New Vision* (Kampala), October 10, 2005.

"Uganda: Museveni Gives Kony Amnesty." *New Vision* (Kampala), July 4, 2006.

"Uganda 'Must Arrest' Rebel Leader." BBC News (May 18, 2006). http://news.bbc.co.uk/2/hi/africa/4992896.stm.

"Uganda: Rebel Leader Rejects Amnesty Offer as America, UN Insist on Arrests." *Monitor* (Kampala), July 7, 2006.

"Uganda: Waiting for Elusive Peace in the War Ravaged North." UN Integrated Regional Information Networks (Nairobi), June 9, 2005.

"UN Airlifts Staff from Darfur as Tension Mounts: Indictment Could Lead to Violence." *Cape Argus* (Cape Town, South Africa), July 15, 2008.

"UN Criminal Court to Target Uganda Rebels, DR Congo Militia." Agence France-Presse, February 8, 2005.

"U.N. Powers Split on Crime Tribunal: France Backs World Court for Genocide and Aggression—Impractical, Britain Says." *New York Times*, November 8, 1952.

"UN Prosecutor to Hold Talks in Paris." Agence France-Presse, May 4, 1999.

"UN to Withdraw Non-Critical Staff from Darfur." Canadian Broadcasting Corporation (CBC) News, July 14, 2008.

"UN War Crimes Team to Probe Atrocities in Northern Ugandan War." Agence France-Presse, August 25, 2004.

"Violence in the East Endangers Stability of Kinshasa's Transitional Government." *SouthScan* (London), March 8, 2004.

"World Crime Court Opposed by Briton." *New York Times*, August 3, 1951. "After Afghan Strike, Charred Flesh and Burning Rage." Reuters, September 4, 2009.

Ackerman, Bruce. "Legal Acrobatics, Illegal War." *New York Times*, June 21, 2011, A27.

Ang, Audra. "China Concerned by International Criminal Court's Move to Seek Arrest of Sudan's President." Associated Press, July 15, 2008.

Arbour, Louise. "Justice v. Politics." *International Herald Tribune*, September 17, 2008, 6.

Barringer, Felicity, and Elisabeth Bumiller. "France Urging U.N. to Suspend Iraq Penalties." *New York Times*, April 23, 2003, A1.

Bolton, John R. "Unsign That Treaty." *Washington Post*, January 4, 2001, A21.

Bone, James. "War Crimes Court Pits United States against the World." *Times* (London), April 11, 2002, 19.

Borger, Julian, Richard Norton-Taylor, and Paul Harris. "Diplomats Meet as Italy Plots Leader's Escape Route." *Guardian* (London), March 29, 2011, 1.

Becker, Elizabeth. "On World Court, U.S. Focus Shifts to Shielding Officials." *New York Times*, September 7, 2002, A4.

Belton, Catherine, and Charles Clover. "West is United in Stand on Georgia." *Financial Times* (London), August 18, 2008, 1.

Beltrano, Damiano. "Life in the World's First Global Jail." *InterDependent* (United Nations Association of the United States), Fall 2009.

Bilefsky, Dan. "Bushes on Trial? Belgium Is Sweating Out Its Own War-Crimes Law." *Wall Street Journal*, March 28, 2003, A11.

Black, Ian. "Belgium Gives in to US on War Crimes Law." *Guardian* (London), June 24, 2003, 13.

Blair, David. "Rebels Murder British Aid Man." *Daily Telegraph* (London), November 8, 2005, 17.

Boudreaux, Richard, and John-Thor Dahlburg. "Crisis in Yugoslavia: NATO Planes Hit Chinese Embassy in Belgrade; 2 Die." *Los Angeles Times*, May 8, 1999, 1.

Bravin, Jess. "International Criminal Court Picks U.S. Lawyer to Lead First Case." *Wall Street Journal*, January 30, 2004, A10.

Bravin, Jess. "U.S. Warms to Hague Tribunal; New Stance Reflects Desire to Use Court to Prosecute Darfur Crimes." *Wall Street Journal*, June 14, 2006, A4.

British Broadcasting Corporation. "Aid Linked to Milosevic Removal." October 8, 1999.

British Broadcasting Corporation. "Milosevic Extradition Unlocks Aid Coffers." June 29, 2001.

Brody, Reed. "Milosevic, Saddam, Taylor. Who's Next? Bringing Tyrants to Justice." *International Herald Tribune*, April 1, 2006.

Butt, Riazat. "Briton Killed as Uganda Rebels Attack Tourists." *Guardian* (London), November 9, 2005, 6.

Cohen, Roger. "How Kofi Annan Rescued Kenya." *New York Times Review of Books*, August 14, 2008.

Connett, David, John Hooper, and Peter Beaumont. "Pinochet Arrested in London." *Guardian*, October 17, 1998.

Copley, Joy, and Chris Stephen. "Milosevic Indicted for War Crimes." *Scotsman* (Edinburgh), May 27, 1999, 1.

Cornwell, Rupert. "US Rebuffed as International War-Crimes Court is Backed." *Independent* (London), July 19, 1998, 17.

Crossette, Barbara. "Helms Vows to Make War on U.N. Court." *New York Times*, March 27, 1998, 9.

Deutsch, Anthony. "Congolese Rebel Leader Extradited to International Criminal Court." Associated Press, March 18, 2006.

Deutsch, Anthony. "ICC Prosecutor Says Sudan Will Assist in Arrest of LRA Leader Kony." Associated Press, October 13, 2005.

DeYoung, Karen. "Bush Uses Exemption on Colombia Forces." *Washington Post*, February 22, 2003, A21.

Dobbs, Michael. "Bosnia Crystallizes U.S. Post-Cold War Role; As Two Administrations Wavered, the Need for U.S. Leadership Became Clear." *Washington Post*, December 3, 1995, A1.

Dobbs, Michael. "U.S. Appoints Envoy on Bosnia War Crimes." *Washington Post*, May 21, 1997.

Donnelly, John. "Up to 192 Killed in Uganda as Rebels Torch Civilian Camp." *Boston Globe*, February 23, 2004, A10.

Dougherty, Carter. "U.S. Aids Uganda against Rebels: Support Seen as Payback for Stance on Iraq." *Washington Times*, October 24, 2003.

Drozdiak, William. "NATO Chiefs Block Call for Pursuit of War Criminals." *Washington Post*, June 13, 1997, A36.

Drozdiak, William. "War Crimes Tribunal Arraigns 1st Suspect; Bosnian Serb Pleads Not Guilty to Charges That He Killed Muslims at Detention Camp." *Washington Post*, April 27, 1995, A31.

Durgham, Raghida. "Ocampo Tells Al-Hayat: 'Al-Bashir is Still Hunted and Justice Will Be Done.'" *Al-Hayat* (London), September 12, 2009.

Edwards, Steven. "Jurists Will Investigate Suspected War Crimes." *Vancouver Sun*, January 27, 2004, A9.

Edwards, Steven. "Try U.S., Britain for Bombings in Iraq, War Crimes Court Urged." *Ottawa Citizen*, January 27, 2004, A9.

Edwards, Steven. "War Crimes Case Planned against U.S: Washington Says Groups' Bid Proves ICC a Political Tool." *National Post* (Toronto), April 15, 2003, A14.

Elman, Colin, and Miriam Fendius Elman. "Diplomatic History and International Relations Theory: Respecting Difference and Crossing Boundaries." *International Security* 22, no. 1 (1997): 5–21.

England, Andrew. "League Rejects Warrant for Bashir." *FT.com* (March 31, 2009).

Erlanger, Steven. "West is Struggling to Unite on Georgia: Russia Agrees to Withdraw, But NATO is Riven by How to Deal with the Crisis." *International Herald Tribune* (Paris), August 18, 2008, 1.

Evans-Pritchard, Ambrose. "Belgium Restricts War Crimes Law." *Daily Telegraph* (London), June 24, 2003, 14.

Evans-Pritchard, Ambrose. "Blair Accused by Greeks of Crimes against Humanity." *Daily Telegraph* (London), July 29, 2003, 12.

Evans-Pritchard, Ambrose. "US Threatens to pull NATO HQ out of Belgium." *Daily Telegraph* (London), June 13, 2003, 15.

Fahim, Kareem, Anthony Shadid, and Rick Gladstone. "Violent End to an Era as Qaddafi Dies in Libya." *New York Times*, October 20, 2011.

Falk, Richard A. "Nuremberg and Vietnam." *New York Times*, December 27, 1970, 165.

Fanton, Jonathan F. "International Justice: Editorial: Mocking the Powerless and the Powerful (September 21, 2007)." *New York Times*, September 28, 2007.

Feller, A. H. "We Move, Slowly, Toward World Law." *New York Times*, June 5, 1949.

Filkins, Dexter. "Flaws in U.S. Air War Left Hundreds of Civilians Dead." *New York Times*, July 21, 2002, 1.

Flint, Julie, and Alex de Waal. "'This Prosecution Will Endanger the People We Wish to Defend in Sudan." *Observer* (London), July 13, 2008.

Forero, Juan. "Colombia Massacre Raises Fear of a Rebel Offensive." *International Herald Tribune*, June 18, 2004.

Forero, Juan. "Rightist Militias in Colombia Offer to Disarm 3,000 of Their Fighters." *New York Times*, October 9, 2004, A5.

Frankel, Glenn. "Belgian War Crimes Law Undone by Its Global Reach; Cases against Political Figures Sparked Crises." *Washington Post*, September 30, 2003, A1.

French, Howard W. "Mobutu Sese Seko, 66, Longtime Dictator of Zaire." *New York Times*, September 8, 1997.

Gall, Carlotta, and Eric Schmitt. "Shocked Afghans Criticize U.S. Strike; Toll Is Some 40 Dead and 100 Wounded." *New York Times*, July 3, 2002, A3.

Gallardo, Eduardo. "Arrest of Former Dictator Rattles Chile's Democratic Transition." Associated Press, October 22, 1998.

Gettleman, Jeffrey. "Under Wraps, Kenya's Bill for Bloodshed Nears Payment." *New York Times*, July 16, 2009, 15.

Gettleman, Jeffrey, and Eric Schmitt. "U.S. Aided a Failed Plan to Rout Ugandan Rebels." *New York Times*, February 7, 2009, A1.

Getz, Arlene. "Rocking the Courtroom." *Newsweek*, March 30, 2009.

Goldsmith, Jack. "Support War Crimes Trials for Darfur." *Washington Post*, January 24, 2005, A15.

Goldstone, Richard. "Prosecuting Aggression." *International Herald Tribune* (Paris), May 27, 2010.

Harman, Danna. "How China's Support of Sudan Shields a Regime Called 'Genocidal.'" *Christian Science Monitor*, June 26, 2007.

Harris, Whitney R. "Justice Jackson at Nuremberg." *International Lawyer* 20, no. 3 (1986): 867–96.

Hedges, Chris. "NATO Troops Kill a Serbian Suspect in War Atrocities." *New York Times*, July 11, 1997, A1.

Hirsch, Afua. "Britain Failing to Make Bashir's Arrest a Priority, says ICC's Chief Prosecutor." *Guardian* (London), May 24, 2009.

Hirsch, Afua. "Libya, France and ICC Compete for Custody of Gaddafi Intelligence Chief: Gaddafi's Brother-in-Law and Spymaster Abdullah al-Senussi Seized after Flying into Mauritania on False Passport." *Guardian* (London), March 18, 2011.

Hofmann, Paul. "Debate on Terror Postponed by U.N.: Recommended by Committee U.S., Canada Seek Law Assembly to Take Up Issue at '75 Session—Definition of Aggression Approved." *New York Times*, December 15, 1974, 21.

Hoge, Warren. "Annan Rebukes U.S. for Move to Give Its Troops Immunity." *New York Times*, June 18, 2004, A10.

Hoge, Warren. "Bosnia Veto by the U.S. is Condemned by Britain." *New York Times*, July 2, 2002, A8.

Hoge, Warren. "U.N. Rights Chief Says Prison Abuse May Be War Crime." *New York Times*, June 5, 2004, A6.

Holligan, Anna. "Invisible Children's Kony Campaign Gets Support of ICC Prosecutor." BBC News, March 8, 2012.

Hooper, John, and Ian Black. "Self-Interest Brings Court into Contempt; Cynicism and Special Pleading are Marring Attempts to Create World Justice." *Guardian* (London), July 15, 1998, 17.

Housego, Kim. "Wave of Slayings and Kidnappings Spreads Fear in Colombia Ahead of Local Elections across Nation." Associated Press, October 18, 2003.

Hurst, Lynda. "Belgium Reins in War-Crime Law; U.S. Threats Finally Sink 'Universal Jurisdiction' Suits Anti-War Activists Used Court to Sue American Leaders." *Toronto Star*, June 29, 2003, F4.

Ibbitson, John. "Canada Condemns World Court Compromise." *Globe and Mail*, July 13, 2002, A11.

Ivanov, Igor. "Russia in the Changing World: The President and the Foreign Ministry Will Seek to Build a Multipolar World." *Ngezavisimaya Gazeta*, June 25, 1999, 1.

Izenberg, Dan, and Herb Keinon. "Israel Will Not Join International Criminal Court." *Jerusalem Post*, July 1, 2002, 1.

Johnson, Scott. "Hard Target the Hunt for Africa's Last Warlord." *Newsweek*, May 25, 2009.

Kamiya, Setsuko. "Chief Justice of ICC Lauds Japan Pledge to Join Tribunal." McClatchy—Tribune Business News, December 7, 2006, 1.

Knickmeyer, Ellen, and Naseer Nouri. "Insurgents Kill 160 in Baghdad; Toll from Day-Long Wave of Attacks Is Largest in Iraqi Capital Since Invasion." *Washington Post*, September 15, 2005, A1.

Kristof, Nicholas D. "Dare We Call It Genocide?" *New York Times*, June 16, 2004, A21.

Kristof, Nicholas D. "If This Is Not Genocide, What Is?" *International Herald Tribune*, June 17, 2004, 9.

Kristof, Nicholas D. "The West Stands by While Genocide Unfolds." *International Herald Tribune*, June 1, 2004, 6.

Lacey, Marc. "White House Reconsiders Its Policy on Crisis in Sudan." *New York Times*, June 12, 2004, A3.

LaFranchi, Howard. "US Opposes ICC Bid to Make 'Aggression' a Crime under International Law." *Christian Science Monitor*, June 15, 2010, 7.

Lambert, Blake. "Tribe Opposes Court Role." *Washington Times*, March 31, 2005, A13.

Lattimer, Mark. "For All Bashir's Bravado, He is Marked as Damaged Goods: The Sudanese President Will Soon Find His Security Council Allies Can't Shield Him from the Impact of Being Cast as Global Pariah." *Guardian* (London), July 16, 2008, 28.

Lauria, Joe. "Canada Launches Campaign for Global War Crimes Court." *Ottawa Citizen*, September 14, 2000.

Lavallee, Guillaume. "Beshir Lashes Out at West as Fears Mount for Darfur." Agence France Presse, March 5, 2009.

Lederer, Edith M. "UN Warns 'Irrevocable Damage' in Darfur Expulsions." Associated Press, March 5, 2009.

Lederer, Edith M. "War Crimes Prosecutor Vows to Win Trust." Associated Press, April 23, 2003.

Lee, Jesse. "President Obama to Those Conducting Violence in Libya: 'It is Their Choice…and They Will Be Held Accountable.'" The White House Blog, March 7, 2011, http://www.whitehouse.gov/blog/2011/03/07/president-obama-those-conducting-violence-libya-it-their-choice-and-they-will-be-hel.

Lehman, Stan. "Judge Who Sought Pinochet Extradition Calls for Ratification of Treaty Creating War Crimes Court." Associated Press, September 23, 2000.

Lekic, Slobodan. "Arrests of War Crimes Suspects Seen as Key to Peace in Bosnia." Associated Press, May 23, 1997.

Lippman, Thomas W. "America Avoids the Stand; Why the U.S. Objects to a World Criminal Court." *Washington Post*, July 26, 1998, C1.

Loyd, Anthony, and Ali Hamdani. "Baghdad's Worst Day of Slaughter." *Times* (London), September 15, 2005, 39.

Lynch, Colum. "European Countries Cut Deal to Protect Afghan Peacekeepers." *Washington Post*, June 20, 2002, A15.

Lynch, Colum. "International Court under Unusual Fire: Africans Defend Sudan's Indicted Leader." *Washington Post*, June 30, 2009, A7.

Lynch, Colum. "Massacre Probe Concerns U.S.; Role of International Court in U.N. Investigation is Cited." *Washington Post*, December 2, 2004, A24.

Lynch, Colum. "US Confronts EU on War Crimes Court; Immunity Pact Issue Threatens Relations." *Washington Post*, June 10, 2003, A17.

Lynch, Colum, and Walter Pincus. "Security Council Set to Debate Blix Role." *Washington Post*, April 22, 2003, A13.

MacArthur Foundation. "MacArthur Announces $1.5 Million in Grants Related to International Criminal Court." News release, Nov. 15, 2002, http://www.macfound.org/press/press-releases/the-macarthur-foundation-announces-15-million-in-grants-related-to-international-criminal-court/.

MacArthur Foundation. "Strengthening the International Criminal Court." News release, Jan. 30, 2004, http://www.macfound.org/press/press-releases/macarthur-provides-more-than-17-million-in-support-of-the-international-criminal-court-january-30-2004/.

MacAskill, Ewen. "U.S. May Face Down Fear of Prosecution and Join International War Crimes Court, Clinton Hints." *Guardian* (London), August 6, 2009, 17.

MacAskill, Ewen, Simon Tisdall, and Nicholas Watt. "Middle East: US Backs No-Fly Zone over Libya but Rebels Fear Aid Will Come Too Late to Stop Gaddafi." *Guardian* (London), March 16, 2011, 18.

MacFarquhar, Neil. "Pursuit of Sudan's Leader Incites Debate." *New York Times*, July 12, 2008, A6.

Macintyre, Ben. "Prosecutor Says French Harbour War Criminals in Bosnia." *Times* (London), December 15, 1997, 11.

Majtenyi, Cathy. "Uganda Joins Forces with the Democratic Republic of Congo to Find Ugandan Rebels in DRC." Voice of America, via *U.S. Fed News*, October 20, 2005.

Maliti, Tom. "Envoy Says US to Attend War Crimes Court Meeting," Associated Press, November 16, 2009.

Marshall, Will. "The Blair Democrats: Ready for Battle." *Washington Post*, May 1, 2003, A27.

Max, Arthur. "International Criminal Court Gets Its First Case: Against Rebels in Uganda." Associated Press, January 29, 2004.

McCarthy, Rory. "Amnesty Details Killing of Civilians by British Soldiers." *Guardian* (London), May 11, 2004.

McCarthy, Rory. "UN Human Rights Chief Accuses Israel of War Crimes." *Guardian* (London), January 10, 2009, 6.

McConnell, Tristan. "A Congo Warlord—Arrested for Crimes against Humanity—Explains Himself." *Christian Science Monitor*, February 15, 2008, 20.

McDonell, Stephen. "China Concerned by ICC's Sudan Arrest Plans." Australian Broadcasting Corporation, July 15, 2008.

McElroy, Damien, Toby Harnden, Richard Spencer, and Matthew Holehouse. "Libya: Cameron Vows Support as Rebels Set Up Government in Tripoli." *Times* (London), August 22, 2011, 1, 5.

McGreal, Chris. "Justice or Reconciliation?: African Search for Peace Throws Court into Crisis: Uganda Fears First Crucial Test for Tribunal Could Prolong Brutal 20-Year Civil War." *Guardian* (London), January 9, 2007, 14.

McKinley, James C. "After a String of Dictators, Ugandans Get to Vote Again." *New York Times*, May 10, 1996.

Moreno-Ocampo, Luis. "A Global Web of Justice is Up and Running: The International Criminal Court." *International Herald Tribune*, June 12, 2006, 8.

Morrison, Patt. "Luis Moreno-Ocampo; 1st Prosecutor." *Los Angeles Times*, November 19, 2011, A17.

Mukasa, Henry. "Kony, Otti Study ICC Rules." *New Vision* (Kampala), November 21, 2006.

Muleme, Geoffrey. "Rebels Kill 192 in Uganda; Many Burned Alive in Huts During Refugee Camp Slaughter." *Chicago Sun-Times*, February 23, 2004, 33.

Murphy, Brian. "Sudan's Leader Arrives in Qatar; Arab League Allies Ignore ICC Warrant, Give Warm Welcome." *Washington Post*, March 30, 2009, A11.

Murphy, Dean E. "Serb General Indicted by U.N. Tribunal." *Los Angeles Times*, March 2, 1996, 1.

Mushtaq, Najum. "Sudan: ICC's Indictment of President Bashir Sparks Hope, Fear." Inter Press Service, July 18, 2008.

Myers, Steven Lee. "Chinese Embassy Bombing: A Wide Net of Blame." *New York Times*, April 17, 2000, A1.

Nyakairu, Frank. "Peace Talks with LRA Face Collapse." *Daily Monitor* (Kampala), October 9, 2005.

Nyakairu, Frank. "Sudan Government Suspends Agreement on Kony on 20 March." *Daily Monitor* (Kampala), March 20, 2007.

Nyakairu, Frank. "Uganda: Government Insists on ICC Trial for Kony." *Daily Monitor* (Kampala), March 19, 2005.

Ohito, David, and Martin Mutua. "The Hague: Cabinet Split over Local Tribunal Website." *Standard* (Nairobi), July 15, 2009.

Olcott, Martha Brill. "Bosnia May Become First Post-Cold War Fatality." *Dayton (OH) Daily News*, September 25, 1993.

Osman, Mohamed. "Sudan Rejects ICC War-Crime Allegations against Two Sudanese." Associated Press, February 27, 2007.

Pace, William. "A Victory for Peace." *International Criminal Court Monitor*, June 2002.

Pallister, David. "Growing Clamour to Remove the Hague Prosecutor Who Wants This Man Arrested: Move to Hold Sudan Leader over Darfur Sparks Outcry: Let the Judges Decide, Says Man at Eye of Storm." *Guardian* (London), August 18, 2008, 13.

Pallister, David. "UN Names Forces in Struggle for Congo Gold Fields." *Guardian* (London), December 4, 2003.

Paul, Rand. "Obama's Unconstitutional Libyan War: By Not Consulting Congress, President Has Violated War Powers Act." *Washington Times*, June 16, 2011, 1.

Perelman, Marc. "International Court Criticized for Uganda Intervention." *Forward* (New York), April 1, 2005, 6.

Perlez, Jane. "Serb Lawyer Vows Not to Cooperate with War Crimes Tribunal." *New York Times*, March 6, 1996, A11.

Peterson, Scott. "Chance for Chechen Peace Wanes; Thursday, Russian Officials Vowed to 'Wipe Out' Commanders of Chechnya's Resistance." *Christian Science Monitor*, November 1, 2002, 6.

Polgreen, Lydia, and Neil MacFarquhar. "Sudanese Protest War Crimes Case against President at Scripted Rally in Capital." *New York Times*, July 14, 2008.

Pomfret, John. "Rwandans Led Revolt in Congo." *Washington Post*, July 9, 1997, A1.

Ponder, Emily. "Child Soldiers Allegedly Helped Pillage Bogoro: Witness Recounts How Child Soldiers Wielding Spears Looted Ituri Village." *Institute for War & Peace Reporting*, ACR Issue 248, February 26, 2010.

Power, Samantha. "Court of First Resort." *New York Times*, February 10, 2005, A23.

Power, Samantha, and John Prendergast. "Break Through to Darfur: Combine Leverage, Internationalism and Aid to Stop the Killing in Sudan." *Los Angeles Times*, June 2, 2004, B13.

Rabkin, Jeremy. Interview by Phil Ponce, *News Hour with Jim Lehrer*, PBS, December 2, 1998, http://www.pbs.org/newshour/bb/latin_america/july-dec98/pinochet_12-2.html.

Ricks, Thomas. "US Signs Treaty on War Crimes Tribunal." *Washington Post*, January 1, 2001, A1.

Rieff, David. "Civil Society and the Future of the Nation-State: The False Dawn of Civil Society." *Nation* 268, no. 7 (February 22, 1999): 11–16.

Rosenberg, Mica. "Doubts Still Shroud UN Peacekeeper Deaths in Congo." Reuters, November 15, 2006, http://uk.reuters.com/article/2006/11/15/uk-guatemala-congo-idUKN1543499920061115.

Rozenberg, Joshua. "Global Court Opens Despite US Fears: International Justice Gets a Permanent Home with 18 Judges at the Hague." *Daily Telegraph* (London), March 12, 2003, 18.

Rubin, Elizabeth. "If Not Peace, Then Justice." *New York Times Magazine*, April 2, 2006, 42–46.

Sanders, Edmund, and Maggie Farley. "To Sudan, Court is Criminal." *Chicago Tribune*, July 12, 2008, 9.

Schmemann, Serge. "U.S. Links Peacekeeping to Immunity from New Court." *New York Times*, June 19, 2002, 3.

Sengupta, Kim. "Judgement Day Dawns after Russia Pledges to Quit Georgia." *Independent* (London), August 18, 2008, 20.

Shanker, Thom, and Seth Mydans. "Rumsfeld Says Threat of War over Kashmir Is Receding." *New York Times*, June 14, 2002, Section A, Column 1, Foreign Desk, p. 17.

Shenker, Israel. "U.N. Struggling with Perennial and Elusive Problem: Defining Aggression." *New York Times*, December 9, 1971, 14.

Simons, Marlise. "As a Wanted Man, Sudan's President Can't Escape His Diplomatic Isolation." *New York Times*, May 2, 2010.

Simons, Marlise. "Palestinians Press International Court for Inquiry on Possible Gaza War Crimes." *New York Times*, February 11, 2009, 13.

Simons, Marlise. "Third Ex-Warlord Sent to U.N. Court." *New York Times*, February 8, 2008.

Simpson, Chris. "UN Criminal Tribunal Chief Banned from Rwanda." Inter-Press Service, November 27, 1999.

Smith, Alex Duval. "Britain Blocks Prosecution of Sudan's Ruler: Human Rights Groups Criticise Strategy on Darfur." *Observer* (London), September 14, 2008, 44.

Smith, David. "New Chief Prosecutor Defends International Criminal Court." *Guardian* (London), May 23, 2012.

Smith, Helena. "Greeks Accuse Blair of War Crimes in Iraq: Athens Lawyers; Hague Case Names PM, Straw and Hoon." *Guardian* (London), July 29, 2003, 11.

Spillmann, Christian. "Paris Denies Inaction on Bosnian War Criminals." Agence France Presse, December 14, 1997.

Stack, Megan K. "Conflict in Caucasus: Ossetians Praise Russians; Blow to U.S. Foreign Policy; Russian Claims Appear Inflated; South Ossetia is Badly Damaged but Bears No Sign of a Genocide by Georgia. Residents Hail Moscow as a Savior." *Los Angeles Times*, August 18, 2008, A1.

Stephen, Chris. "International Criminal Court to Open in Face of US Opposition; Hopes Are High for the New International Criminal Court Despite US Hostility." *Irish Times* (Dublin), March 8, 2003, 13.

Stephen, Chris. "Jury Is Out on Future of Hague War Crimes Court." *Scotland on Sunday* (Edinburgh), March 9, 2003, 27.

Stephen, Christopher. "ICC Competes with Libya and France for Senussi." Radio Netherlands Worldwide, March 19, 2012.

Sulaiman, Tosin. "Group Investigating Whether U.S., British Troops Committed War Crimes." *Knight Ridder Tribune Business News*, April 24, 2003, 1.

Timberg, Craig. "Liberia's Taylor Found and Arrested." *Washington Post*, March 30, 2006.

Tisdall, Simon. "West Faces Clash with Africa on War Crime Indictment." *Guardian* (London), February 17, 2008.

Trickey, Mike. "Canada, U.S. at Odds over World Court." *Gazette* (Montreal), June 12, 2000, A10.

Trueheart, Charles. "Bosnian Serb Wanted for Genocide Arrested; War Crimes Tribunal Charges General Led Massacre of Muslims." *Washington Post*, December 3, 1998, A1.

Trueheart, Charles. "France Splits with Court Over Bosnia; Generals Won't Testify in War Crimes Cases." *Washington Post*, December 16, 1997, A22.

Tweedie, Neil, and Joshua Rozenberg. "New International Criminal Court Set Up: UN Ratifies its Ground-Breaking Treaty for Global Justice, Despite Being Snubbed by America and China." *Daily Telegraph* (London), April 12, 2002, 16.

Usborne, David. "Hans Blix vs the US; 'I Was Undermined,' Says Chief Weapons Inspector; Evidence for War Was 'Very, Very Shaky'; America Challenged to Step up Hunt for Weapons." *Independent* (London), April 23, 2003, 1.

VandeHei, Jim. "In Break with U.N., Bush Calls Sudan Killings Genocide." *Washington Post*, June 2, 2005.

Vulliamy, Ed, and Patrick Wintour. "War in the Balkans: Hawks Smell a Tyrant's Blood: NATO's New Confidence Suggests That the Neck of Slobodan Milosevic, the Butcher of Belgrade, May Itself Now Be on the Block." *Observer* (London), May 30, 1999, 15.

Ward, Olivia. "Prosecutor Points the Finger of Guilt; International Criminal Court Counsel Frustrated in His Bid to Bring Sudanese Minister to the Hague." *Toronto Star*, September 9, 2007, A13.

Watson, Roland. "Rumsfeld's Threat to Belgium over War Crimes Law." *Times* (London), June 13, 2003, 20.

Watson, Roland, Sam Coates, Tom Coghlan, Michael Evans, and James Bone. "Gaddafi's Way Out: Rebel Saloon-Car Army Drives on Towards Sirte: Allies May Allow Dictator to Leave Libya International Coalition Split over Ceasefire." *Times* (London), March 29, 2011, 1, 5.

Watt, Nicholas, and James Meikle. "Libya Officials Bribed by Britain to Help Evacuate UK Citizens." *Guardian* (London), February 25, 2011.

Wilson, Janet. "Prosecutor Arbour on Verge of Indicting Milosevic." *Los Angeles Times*, May 27, 1999, A1.

Wilson, Scott. "U.S. Moves Closer to Colombia's War; Involvement of Special Forces Could Trigger New Wave of Guerrilla Violence." *Washington Post*, February 7, 2003, A22.

Wilson, Scott, and Warrick, Joby. "Obama Appeals Directly to Top Libyan Officials." *Washington Post*, March 8, 2011, A8.

Wong, Edward. "Scores Killed in Iraq as Two Mosques Are Hit; Attacks in North Follow Baghdad Carnage." *International Herald Tribune*, November 19, 2005, 5.

Woolf, Marie. "Iraq in Crisis: CPS [Crown Prosecution Service] Considers Charges over Death of Iraqi." *Independent* (London), May 27, 2004.

World Federalist Movement. "Views of the World Federalist Movement on the Establishment of a Permanent International Criminal Court." News release, March 25, 1996, http://www.iccnow.org/documents/1PrepCmtViewsonICCWFM.pdf.

Wright, Robin. "When No One is Prepared to Say 'No' to Aggression: Bosnia: The Failure to Halt Ethnic Strife is Having a Deep and Destructive Impact on the Post-Cold War World. Goodby Desert Storm Principles." *Los Angeles Times*, May 23, 1993, 1.

Zarembo, Alan. "Museveni Juggles Ugandan Democracy: President Says Western Donors Shouldn't Tell Africans How They Should Be Running Their Affairs." *Globe and Mail* (Toronto), May 13, 1996.

SCHOLARLY AND SPECIALIST ARTICLES

Abbott, Kenneth W., and Duncan Snidal. "Why States Act through Formal International Organizations." *Journal of Conflict Resolution* 42, no. 1 (1998): 3–32.

Aberbach, Joel D., and Bert A. Rockman. "Conducting and Coding Elite Interviews." *PS: Political Science and Politics* 35, no. 4 (2002): 673–76.

Akhavan, Payam. "Beyond Impunity: Can International Criminal Justice Prevent Future Atrocities?" *American Journal of International Law* 95, no. 1 (2001): 7–31.

Alexander, James F. "The International Criminal Court and the Prevention of Atrocities: Predicting the Court's Impact." *Villanova Law Review* 54, no. 1 (2009): 1–56.

Alter, Karen J. "Agents or Trustees? International Courts in their Political Context." *European Journal of International Relations* 14, no. 1 (March 2008): 33–63.

Arbour, Louise. "The Need for an Independent and Effective Prosecutor in the Permanent International Criminal Court." *Windsor Yearbook of Access to Justice* 17 (1999): 207–95.

Bassiouni, M. Cherif, and Daniel H. Derby. "Final Report on the Establishment of an International Criminal Court for the Implementation of the Apartheid Convention and Other Relevant International Instruments (Symposium on the Future of Human Rights)." *Hofstra Law Review* 9, no. 2 (1980-81): 523–92.

Benedetti, Fanny, and John L. Washburn. "Drafting the International Criminal Court Treaty: Two Years to Rome and an Afterword on the Rome Diplomatic Conference." *Global Governance* 5, no. 1 (1999): 1–37.

Bolton, John R. "American Justice and the International Criminal Court." *DISAM (Defense Institute of Security Assistance Management) Journal of International Security Assistance Management* 26, no. 2 (2003): 28–32.

Bolton, John R. "Courting Danger: What's Wrong with the International Criminal Court." *National Interest*, no. 54 (Winter 1998/1999): 60–71.

Bolton, John R. "The Risks and Weaknesses of the International Criminal Court from America's Perspective." *Law and Contemporary Problems* 64, no. 1 (2001): 167–80.

Bolton, John R. "Should We Take Global Governance Seriously?" *Chicago Journal of International Law* 1, no. 2 (Fall 2000): 205–21.

Bosco, David L. "The International Criminal Court and Crime Prevention: Byproduct or Conscious Goal?" *Michigan State University College of Law Journal of International Law* 19, no. 2 (2011): 163–200.

Brubacher, Matthew. "Prosecutorial Discretion within the International Criminal Court." *Journal of International Criminal Justice* 2, no. 1 (March 2004): 71–95.

Buchanan, Allen, and Robert O. Keohane. "The Legitimacy of Global Governance Institutions." *Ethics & International Affairs* 20, no. 4 (2006): 405–38.

Burke-White, William W. "Complementarity in Practice: The International Criminal Court as Part of a System of Multi-level Global Governance in the Democratic Republic of Congo." *Leiden Journal of International Law* 18, no. 3 (2005): 557–90.

Cayley, Andrew T. "The Prosecutor's Strategy in Seeking the Arrest of Sudanese President Al Bashir on Charges of Genocide." *Journal of International Criminal Justice* 6, no. 5 (November 2008): 829–40.

Cerone, John P. "Dynamic Equilibrium: The Evolution of US Attitudes toward International Criminal Courts and Tribunals." *European Journal of International Law* 18, no. 2 (April 1, 2007): 277–315.

Chapman, Terrence L., and Stephen Chaudoin. "Ratification Patterns and the International Criminal Court." *International Studies Quarterly* (2012): 1–10.

Chung, Christine. "A Prosecutor without Borders." *World Affairs* 172, no. 1 (Summer 2009): 104.

Coalition for an International Criminal Court. "Brazil Formally Joins Supporters of the International Criminal Court: More Ratifications Expected Before July 1st Entry into Force." News release, June 20, 2002, http://www.iccnow.org/documents/pressrelease20020620.pdf.

Cogan, Jacob Katz. "Competition and Control in International Adjudication." *Virginia Journal of International Law* 48, no. 2 (2008): 411–49.

Côté, Luc. "Reflections on the Exercise of Prosecutorial Discretion in International Criminal Law." *Journal of International Criminal Justice* 3, no. 1 (March 2005): 162–86.

Cryer, Robert. "Sudan, Resolution 1593, and International Criminal Justice." *Leiden Journal of International Law* 19, no. 1 (March 2006): 195–222.

Danner, Allison Marston. "Navigating Law and Politics: The Prosecutor of the International Criminal Court and the Independent Counsel." *Stanford Law Review* 55, no. 5 (2003): 1633–65.

deGuzman, Margaret M. "Gravity and the Legitimacy of the International Criminal Court." *Fordham International Law Journal* 32, no. 5 (May 2009): 1400–65.

Flint, Julie, and Alex de Waal. "Case Closed: A Prosecutor Without Borders." *World Affairs* 171, no. 4 (Spring 2009): 23–38.

Furley, Oliver, and James Katalikawe. "Constitutional Reform in Uganda: The New Approach." *African Affairs* 96, no. 383 (1997): 243–60.

Glasius, Marlies. "Global Justice Meets Local Civil Society: The International Criminal Court's Investigation in the Central African Republic." *Alternatives: Global, Local, Political* 33, no. 4 (2008): 413–33.

Glassborow, Katy. "Darfuris' Mixed Feelings over Bashir Warrant: Some Unhappy that Genocide Charges against Sudanese President Weren't Included in Indictment." *Institute for War & Peace Reporting*, ACR Issue 207, April 29, 2009.

Goodliffe, Jay, and Darren Hawkins. "A Funny Thing Happened on the Way to Rome: Explaining International Criminal Court Negotiations." *Journal of Politics* 71, no. 3 (2009): 977–97.

Goodliffe, Jay, Darren Hawkins, Christine Horne, and Daniel L. Nielson. "Dependence Networks and the International Criminal Court." *International Studies Quarterly* 56, no. 1 (2012): 131–47.

Graubart, Jonathan. "Rendering Global Criminal Law an Instrument of Power: Pragmatic Legalism and Global Tribunals." *Journal of Human Rights* 9, no. 4 (2010): 409–26.

Hall, Christopher Keith. "The First Two Sessions of the UN Preparatory Committee on the Establishment of an International Criminal Court." *American Journal of International Law* 91, no. 1 (1997): 177–87.

Haq, Farhan. "Alliances Cut through North-South Divide." *Terra Viva*, June 22, 1998.

Harbom, Lotta, Erik Melander, and Peter Wallensteen. "Dyadic Dimensions of Armed Conflict, 1946–2007." *Journal of Peace Research* 45, no. 5 (2008): 697–710.

Hehir, J. Bryan. "Just War Theory in a Post-Cold War World." *Journal of Religious Ethics* 20, no. 2 (1992): 237–57.

Helfer, Laurence R. "Exiting Treaties." *Virginia Law Review* 91, no. 7 (2005): 1579–648.

Helfer, Laurence R., and Anne-Marie Slaughter. "Why States Create International Tribunals: A Response to Professors Posner and Yoo." *California Law Review* 93, no. 3 (2005): 899–956.

Hetesy, Zsolt. "Completing the Work of the Preparatory Commission: The Making of the Basic Principles of the Headquarters Agreement." *Fordham International Law Journal* (March 2002).

Janashia, Eka. "Georgian Government to Probe August 2008 War." *Central Asia-Caucasus Institute Analyst*, April 17, 2003, http://www.cacianalyst.org/publications/field-reports/item/12708-georgian-government-to-probe-august-2008-war.html.

Jaura, Ramesh, and Alison Dickens. "US Speak More Softly." *Terra Viva*, July 16, 1998.

Johnson, Larry D. "The Lubanga Case and Cooperation between the UN and the ICC: Disclosure Obligation v. Confidentiality Obligation." *Journal of International Criminal Justice* 10, no. 4 (September 2012): 887–903.

Kaye, David. "America's Honeymoon with the ICC: Will Washington's Love for International Law Last?" *Foreign Affairs*, April 16, 2013.

Keppler, Elise. "Grave Crimes: Darfur and the International Criminal Court." Human Rights Watch and *The World Today* (Chatham House, UK), January 2, 2005, http://www.hrw.org/news/2005/01/01/grave-crimes-darfur-and-international-criminal-court.

Kirsch, Philippe, and John T. Holmes. "The Birth of the International Criminal Court: The 1998 Rome Conference." *Canadian Yearbook of International Law* 36 (1998).

Kirsch, Philippe, and John T. Holmes. "The Rome Conference on an International Criminal Court: The Negotiating Process." *American Journal of International Law* 93, no. 1 (1999): 2–12.

Koremenos, Barbara, Charles Lipson, and Duncan Snidal. "The Rational Design of International Institutions." *International Organization* 55, no. 4 (2001): 761–99.

Ku, Julian, and Jide Nzelibe. "Do International Criminal Tribunals Deter or Exacerbate Humanitarian Atrocities?" *Washington University Law Review* 84, no. 4 (2006).

Lacina, Bethany, and Nils Petter Gleditsch. "Monitoring Trends in Global Combat: A New Dataset of Battle Deaths." *European Journal of Population / Revue Européenne de Démographie* 21, no. 2/3 (2005): 145–66.

Lacina, Bethany, Nils Petter Gleditsch, and Bruce Russett. "The Declining Risk of Death in Battle." *International Studies Quarterly* 50, no. 3 (2006): 673–80.

Levy, Jack S. "Qualitative Methods in International Relations." In *Millennial Reflections on International Studies*, edited by Michael Brecher and Frank P. Harvey, 432–54. Ann Arbor: University of Michigan Press, 2002.

Ling, Yan. "The Beijing Symposium on the Comparative Study of International Criminal Law and the Rome Statute." *Chinese Journal of International Law* 3, no. 1 (January 2004): 305–18.

Mackenzie, Ruth, and Philippe Sands. "International Courts and Tribunals and the Independence of the International Judge." *Harvard International Law Journal* 44 (2003): 271–85.

Mavroidis, Petros C. "Remedies in the WTO Legal System: Between a Rock and a Hard Place." *European Journal of International Law* 11, no. 4 (January 1, 2000): 763–813.

McMahan, Jeff. "Just Cause for War." *Ethics & International Affairs* 19, no. 3 (2005): 1–21, 119.

McNamara, Robert S., and Benjamin B. Ferencz. "For Clinton's Last Act." *New York Times*, December 12, 2000, A33.

Mearsheimer, John J. "The False Promise of International Institutions." *International Security* 19, no. 3 (1994): 5–49.

Mendez, Juan E. "National Reconciliation, Transnational Justice, and the International Criminal Court." *Ethics & International Affairs* 15, no. 1 (2001): 25–44.

Meron, Theodor. "Answering for War Crimes: Lessons from the Balkans." *Foreign Affairs* 76, no. 1 (January/February 1997): 2–8.

Meron, Theodor. "Defining Aggression for the International Criminal Court." *Suffolk Transnational Law Review* 25, no. 1 (Winter 2001): 1–15.

Meron, Theodor. "Judicial Independence and Impartiality in International Criminal Tribunals." *American Journal of International Law* 99, no. 2 (2005): 359–69.

Mertens, Mitja. "The International Criminal Court: A European Success Story." *EU Diplomacy Papers* (January 2011).

Muller, A. S. "Setting Up the International Criminal Court: Not One Moment but a Series of Moments." *International Organizations Law Review* 1, no. 1 (2004): 189–96.

Murphy, Ray. "Gravity Issues and the International Criminal Court." *Criminal Law Forum* 17, no. 3-4 (2006): 281–315.

Murphy, Sean D. "Aggression, Legitimacy and the International Criminal Court." *European Journal of International Law* 20, no. 4 (November 1 2009): 1147–56.

Neumayer, Eric. "A New Moral Hazard? Military Intervention, Peacekeeping and Ratification of the International Criminal Court." *Journal of Peace Research* 46, no. 5 (2009): 659–70.

Open Society Foundations, "Open Society Justice Initiative Highlighting Complementarity and Outreach at ICC Review." News release, May 26, 2010, http://www.opensocietyfoundations.org/press-releases/open-society-justice-initiative-highlighting-complementarity-and-outreach-icc-review.

Orentlicher, Diane F. "Unilateral Multilateralism: United States Policy toward the International Criminal Court." *Cornell International Law Journal* 36 (January 2004): 415–521.

Paul, Joel Richard. "Is Global Governance Safe for Democracy?" *Chicago Journal of International Law* 1, no. 2 (Fall 2000).

Pellet, Alain. "The Palestinian Declaration and the Jurisdiction of the International Criminal Court." *Journal of International Criminal Justice* 8, no. 4 (September 2010): 981–99.

Posner, Eric A. "The Decline of the International Court of Justice." University of Chicago Law School, John M. Olin Law & Economics Working Paper Series, 2004.

Posner, Eric A., and John C. Yoo. "Judicial Independence in International Tribunals." *California Law Review* 93, no. 1 (2005): 1–74.

Rabkin, Jeremy. "Is EU Policy Eroding the Sovereignty of Non-Member States?" *Chicago Journal of International Law* 1, no. 2 (Fall 2000): 273–90.

Rudolph, Christopher. "Constructing an Atrocities Regime: The Politics of War Crimes Tribunals." *International Organization* 55, no. 3 (2001): 655–91.

Ryngaert, Cedric. "The International Criminal Court and Universal Jurisdiction: A Fraught Relationship?" *New Criminal Law Review: An International and Interdisciplinary Journal* 12, no. 4 (2009): 498–512.

SáCouto, Susana, and Katherine Cleary. "The Gravity Threshold of the International Criminal Court." *American University International Law Review* 23, no. 5 (2008): 807–54.

Schabas, William A. "Prosecutorial Discretion v. Judicial Activism at the International Criminal Court." *Journal of International Criminal Justice* 6, no. 4 (September 2008).

Scheffer, David. "Article 98(2) of the Rome Statute: America's Original Intent." *Journal of International Criminal Justice* 3, no. 2 (May 2005): 333–53.

Scheffer, David J. "Staying the Course with the International Criminal Court." *Cornell International Law Journal* 35, no. 1 (2002): 47–100.

Schonberg, Karl K. "The General's Diplomacy: U.S. Military Influence in the Treaty Process, 1992–2000." *Seton Hall Journal of Diplomacy and International Affairs* 68, no. 3 (2002): 68–85.

Simmons, Beth A., and Allison Danner. "Credible Commitments and the International Criminal Court." *International Organization* 64, no. 2 (Spring 2010): 225–56.

Simmons, P. J. "Learning to Live with NGOs." *Foreign Policy*, no. 112 (Autumn 1998): 82–96.

Skidelsky, Robert, and Michael Ignatieff. "Is Military Intervention over Kosovo Justified?" *Prospect*, May 3–4, June 20, 1999.

Smidt, Michael L. "The International Criminal Court: An Effective Means of Deterrence?" *Military Law Review* 167 (2001): 156–240.

Stephan, Paul B. "International Governance and American Democracy." *Chicago Journal of International Law* 1, no. 2 (Fall 2000): 237–56.

Swart, Mia. "[Review] Ruth Mackenzie, Kate Malleson, Penny Martin, and Philippe Sands QC (eds.), *Selecting International Judges: Principle, Process, and Politics*." *Leiden Journal of International Law* 24, no. 3 (2011): 789–92.

Tamaki, Taku. "Recasting 'Nuclear-Free Korean Peninsula' as a Sino-American Language for Co-ordination." *Japanese Journal of Political Science* 13, no. 1 (2012): 59–81.

Totten, Samuel. "The UN International Commission of Inquiry on Darfur: New and Disturbing Findings." *Genocide Studies and Prevention* 4, no. 3 (2009): 354–78.

Vinci, Anthony. "The Strategic Use of Fear by the Lord's Resistance Army." *Small Wars & Insurgencies* 16, no. 3 (2005): 360–81.

Voeten, Erik. "The Impartiality of International Judges: Evidence from the European Court of Human Rights." *American Political Science Review* 102, no. 4 (2008): 417–33.

Wedgwood, Ruth. "Fiddling in Rome: America and the International Criminal Court." *Foreign Affairs* 77, no. 6 (November/December 1998): 20–24.

Whitbeck, John V. "Palestine and the ICC." *Palestine Chronicle*, April 6, 2013.

Wippman, David. "Atrocities, Deterrence, and the Limits of International Justice." *Fordham International Law Journal* 23 (1999): 473.

UNITED NATIONS DOCUMENTS

"Assessment of Member States' Contributions for the Financing of the International Criminal Tribunal for the Prosecution of Persons Responsible for Serious Violations of International Humanitarian Law Committed in the Territory of the Former Yugoslavia since 1991 from 1 January 1994 to 31 December 2003." New York: UN Secretariat, 2003.

"Assessment of the Contributions of Member States for the Financing of the International Criminal Tribunal for the Prosecution of Persons Responsible for Genocide and Other Serious Violations of International Humanitarian Law Committed in the Territory of Rwanda and Rwandan Citizens Responsible for Genocide and Other Such Violations Committed in the Territory of Neighbouring States between 1 January and 31 December 1994, for the Period up to 31 October 1995 through 31 December 2003." New York: UN Secretariat, 2003.

"Daily Press Briefing by the Office of the Spokesman for the Secretary-General [Stéphane Dujarric, Associate Spokesman]." http://www.un.org/News/briefings/docs/2004/db061704.doc.htm.

"Legal Consequences of the Construction of a Wall in the Occupied Palestinian Territory." International Court of Justice Advisory Opinion, July 9, 2004, http://www.icj-cij.org/docket/files/131/1671.pdf.

"Letter dated 26 July 2002 from the President of the International Criminal Tribunal for the Prosecution of Persons Responsible for Genocide and Other Serious Violations of International Humanitarian Law Committed in the Territory of Rwanda and Rwandan Citizens Responsible for Genocide and Other Such Violations Committed in the Territory of Neighbouring States between 1 January and 31 December 1994 addressed to the President of the Security Council." July 29, 2002, UN Doc. S/2002/847, http://www.un.org/Docs/journal/asp/ws.asp?m=S/2002/847.

"New Significant Outflow of Sudanese Refugees into Chad." UN High Commissioner for Refugees, August 17, 2004, http://www.unhcr.org/cgi-bin/texis/vtx/search?page=search&docid=412206084&query=+sudan%20+chad%20+darfur.

Annan, Kofi. Press Release, "Secretary-General, Secretary-General Welcomes Arrest Warrants, First from International Criminal Court, as 'Powerful Signal Around World,'" U.N. Press Release SG/SM/10167, L/3095 (Oct. 14, 2005), http://www.un.org/News/Press/docs/2005/sgsm10167.doc.htm.

Centre, UN News. "Sudan Not Cooperating on Arrests of War Crimes Suspects, Says Prosecutor." Published electronically August 28, 2007. http://www.un.org/apps/news/story.asp?NewsID=23625&Cr=sudan&Cr1=icc#.UZf4S8pQVjo.

Centre, UN News. "UN Calls for More Offers of Troops, Specialist Units for Hybrid Force in Darfur." Published electronically September 20, 2007. http://www.un.org/apps/news/story.asp?NewsID=23889&Cr=sudan&Cr1#.UEfGgaPoxqI.

Charter of the International Military Tribunal—Annex to the Agreement for the Prosecution and Punishment of the Major War Criminals of the European Axis ("London Agreement"), U.S.-Fr.-U.K.-U.S.S.R., Aug. 8, 1945, 59 Stat. 1544, 82 U.N.T.S. 279, http://www.unhcr.org/refworld/docid/3ae6b39614.html.

Corfu Channel (U.K. v. Alb.), 1949 I.C.J., http://www.icj-cij.org/docket/index.php?p1=3&p2=3&k=cd&case=1.

De la Sablière, Jean-Marc. "Statement by French Ambassador De la Sablière after the Vote of Resolution 1593." http://www.iccnow.org/documents/France_Darfur1593_Press31Mar05.pdf.

G.A. Res. 3314 (XXIX), Annex (Dec. 14, 1974), http://www.un.org/documents/ga/res/29/ares29.htm.

Geneva Convention Relative to the Protection of Civilian Persons in Time of War (Fourth Geneva Convention), Aug. 12, 1949, 6 U.S.T. 3516, 75 U.N.T.S. 287, http://www.unhcr.org/refworld/docid/3ae6b36d2.html.

International Court of Justice. "Basis of the Court's Jurisdiction," http://www.icj-cij.org/jurisdiction/index.php?p1=5&p2=1&p3=2.

International Criminal Tribunal for Rwanda. "Prosecutor Outlines Future Plans." News release ICTR/INFO-9-2-254, December 13, 2000, http://www.unictr.org/tabid/155/Default.aspx?id=362.

International Criminal Tribunal for the Former Yugoslavia. "Statement by the Prosecutor Louise Arbour Following Her Meeting with the French Minister of Foreign Affairs, Mr. Hubert Vedrine." News release, December 15, 1997, http://www.icty.org/sid/7429/en.

International Labor Organization. 105th Session, Administrative Tribunal Judgment No. 2757, issued in Geneva, July 9, 2008, http://www.ilo.org/dyn/triblex/triblexmain.fullText?p_lang=fr&p_judgment_no=2757&p_language_code=EN.

Karl Doenitz Judgment (International Military Tribunal), http://avalon.law.yale.edu/imt/juddoeni.asp.

Motoc, Iulia. "Report on the Situation of Human Rights in the Democratic Republic of the Congo, Submitted by the Special Rapporteur." March 10, 2004, Commission on Human Rights, 60th Sess., U.N. Doc. E/CN.4/2004/34 http://www.unhchr. ch/Huridocda/Huridoca.nsf/0/e17f022df5c7829dc1256e9800380663/$FILE/ G0411748.pdf.

Press Release, Secretary-General. "Secretary-General Says Establishment of International Criminal Court is Major Step in March Towards Universal Human Rights, Rule of Law," U.N. Press Release L/2890 (July 18/20, 1998), http://www. un.org/News/Press/docs/1998/19980720.l2890.html.

S. Con. Res. 99, H.Con.Res.467, 108th Cong. (2004) Declaring Genocide in Darfur, Sudan, http://www.gpo.gov/fdsys/pkg/BILLS-108sconres99es/pdf/ BILLS-108sconres99es.pdf.

S.C. Pres. Statement 2004/18, U.N. Doc. S/PRST/2004/18 (May 25, 2004), http:// www.un.org/ga/search/view_doc.asp?symbol=S/PRST/2004/18.

S.C. provisional verbatim record, 3175th mtg. at 11, U.N. Doc. S/PV.3175 (Feb. 22, 1993).

S.C. Res. 1422, U.N. Doc. S/RES/1422 (July 12, 2002), http://www.un.org/Docs/ journal/asp/ws.asp?m=S/RES/1422.

S.C. Res. 1564, para. 12, U.N. Doc. S/RES/1564 (Sept. 18, 2004), http://www.un.org/ docs/sc/unsc_resolutions04.html.

S.C. Res. 780, U.N. Doc. S/RES/780 (Oct. 6, 1992), http://www.un.org/documents/ sc/res/1992/scres92.htm.

S.C. Res. 808, ¶ 1, U.N. Doc. S/RES/808 (Feb. 22, 1993), http://www.un.org/Docs/ scres1993/scres93.htm.

S.C. Res. 955, U.N. Doc. S/RES/955 (Nov. 8, 1994), http://www.un.org/Docs/ scres1994/scres94.htm.

Trial of the Major War Criminals before the International Military Tribunal. Nuremberg ("Blue Series"), Nov. 14, 1945 to Oct. 1, 1946, vol. I, http://www.loc.gov/rr/frd/ Military_Law/pdf/NT_Vol-I.pdf.

UN Assistance Mission in Afghanistan. Statement by the Special Representative of the Secretary-General for Afghanistan, Kai Eide, August 26, 2009.

UN Diplomatic Conference of Plenipotentiaries on the Establishment of an International Criminal Court, Rome, 15 June—1 7 July 1998. Official Records vol. 2, p. 129, http://untreaty.un.org/cod/icc/rome/proceedings/E/Rome%20 Proceedings_v2_e.pdf.

UN Diplomatic Conference of Plenipotentiaries on the Establishment of an International Criminal Court, Rome, 15 June-17 July 1998. Official Records vol. 2, Summary records of the plenary meetings and of the meetings of the Committee of the Whole, http://untreaty.un.org/cod/icc/rome/proceedings/E/Rome%20 Proceedings_v2_e.pdf.

UN G.A. Res 67/19, U.N. Doc. A/RES/67/19 (Nov. 29, 2012), http://www.un.org/ Depts/dhl/resguide/r67.shtml

UN Information Service. "Eight UN Human Rights Experts Gravely Concerned About Reported Widespread Abuses in Darfur, Sudan." Statement issued in Geneva on March 26, 2004; press release AFR/873, HR/CN/1065 issued March 29, 2004.

UN Integrated Regional Information Networks. "Congo-Kinshasa; Interview With UN Under-Secretary for Peacekeeping Operations." (June 5, 2003).

UN Integrated Regional Information Networks. "US Aid for Fight Against Lord's Resistance Army." (October 28, 2003).

UN Office of the High Commissioner for Human Rights. "UN Human Rights Chief Expresses Her Grave Concern in the Escalating Violence in Gaza" news release, December 28, 2008, http://www.unhchr.ch/huricane/huricane.nsf/view01/F5307 C1E012294F6C125752D005CD71F?opendocument.

UN Organization Mission in the Democratic Republic of the Congo (MONUC) and Office of the United Nations High Commissioner for Human Rights. "The Human Rights Situation in the Democratic Republic of Congo (DRC) During the Period January to June 2007," September 27, 2007, http://www.ohchr.org/Documents/Countries/UNHROBiannualReport01to062007.pdf.

UN Organization Mission in the Democratic Republic of the Congo and Office of the High Commissioner for Human Rights, "Summary of Fact Finding Missions on Alleged Human Rights Violations Committed by the Lord's Resistance Army (LRA) in the Districts of Haut-Uélé and Bas-Uélé in Orientale Province of the Democratic Republic of Congo," December 2009, http://www2.ohchr.org/SPdocs/Countries/LRAReport_December2009_E.pdf.

UN S.C. Res. 1970, U.N. Doc. S/RES/1970 (February 26, 2011), http://www.un.org/Docs/journal/asp/ws.asp?m=s/res/1970%282011%29.

UN S.C. Res. 1973, U.N. Doc. S/RES/1973 (March 17, 2011), http://www.un.org/Docs/journal/asp/ws.asp?m=S/RES/1973%20%282011%29.

UN Secretary-General. "Historical Survey of the Question of International Criminal Jurisdiction—Memorandum Submitted by the Secretary-General," 1949, A/CN.4/7Rev.1, http://untreaty.un.org/ilc/documentation/english/a_cn4_7_rev1.pdf.

U.N. Secretary-General. *Report of the Secretary-General's Internal Review Panel on United Nations Action in Sri Lanka* (November 2012), http://www.un.org/News/dh/infocus/Sri_Lanka/The_Internal_Review_Panel_report_on_Sri_Lanka.pdf.

UN Secretary-General. *Report of the Secretary-General Pursuant to Paragraph 2 of Security Council Resolution 808 (1993)*, ¶ 87 (p. 22), U.N. Doc. S/25704 (May 3, 1993), http://www.un.org/Docs/journal/asp/ws.asp?m=S/25704.

UN Secretary-General. *Report of the Secretary-General, Financing of the International Criminal Tribunal for the Prosecution of Persons Responsible for Genocide and Other Serious Violations of International Humanitarian Law Committed in the Territory of Rwanda and Rwandan Citizens Responsible for Genocide and Other Such Violations Committed in the Territory of Neighbouring States Between 1 January and 31*

December 1994, ¶ 33, U.N. Doc. A/C.5/51/29/Add.1 (May 12, 1997), http://www. un.org/Docs/journal/asp/ws.asp?m=A/C.5/51/29/Add.1.

UN Secretary-General. Secretary-General Urges "Like-Minded" States to Ratify Statute of International Criminal Court, U.N. Press Release SG/SM/6686 (Sept. 1, 1998), http://www.un.org/news/Press/docs/1998/19980901.sgsm6686.html.

UN Security Council Resolution 1593, U.N. Doc. S/RES/1593 (March 31, 2005), http://www.un.org/Docs/journal/asp/ws.asp?m=S/RES/1593.

UN Security Council, 55th Sess. 4150th mtg. at 3, U.N. Doc. S/PV.4150 (June 2, 2000), http://www.un.org/ga/search/view_doc.asp?symbol=S/PV.4150. See also International Criminal Tribunal for the former Yugoslavia, "Prosecutor's Report on the NATO Bombing Campaign," news release, June 13, 2000, http://www.icty.org/sid/7846.

UN Security Council, 5934th mtg. U.N. Doc. S/PV.5905 (July 16, 2008), http://www. un.org/ga/search/view_doc.asp?symbol=S/PV.5934.

UN Security Council, 60th year, 5158th mtg. U.N. Doc. S/PV.5158 (March 31, 2005), http://www.un.org/ga/search/view_doc.asp?symbol=S/PV.5158.

UN Security Council, 62nd year, 5789th mtg. p. 5, U.N. Doc. S/PV.5789 (Dec. 5, 2007), http://www.un.org/ga/search/view_doc.asp?symbol=S/PV.5789.

UN Security Council, 63rd year, 5905th mtg, p. 4, U.N. Doc. S/PV.5905 (June 5, 2008), http://www.un.org/ga/search/view_doc.asp?symbol=S/PV.5905.

UN Security Council, 63rd year, 5947th mtg, p. 8, U.N. Doc. S/PV.5947 (July 31, 2008), http://www.un.org/ga/search/view_doc.asp?symbol=S/PV.5947.

United Nations. "Secretary-General Says Establishment of International Criminal Court is Major Step in March Towards Universal Human Rights, Rule of Law," news release L/ROM/23, July 20, 1998 (remarks from July 18, 1998), http://www. un.org/News/Press/docs/1998/19980720.l2890.html.

ICC DOCUMENTS

Agreement between the International Criminal Court and the European Union on Cooperation and Assistance, http://eur-lex.europa.eu/LexUriServ/site/en/oj/2006/l_115/l_11520060428en00500056.pdf.

Al-Hussein, [HRH Prince] Zeid Ra'ad Zeid. Statement by the President of the Assembly of States Parties to the Rome Statute of the International Criminal Court at the Inaugural Meeting of Judges of the International Criminal Court, March 11, 2003, http://www.icc-cpi.int/NR/rdonlyres/6D0FE045-1D39-4CD3-BA77-B9517380EC18/144080/Statement_by_HRH_Prince_Zeid_Ra_EN.pdf.

Draft Statute for an International Criminal Court, adopted by the UN International Law Commission, 46th session, 1994, and submitted to the General Assembly, http://untreaty.un.org/ilc/texts/instruments/english/draft%20articles/7_4_1994.pdf.

"Election of the Judges of the International Criminal Court, First election (first resumed session of the Assembly of States Parties, held from 3 to 7 February 2003) Results." United Nations, http://untreaty.un.org/cod/icc/asp/aspfra.htm.

ICC Assembly of States Parties, 10th Sess. "Closing Remarks by Christian Wenaweser as ASP President," p. 2 (December 2011), http://www.icc-cpi.int/iccdocs/asp_docs/ASP10/Statements/ASP10-ST-PASP-CW-CLRemarks-ENG.pdf.

ICC Assembly of States Parties, 10th Sess. "Report of the Committee on Budget and Finance on the Work of Its Tenth Session." ICC-ASP/7/20 (April 2008), http://www.icc-cpi.int/iccdocs/asp_docs/B.pdf.

ICC Assembly of States Parties, 4th Sess. "Report of the Committee on Budget and Finance on the Work of Its Fourth Session." ICC-ASP/4/2 (April 15, 2005), http://www.icc-cpi.int/iccdocs/asp_docs/library/asp/ICC-ASP-4-2_English.pdf.

ICC Assembly of States Parties, 5th Sess. "Report of the Bureau on Ratification and Implementation of the Rome Statute and on Participation in the Assembly of States Parties." ICC-ASP/5/26 (November 17, 2006), http://www.icc-cpi.int/iccdocs/asp_docs/library/asp/ICC-ASP-5-26_English.pdf.

ICC Assembly of States Parties. States Parties—Chronological List, updated March 15, 2013, http://www.icc-cpi.int/en_menus/asp/states%20parties/Pages/states%20parties%20_%20chronological%20list.aspx.

ICC Assembly of States Parties. "Report of the Committee on Budget and Finance." August 13, 2004.

ICC Assembly of States Parties. Resolution ICC-ASP/1/Res.3 (September 9, 2002), http://untreaty.un.org/cod/icc/elections/texts/electionofjudges%28e%29.pdf.

ICC Assembly of States Parties. Third session, The Hague, September 6–10, 2004 Official Records, ICC-ASP/3/25, http://www.icc-cpi.int/NR/rdonlyres/EEF8F8E2-6AF9-47F7-859E-1C1AE1359ED3/140538/ICCASP325IIB_English.pdf.

ICC Office of the Prosecutor and Pre-Trial Chamber I. "Warrant of Arrest" for Bosco Ntaganda (issued under seal), ICC-01/04-02/06 (August 22, 2006), http://www.icc-cpi.int/iccdocs/doc/doc305330.PDF.

ICC Office of the Prosecutor and Pre-Trial Chamber I. "Warrant of Arrest for Ali Kushayb." ICC-02/05–01/07 (April 27, 2007), http://www.icc-cpi.int/iccdocs/doc/doc279858.PDF.

ICC Office of the Prosecutor and Pre-Trial Chamber I. "Warrant of Arrest for Mathieu Ngudjolo Chui," ICC-01/04-02/07 (July 6, 2007), http://www.icc-cpi.int/iccdocs/doc/doc453054.PDF.

ICC Office of the Prosecutor and Pre-Trial Chamber II. "Warrant of Arrest for Joseph Kony Issued on 8 July 2005 as Amended on 27 September 2005." ICC-02/04–01/05 (September 27, 2005), http://www.icc-cpi.int/iccdocs/doc/doc97185.PDF.

ICC Office of the Prosecutor and Pre-Trial Chamber III. "Warrant of Arrest for Jean-Pierre Bemba Gombo" ICC-01/05-01/08 (May 23, 2008), http://www.icc-cpi.int/iccdocs/doc/doc504390.PDF.

ICC Office of the Prosecutor and Pre-Trial Chamber III. "Warrant of Arrest for Laurent Koudou Gbagbo." ICC-02/11 (November 23, 2011), http://www.icc-cpi.int/iccdocs/doc/doc1276751.pdf.

ICC Office of the Prosecutor. "Prosecutor's Statement on the Prosecutor's Application for a Warrant of Arrest under Article 58 against Omar Hassan Ahmad al Bashir" (July 14, 2008), http://www.icc-cpi.int/iccdocs/asp_docs/library/organs/otp/ICC-OTP-ST20080714-ENG.pdf.

ICC Office of the Prosecutor. "Report on Preliminary Examination Activities 2012" (November 2012), http://www.icc-cpi.int/iccdocs/otp/OTP2012ReportonPreliminaryExaminations22Nov2012.pdf.

ICC Office of the Prosecutor. "Situation in Palestine" (April 3, 2012), http://www.icc-cpi.int/NR/rdonlyres/C6162BBF-FEB9-4FAF-AFA9-836106D2694A/284387/SituationinPalestineo30412ENG.pdf.

ICC Office of the Prosecutor. "Statement to the United Nations Security Council on the situation in the Libyan Arab Jamahiriya, pursuant to UNSCR 1970 (2011)" (May 4, 2011), http://www.icc-cpi.int/en_menus/icc/structure%20of%20othe%20court/office%20of%20the%20prosecutor/reports%20and%20statements/statement/Pages/statement%20to%20the%20united%20nations%20security%20council%20on%20the%20situation%20in%20the%20libyan%20.aspx.

ICC Office of the Prosecutor. "Third Report of the Prosecutor of the International Criminal Court to the UN Security Council Pursuant to UNSCR 1593 (2005)" (June 14, 2006).

ICC Office of the Prosecutor. Press Conference on Libya, May 16, 2011, http://www.icc-cpi.int/en_menus/icc/structure%20of%20othe%20court/office%20of%20the%20prosecutor/reports%20and%20statements/statement/Pages/statement%20icc%20prosecutor%20press%20conference%20on%20olibya%2016%20may%202011.aspx.

ICC Preparatory Commission. *Proposal submitted by Bahrain, Iraq, Lebanon, the Libyan Arab Jamahiriya, Oman, the Sudan, the Syrian Arab Republic and Yemen,* U.N. Doc. PCNICC/1999/DP.11 (February 26, 1999), http://untreaty.un.org/cod/icc/documents/aggression/english/1999.dp11.pdf.

ICC Pre-Trial Chamber I. "Situation in the Democratic Republic of the Congo: In the Case of the Prosecutor v. Thomas Lubanga Dyilo: Reasons for Oral Decision Lifting the Stay of Proceedings," ICC-01/04–01/06–1644 (January 23, 2009), http://www.icc-cpi.int/iccdocs/JUDSUMM/JSV_ICC_0104_0106_1644.pdf.

ICC Pre-Trial Chamber I. "Decision on the Consequences of Non-Disclosure of Exculpatory Materials Covered by Article 54(3)(e) Agreements and the Application to Stay the Prosecution of the Accused, Together with Certain Other Issues Raised at the Status Conference on 10 June 2008" ICC-01/04–01/06–1401 (June 13, 2008), http://www.icc-cpi.int/iccdocs/doc/doc511249.pdf.

ICC Pre-Trial Chamber II. "Decision Pursuant to Article 15 of the Rome Statute on the Authorization of an Investigation into the Situation in the Republic of Kenya," ICC-01/09 (March 31, 2010), http://www.icc-cpi.int/iccdocs/doc/doc854287.pdf.

ICC Public Information Office. "Press-Kit: Inaugural Ceremony: Swearing-in of the Judges of the ICC." March 11, 2003.

Kaul, Hans-Peter. "Dissenting Opinion of Judge Hans-Peter Kaul," in Pre-Trial Chamber II, "Decision Pursuant to Article 15 of the Rome Statute on the Authorization of an Investigation into the Situation in the Republic of Kenya," ICC-01/09–19-Corr 01–04-2010 (March 31, 2010), http://www.icc-cpi.int/iccdocs/doc/doc854562.pdf.

Kirsch, Philippe. "Fifth Session of the Assembly of States Parties: Opening Remarks," November 23, 2006, http://www.icc-cpi.int/iccdocs/asp_docs/library/organs/presidency/PK_20061123_en.pdf.

Kirsch, Philippe. "Statement by Judge Philippe Kirsch, President of the International Criminal Court, at the Inaugural Meeting of the Judges," March 11, 2003, http://www.icc-cpi.int/NR/rdonlyres/48D76A79-7315-49C2-A16F-86D7CFAAE721/143846/PK_20030311_En.pdf.

Kofi Annan remarks to the Preparatory Commission for the International Criminal Court, "Preparatory Committee-3-1st Meeting (AM)" news release L/2907, February 16, 1999, http://www.un.org/News/Press/docs/1999/19990216.l2907.html.

Moreno-Ocampo, Luis. "Election of the Prosecutor, Statement," April 22, 2003. http://www.icc-cpi.int/Menus/ICC/Structure+of+the+Court/Office+of+the+Prosecutor/Reports+and+Statements/Press+Releases/Press+Releases+2003/.

Moreno-Ocampo, Luis. "Letter from ICC Prosecutor to President Philippe Kirsch." The Hague, June 17, 2004.

Moreno-Ocampo, Luis. "Statement by the Prosecutor Related to Crimes Committed in Barlonya Camp in Uganda." http://www.icc-cpi.int/NR/rdonlyres/47964D88-9 3C8-4E71-9119-4DA540EF5EE2/143705/PIDSOTP0022004EN2.pdf.

Moreno-Ocampo, Luis. (Untitled statement.) February 9, 2006, http://www.icc-cpi.int/NR/rdonlyres/04D143C8-19FB-466C-AB77-4CDB2FDEBEF7/143682/OTP_letter_to_senders_re_Iraq_9_February_2006.pdf.

Moreno-Ocampo, Luis. "Communications Received by the Office of the Prosecutor of the ICC," news release 009.2003-EN, July 16, 2003, http://www.icc-cpi.int/NR/rdonlyres/9B5B8D79-C9C2-4515-906E-125113CE6064/277680/16_july__english1.pdf.

Moreno-Ocampo, Luis. "International Criminal Court Prosecutor Opening Remarks on the Situation in Darfur." News release ICC-OTP-20070227–208, February 27, 2007, http://www.icc-cpi.int/en_menus/icc/situations%20and%20cases/situations/situation%20icc%200205/press%20releases/Pages/prosecutor%20opening%20remarks.aspx.

Moreno-Ocampo, Luis. "Press Conference in Relation with the Surrender to the Court of Mr. Thomas Lubanga Dyilo." March 18, 2006, http://www.icc-cpi.int/NR/rdonlyres/4760D87D-750C-4BFD-9CD0-1AE171DFC553/143842/LMO_20060318_En1.pdf.

Moreno-Ocampo, Luis. "Press Conference on the Uganda Arrest Warrants." News release ICC-OTP-20051014–109, October 14, 2005, http://www.icc-cpi.int/en_menus/icc/press%20and%20media/press%20releases/2005/Pages/press%20conference%20on%20the%20uganda%20arrest%20warrants.aspx.

Moreno-Ocampo, Luis. "Statement by Chief Prosecutor Luis Moreno-Ocampo." October 14, 2005, http://www.icc-cpi.int/NR/rdonlyres/2919856F-03E0-403F-A 1A8-D61D4F350A20/277305/Uganda_LMO_Speech_141020091.pdf.

Moreno-Ocampo, Luis. "Statement Made at the Ceremony for the Solemn Undertaking of the Chief Prosecutor of the ICC," June 16, 2003, http://www.icc-cpi.int/nr/rdonlyres/d7572226-264a-4b6b-85e3-2673648b4896/143585/030616_moreno_ocampo_english.pdf.

Moreno-Ocampo, Luis. "Statement: ICC Prosecutor Press Conference on Libya," May 16, 2011, http://www.icc-cpi.int/en_menus/icc/structure%20of%20the%20court/office%20of%20the%20prosecutor/reports%20and%20statements/statement/Pages/statement%20icc%20prosecutor%20press%20conference%20on%20libya%2016%20may%202011.aspx.

Moreno-Ocampo, Luis. "The Prosecutor of the ICC Opens Investigation in Darfur." News release ICC-OTP-0606–104, June 6, 2005, http://www.icc-cpi.int/en_menus/icc/press%20and%20media/press%20releases/2005/Pages/the%20prosecutor%20of%20the%20icc%20opens%20investigation%20in%20darfur.aspx.

Moreno-Ocampo, Luis. Decision Assigning the Situation in the Libyan Arab Jamahiriya to Pre-Trial Chamber I (ref: 2011/017/LMO/JCCD-rr), March 2, 2011, http://www.icc-cpi.int/iccdocs/doc/doc1032133.pdf.

Moreno-Ocampo, Luis. First Public Hearing of the Office of the Prosecutor, June 17–18, 2003, http://www.icc-cpi.int/en_menus/icc/structure%20of%20the%20court/office%20of%20the%20prosecutor/network%20with%20partners/public%20hearings/Pages/first%20public%20hearing.aspx.

"Observations of the United Nations High Commissioner for Human Rights invited in Application of Rule 103 of the Rules of Procedure and Evidence," ICC-02/05, October 10, 2006, http://www.icc-cpi.int/iccdocs/doc/doc259768.pdf.

Russian Federation. Proposal submitted to the Preparatory Commission for the International Criminal Court by the Russian Federation on the definition of the crime of aggression, U.N. Doc. PCNICC/1999/DP.12 (July 29, 1999), http://www.un.org/Docs/journal/asp/ws.asp?m=PCNICC/1999/DP.12.

Song, Sang-Hyun. "Remarks at Groundbreaking Ceremony for ICC Permanent Premises," April 16, 2013, http://www.icc-cpi.int/en_menus/icc/press%20and%20media/press%20releases/Documents/pr898/Groundbreaking-Ceremony-ICC-President-Statement.pdf.

Statement from Brazilian representative to the Review Conference on the Rome Statute of the International Criminal Court (ICC) in Kampala, Uganda, May 31-June 11, 2010, http://www.iccnow.org/documents/ICC-RC-gendeba-Brazil-ENG.pdf.

AFRICAN UNION DOCUMENTS

African Union Assembly. Decisions and Declarations reached by the Assembly of the African Union, July 1–3, 2009, Sirte, Libya, Assembly/AU/Dec. 243–267 (XIII) Rev.1 Assembly/AU/Decl.1- 5(XIII), http://www.au.int/en/sites/default/files/ ASSEMBLY_EN_1_3_JULY_2009_AUC_THIRTEENTH_ORDINARY_ SESSION_DECISIONS_DECLARATIONS_%20MESSAGE_ CONGRATULATIONS_MOTION_0.pdf.

African Union Executive Council, 19th Ordinary Sess. "Decision on African Candidatures for Posts Within the International System," Doc. EX.CL/673(XIX) (June 23–28, 2011) http://www.au.int/en/sites/default/files/EX%20CL%20Dec% 20644-667%20%28XIX%29%20_E.pdf.

African Union Peace and Security Council. "Report of the Chairperson of the Commission on the Activities of the AU High Leven Ad Hoc Committee on the Situation in Libya," April 26, 2011, http://www.au.int/en/sites/default/ files/275%20-%20Report%20on%20Libya%20_Eng%20_%20%283%29.pdf.

TREATIES AND AGREEMENTS

Inter-Congolese Dialogue: Political Negotiations on the Peace Process and on Transition in the DRC: Global and Inclusive Agreement on Transition in the Democratic Republic of the Congo, Dec. 16, 2002, http://www.ucdp.uu.se/gpda- tabase/peace/DRC%2020021216.pdf.

International Criminal Court Article 98 Agreement, U.S.-Uganda, June 12, 2003, T.I.A.S. 03–1023, http://www.state.gov/documents/organization/152670.pdf.

Military Technical Agreement between the International Security Assistance Force and the Interim Administration of Afghanistan, Jan. 4, 2002, http://webarchive. nationalarchives.gov.uk/+/http://www.operations.mod.uk/isafmta.pdf

Negotiated Relationship Agreement between the International Criminal Court and the United Nations, ICC-ASP/3/Res.1, adopted October 4, 2004, entered into force July 22, 2004, http://www.icc-cpi.int/NR/rdonlyres/916FC6A2-7846-4 177-A5EA-5AA9B6D1E96C/0/ICCASP3Res1_English.pdf.

Palestinian National Authority, Ministry of Justice, Office of Minister, "Declaration Recognizing the Jurisdiction of the International Criminal Court," January 21, 2009, http://www.icc-cpi.int/NR/rdonlyres/74EEE201-0FED-4481-9 5D4-C8071087102C/279777/20090122PalestinianDeclaration2.pdf.

Rome Statute on an International Criminal Court, July 17, 1998, UN Doc. A/CONF. 183/9, 2187 U.N.T.S. 90, http://untreaty.un.org/cod/icc/statute/romefra.htm.

Versailles Peace Treaty, June 28, 1919, 13 A.J.I.L. Supp. 151, 385, http://avalon.law.yale. edu/subject_menus/versailles_menu.asp.

DATA SETS

Iraq Body Count. http://www.iraqbodycount.org/.

Peace Research Institute, Oslo (PRIO). Battle Deaths Data set, version 3.0, released October 2009. http://www.prio.no/CSCW/Datasets/Armed-Conflict/Battle-Deaths/The-Battle-Deaths-Dataset-version-30/.

Project Ploughshares. http://ploughshares.ca/publications/.

World Bank World Development Indicators, http://databank.worldbank.org/data/home.aspx.

Index

Numbers in *italics* indicate figures and tables.